The Bank for International Settlements Arbitration Awards of 2002 and 2003

L'arbitrage concernant la Banque des règlements internationaux Sentences de 2002 and 2003

PERMANENT COURT OF ARBITRATION AWARD SERIES

The Bank for International Settlements Arbitration Awards of 2002 and 2003

With an Introduction by V.V. Veeder

L'arbitrage concernant la Banque des Règlements internationaux Sentences de 2002 et 2003

Avec une Introduction de V.V. Veeder

Series Editor

BELINDA MACMAHON

Legal Counsel/Chief Editor
Permanent Court of Arbitration

Responsable de série

BELINDA MACMAHON

Conseillere juridique/Rédactrice en chef
Court permanente d'arbitrage

T·M·C·ASSER PRESS

Published by T·M·C·Asser press
P.O. Box 16163, 2500 BD The Hague, The Netherlands
<www.asserpress.nl>

ISBN 90-6704-943-3
ISBN 978-90-6704-943-6

Softcover re-print of the Hardcover 1st edition 2007

The Permanent Court of Arbitration (PCA) is an intergovernmental organization, founded at the first Hague Peace Conference in 1899, and based in the Peace Palace in The Hague. It provides a wide range of dispute resolution mechanisms – including arbitration, conciliation and fact finding – in disputes involving various combinations of states, private parties and intergovernmental organizations. The PCA is committed to meeting the rapidly evolving dispute resolution needs of its member states and the international community.

International Bureau
Permanent Court of Arbitration
Peace Palace
Carnegieplein 2
2517 KJ The Hague
The Netherlands
Telephone: +31 70 302 4165
Facsimile: +31 70 302 4167
Email: bureau@pca-cpa.org
Website: www.pca-cpa.org

SUMMARY OF CONTENTS
SOMMAIRE DES MATIÈRES

The English versions are the official texts of the Awards.
In the case of any discrepancy between the English versions and the French translations, the English texts shall govern.

FOREWORD

This volume contains the two Awards of the Arbitral Tribunal Concerning the Bank for International Settlements, rendered in 2002 and 2003. The Swiss-based Bank, established in 1930, describes itself as the world's oldest international financial organization. The world's oldest intergovernmental organization for international dispute resolution, the Permanent Court of Arbitration, served as Registry for the arbitration. Three Claimants – private shareholders of the Bank – sought compensation for their shares which the Bank had recalled on 8 January 2001.

A distinguished arbitral tribunal, comprised of Professor W. Michael Reisman (President) (U.S.A.), Professor Dr. Jochen A. Frowein (Germany), Professor Dr. Mathias Krafft (Switzerland), Professor Dr. Paul Lagarde (France) and Professor Dr. Albert Jan van den Berg (Netherlands), was appointed by five governments (Belgium, France, Germany, Italy and the United Kingdom) that are parties to the Agreement regarding the Complete and Final Settlement of the Question of Reparations, signed in 1930 at The Hague. The Arbitral Tribunal that is provided for in this 1930 Hague Agreement is referred to in various international agreements and related texts regarding the Bank.

The Tribunal's Partial Award, rendered on 22 November 2002, dealt with the international status of the Bank and its competence to amend the Bank's Statutes, the lawfulness of the recall of the privately held shares and the applicable standards for valuation of those shares. In its Final Award, rendered on 19 September 2003, the Tribunal determined the amount of compensation to be paid.

The Tribunal also decided the counterclaim of the Bank against Claimant No. 2, First Eagle SoGen Funds, Inc. That Claimant had commenced litigation against the Bank in New York, and only pursued arbitration under the Bank's constituent documents following the decision of the Federal District Court in New York. In its Final Award, the Tribunal awarded the Bank its costs in defending the U.S. law suit brought by First Eagle, in violation of the agreement to arbitrate.

In his erudite yet highly readable Introduction to this volume, V.V. Veeder QC demonstrates how the significance of a major international commercial arbitration can extend beyond the substantive to the procedural and practical. He also explains the great significance of the Tribunal's Awards to existing jurisprudence on matters such as valuation of an expropriated asset, the award of interest, and the right to damages for breach of an arbitration agreement where a claim on the merits is brought by one party before a domestic court.

The Rules of Procedure provided for written proceedings in either English or French, with translations as deemed necessary by the arbitrators. The Parties were permitted to address the Tribunal orally in their own languages, subject to translation requirements, and this introduced a third language into the proceedings, as Claimant No. 1, Dr. Horst Reineccius, was German. The Awards were rendered in English, and the Tribunal arranged for a translation into French. The English versions are however the official texts of the Awards.

Mrs. Phyllis Pieper Hamilton, then Deputy Secretary-General of the PCA, served as Tribunal Secretary, assisted by the PCA's current Deputy Secretary-General, Mr. Brooks W. Daly. The Awards were translated into French by Ms. Carine Wertz-Midré. Mr. Veeder's Introduction was translated by Mr. Nicolas Ramade. The PCA expresses its sincere gratitude to Mr. Veeder for his valuable contribution to this publication.

The Hague, January 2007

Tjaco T. van den Hout
Secretary-General
Permanent Court of Arbitration

AVANT-PROPOS

Ce volume contient les deux sentences rendues en 2002 et 2003 par le tribunal arbitral institué dans l'affaire concernant la Banque des règlements internationaux. Cette Banque, établie en 1930 et dont le siège est en Suisse, se qualifie elle-même de plus ancienne organisation financière internationale. La plus ancienne organisation internationale pour la résolution des différends internationaux, la Cour permanente d'arbitrage, a agit comme greffe de la procédure arbitrale. Trois demandeurs – actionnaires privés de la Banque – demandaient le paiement d'une indemnité en compensation du retrait par la Banque de leurs actions, le 8 janvier 2001.

Un éminent tribunal arbitral, composé du Professeur W. Michael Reisman (Président – États-Unis), du Professeur Jochen A. Frowein (Allemagne), du Professeur Mathias Krafft (Suisse), du Professeur Paul Lagarde (France) et du Professeur Albert Jan van den Berg (Pays-Bas), fut nommé par cinq gouvernements partis à l'Accord sur le règlement complet et définitif des réparations signé à La Haye en 1930. Il est fait référence au tribunal arbitral prévu par cet accord dans plusieurs conventions internationales et autres documents se rapportant à la Banque.

La sentence partielle rendue par le tribunal le 22 novembre 2002 traitait du caractère international de la Banque, de sa compétence pour amender les statuts de la Banque, de la licéité du retrait des actions détenues par des actionnaires privés et des principes applicables à l'évaluation de ces actions. Dans sa sentence définitive, rendue le 19 septembre 2003, le tribunal a déterminé le montant de l'indemnité à payer.

Le tribunal a également jugé la question de la demande reconventionnelle de la Banque contre le Demandeur No. 2, First Eagle SoGen Funds, Inc. Ce demandeur avait engagé une action contre la Banque à New York et n'avait eu recours à l'arbitrage en application des instruments constitutifs de la Banque qu'après une décision d'un tribunal fédéral de New York. Dans sa sentence définitive, le tribunal a accordé à la Banque les frais engagés pour se défendre dans la procédure américaine engagée par First Eagle, en violation de la convention d'arbitrage.

Dans son introduction érudite mais néanmoins éminemment lisible au présent volume, V.V. Veeder QC démontre comment la portée d'un arbitrage commercial international majeur peut s'étendre au delà des questions de fond et jusqu'aux questions de procédure et de pratique arbitrale. Il explique également l'apport considérable des sentences rendues par le tribunal à des thèmes tels que l'évaluation d'un actif exproprié, l'octroi d'intérêts et le droit à réparation pour violation d'une convention d'arbitrage lorsqu'une demande au fond est engagée par une partie devant des tribunaux nationaux.

Le règlement de procédure prévoyait une procédure écrite en anglais ou français, avec traduction si les arbitres le jugeaient nécessaire. Au cours des plaidoiries, les parties pouvaient s'exprimer dans leur propre langue, sous réserve des exigences d'interprétation, ce qui conduisit à l'apparition d'une troisième langue dans la procédure, car le Demandeur No. 1, le Dr. Horst Reineccius, était Allemand. Les sentences furent rendues en anglais et le tribunal en supervisa la traduction en français. La version anglaise des sentences demeure cependant le texte de référence.

Mme Phylis Pieper Hamilton, alors Secrétaire général adjoint de la CPA, agît comme secrétaire du tribunal, assistée de l'actuel Secrétaire général adjoint de la CPA, M. Brooks W. Daly. Les sentences furent traduites en français par Mme Carine Wertz-Midré. L'introduction de M. Veeder à été traduite par M. Nicolas Ramade. La CPA exprime ses sincères remerciements à M. Veeder pour sa contribution précieuse à cette publication.

La Haye, janvier 2007

Tjaco T. van den Hout
Secrétaire général
Cour permanente d'arbitrage

THE BANK FOR INTERNATIONAL SETTLEMENTS ARBITRATION

Its Contribution to International Law

by

V.V.Veeder*

Under the laws of nature, banks are claimants and creditors, not respondents. Banks do not like being sued by anyone; and central banks still more so, as the recent litigation in London more than demonstrates in the claims brought against the Bank of England by thousands of depositors of the failed Bank of Credit and Commerce International ("BCCI").[1] It can therefore hardly be imagined how the central bank of central banks, the Bank for International Settlements ("BIS") in Basel, must have felt when sued by one of its private shareholders in January 2001. In that month, First Eagle (a mutual fund registered in the United States) filed suit and applied for a temporary restraining order before the Federal District Court in New York to stop the Bank's compulsory buy-back of all its privately held shares.

As a financial institution, the Bank was founded in 1930 in accordance with the provisions of the Agreement regarding the Complete and Final Settlement of the Question of Reparations from Germany made at The Hague on 20 January 1930 ("1930 Hague Agreement").[2] The Convention respecting the Bank for International Settlements was concluded on the same day in The Hague by Belgium, France, Germany, the United Kingdom, Italy, Japan and Switzerland. This

* Queen's Counsel, England and Wales, Essex Court Chambers, London; Visiting Professor of International Law, King's College, University of London.

[1] The BCCI litigation in the Commercial Court in London, *Three Rivers et al v. The Bank of England*, was concluded in mid-2006 long short of final judgment after almost two years of trial (to the mutual dissatisfaction of all concerned, including the trial judge, albeit for different reasons). The proceedings had lasted more than twelve years overall and given rise to more than twenty-five reported judgments of the English courts (including numerous excursions from the Commercial Court to the Court of Appeal and the House of Lords), at a cost to the parties rumoured to exceed £130 million.

[2] 104 League of Nations Treaty Series (L.N.T.S.) p. 441.

Convention included the Bank's foundation documents, its Constituent Charter and its Statutes; and their stated purpose was to facilitate the collection and distribution of Germany's war reparations from the First World War. This was still a vast undertaking under the new Young Plan,[3] with global economic consequences. Prior to the Bank's foundation, under the previous Dawes Plan, Germany's reparations were administered in Berlin by J.P. Morgan where it collected from Germany more than 1 billion marks in 1924–1925, more than 1.22 billion marks in 1926–1927, 2 billion marks in 1927–1928 and 2.5 billion marks in 1928–1929, which J.P. Morgan deposited in a Berlin bank in return for which Germany was permitted to borrow, on long term and for the mutual benefit of debtor and creditors, more than she paid out.[4] Fortunately, for the present day, the Bank's purpose was also more broadly promoted as the general cooperation between central banks to carry out their international financial operations, functions of still greater global economic importance in the 21st century. The Bank was formed under Swiss law and located in Basel; the Bank's foundation documents, however, provided that it was not subject to the municipal law of any of its signatory States or of its corporate seat, but it was to be treated as an international legal person subject to its own foundation documents. Significantly, for present purposes, Article 55(1)(b) of the 1930 BIS Statutes conferred jurisdictional immunity on the Bank in civil or commercial suits arising from banking or financial transactions initiated by its contractual counterparties "except in those cases in which provision for arbitration has been or shall have been made".

In September 2000 the Bank announced that it would hold a meeting of its central bank shareholders on 8 January 2001 to vote on an amendment to its Statutes allowing a mandatory redemption of all its outstanding shares held by its private, non-voting, shareholders. These private shares amounted at that time to approximately 14% of the Bank's total shares, of which 12.5% were in turn held by First Eagle. Historically, it had not been unusual even for central banks to have private shareholders, but by 2000, this was no longer true and their private shares had been repurchased under compulsion in many countries, including Canada, France, Norway, Spain, New Zealand, Portugal and Venezuela. Likewise, the Bank's mandatory redemption plan had been prompted by a growing tension between the Bank's public purpose in promoting international financial

---

[3] The Young Plan (1930) dealt with the issue of the reparation payments imposed on Germany by the Treaty of Versailles following World War I.

[4] LOUIS FISCHER, MEN AND POLITICS p. 103 (New York 1941).

cooperation between central banks in the general public interest and what might be assumed to be a selfish mercantile duty to maximise its own corporate profits, particularly by its private shareholders. Accordingly, the Bank wanted to cancel the registration of all its privately held shares (which would be redistributed to the Bank's central bank shareholders) and then as compensation to issue to each private shareholder a right to payment of 16,000 Swiss francs per share (then approximately US$ 10,000), a valuation established on the expert advice of J.P. Morgan, as the Bank's financial adviser.

First Eagle filed suit in the Federal District Court on 5 January 2001; and immediately following the central banks' approval of the Bank's redemption plan on 8 January 2001, First Eagle filed an amended complaint seeking a preliminary injunction and simultaneously applied for a temporary restraining order. Its amended complaint claimed that the Bank had exceeded its authority in amending its Statutes, that J.P. Morgan's valuation was flawed and lastly, that the Bank had violated mandatory disclosure obligations under U.S. securities law. The District Court heard the motion for the temporary restraining order on the same day it was filed and denied it on 24 January 2001 on the ground that First Eagle had not established any risk of irreparable harm. First Eagle then filed a notice of appeal which was argued on 5 March 2001 before the United States Court of Appeals, Second Circuit. That court dismissed the appeal on 7 June 2001, deciding that the appeal was interlocutory (not therefore ordinarily subject to any appeal) and that First Eagle would not suffer any serious or irreparable injury that could not be adequately addressed by money damages.[5]

Before the appeal, the District Court had also justified its decision on the basis that First Eagle had an adequate remedy at law which it could pursue by arbitration under the arbitration clause in the Bank's Statutes. In response, the Bank had then filed a motion before the District Court to compel arbitration under the U.S. Federal Arbitration Act. Leaving aside its separate securities claims, First Eagle then chose to pursue its other claims against the Bank by arbitration, by notice of arbitration dated 31 August 2001. There was nonetheless more legal skirmishing before the District Court in September 2001, which decided that the Bank's motion to compel arbitration was now moot (given that First Eagle had now commenced arbitration proceedings), that First Eagle's securities claims in the District Court would be stayed pending the outcome of the arbitration proceedings,

---

[5] *First Eagle SoGen Funds, Inc. v. Bank for Int'l Settlements*, 252 F.3d 604 (2d Cir. 2001).

and that First Eagle's application to amend its complaint to add class action claims would be denied.[6]

The scene therefore shifted from litigation in New York to arbitration at The Hague. The relevant arbitration clause was contained in Article 54(1) of the Bank's Statutes, which all shareholders were treated as having accepted under Article 17 of the Statutes. This arbitration clause provided that if any dispute arose between the Bank and (*inter alios*) any of its shareholders with regard to the interpretation or application of the Bank's Statutes, that dispute would be referred for final decision to the Tribunal provided by Article XV of the 1930 Hague Agreement (reproduced as Appendix B to the first Partial Award). The arbitral procedure was prescribed by Annex XII to the 1930 Agreement (reproduced as Appendix A to the first Partial Award), which incorporated Chapter III of the 1907 Hague Convention for the Pacific Settlement of International Disputes (one of the two founding conventions of the Permanent Court of Arbitration). In addition, the Tribunal adopted rules of procedure for arbitration between the Bank and private persons, the emergence of which in March 2001 was doubtless prompted by the Bank's disputes with its private shareholders.[7] Article XV of the 1930 Hague Agreement provided for an arbitration tribunal comprised, in this case, of five arbitrators from the United States, Germany, Switzerland, France and the Netherlands, appointed by the governments of Belgium, France, Germany, Italy and the United Kingdom (Japan having waived its rights to do so in 1951). None of the arbitrators were appointed by the Bank's private shareholders, including any of the three Claimants in the arbitration; and all five were therefore appointed by States whose central banks were both shareholders of the Bank and indirect beneficiaries of the Bank's redemption of the Claimants' shares. Annex XII required, ostensibly, each party to the arbitration proceedings to "pay its own expenses and an equal share of those of the Tribunal" (Article 1). It also required oral debates to be "public" (Article 4). A party could not instruct more than two advocates for "each separate question submitted to arbitration" (Article 10). There was a right to intervene to the State parties to the 1930 Agreement (Article 19).

---

[6] This judgment is reported at 2001 U.S. Dist. LEXIS 15574.

[7] These special procedural rules, the Rules for Arbitration between the Bank for International Settlements and Private Parties of 23 March 2001 [hereinafter Procedural Rules], are available on the website of the Permanent Court of Arbitration (PCA) at <http://www.pca-cpa.org>, together with the Tribunal's procedural orders and other materials.

The end-result was two arbitration awards made in these arbitration proceedings: the first Partial Award dated 22 November 2002 and the second Final Award dated 19 September 2003. These are both lengthy documents which repay close study for several reasons. First, the reasoning is completely transparent, comprehensible and succinct. It is clear to the disputing Parties (but also to readers less acquainted with the dispute) exactly why the Tribunal reached its decision on the issues without having to guess at which of the Parties' arguments might have been accepted or rejected by the Tribunal and why. It therefore represents a salutary lesson to all arbitrators in the drafting of awards, both to those who use too few words and to those who use too many, but of the wrong kind.

Second, the Tribunal's reasoning extends to a number of important procedural issues, probably of greater long term interest than even the substantive issues decided by these two Awards. These procedural issues include multiple claims by different parties, consolidation (de facto), equality of arms in regard to the appointment of the arbitration tribunal (the *Dutco* point[8]), bifurcation, confidentiality, document production (including the use of the International Bar Association Rules on the Taking of Evidence in International Commercial Arbitration, attorney-client privilege and implied waiver of such privilege), expert evidence, visual aids, unrepresented parties and parties represented by *pro bono* attorneys, challenges to an arbitrator based on his former affiliation to a law firm representing a party in the arbitration and trilinguism.

Third, as regards substantive issues, the Tribunal's reasoning is a significant addition to the existing jurisprudence on the valuation of an expropriated asset (including the role of human rights law, as a distinct branch of international law), the award of compound interest, orders for legal costs and in particular the right of one party to damages against another party for the latter's breach of their arbitration agreement in bringing a claim on the merits before a State court. However, the primary issue confronting the U.S. courts and the Arbitral Tribunal was the nature of the multiparty arbitration agreement binding the Bank and its former private shareholders to refer their disputes to arbitration.

---

[8] *Siemens AG & BKMI Industrienlagen GmbH v. Dutco Consortium Construction Co.*, *Cour de cassation* (France), 7 January 1992, reprinted in XVIII Y.B. COMM. ARB. p. 140 and Article 6 of the European Convention on Human Rights: see FOUCHARD, GAILLARD & GOLDMAN ON INTERNATIONAL COMMERCIAL ARBITRATION pp. 468–470 (E. Gaillard & J. Savage eds., 1999).

Historically under English company law (as with many common law countries), a corporation's foundation documents (i.e., its memorandum and articles of association) bound the corporation and its shareholders to the same extent as if these documents respectively had been "signed and sealed" by each shareholder and contained promises by each shareholder to observe all the provisions contained in those documents.[9] In the early days of English arbitration, it was not uncommon to insert an arbitration clause in the rules of a trade association and later the articles of a corporation, intended to oblige its shareholders to refer their disputes to private arbitration, rather than litigation. As to legal principle, there was no difficulty in multiparty arbitration agreements formed by individual non-contemporaneous acts of acceptance without the formal process of offer and acceptance by all contracting parties; and indeed it would be an act of despair if the position were otherwise because it would make such multiparty arbitration agreements impossible in practice.[10]

Yet questions arose whether such an arbitration clause was valid under the law and practice of English arbitration. A corporation's shareholder might acquire his share on a stock exchange without actually signing or agreeing or even knowing of the arbitration clause; and a corporation's articles could be amended after a shareholder's acquisition of shares so as to insert or delete any reference to arbitration, notwithstanding his active opposition and disagreement. Moreover, by this legal fiction, English company legislation treated shareholders as having signed and sealed the corporation's articles, but not (expressly) the corporation itself; and the fiction did not address at all the position of the corporation's directors, officers or other third persons. These and other difficulties gave rise to much controversy in the English courts, culminating in the English Court of Appeal's decision, in *London Sack & Bag Company* (1943),[11] that such an

---

[9] Now Section 14 of the Companies Act 1985, being derived from Section 16 of the Companies Act 1862.

[10] See generally *Clarke v. Dunraven* (The "Satanita") [1897] A.C. 59, as applied to a multiparty arbitration clause in *Walkinshaw v. Pedro Diniz* (1999), reported in 17(2) ARB. INT'L p. 193 (2001). See also Gabrielle Kaufmann-Kohler & Henry Peter, *Formula 1 Racing and Arbitration: The FIA Tailor-Made System for Fast Track Dispute Resolution*, 17(2) ARB. INT'L p. 173 (2001). Under Swiss law, a similar approach was taken by the Swiss Federal Tribunal over the multiparty partnership and corporate dispute in *Andersen Consulting v. Arthur Andersen* (8 December 1989), reported at 18 ASA BULLETIN p. 546 (2000, No. 3).

[11] *London Sack & Bag Company Limited v. Dixon & Lugton Limited* (1944) 170 L.T. 70; [1943] 2 All E.R. 763 (Court of Appeal). Other cases may be found in MUSTILL & BOYD, THE LAW AND PRACTICE OF COMMERCIAL ARBITRATION p. 75, n.2 (1st ed. 1982), including *Hickman v. Kent & Romney Marsh Sheepbreeders' Association* [1915] 1 Ch. 881.

arbitration clause could not generally satisfy the test for a written arbitration agreement under Section 4 of the English Arbitration Act 1889. In the leading judgment, Lord Justice Scott (an experienced judge well-versed in commercial law) openly mocked the idea that "a purely oral agreement expressed to include a printed arbitration clause on the wall could satisfy the [1889] statute".[12] Nonetheless, the learned Judge was prepared to accept that the arbitration clause might operate as between shareholders in their capacity as shareholders, but not in a matter entirely outside that relationship. It was a prescient qualification because the English Arbitration Act 1996 would now recognise as effective his example of an arbitration clause in the form of wall-graffiti, incorporated by reference into an oral contract (Sections 5 and 6); the exigencies of commerce require effective arbitration agreements; and as a result judicial and legislative attitudes have changed substantially.

Likewise, the uniform application of arbitration clauses is required for effective use in transnational commerce, under Article II of the New York Arbitration Convention[13] and Article 7 of the UNCITRAL Model Law. In regard to an arbitration agreement in the statutes of a corporation, this necessity is well illustrated by the analogous treatment of exclusive jurisdiction clauses in transnational trade within the European Union. In *Powell Duffryn v. Wolfgang Petereit* (1992),[14] the European Court of Justice decided that an exclusive jurisdiction clause in the statutes of a German company, to which the shares were subject under German law, was effective to bind the company and a foreign shareholder under Article 17 of the Brussels Convention (now Article 23 of the Judgments Regulation No. 44/2001). That was so, even though German law might not recognise the clause as a jurisdiction clause under its national law, because the issue was to be decided under the Brussels Convention as an autonomous concept under the Convention and (on the facts of that case) despite shareholders having opposed and voted against the introduction of the arbitration clause at the company's general meeting. Accordingly, the efficacy of both jurisdiction and arbitration clauses, as regards a corporation's statutes, may now depend not on national laws but on international treaties and conventions.

---

[12] At p. 72. Prior to his appointment to the bench, Sir Leslie Scott (1869–1950) had been the English arbitrator appointed by the claimant in *Lena Goldfields Co. Ltd. v. U.S.S.R.* (1930), Arbitration Award of 2 September 1930, in LAUTERPACHT, ANNUAL DIGEST OF PUBLIC INTERNATIONAL LAW CASES p. 426 (1929/30) and 47 INT'L COMP. L.Q. p. 747 (1998).

[13] United Nations Convention on the Recognition and Enforcement of Foreign Arbitral Awards, New York, 10 June 1958, 21 U.S.T. p. 2517, 330 U.N.T.S. p. 38.

[14] Case C-214/89, *Powell Duffryn plc v. Wolfgang Petereit*, 1992 E.C.R. 1-1745.

It is significant that none of these historical difficulties caused any substantial problems in this case, neither for the U.S. courts in New York nor the Arbitral Tribunal at The Hague: all decision-makers treated the arbitration clause, as between the private shareholders and the Bank, as being governed by international law. The national dog did not therefore bark in the night. First Eagle contended that the general principles of international law applied to the dispute, including the interpretation of the Bank's Statutes. The other Claimants, although advancing additional arguments, did not materially disagree on this particular point (which was to them less relevant than First Eagle, as the sole Respondent to the Bank's counterclaim). In regard to its counterclaim, the Bank contended before the Tribunal that the arbitration clause was not the subject of any private agreement but resulted directly from the 1930 Hague Agreement, without reference to any municipal law. The Tribunal agreed, treating the arbitration clause as a *lex specialis*, created by the Bank's foundation documents solely under international law. Having considered the terms of Articles 17, 54 and 55 of the Bank's Statutes, the Tribunal concluded:

> The regime that emerges is quite unique. Article 55 of the Statutes is, besides being part of the international legal structure of the Bank, a bilateral commitment that operates parallel to Article 54 and Article 17. By accepting the Statutes pursuant to Article 17, shareholders also accept Article 54 and thus the jurisdiction of a Tribunal established under the 1930 [Hague] Agreement, and agree not to pursue actions within the jurisdiction of such a Tribunal before national courts. The regime that emerges from these provisions makes clear that disputes between, *inter alia*, the Bank and its shareholders with regard to the interpretation or application of the Statutes were to be referred to a Tribunal established in accordance with the 1930 Hague Agreement. Such a Tribunal was empowered to decide "all questions (including the question of its own jurisdiction)" and, in addition, to "order any appropriate provisional measures in order to safeguard the respective rights of the parties." Article 55 underlines the exclusive character of the Bank from other national jurisdictions, with two explicit exceptions, neither of which is relevant to the case at bar.
>
> A private shareholder of the Bank could not be a formal party to the 1930 Hague Agreement. But a private shareholder, purchasing shares, acquired a special and equally binding type of privity with respect to the dispute resolution regime described above. Article 17 of the Bank's Statutes states that "[o]wnership of shares of the Bank implies acceptances of the Statutes of the Bank." Each share certificate carried the same notice. The Prospectus for shares stated the exclusive jurisdictional regime. A Declaration of Acceptance of Shares included an agreement to accept the dispute resolution regime. In sum, private actors, purchasing shares, accepted, through manifold instruments whose multiplicity and reiteration belie any

> possibility of misunderstanding, the dispute resolution regime, including the immunity of the Bank from national courts and the competence of a Tribunal formed under the 1930 Hague Agreement and the Statutes to decide its own jurisdiction and to issue provisional measures. The Tribunal would emphasize the critical factor of *acceptance* of the regime. With respect to the question of the competent jurisdiction, private shareholders accepted the international legal status of the Bank unconditionally.[15]

By that process of reasoning, it is clear that arbitration between private persons and international persons or States has come fully of age, establishing the independent right of a private person to pursue an arbitral remedy under international law, without dependence on any national law or derivation from any diplomatic protection by his home State. Accordingly, in Professor Rosalyn Higgins' terminology, such a private person is now neither a subject nor an object of international law, but a "participant".[16] It is a radical departure from the orthodox position that if this was ever to be or become the position for a private person, it could only result from the application of a national law prescribing that precise result.[17] The Tribunal's reasoning has since been confirmed by the recent decision of the English Court of Appeal, in *Ecuador v. Occidental* (2006), in legal proceedings ancillary to an arbitration between a private U.S. investor and a State under a bilateral investment treaty ("BIT"), held in London. The court there accepted international law as the law directly applicable to the arbitration agreement formed from the arbitration clause in the U.S.-Ecuador BIT and the investor's invocation of arbitration thereunder, thereby decisively rejecting the traditional approach that an investor can only exercise procedural rights under a treaty deriving from a State party to that BIT.[18] In this case, however, the arbitration clause in the Bank's Statutes, as a *lex specialis*, bound First Eagle even before its commencement of the arbitration proceedings at The Hague.

---

[15] See Final Award, paras. 114–115.

[16] ROSALYN HIGGINS, PROBLEMS & PROCESS: INTERNATIONAL LAW AND HOW WE USE IT p. 50 (1994); see also Stephen Schwebel, *The Law Applicable in International Arbitration: Application of Public International Law*, ICCA Series No. 7, pp. 562–564 (1994).

[17] For example, as regards the Iran-United States Claims Tribunal under the Algiers Declarations, see *Dallal v. Bank Mellat* [1986] Q.B. p. 441; XI Y.B. COM. ARB. p. 547 (1986); and generally Francis Mann QC, *State Contracts and International Arbitration*, 42 BRITISH Y.B. OF INT'L L. pp. 1, 8 (1967).

[18] *Ecuador v. Occidental* [2006] 2 W.L.R. p. 70 (CA); see also Zachary Douglas, *Nothing if Not Critical for Investment Treaty Arbitration*: *Occidental, Eureko and Methanex*, 22(1) ARB. INT'L pp. 27, 30 ff. (2006).

At The Hague, the Tribunal was confronted by two other private Claimants who also disputed the Bank's level of compensation for their recalled shares, on different grounds: Dr. Reineccius (of Germany) and Mr. Mathieu and *la Société de concours hippique de la Châtre (*from France). Mr. Mathieu, alone of the three Claimants, challenged the lawfulness of the Bank's share-recall. The former, a non-lawyer, was to act in person throughout the arbitration proceedings, with manifest distinction; and the latter were represented, *pro bono*, by distinguished lawyers from Paris. The Bank was represented by equally distinguished lawyers, as was First Eagle. The Tribunal consolidated these different proceedings into "parallel" arbitrations for practical reasons; and, by its third procedural order, the Tribunal proceeded to decide in a first phase upon the lawfulness of the recall and the identification of applicable standards for the valuation of the recalled shares, by a first partial award; and in a second phase (if necessary, as it eventually was) the application of those standards, in a final award.

There was a preparatory conference on 7 September 2001 and a procedural meeting at The Hague on 26 February 2002. For the arbitration's first phase, public hearings were organised by the PCA in the Great Hall of Justice of the Peace Palace at The Hague on 26 to 28 August 2002 and further public hearings on 28 to 29 May 2003 for the second phase. In accordance with the requirements of the 1930 Hague Agreement, these hearings were simultaneously translated into English, French and German. Of all the many minor procedural orders issued by the Tribunal, from the practical perspective, the most interesting related to electronic technology used by the Parties' legal representatives at the hearings. For many years, like Roman Emperors at the Coliseum, arbitrators would rub their hands with anticipation as a party's legal representative braved the perils of PowerPoint, only to fall as the software broke down, electrical power failed, the order of slides rearranged by unknown hands – or worse. It was also not unknown for an arbitrator unwittingly to require, in mid-stream, a different order or treatment of the issues to be addressed by that legal representative, with equally fatal results. Today, electronic technology is vastly improved, as have arbitral facilities generally; and as a result the increased use of visual aids has led to new procedural difficulties. The Tribunal's eighth procedural order is therefore a model for others to follow. It states:

> 1. Use of demonstrative exhibits and other visual aids, whether computer assisted or otherwise, is not unusual in international arbitration hearings. Such visual aids may be employed by the Parties so long as the material concerned is based solely on evidence already in the record and has been shown to the opposing party prior to the Hearing for purposes of verification.

2. Introduction of new evidence will not be permitted unless a proper application has been made to the Tribunal, the latter has granted leave, and the opposing party has sufficient opportunity to present its comments thereon.[19]

As here suggested, whenever visual aids are used in oral argument, the tribunal should require beforehand the distribution to all parties and itself of hard copies (arbitrators make notes on hard copies); and for ease of reference later, parties should mark all their visual aids with specific reference numbers, particularly so as to make a written transcript subsequently intelligible. In most cases, however, it will not be possible to limit, as in this case, the use of visual aids to "evidence already in the record": it may be useful to present visually argument, other legal materials and demonstrative non-evidential aids. In that event, there may still remain procedural difficulties as to the precise lines to be drawn between old written argument, new oral argument in support of an existing case and a fresh case. The first is permissible, the last usually impermissible; and the second may be one or the other; but even if otherwise permissible, it may become impermissible if the visual aid conflicts with an earlier procedural order by the tribunal regarding the timing for the exchange of written memorials or written submissions before the oral hearing.

During the first phase, the Tribunal addressed the first two questions. As regards the first question, raised by Mr. Mathieu, the Tribunal determined that the Statutes of the Bank had been lawfully amended on 8 January 2001, thereby excluding all private shareholders as shareholders of the Bank. As to the second question, the Tribunal decided that the three Claimants were entitled to compensation from the Bank for each of their recalled shares corresponding to a proportionate share, discounted by 30%, of the Net Asset Value of the Bank ("NAV"). The Tribunal also recorded that the Claimants accepted that NAV to be US$ 10.072 billion, corresponding to US$ 19,034 per share (equivalent to 33,820 Swiss francs), not counting the value of the Bank's real estate. These decisions required the Tribunal to address several issues, including the legal character and status of the Bank, the law applicable to that issue, the Bank's amendment of its Statutes and Mr. Mathieu's allegation of unlawful conduct.

As regards the second question, the Tribunal had to consider the legal principles applying to the valuation of the recalled shares whether as "reparations",

[19] Procedural Order No. 8 (Computer Assisted Projections, Requirements for Late Submissions of Evidence of Authorities), 23 August 2002. See the PCA website, *supra* note 7, and the first Partial Award, para. 49.

implying that the recall was unlawful, or as "compensation", implying that the recall was expropriatory and that its unlawfulness was contingent only upon the Bank's not paying the proper measure of compensation and whether any such reparations or compensation was to be full, just, equitable or appropriate under the various golden formulae. It is here that the first Partial Award records the Tribunal's useful survey of international jurisprudence on the valuation of the fair market value for expropriated shares of foreign investors.[20] The complication in this case was that there was no reliable market value established by the operations of an efficient market because the market for the Bank's private shares was materially illiquid, these shares carried no voting rights and their market value, where ascertainable, was known to be undervalued because of the small dividends paid by the Bank and their other legal characteristics.

The Bank, guided by J.P. Morgan's report, had used a valuation method based on a dividend perpetuity model ("DPM"), thereby arriving at a share price double their prevailing market price in certain stock exchanges. Dr. Reineccius submitted that the appropriate model for valuation was not DPM, because the Bank traditionally distributed as dividends to its shareholders only a small proportion of its actual profits, but an earning power method ("EPM"). The other two Claimants (here joined by Dr. Reineccius in the subsidiary alternative) submitted that the appropriate method for valuation was a per share proportionate part of the undiscounted NAV. The Tribunal decided upon the NAV method; and it then turned to the question of whether and to what extent that proportionate NAV should be discounted because of the legal nature of the private shares. The Tribunal decided eventually upon thirty percent as the appropriate discount, given the shares' legal characteristics, subject to a further calculation for the additional NAV in respect of the Bank's real estate (which had not been included in the J.P. Morgan report). As the Bank's valuation of the Claimants' shares was, on any possible calculation, less than this amount, the Tribunal decided that the Bank was liable to pay the difference to each of the Claimants, to be finally assessed in its Final Award.

---

[20] It is significant how issues of quantum have recently assumed greater interest in this field, as demonstrated by the recently established website of the British Institute for International and Comparative Law especially devoted to damages awarded in investor-state arbitrations: see <http://www.biicl.org/damages_investment_law>; and see also Wilson, Cain & Gray, *ICSID Arbitration Awards and Cost*, TRANSNATIONAL DISPUTE MANAGEMENT (2006). See also Irmgard Marboe, *Compensation and Damages in International Law*, 7(5) J. WORLD INVESTMENT & TRADE (2006).

Accordingly, during the second phase, the Tribunal addressed the amount of compensation payable to each Claimant, determining that the Bank should pay to each 7,977.56 Swiss francs per share, together with 5% simple interest from 8 January 2001 until the date of the Final Award. In assessing the calculation of compensation, the Tribunal received a valuation from its appointed expert as to the value of the Bank's real estate. As regards the Bank's counterclaim against First Eagle for breach of the arbitration agreement, the Tribunal ordered First Eagle to reimburse the Bank in the sum of US$ 587,413.49 (representing the Bank's reasonable legal costs incurred in the legal proceedings in New York). As regards the Parties' own costs, the Tribunal ordered the Bank to bear only Mr. Mathieu's modest costs (as a *pro bono* client); and as regards the arbitration costs, by an ingenious but rational interpretation of Annex XII, the Tribunal decided that the Bank should bear these costs in full (albeit rejecting the Claimants' claims for interest on their advance deposits towards such arbitration costs). There were further issues regarding the currency of the award and starting dates for the calculation of interest.

As regards interest, the Claimants had claimed interest varying from 3¼% to 7% on the additional compensation found due to them, the first for simple interest at the money market rate for Swiss francs and the others for compound interest. Their claims were advanced under general principles of unjust enrichment (given that the Bank had received a return on the retained compensation), comparative commercial law and Swiss banking practice. As regards compound interest, it was argued that "recent arbitral decisions" had made the award of such interest part of customary international law. In response, the Bank contended that neither the 1930 Hague Agreement, nor the 1907 Hague Convention, nor the Bank's Statutes (including the arbitration clause) provided for any award of interest, nor was interest "required" under general principles of international law; but that if interest was to be awarded by the Tribunal, it should only be simple interest at three-month LIBOR rates for Swiss francs because the compensation was payable in Swiss currency and Switzerland was the place where such payment fell due, in Basel as the Bank's seat.

The Tribunal decided in the Partial Award, confirmed by its Final Award, that the Bank would be liable to pay interest, because "it is a general rule that interest is owed where payments are to be made on a specific date but are not made".[21]

[21] Partial Award, para. 204; Final Award, para. 90.

This rule of international law was regarded by the Tribunal as too obvious to warrant any citation of authority; and it therefore concentrated in its Final Award on the appropriate rate of interest. Recognising that international law did not prescribe any specific rate, the Tribunal identified Swiss law as the national legal system with which this issue had "the closest contacts", given principally the Bank's seat and the role of Swiss currency both for historical dividends paid and the compensation payable by the Bank. Applying Articles 73 and 104 of the Swiss Code of Obligations, the Tribunal chose a simple pre-award interest rate of 5% per annum, with no order for post-award interest.

In the circumstances, this was a safe and uncontroversial result. As noted in the commentary to Article 38 of the International Law Commission's Articles on State Responsibility, the "general view of courts and tribunals has been against the award of compound interest".[22] The ancient laws of usury can still influence commercial litigation and arbitration everywhere; and the actual difference between compound and simple interest over a short period cannot always justify the jurisprudential *fureur* created by an award of compound interest. Less significantly, whilst a common lawyer might quibble with a conflict rule based on the concept that a creditor should seek out its debtor at the latter's place of business (as opposed to the debtor seeking out its creditor for payment), the only candidate for an applicable national law was here clearly Switzerland; and doubtless this Bank could be expected to honour the award promptly, making any order for post-award interest unnecessary in practice. However, the Tribunal also added an important caveat which suggests that the actual reasons for this common-sense result may have been awkward for the five arbitrators to reach unanimously; namely:

> the decision to apply Swiss moratory interest is the result of the application of a number of factors with respect to the practice of the Bank and the preponderance of contacts with Swiss law. It is not based upon any assumption of subjection of the Bank to Swiss law. Nor should the Tribunal's decision be taken as indicating any position for or against recent trends with respect to the application of compound interest in contemporary international law; that is a question that does not arise in this case, in view of the dispositive effect of the Bank's practice and the preponderance of contacts with the Swiss legal system insofar as interest in the present case is concerned.[23]

[22] James Crawford, The International Law Commission's Articles on State Responsibility p. 237 (Cambridge University Press 2002); see also Christoph Schreuer, The ICSID Convention pp. 733–734 (Cambridge University Press 2001).

[23] Final Award, para. 93.

Accordingly, with this magisterial mantra, future practitioners are firmly warned off citing this case as any authority for or against the award of compound interest before other international tribunals, in particular ICSID arbitrations subject to Article 42(1) of the Washington Convention.[24] It cannot, however, prevent still more *fureur*, particularly in the wake of the analogous award in *Wena Hotels v. Egypt*[25] (ordering, in contrast, compound interest notwithstanding Egyptian laws to the contrary). That debate was taking place simultaneously with the Tribunal's deliberations and drafting of its Final Award; and it continues.[26] Nor should this mantra still the growing consensus over the last decade that, almost invariably, only compound interest can properly compensate for a claimant's monetary loss. That is the approach finally adopted for commercial arbitration in Section 49(3) of the English Arbitration Act 1996;[27] and as regards international tribunals, there seems to be an increasing trend to award compound interest as a general principle of international law, particularly where the respondent's conduct has been egregious.[28] It is hardly an unfair rule economically; and it is certainly not for any bank to complain. There is no doubt that, if these three claimants had owed any monies to this Bank, the Bank would have applied to their debts compound

[24] Convention on the Settlement of Investment Disputes Between States and Nationals of Other States, Washington, 14 October 1966, 575 U.N.T.S. p. 159. See also Article 54(1) of the ICSID Arbitration (Facility) Rules.

[25] *Wena Hotels v. Egypt*, ICSID Award, 8 December 2000 (Ibrahim Fadlallah; Don Wallace and Monroe Leigh); and Decision of ICSID *ad hoc* committee, 28 January 2002 (K.D. Kerameus; Andreas Bucher and Francisco Orrego Vicuòa), 41 I.L.M. pp. 896 & 933 (2002).

[26] See especially Emmanuel Gaillard & Yas Banifatemi, *The Meaning of "and" in Article 42(1), Second Sentence, of the Washington Convention: The Role of International Law in the ICSID Choice of Law Process*, 18 ICSID REV. – FOREIGN INVESTMENT LAW JOURNAL p. 375 (2003); and Eric Schwartz, *Finality at What Cost? The Decision of the Ad Hoc Committee in Wena Hotels v. Egypt*, in ANNULMENT OF ICSID AWARDS p. 43, at pp. 68 ff (E. Gaillard & Y. Banifatemi eds., International Arbitration Institute 2004).

[27] The Law Commission of England and Wales has proposed extending the general power of arbitrators to order compound interest to the English Courts: see its Consultation Paper No. 167 (2002) and Report No. 287 (2004). As to its genesis under the law and practice of English commercial arbitration, see this author's *Whose Arbitration Is It Anyway: The Parties or the Arbitration Tribunal – An Interesting Question?*, in THE LEADING ARBITRATORS' GUIDE TO INTERNATIONAL ARBITRATION p. 347, at pp. 354–367 (Newman & Hill eds., 2004).

[28] Stephen Schwebel, *Compound Interest in International Law*, Vol. 2, Issue 5 TRANSNATIONAL DISPUTE MANAGEMENT p. 1 (2005); and RAYMOND DOAK BISHOP, JAMES CRAWFORD & MICHAEL REISMAN, FOREIGN INVESTMENT DISPUTES pp. 1373 ff (2005). Over the last five years, it is not insignificant that the literature on compound interest has grown extensively.

and not simple interest as a banking trade usage.[29] That, too, is a law of nature; and what is sauce for goose, should usually be sauce for the gander – but not in this case.

However, the most interesting aspect of this Final Award is the Tribunal's reasoning on the Bank's counterclaim for First Eagle's breach of the arbitration agreement in bringing legal proceedings in New York. The Tribunal accepted that the New York courts might provide a procedure to First Eagle to test the validity of the arbitration clause but that it was not a "legal imperative, which required resort to that procedure".[30] It was a mere power or option available to First Eagle, but not an obligation; and as provided by national law, it could not be used to justify First Eagle's violation of a commitment operating at the level of international law. Under the arbitration agreement binding on First Eagle, the Tribunal had exclusive competence to determine its own jurisdiction; and a contrary decision of the New York courts could not have pre-empted the Tribunal's decision as to the validity or scope of its jurisdiction. The Tribunal also rejected First Eagle's submission that the Tribunal did not exist at the time of its legal proceedings, given that there was always "a workable mechanism for establishing the tribunal". It was here doubtless significant, on the facts of this case, that First Eagle's application for a temporary restraining order had so lamentably failed before the New York courts. If such an order had been granted by the New York Federal Court, at a time when the Tribunal did not exist and could not therefore decide urgently upon any application for provisional measures by First Eagle,[31] would the Tribunal have decided that such an application was still a breach of the arbitration agreement? The answer is not wholly clear from the Tribunal's reasoning (because that question did not arise); but the likely assumption is that it would.

---

[29] At common law, such a trade usage has long been recognised: under English law, see *National Bank of Greece v. Pinios Shipping Co. (No. 1)* [1990] 1 AC 637.

[30] Final Award, para. 116.

[31] Article 21 of the Procedural Rules, *supra* note 7, provided for provisional measures to be ordered by the Tribunal's President or any arbitrator designated by the President, with a power to require from the applicant security for the costs of such measures. That power assumes the prior appointment of the Tribunal's President; and in any event these rules post-dated First Eagle's application for a temporary restraining order in New York on 8 January 2001. However, this practical problem will not arise again: the Tribunal has been reconstituted as a permanent body (for five year periods), as confirmed by the letter dated 19 September 2006 to the PCA from the French Ministry of Foreign Affairs sent on behalf of all interested States.

These arbitration proceedings having been concluded at The Hague in 2003, their coda followed in France in 2004 where the Paris *Cour d'appel*, overturning the judgment of the Paris *tribunal de commerce*, likewise recognised the efficacy of the arbitration agreement in the Bank's Statutes.[32] The lower court had decided that more than 200 former private shareholders in the Bank could bring legal proceedings to the French courts against the Bank because, having now ceased to be shareholders, none remained bound by Article 54 of the Bank's Statutes containing the arbitration agreement. The appellate court, recognising the provisional validity of the arbitration agreement (which had originally been accepted by these former shareholders and which had remained unamended thereafter) and rejecting further arguments based on *ordre public international*, declared the French courts' lack of jurisdiction on the merits of these claims and directed the claimants to their arbitral remedy at The Hague.

*

In conclusion, by these two Awards, international arbitration can be seen to work for the best in the best of all possible worlds. Although potentially beset by procedural and substantive difficulties, this arbitration was final and relatively quick (two years from beginning to end, with only five days of hearings); relatively inexpensive (arbitration costs were about EUR 810,000, to which the Parties' own costs and expenses must be added); but above all fair, as manifestly demonstrated by the care, attention and transparency of the Tribunal's reasoning. Moreover, the alternative of litigation of this dispute in a national court, particularly if translated into a class action, could only have been much less effective on almost all counts, without even the need to refer to the abortive multiparty proceedings in the New York and Paris courts, still less the recent travails of the BCCI litigation in the English courts. That too, perhaps, is becoming a law of nature.

[32] *Madame Alhinc et al c/ S.A. Banque de France & S.A. Banque des Règlements Internationaux:* judgment of the *Cour d'appel* of Paris dated 25 February 2004, overturning the judgment of the *tribunal de commerce* of Paris dated 17 March 2003. As regards the *Dutco* point, the *Cour d'appel* stressed that the five arbitrators had all been appointed by States and not by their central banks as shareholders in the Bank or the Bank itself. Further appeal was rejected by the *Cour de cassation* (Cass. 1re civ., 23 May 2006, *pourvoi* No. 04-13800).

PERMANENT COURT OF ARBITRATION

ARBITRATION TRIBUNAL ESTABLISHED PURSUANT
TO ARTICLE XV OF THE AGREEMENT SIGNED AT
THE HAGUE ON 20 JANUARY 1930

Prof. W. Michael Reisman
Prof. Dr. Jochen A. Frowein
Prof. Dr. Mathias Krafft
Prof. Dr. Paul Lagarde
Prof. Dr. Albert Jan van den Berg

Phyllis Hamilton, Secretary
Permanent Court of Arbitration, Registry

DR. HORST REINECCIUS, CLAIMANT (CLAIM NO. 1)
FIRST EAGLE SOGEN FUNDS, INC., CLAIMANT (CLAIM NO. 2)
MR. PIERRE MATHIEU AND LA SOCIÉTÉ DE CONCOURS HIPPIQUE
DE LA CHÂTRE, CLAIMANTS (CLAIM NO. 3)
-VERSUS-
BANK FOR INTERNATIONAL SETTLEMENTS, RESPONDENT

PARTIAL AWARD
ON THE LAWFULNESS OF THE RECALL OF THE PRIVATELY HELD SHARES ON 8 JANUARY 2001 AND THE APPLICABLE STANDARDS FOR VALUATION OF THOSE SHARES

The Hague, 22 November 2002

Table of Contents

TABLE OF CONTENTS
PARTIAL AWARD

TABLE OF CONTENTS
PARTIAL AWARD

CHAPTER I – INTRODUCTION

1. On 20 January 1930, the Governments of Germany, Belgium, Great Britain, Italy, Japan and Switzerland concluded at The Hague, the Convention respecting the Bank for International Settlements. The Convention included the Constituent Charter and the Statutes of the Bank (hereafter the Convention, the Constituent Charter and the Statutes of the Bank will be referred to collectively as the "Constituent Instruments"). The Bank for International Settlements (hereafter the "Bank" or "BIS") was organized, by Article 1 of the Statutes, as "a Company limited by shares" and its objects, according to Article 3, were

> to promote the co-operation of central banks and to provide additional facilities for international financial operations; and to act as trustee or agent in regard to international financial settlements entrusted to it under agreements with the parties concerned.

2. In extending invitations to subscribe to capital in the Bank, Article 10 of the Statutes prescribed that "consideration shall be given by the Board [of Directors of the Bank] to the desirability of associating with the Bank the largest possible number of central banks."

3. The shares did not convey any rights in the governance of the Bank. Article 15 of the Statutes provided, in part:

> The ownership of shares of the Bank carries no right of voting or representation at the General Meeting. The right of representation and of voting, in proportion to the number of shares subscribed by each country, may be exercised by the central bank of that country or by its nominee.

4. Because some of the central banks were not, at the time of the founding of the Bank, in a position to subscribe and hold shares and others would have found the financial burden of acquiring and holding the shares onerous, Article 16 of the Statutes stated that "[a]ny subscribing institution or banking group may issue, or cause to be issued to the public the shares which it has subscribed." In accordance with this option, the United States Federal Reserve, the French Central Bank and the Belgian Central Bank issued all or some of the shares which they had subscribed for sale to private parties. At the time of the founding of the

Bank, "a substantial part of [the] share holdings"[1] were held by private parties. French-issued shares were traded on the Paris marché au comptant; Belgian and American shares were traded on the Zurich Nebensegment/marché annexe.[2]

5. As of 2000, there were 529,165 shares of the Bank in issue of which 72,648 were held by private shareholders, *i.e.* 13.73% of the Bank's shares. On 11 September 2000, the Board of Directors of the Bank proposed to restrict in the future the right to hold shares in the Bank to central banks and, to this end, to call an Extraordinary General Meeting on 8 January 2001 to amend the Statutes so as to exclude private shareholders against payment of compensation of CHF 16,000, an amount, which the Board stated, represented a premium of 95% for the American shares, 105% for the Belgian shares and 155% for the French shares. The level of compensation was based on a recommendation of J.P. Morgan, which had prepared a report for the Bank.

6. Three claimants who have disputed the level of compensation, one of whom has also disputed the lawfulness of the Bank's recall of the privately held shares, have invoked the jurisdiction of the Arbitration Tribunal established pursuant to Article XV of the Agreement regarding the Complete and Final Settlement of the Question of Reparations, signed at The Hague on 20 January 1930 (see Appendix B to this Award).

---

[1] Henry H. Schloss, The Bank for International Settlements, p. 40 (North-Holland Publishing Company, Amsterdam, 1958).

[2] "In February, 1956, average quotations of Bank for International Settlements shares of the French issue on the Paris Bourse were ffrs. 88,140; unofficial quotations on the Brussels Bourse in February, 1956, were bfrs. 10,050 and 10,100 for the American and Belgian issue respectively. Source: Bank for International Settlements." *Id.*, at fn. 7.

CHAPTER II – PROCEDURAL HISTORY

7. This Tribunal Concerning the Bank for International Settlements (hereafter the "Tribunal") was constituted pursuant to Article XV of the Agreement regarding the Complete and Final Settlement of the Question of Reparations, signed at The Hague on 20 January 1930 (hereafter the "1930 Hague Agreement").

8. Article XV of the 1930 Hague Agreement provides as follows:

> 1. Any dispute, whether between the Governments signatory to the present Agreement or between one or more of those Governments and the Bank for International Settlements, as to the interpretation or application of the New Plan shall, subject to the special provisions of Annexes I, Va, VIa and IX be submitted for final decision to an arbitration tribunal of five members appointed for five years, of whom one, who will be the Chairman, shall be a citizen of the United States of America, two shall be nationals of States which were neutral during the late war; the two other shall be respectively a national of Germany and a national of one of the Powers which are creditors of Germany.
>
> For the first period of five years from the date when the New Plan takes effect this Tribunal shall consist of the five members who at present constitute the Arbitration Tribunal established by the Agreement of London of 30 August, 1924.
>
> 2. Vacancies on the Tribunal, whether they result from the expiration of the five-yearly periods or occur during the course of any such period, shall be filled, in the case of a member who is a national of one of the Powers which are creditors of Germany, by the French Government, which will first reach an understanding for this purpose with the Belgian, British, Italian and Japanese Governments; in the case of the member of German nationality, by the German Government; and in the cases of the three other members by the six Governments previously mentioned acting in agreement, or in default of their agreement, by the President for the time being of the Permanent Court of International Justice.

3. In any case in which either Germany or the Bank is plaintiff or defendant, if the Chairman of the Tribunal considers, at the request of one or more of the Creditor Governments parties to the proceedings, that the said Government or Governments are principally concerned, he will invite the said Government or Governments to appoint – and in the case of more Governments than one by agreement – a member, who will take the place on the Tribunal of the member appointed by the French Government.

   In any case in which, on the occasion of a dispute between two or more Creditor Governments, there is no national of one or more of those Governments among the Members of the Tribunal, that Government or those Governments shall have the right to appoint each a Member who will sit on that occasion. If the Chairman considers that some of the said Governments have a common interest in the dispute, he will invite them to appoint a single member. Whenever, as a result of this provision, the Tribunal is composed of an even number of members, the Chairman shall have a casting vote.

4. Before and without prejudice to a final decision, the Chairman of the Tribunal, or, if he is not available in any case, any other Member appointed by him, shall be entitled, on the request of any Party who makes the application, to make any interlocutory order with a view to preventing any violation of the rights of the Parties.

5. In any proceedings before the Tribunal the Parties shall always be at liberty to agree to submit the point at issue to the Chairman or any one of the Members of the Tribunal chosen as a single arbitrator.

6. Subject to any special provisions which may be made in the Submission – provisions which may not in any event affect the right of intervention of a Third Party – the procedure before the Tribunal or a single arbitrator shall be governed by the rules laid down in Annex XII.

The same rules, subject to the same reservation, shall also apply to any proceedings before this Tribunal for which the Annexes to the present Agreement provide.

7. In the absence of an understanding on the terms of Submission, any Party may seize the Tribunal directly by a proceeding *ex parte*, and the Tribunal may decide, even in default of appearance, any question of which it is thus seized.

8. The Tribunal, or the single arbitrator, may decide the question of their own jurisdiction, provided always that, if the dispute is one between Governments and a question of jurisdiction is raised, it shall, at the request of either Party, be referred to the Permanent Court of International Justice.

9. The present provisions shall be duly accepted by the Bank for the settlement of any dispute, which may arise, between it and one or more of the signatory Governments as to the interpretation or application of its Statutes or the New Plan.

9. In accordance with the procedures prescribed in Article XV of the 1930 Hague Agreement, the Governments of Belgium, France, Germany, Italy and the United Kingdom appointed the five members of the Tribunal for a term of five years. The Government of France, in agreement with the Governments of Belgium, Italy and the United Kingdom, designated the Chairman of the Tribunal.[3] The procedures of the Tribunal are set out in Annex XII of the 1930 Hague Agreement (the full text may be found in Appendix A to this Award), which incorporates Chapter III of the Hague Convention of 1907 for the Pacific Settlement of International Disputes, except as modified by the 1930 Hague Agreement.

[3] Japan waived all its rights under the Agreement with Germany of 20 January 1930, including the Annexes to it, see Art. 8c of the Peace Treaty of 8 September 1951.

10. The members of the Tribunal, appointed in accordance with Article XV of the 1930 Hague Agreement, are Prof. W. Michael Reisman (United States of America), Chairman, Prof. Dr. Jochen A. Frowein (Germany), Prof. Dr. Mathias Krafft (Switzerland), Prof. Dr. Paul Lagarde (France) and Prof. Dr. Albert Jan van den Berg (The Netherlands). On 17 January 2001, the Tribunal designated Mrs. Phyllis Hamilton of the Permanent Court of Arbitration (hereafter the "PCA") as its Secretary and the International Bureau of the PCA as Registry.

11. The present dispute between the Claimants named herein and the Bank arises under the Statutes of the Bank for International Settlements of 20 January 1930, as amended on 8 January 2001 (hereafter the "Statutes").

12. Article 54(1) of the Statutes provides as follows:

> If any dispute shall arise between the Bank, on the one side, and any central bank, financial institution, or other bank referred to in the present Statutes, on the other side, or between the Bank and its shareholders, with regard to the interpretation or application of the Statutes of the Bank, the same shall be referred for final decision to the Tribunal provided for by the Hague Agreement of January, 1930.

13. By a Notice of Arbitration and Statement of Claim dated 7 March 2001, Dr. Horst Reineccius (hereafter "Dr. Reineccius") notified the Tribunal of his dispute with the Bank. Dr. Reineccius claimed that the compensation for his shares in the Bank, which had been cancelled when the Bank amended its Statutes at an Extraordinary General Meeting on 8 January 2001, was less than the value to which he was entitled (Claim No. 1).

14. On 23 March 2001, the Tribunal, in accordance with Article 54 of the Statutes, Article XV and Annex XII of the 1930 Hague Agreement (which incorporates Chapter III of the Hague Convention of 1907 for the Pacific Settlement of International Disputes, except as modified by the 1930 Hague Agreement), adopted Rules of Procedure for Arbitration between the Bank and Private Parties (hereafter "Rules for Arbitration"). Pursuant to Article 10(1) of the Rules for Arbitration, the Tribunal has its site at The Hague.

15. On 25 July 2001, Mr. Reginald Howe, a former private shareholder of the Bank, requested information from the Registry about the Bank's former private shareholders. The Registry in a letter dated 30 July 2001 requested the Bank's comments on Mr. Howe's request. Counsel for the Bank responded in a letter dated 2 August 2001 that the type of information Mr. Howe requested would be dealt with at the preliminary conference of the Parties. Pursuant to the Rules for Arbitration, Counsel for the Bank continued, participation in the preliminary conference and exchange of the type of information sought by Mr. Howe would only be possible after Mr. Howe filed a Notice of Arbitration and Statement of Claim against the Bank. In a letter from the Registry on 2 August 2001, Mr. Howe was asked to comment on the Bank's letter.

16. In a letter to the Secretary of the Tribunal dated 17 August 2001, Mr. Howe responded requesting "advice, clarification or information" from the Tribunal. Mr. Howe noted that he was aware of the procedure for joining the arbitration but that he did not at that time intend to file a Notice of Arbitration. The Registry on 21 August 2001 requested the Bank's comments on the new requests in Mr. Howe's letter. The Bank responded on 23 August 2001 that it was inappropriate for Mr. Howe to be requesting *ex parte* extraordinary relief and access to information without submitting to the jurisdiction of the Tribunal by submitting a Notice of Arbitration.

17. On 31 August 2001 the Tribunal responded with a Procedural Order that denied Mr. Howe's request to be allowed to attend the preliminary conference of the Parties without filing the requisite Notice of Arbitration. But the Order further directed the Secretary of the Tribunal to make available on the PCA website certain information regarding claims by former private shareholders against the Bank as well as a schedule of pending proceedings before the Tribunal.

18. By a Notice of Arbitration dated 31 August 2001, Claimant First Eagle SoGen Funds, Inc. (hereafter "First Eagle") initiated its proceedings against the Bank claiming that the compensation for its shares in the Bank which had been recalled by the Extraordinary General Meeting on 8 January 2001 was less than the value to which they were entitled (Claim No. 2).

19. On 7 September 2001, pursuant to Article 12 of the Rules for Arbitration, the Tribunal held a preparatory conference, at which it directed the Parties to confer with respect to the scheduling of proceedings, the terms of a confidentiality order and the production of requested documents relevant to the issues to be arbitrated and to report on those discussions by, as later extended, 21 September 2001.

20. On 10 October 2001, Mr. Pierre Mathieu submitted a Notice of Arbitration to the Tribunal claiming that the Bank had acted unlawfully in forcibly repurchasing his shares and a share held by the Société Hippique de La Châtre (hereafter collectively "Mr. Mathieu") (Claim No. 3).

21. On 11 October 2001, the Tribunal, having considered letters from the Parties regarding the subject of the allocation of the costs and deposits for the arbitrations, issued an Order on Costs directing that:

> 1. The Bank would immediately deposit half of the projected costs of the arbitration as detailed in the estimate submitted to the Parties at the First Preparatory Conference.
>
> 2. Each Claimant would immediately deposit an amount equal to its pro-rata share (based on the number of shares held by each Claimant) of the remaining half of the estimated costs of the arbitration. Further that the same formula based on the number of privately held shares would be used to allocate costs for any additional claimants in the arbitration taking into account the possibility that additional parties might increase the costs of the arbitration.

22. The Tribunal noted in its Order on Costs that, on 5 October 2001, the Bank had submitted its position concerning the distribution of costs among all the owners of privately held shares should they benefit from an Award made to the Claimants in the arbitration. In this eventuality, the costs of Claimant No. 1 and Claimant No. 2 could be reduced proportionally. The Tribunal also reserved the right to order a further deposit for costs should circumstances (such as, but not limited to, the complexity of issues raised in the Statements of Claim or Defense, the

length of time required for the scheduling of testimony or analysis of reports from expert witnesses, the extension of the number of days required for hearings, or a need for more meetings than presently projected) increase the costs of the arbitration.

23. On 17 October 2001, the Tribunal issued Procedural Order No. 1 (On Consent) containing a schedule of submissions including requirements for the timing and substance of each Claimant's Statement of Claim, Application for the Production of Documents, and Proposed Scheduling Order including the submission of pre-hearing Memorials of law and fact and of evidence in support of the claims. The Order directed the Bank to submit a Statement of Defense, a Response to the Application for the Production of Documents, and a Response to the Proposed Scheduling Order. The Order further provided that the Tribunal would convene a meeting, either in person or by telephone, to hear the Parties on the points in dispute arising from the Application for Production of Documents and Proposed Scheduling Orders and to make such orders and set such further proceedings as it deemed appropriate.

24. In addition, Procedural Order No.1 directed the Secretary to post on the Registry's website a notice advising that any prospective claimant that intended that its claims be subject to proceedings coordinated with those on claims filed as of 17 October 2001 (the date of the Order) should file a Statement of Claim by 15 November 2001. The Order noted that this provision did not constitute consent to any form of consolidation or coordination with any claims filed as of the date of the Order or claims that might be filed prior to 15 November 2001. The Order noted that in the event of additional Statements of Claim, the Bank reserved its right to request an extension of time to file its Statement of Defense. Claimant First Eagle reserved its right to oppose any such extension of time.

25. On 17 October 2001, the Parties jointly submitted an agreed confidentiality order governing the production of documents. Subject to that confidentiality order, the Bank produced to First Eagle the J.P. Morgan Report described in the Note to Private Shareholders dated 15 September 2000.

26. On 7 February 2002, the Tribunal issued Procedural Order No. 2 (On Consent) noting that First Eagle had submitted on 12 November 2001, pursuant to Procedural Order No. 1, a Statement of Claim against the Bank and an Application for the Production of Documents; pursuant to the same Order, the Bank submitted its Statement of Defense and a Response to the Application for the Production of Documents on 14 January 2002, as well as an Application for the Production of Documents from First Eagle. First Eagle and the Bank further agreed that on or before 11 February 2002, First Eagle would submit a Memorandum responding to the Bank's Application for the Production of Documents and that on or before 20 February 2002, the Bank would submit a Memorandum concerning First Eagle's Response to the Bank's Application for the Production of Documents. The Parties agreed that the Tribunal would meet with the Parties on 26 February 2002 in a conference on the Terms of Submission, at which time the Tribunal would also hear the Parties on any unresolved issues of procedure.

27. The Tribunal met with the Parties and their counsel on 26 February 2002 at The Hague for the purposes of establishing the Terms of Submission in accord with Article 12 of the Rules for Arbitration Between the Bank and Private Parties (effective 23 March 2001).

28. At the 26 February conference, the Chairman referred to a 22 February 2002 letter from the Bank and a 25 February 2002 response from the Freshfields law firm in Paris that dealt with questions concerning a potential conflict of interest should counsel from the Freshfields firm in Paris represent Mr. Mathieu. Counsel for Mr. Mathieu discussed with counsel for the Bank and the Tribunal the Freshfields firm's representation of the Bank of England and Prof. van den Berg's previous association with the Freshfields firm in Amsterdam. Prof. van den Berg indicated that the association had been terminated. Counsel for the Bank then indicated the Bank was satisfied that a conflict of interest did not exist.

29. On 5 March 2002 the Tribunal issued Procedural Order No. 3 on the Terms of Submission. In the Order, the Tribunal noted that the Parties had stated they had no jurisdictional objections, but that the following matters remained at issue between all or a number of the Parties:

(i) the lawfulness of the compulsory recall of the shares, including the procedures by which it was accomplished and the possible scope of the consequences of a finding of unlawfulness for all those who were private shareholders as of 8 January 2001;

(ii) the identification of the applicable standards for the valuation of the compulsorily recalled shares;

(iii) the application of the standards in (ii) above to the shares which were compulsorily recalled.

The Tribunal found it most economical to treat the first two issues in a single phase and to defer the third issue to a second, final phase, if it should prove necessary.

30. Although only Mr. Mathieu and the Bank had raised issue (i) above, both contended that a finding of unlawfulness would affect the recall program and all those who were shareholders as of 8 January 2001. A finding of unlawfulness of the compulsory recall of shares could therefore have affected all Claimants. Accordingly,

(i) the Tribunal requested Mr. Mathieu and the Bank to address all matters they deemed relevant to their contentions with respect to the lawfulness of the recall program including its consequences for those who were shareholders as of 8 January 2001;

(ii) the Tribunal requested Dr. Reineccius and First Eagle to address all matters they deemed relevant to the scope of the possible consequences of a finding of unlawfulness of the recall program for those who were shareholders as of 8 January 2001;

(iii) all the Parties were requested to address all matters they deemed relevant to the nature and extent of the rights of the private shareholders and the applicable standards for the valuation of the compulsorily recalled shares.

31. Procedural Order No. 3 further directed that (1) Mr. Mathieu should submit a consolidated Statement of Claim no later than 12 March 2002; (2) the three Claimants should submit Memorials no later than 20 April 2002; (3) the Respondent should submit Counter-Memorials no later than 15 July 2002; and (4) Hearings in this phase of the arbitration would take place in the Peace Palace in The Hague during the week of 26 August 2002.

32. The Tribunal granted the following requests of First Eagle for discovery from the Bank to be provided by 15 March 2002:

(i) documents relating to the Bank's offer to purchase shares held by private shareholders in or about 1975, including offering memoranda and other communications with shareholders, and valuations or other methods or analyses considered by the Bank in determining the offering price for such shares;

(ii) all subscription agreements relating to the Bank's issuance of new shares since 1969;

(iii) all documents relating to the Bank's determination of subscription prices for shares issued since 1969, including any valuations;

(iv) all documents provided to subscribers of shares since 1969, to the extent that they were offering memoranda, prospectuses, solicitation letters and financial statements;

(v) all documents since 1990 relating to the Bank's valuation of the Bank's shares;

(vi) all documents since 1990 concerning any transfer of its shares by the Bank including the price therefor;

(vii) all versions of the Bank's Statutes, as amended, since and including the original version adopted in or about 1930.

33. The Tribunal noted that Dr. Reineccius, Mr. Mathieu, and the Bank had stated that they had no discovery requests in this phase.

34. Pursuant to D.5 of Procedural Order No. 3 (Terms of Submission) dated 5 March 2002, the Parties agreed to modify the schedule for submissions contained in D.2-3 of that Order. Therefore, on 1 April 2002, the Tribunal issued Procedural Order No. 4 (On Consent) recording the Parties' agreement that:

(i) First Eagle should submit its Memorial no later than 6 May 2002;

(ii) Mr. Mathieu should submit his Memorial no later than 13 May 2002;

(iii) Dr. Reineccius should submit his Memorial or additions to the First Eagle Memorial no later than 13 May 2002;

(iv) the Respondent (the Bank) should submit Counter-Memorials no later than 22 July 2002.

35. The Tribunal further noted that having received pursuant to D.1 and E.3 of Procedural Order No. 3 the consolidated Statement of Claim of Mr. Mathieu on 12 March 2002 and both his Request for the Production of Documents dated 20 March 2002 and the Bank's Reply dated 26 March 2002, the Tribunal would grant the following requests of Mr. Mathieu for discovery on or before 5 April 2002 from the Bank:

(i) documents relating to the Bank's offer to purchase shares held by private shareholders in or about 1975, including offering memoranda and other communications with shareholders, and valuations or other methods or analyses considered by the Bank in determining the offering price for such shares;

(ii) all subscription agreements relating to the Bank's issuance of new shares since 1969;

(iii) all documents relating to the Bank's determination of subscription prices for shares issued since 1969, including any valuations;

(iv) all documents provided to subscribers of shares since 1969, to the extent that they are offering memoranda, prospectuses, solicitation letters and financial statements;

(v) all documents since 1990 relating to the Bank's valuation of the Bank's shares;

(vi) all documents since 1990 concerning any transfer of its shares by the Bank including the price therefor;

(vii) all versions of the Bank's Statutes, as amended, since and including the original version adopted in or about 1930;

(viii) documents described in paragraph 2(h) of Mr. Mathieu's 20 March 2002 Request.

36. The Tribunal received letters from the Parties concerning the production of documents in the arbitration in the course of April 2002. On 3 May 2002, the Tribunal issued Procedural Order No. 5 (Exchange of Documents Among Claimants, Access to BIS Archives, Assertion of Privilege) noting that the Parties had agreed that the Claimants would exchange documents with each other as well as sending copies to the Bank. However, all communications remained subject to the provisions of the Confidentiality Agreements between the Bank and Dr. Reineccius, First Eagle and Mr. Mathieu which had been concluded pursuant to paragraph 4 of Procedural Order No. 1 (On Consent).

37. Regarding First Eagle's Application dated 5 April 2002 for an Order directing the Bank to grant access to the Bank's archives and the Response thereto from the Bank dated 11 April 2002 opposing the Application, the Tribunal found that First Eagle's Application did not comply with the schedule agreed between the Parties in Procedural Order No. 1 nor with the schedule in Procedural Order No. 3, paragraph E, and was therefore out of order. The Application was therefore denied.

38. Procedural Order No. 5 granted First Eagle's Application for the Production of Documents as follows:

> 1. Non-production or redaction of the documents responsive to Procedural Order No. 3, paragraph E, based upon assertions of attorney-client privilege or special political or institutional sensitivity or other reasons consistent with those set forth in Article 9(2) of the IBA Rules on the Taking of Evidence in International Commercial Arbitration (1999) should be recorded by the Bank in a listing to be provided to First Eagle by 8 May 2002.
>
> 2. That listing should identify: (i) the bates number of the document, its author and recipients, (ii) the part of the document withheld or redacted, and (iii) the specific reason for non-production or redaction and the basis for the invocation of that reason. Any part of an otherwise responsive document withheld because the part is deemed not to be responsive should also be listed.
>
> 3. First Eagle should submit any objections to the reasons stated under paragraph 1 by 10 May 2002.
>
> 4. The Tribunal would dispatch its Secretary on 13 May 2002 to the place where the documents were retained by the Bank to resolve, in consultation with First Eagle and the Bank, the objections raised. Issues concerning document production under Procedural Order No. 3, paragraph E, which remained unresolved after the above review and consultation would be addressed to the Tribunal on or before 17 May 2002.

39. Pursuant to Procedural Order No. 5, First Eagle and the Bank resolved certain questions concerning the production of documents under the terms of Procedural Order No. 3. They then contacted the Secretary of the Tribunal to set up a conference call to address First Eagle's remaining concerns. At the telephone conference on 13 May 2002, attended by counsel for First Eagle and the Bank and the Secretary of the Tribunal, First Eagle indicated that still at issue with respect to their relevance were nine (9) documents, portions of which had been withheld

by the Bank for alleged lack of relevance under Procedural Order No. 3 or because of assertions of attorney-client privilege. Counsel for First Eagle and the Bank requested that the Secretary review the nine documents (as numbered in the document log dated 8 May 2002, prepared by the Bank to which First Eagle appended its Objections on 10 May 2002) that were kept in the Bank's offices in Basle, Switzerland, and then discuss by telephone conference with counsel for First Eagle and the Bank her recommendations regarding the relevance of the redacted portions. Counsel also agreed that they would submit legal memoranda to the Tribunal concerning the Bank's assertions of attorney-client privilege.

40. The Secretary reviewed the nine documents in question at the Bank's offices on 15 and 16 May 2002 and discussed with counsel the possible relevance of some parts of five documents to Section E.1.f of Procedural Order No. 5; counsel for the Bank agreed to produce portions of those five documents which had been previously redacted for lack of relevance. In a telephone conference with First Eagle's counsel and the Secretary on 16 May 2002, the Bank indicated to First Eagle that it would immediately produce those portions of the five documents. The Parties agreed that four other documents had been appropriately redacted. On 22 May 2002, the Bank submitted a Memorandum to the Tribunal on attorney-client privilege issues raised in First Eagle's 10 May 2002 Objections. First Eagle responded with a Memorandum in support of its Objections on 29 May 2002.

41. Seventeen documents that fell within the purview of Section E of Procedural Order No. 3 (Terms of Submission) were listed by the Bank; five documents were partially redacted and twelve documents were withheld entirely on the ground of attorney-client privilege. The documents were described in the log assembled by the Bank in compliance with Procedural Order No. 5 along with summaries of First Eagle's objections.

42. In its Objections submitted on 10 May 2002, First Eagle contended that the Bank was not entitled to invoke the attorney-client privilege because a company was not permitted to invoke the privilege against its own shareholders.

43. On 22 May 2002, the Bank stated in its Memorandum that attorney-client communications between the Bank and its counsel are protected by privilege in disputes between the Bank and its private shareholders under settled principles of law.

44. In its Memorandum of 29 May 2002, First Eagle contended that the differential treatment accorded by the Bank to its private shareholders with respect to the communications that First Eagle sought to discover was inconsistent with the principles of international law upon which First Eagle relied. Six of the documents the Bank withheld, First Eagle stated, would not benefit from privilege as they were created prior to the Board's announcement of the compulsory repurchasing program. First Eagle also contended that the Bank could not unilaterally withdraw documents that it had "inadvertently" produced.

45. On 11 June 2002, the Tribunal issued Procedural Order No. 6 (Order with Respect to the Discovery of Certain Documents for Which Attorney-Client Privilege Has Been Claimed) ordering the Bank to produce Document No. 34 to each of the Claimants in accordance with Procedural Order No. 5, insofar as it was disclosed at a press conference. The Tribunal determined that sixteen documents were subject to the attorney-client privilege.

46. In a letter dated 28 May 2002 to the Tribunal with copies to counsel for First Eagle and Respondent, the Bank, Dr. Reineccius requested that a banking expert be appointed. The Tribunal received in response to the letter from Dr. Reineccius comments from First Eagle on 4 June 2002, Mr. Mathieu on 10 June 2002, the Bank on 10 June 2002, and a further submission from Dr. Reineccius dated 11 June 2002. First Eagle and Mr. Mathieu, as well as the Bank, indicated that they considered the appointment of a banking expert at this stage of the arbitration to be premature since the matters that Dr. Reineccius proposed be submitted to a banking expert would not arise in the current phase of the arbitration.

47. The Tribunal reviewed the submissions of the Parties and on 17 June 2002 issued Procedural Order No. 7 (Order with Respect to the Request from Dr. Horst Reineccius, Claimant No. 1, that the Tribunal Appoint an

Expert) finding the request from Dr. Reineccius for the appointment of an expert to be premature.

48. Having conferred with the Parties and received from each Party its agreement to a proposed schedule, the Secretary, pursuant to Article 20 of the Rules for Arbitration, on 10 August 2002, transmitted the Agenda for the Hearings on 26-29 August 2002 to the Tribunal and Parties and published the Agenda on the Registry's website.

49. On 23 August 2002, the Tribunal issued Procedural Order No. 8 (Computer Assisted Projections, Requirements for Late Submissions of Evidence or Authorities) in response to: (1) a letter from the Bank dated 19 August 2002; (2) a letter from First Eagle dated 20 August 2002; and (3) a letter from the Bank dated 21 August 2002. This correspondence indicated that the Bank and First Eagle were unable to agree on the procedural requirements for (1) the employment of computer technology to project evidence and illustrate oral argument during the Hearings; and (2) the submission of evidence or legal authorities after the deadlines established in consultation with the Parties and set forth in Procedural Orders Nos. 3 and 4. The Tribunal found that:

(i) Use of demonstrative exhibits and other visual aids, whether computer assisted or otherwise, is not unusual in international arbitration hearings. Such visual aids may be employed by the Parties so long as the material concerned is based solely on evidence already in the record and has been shown to the opposing party prior to the Hearing for purposes of verification.

(ii) Introduction of new evidence will not be permitted unless a proper application has been made to the Tribunal, the latter has granted leave, and the opposing party has sufficient opportunity to present its comments thereon.

(iii) New legal authorities can be referred to at the Hearing as rebuttal or additional authorities, provided that they are not excessive in number.

(iv) Issues concerning allegedly truncated copies of legal authorities are in the first instance to be resolved between counsel. The Party alleging that authorities are incomplete has the duty to identify them to the Party that submitted them.

50. The full text of all of the above referenced Procedural Orders can be found at www.pca-cpa.org.

51. Public Hearings pursuant to Article XV of the 1930 Hague Agreement and Article 20 of the Rules for Arbitration were held in the Great Hall of Justice at the Peace Palace in The Hague from 26-28 August 2002. At the request of the Parties, their separate claims were heard in parallel with some integration for efficiency and the convenience of the Parties. First Eagle was represented, throughout the hearings, by Mr. Donald Francis Donovan and Mr. Dietmar W. Prager of the Debevoise & Plimpton firm. Mr. Mathieu was represented by Mr. Elie Kleiman and Mr. Guillaume Tattevin of the Freshfields Bruckhaus Deringer firm. The Bank was represented by Mr. Jonathan I. Blackman, Mr. Laurent Cohen-Tanugi and Ms. Claudia Annacker of the Cleary, Gottlieb, Steen & Hamilton firm. Prof. Dr. Mario Giovanoli and Dr. James Freis were also present on behalf of the BIS Secretariat and Prof. Giovanoli intervened in response to a question from the Tribunal on the first day of the Hearings.[4] Dr. Reineccius, appeared *pro se*, on 27 and 28 August; he declined to exercise his right to attend on 26 August during the presentations on the legality of the Bank's actions since the Bank's right to repurchase the shares was not at issue in his claim.

52. In accordance with the 1930 Hague Agreement, simultaneous translations in English, French and German were provided for the Hearings.

53. On the first day of the Hearings, pursuant to Procedural Order No. 8, First Eagle requested permission to submit a binder with additional legal authorities and the Bank requested the Tribunal's permission to submit as additional evidence three annual reports of First Eagle. The Tribunal agreed to receive the late submitted materials on the condition that

[4] Transcript, at p. 79.

counsel refrain from referring to the materials introduced as new evidence until the following day's presentations, when Question 2 of Procedural Order No. 3 would be taken up, so as to allow time for opposing counsel to examine the late-submitted material.[5]

[5] *Id.*, at p. 83.

CHAPTER III – THE PARTIES AND THEIR CLAIMS

A. IDENTITY OF THE PARTIES

54. Claimant No. 1, Dr. Horst Reineccius, resides in Hannover, Germany, and owned 20 shares of the Bank.

55. Claimant No. 2, First Eagle SoGen Funds, Inc., is a U.S.-registered mutual fund group organized under the laws of the State of Maryland, United States of America. First Eagle is managed by Arnhold and S. Bleichroeder Advisers, Inc., a U.S.-registered investment advisor. First Eagle has its address and principal place of business at 1345 Avenue of the Americas, New York, New York 10105. First Eagle owned 9085 of the shares of the Bank.

56. Claimant No. 3, Mr. Pierre Mathieu, resides at Urmont, F-36400 Montgivray, France, and owned 8 of the shares of the Bank; la Société Hippique de La Châtre is a non-profit association which owned one share and for purposes of this arbitration shares the same address as Mr. Mathieu.

57. Respondent, the Bank, was established, as stated above, pursuant to the 1930 Hague Agreement as a company limited by shares. The Bank's headquarters are in Basle, Switzerland.

B. TERMS OF SUBMISSION

58. Article 3(g) of the Rules for Arbitration contains the definition: "'Terms of Submission': as understood in the 1930 Agreement, the question or questions to be submitted to the Tribunal and the specific procedures to be followed."

59. In Procedural Order No. 3 on the Terms of Submission, dated 5 March 2002, the Tribunal noted that although the Parties had stated they had no jurisdictional objections, the following matters remained at issue between all or a number of the Parties:

(i) the lawfulness of the compulsory recall of the shares, including the procedures by which it was accomplished and the possible scope of the consequences of a finding of unlawfulness for all those who were private shareholders as of 8 January 2001;

(ii) the identification of the applicable standards for the valuation of the compulsorily recalled shares;

(iii) the application of the standards in (ii) above to the shares which were compulsorily recalled.

The Tribunal found it most economical to treat the first two issues in a single phase and to defer the third issue to a second, final phase, if it should prove necessary.

C. THE PARTIES' SUBMISSIONS

1. Claimant No. 1, Dr. Reineccius

a. ARGUMENTS

60. "[The Bank's use of] the dividend perpetuity (DPM) model for the valuation of the shares applied by the experts charged by the Bank . . . is suitable if a company distributes the major portion of its net profits totally . . . . For the last two financial years, the Bank for International Settlements distributed less than a fifth of the net profit, the DPM is, therefore, not acceptable."

61. "As additional arguments, . . . the Bank refers to the low prices on the stock exchange and the lack of voting right of the private shareholders. The extreme undervaluation of the BIS shares was, first of all, caused by the small dividends and, therefore by the Bank itself. The business policy of the Bank is ruled by the founder members as major shareholders. There is no divisive voting in the General Meetings of the BIS, the exclusion of the private shareholders was decided unanimously, too. Therefore, no particular importance should be attached to the lack of voting right of the private shareholders."

62. "The earning-power value method gives the value of a share as the quotient of the net profit per share and the bond yield . . . . The method of adjusted net asset value for the valuation of the BIS share is, likewise, suitable – not, however, the discount of 45% 'estimated' by the experts of J.P. Morgan & Cie SA. On the contrary, in the case of a well earning bank, we have to think of a premium because the Bank will increase the net assets by its future profits."

63. Dr. Reineccius indicated at the Hearings[6] that he would stipulate that the J.P. Morgan calculations of net asset value ("NAV") were correct.

b. RELIEF REQUESTED

64. Dr. Reineccius requested the Tribunal to find that:

(i) compensation should be based on the full value of the shares (the higher of an NAV analysis or earning power method analysis) including interest of 3¼% per annum from 8 January 2001;

(ii) the value of these shares cannot be smaller or lower than the NAV;

(iii) a first payment of 17,000 Swiss francs per share should be made to him; and

(iv) an expert should be appointed to calculate the earning power and the NAV of the Bank's shares on 8 January 2001 and explain which of the two results reflects the value of the shares correctly.

---

[6] *Id.*, at p. 331.

2. *Claimant No. 2, First Eagle*

a. ARGUMENTS

65. In its Memorial, First Eagle asserts:

> Under the Statutes, as well as international law, First Eagle is entitled to compensation equal to the full value of its proportionate interest in the Bank as a whole . . . . To measure the level of compensation due First Eagle, the Bank used a dividend perpetuity model, a variant of the discounted cash flow method. It used the model to value only the flow of dividends, however, even though the Bank regularly allocates the major portion of its profits to build up its assets. By valuing only the dividends, the Bank violated the excluded shareholders' right to participate equally in "the profits" of the Bank – all the profits.[7]
>
> The Bank also calculated its net asset value per share, which came to twice the level of compensation it paid. Rather than returning to the excluded shareholders their pro rata share of net asset value upon their exclusion from the company, the Bank applied discounts for lack of voting rights and non-marketability in the aggregate amount of 45%, which reduced the net asset value per share to roughly the level of compensation yielded by the valuation of the dividend flow . . . . [T]he Bank's shares are identical, and application of the discounts therefore violated the equal-rights guarantee of Article 13 of the Statutes.[8]

66. Exhibit 23, prepared by the Bank in 1969 for the benefit of the Board of Directors, was "an earlier instance of the distribution of profits and assets in which all shareholders were treated alike."[9] First Eagle asserts that the purpose of this memorandum was to determine the premium at which the third tranche would be priced . . . the value of the shares above their par value. In the memo the Bank considered three ways of valuing the shares: (1) a discounted cash flow analysis; (2) the market value; and (3) "the mathematical method". First Eagle argues that the memo records

---

[7] FE Memorial, at paras. 15-16.
[8] *Id.*, at paras. 17-18.
[9] Transcript, at p. 170.

that the Bank rejected methods (1) and (2) as flawed and recommended the mathematical method which First Eagle finds to be the NAV method.[10] First Eagle stated that the method determined in 1969 "has governed each of the issuances of shares to central bank shareholders and the Bank only departed from that method in the exclusion [of private shareholders] transaction . . . . In each of those [previous] cases the Bank used NAV minus 30 per cent."[11]

67. Exhibit 15, an internal BIS memorandum written in 1998, states that in a possible buy back, the price offered "should not be viewed as being less than the patrimonial value of each share."[12]

68. The imposition of the discounts would have violated international law even in the absence of the Article 13 guarantee. International Tribunals recognize that in an expropriation setting, the coercive character of the taking precludes the use of discounts for lack of voting rights or non-marketability to reduce the compensation due.[13]

69. First Eagle asserts that the Bank does not urge reliance on the dividend perpetuity model by which it set the excluded shareholders' compensation or the alternative measure of discounted net asset value. "Instead, [the Bank] argues that [it] has satisfied any obligation to the excluded shareholders by paying them compensation that exceeded the stock market trading prices . . . . [B]ecause the market for its shares is structurally flawed, trading prices do not provide reliable evidence of their value."

70. Market price, First Eagle asserts, is what the Bank offered in voluntary buy-back offers in 1936 and 1975; in both cases "they utterly failed."[14]

---

[10] *Id.*, at p. 171.
[11] *Id.*, at p. 172.
[12] *Id.*
[13] *Id.*, at p. 199.
[14] *Id.*, at p. 141.

71. First Eagle asserted that the transfer of the shares was illegal because the taking of that property "was not accompanied by full compensation for the property interest that was taken."[15]

> Full compensation for the taking . . . should be more than the Bank's net asset value, or NAV, per share.[16]
>
> Recognizing that NAV is both reliable and conservative, international tribunals have regularly granted compensation measured by NAV when requested to do so by the claimant. Using its own figures, the Bank has therefore deprived First Eagle of some $84 million.[17]

72. First Eagle further argued that:

> All shareholders of the Bank had an equal right, protected by international law, to participate in the fruits of the enterprise earned on the capital they contributed. If the non-central bank shareholders may now be excluded, their equal right to participate can only be vindicated by payment of compensation equal to their proportionate share of the value of the Bank as a whole, in the form of net assets, goodwill, and future prospects. The excluded shareholders, along with the other shareholders, owned the Bank, and that ownership cannot be overridden by the exclusion transaction.[18]

b. APPLICABLE LAW

73. In its Memorial, First Eagle stated that "general principles of international law govern this dispute" and that it, as well as the Bank, agrees that "the rules of general public international law apply to the interpretation of the Statutes and hence to the determination of the excluded shareholders' property interest in the Bank."[19] First Eagle added that "in particular the relevant provisions of the Bank's Statutes

---

[15] *Id.*, at p. 29.
[16] FE Memorial, at para. 22.
[17] *Id.*, at para. 25.
[18] *Id.*, at para. 30.
[19] *Id.*, at para. 205.

should be interpreted in accordance with general principles of international law governing the interpretation of treaties, which are expressed in Articles 31, 32 and 33 of the Vienna Convention on the Law of Treaties of 1969."[20]

74. Further First Eagle referred to and itself relied on a statement of the Bank that the relations of the Bank "with its shareholders are governed by its constituent instruments . . . supplemented as appropriate by general public international law."[21]

c. RELIEF REQUESTED

75. In response to the Tribunal's request during the Hearings for the written, final submissions of the Parties, First Eagle submitted the request that the Tribunal issue an award declaring that:

(i) The Bank has an obligation to pay First Eagle the full, undiscounted value of its proportionate interest in the Bank as a whole;

(ii) The full value of First Eagle's proportionate interest in the Bank must, as a matter of law, equal, at a minimum, First Eagle's pro rata share of the Bank's undiscounted net asset value;

(iii) The Bank's undiscounted net asset value must equal, at a minimum, the undiscounted net asset value calculated by the Bank in consultation with J.P. Morgan (that is, CHF 32,846 as of 30 November 2000), and First Eagle shall have the opportunity to present evidence as to the correct calculation of the Bank's net asset value in the next phase of this proceeding;

(iv) First Eagle is also entitled to additional compensation representing the amount by which its proportionate interest in the Bank's value as a going concern exceeds

20 *Id.*, at para. 206.
21 *Id.*, at para. 205.

its pro rata share of the Bank's undiscounted net asset value;

(v) On the basis of the evidence before the Tribunal, and as a matter of law, the trading prices of the publicly traded shares cannot be considered in determining the full value of First Eagle's proportionate interest in the Bank as a whole;

(vi) As a matter of law, the dividend perpetuity model cannot be used to determine the full value of First Eagle's proportionate interest in the Bank as a whole, and if any variant of the discounted cash flow method is used, the method must take account of the full profit making capacity of the Bank;

(vii) If the dividend perpetuity model were to be used to determine the value of First Eagle's property interest in the Bank, First Eagle shall have the opportunity to present evidence on the proper application of that model in the next phase of this proceeding;

(viii) First Eagle shall have the right to appropriate interest on the amounts awarded;

(ix) First Eagle shall be awarded the costs of the proceedings.

d. STIPULATION REGARDING CALCULATION OF NET ASSET VALUE

76. First Eagle stated during the oral hearings[22] that it was prepared to stipulate, if the Bank also so stipulated, that the net asset value is as determined by J.P. Morgan in Exhibit 43 of its report. However, since the J.P. Morgan Report did not contain a calculation of the value of the Bank's real estate, First Eagle proposed that the Tribunal appoint a Tribunal expert to determine the real estate value whose valuation would be final and would be added to the net asset value.

---

[22] Transcript, at p. 329.

3. *Claimant No. 3, Mr. Mathieu*

a. ARGUMENTS

77. The resolution of 8 January 2001 amending the Statutes (modifying Articles 6, 12, 15-18, adding Article 18A) was illegal because it did not conform to the Constituent Instruments of the Bank. "An analysis of the Statutes and the Charter of the Bank in conformity with settled principles of international law regarding the interpretation of treaties,[23] does not authorize the addition of an article. Even if such an addition had been authorized, it should not have been effected pursuant to Article 57 of the Bank's Statutes which provides that amendments may be 'adopted by a majority of the General Meeting', but rather pursuant to Article 58 of the Statutes which provides that: 'the amendment must be adopted by a two-thirds majority of the Board, approved by a majority of the General Meeting and sanctioned by a law supplementing the Charter of the Bank'."[24]

78. Mr. Mathieu concluded that the resolution purporting to amend the Statutes, as an act of an international organization not in conformity with its Constituent Instruments, was null and void. Thus, the recall of the privately held shares is null and void as to all the private shareholders. Mr. Mathieu cited as evidence that the Bank did not have the power to exclude the private shareholders, an internal memo authored by Mr. Weiser in 1936 that stated: "one thing the General Meeting cannot do is to deprive shareholders of their membership in the common venture."[25]

79. The illegality of the Bank's resolution also constitutes an unlawful act (*acte illicite*) under international law subjecting the Bank to a claim for damages.

80. Further, even should the Tribunal not find the Bank's resolution to have been illegal, the compulsory recall of the shares constitutes an unlawful expropriation. The compulsory recall was carried out by a subject of

[23] Vienna Convention on the Law of Treaties, 23 May 1969, 1155 UNTS 331, Art. 31(3)(c).
[24] Transcript, at pp. 17-19, 25-26.
[25] Exhibit 35, Transcript, at p. 12.

international law, deprived the claimant of his property, *i.e.* his shares, and was inspired by economic and financial rather than political considerations. Further, the Bank has violated general principles of international law because the conditions necessary for the lawful expropriation of property – the existence of a legislative foundation, service to the public interest, respect for the principle of non-discrimination, and just and fair compensation – were not met.

b. APPLICABLE LAW

81. Mr. Mathieu asserted that the present dispute is governed by the Constituent Instruments of the Bank. He further stated that "en l'absence de précision ou dispositions contraires des Instruments constitutifs de la BRI, le droit international général est également applicable".

82. Mr. Mathieu also contended that, since the award will be rendered in The Netherlands and since the award can conceivably be enforced in Switzerland where the Bank is located, the Tribunal must consider the international public policy of these two countries.

c. RELIEF REQUESTED

83. Mr. Mathieu, in his submission "Conclusions modificatives" of 28 August 2002, asked the following:

> M. Mathieu et la Société de Concours Hippique de La Châtre (ci après, *"le Demandeur"*) requièrent qu'il plaise au Tribunal Arbitral recevoir les présentes conclusions modificatives qui annulent et remplacent les conclusions figurant en pages 56 à 58 du Mémoire en demande en date du 13 mai 2002 et, y faisant droit, statuer comme suit:
>
> 1. A titre principal:
>
>   1.1. Dire et juger que la résolution du 8 janvier 2001 est illégale;
>
>   1.2. La dire en conséquence nulle;

1.3. Constater le caractère irréversible des opérations de mise en œuvre de ladite résolution et, en particulier, l'impossibilité de réinscrire les actions de la Banque des Règlements Internationaux (ci-après *"la BRI"*) à la cote des marchés boursiers réglementés de Paris et de Zurich; dire que cette impossibilité fait dès lors obstacle à toute restitution à l'identique;

1.4. Ordonner, en conséquence de l'illégalité de la résolution du 8 janvier 2001 et de la nullité l'invalidant, une restitution intégrale par équivalent, et en conséquence condamner la BRI au paiement au Demandeur d'une compensation financière correspondant: (i) à la valeur patrimoniale des actions dont le Demandeur a été privé, estimée au 8 janvier 2001, date de la résolution invalidée, augmentée des intérêts capitalisés ayant couru depuis cette date jusqu'à la date du parfait paiement au Demandeur; et (ii) au montant des dividendes dont le Demandeur a été privé depuis le 8 janvier 2001, avec intérêts capitalisés depuis la date de leur mise en versement jusqu'à la date de parfait paiement au Demandeur;

2. En outre:

2.1. Dire et juger qu'en adoptant une résolution illégale, la BRI a engagé sa responsabilité internationale;

2.2. Dire et juger que l'opération de retrait forcé constitue une expropriation illicite de nature à engager la responsabilité de la BRI;

2.3. Dire et juger que le Demandeur a subi un dommage du fait des actes illicites de la BRI;

2.4. En conséquence, condamner la BRI au paiement au Demandeur d'une compensation financière correspondant: (i) dans l'hypothèse où le Tribunal ne ferait pas droit aux demandes sollicitées au point 1. ci-dessus, à la valeur patrimoniale des actions dont le Demandeur a été privé, estimée au 8 janvier 2001, date de la résolution querellée, augmentée des intérêts capitalisés ayant couru depuis cette date jusqu'à la date du parfait paiement au Demandeur; et en toute hypothèse (ii) au préjudice matériel et moral subi par le Demandeur;

3. Dans tous les cas, aux fins de calcul de la réparation par équivalent pour la privation de la propriété des actions:

   3.1. Rejeter les estimations de la BRI; et:

   3.2. Ordonner, le cas échéant par une sentence intérimaire, qu'il soit fait application de la méthode de l'actif net réévalué pour estimer à la date du 8 janvier 2001 la valeur des actions reprises;

   3.3. Dire qu'aucune décote ne viendra diminuer les estimations retenues;

   3.4. Dire en conséquence que le montant du supplément d'indemnisation que devra verser la BRI au Demandeur, venant s'ajouter aux sommes que la BRI a d'ores et déjà reconnu devoir, correspondra à la différence entre le montant de l'indemnisation reconnue et celui qui sera établi par application de la méthode de l'actif net réévalué;

4. Subsidiairement:

   4.1. Dire et juger qu'en tout état de cause la BRI doit aux actionnaires évincés la valeur de leurs actions;

   4.2. Constater que cet engagement n'a pas été rempli;

4.3. Retenir en conséquence une méthode plus appropriée pour évaluer la valeur des actions reprises;

4.4. Dire que cette valeur doit être déterminée par la méthode de l'actif net réévalué;

5. Dans l'hypothèse où la Sentence du Tribunal serait définitive, dire et juger que la BRI paiera au Demandeur les frais de toute nature exposés dans le cadre de la procédure arbitrale, et en particulier mettre à sa charge les honoraires des Conseils du Demandeur.

84. Mr. Mathieu indicated that he joined the other Claimants in the stipulation described in paragraph 76 above regarding the use of the NAV as determined in Exhibit 43 of the J.P. Morgan Report with the addition of the value of the Bank's real estate.[26]

4. Respondent, The Bank for International Settlements

a. ARGUMENTS

(i) Lawfulness of the Share Redemption

85. The Bank filed its Statement of Defense and Counterclaim on 14 January 2002 and its Counter-Memorial on 22 July 2002. Pursuant to Procedural Order No. 3, the Bank first addressed the lawfulness of the compulsory redemption of the privately held shares. The Bank maintained that it had the authority to amend the Statutes of the Bank under Article 57 of the Statutes. The Bank asserted that "any Article of the Statutes", other than the "reserved" articles listed in Article 58, might be amended by a two-thirds majority of its Board of Directors and adoption of such proposal by a majority of the General Meeting "provided that such amendments are not inconsistent with the provisions of the Articles enumerated in Article 58."[27]

---

[26] Transcript, at p. 318.
[27] Counter-Memorial, at para. 8.

86. The Bank denied that a valid distinction existed between "adding" an article or "amending" an article as Mr. Mathieu contended. "'Amendment' includes any change, including by way of adding new terms to an existing instrument or agreement."[28] Further, there is no basis for Mr. Mathieu's argument that the Article 58 procedure for the amendment of reserved articles, requiring a supplement to the Bank's Charter and Swiss legislative approvals, should be applied to the unreserved articles. The Statutes explicitly distinguish between amendment of the unreserved articles by the procedures of Article 57 and amendment of the reserved articles under Article 58. The Bank has made no amendment of the reserved articles.[29]

(ii) The Consequences of a Finding of Unlawfulness

87. The Bank asserted that if the Tribunal finds the transaction illegal, (1) the Bank would have to restore the recalled shares to the private shareholders; or (2) the private shareholders could only elect to retain the compensation that they had been paid for their shares on the basis of a voluntary agreement with the Bank. The Bank argued that a finding of unlawfulness would render impossible the increase in compensation for the recalled shares sought by First Eagle.[30]

(iii) The Standard of Valuation

88. The Bank disputes First Eagle's assertion that the private shareholders possessed "a proportionate interest in the Bank as a whole".[31] The Bank contended that the shareholders of the Bank lack the fundamental characteristics of equity ownership; they lack: voting rights (Statutes, Article 14), the right "to elect members of the board (id)", and the right to "transfer shares without the approval of the Bank and the central bank of the state to whose national issue the shares belong (Statutes, Art. 12)."[32] New central banks have paid more than the market price for

[28] *Id.*, at para. 9.
[29] *Id.*, at para. 11.
[30] *Id.*, at para. 90.
[31] FE Memorial, at para. 15.
[32] Counter-Memorial, at para. 20.

shares of their own new national issue because "these shares could give them what no other shareholder could ever obtain, participation in the governance and control of the Bank through the voting rights that the existence of these new shares uniquely provided to them."[33]

89. As regards the method of valuation applied by the Bank in awarding compensation for the repurchased shares, the Bank asserted that the standard of valuation to be applied is the fair market value represented by the market price of the Bank's publicly traded shares rather than the value of the proportionate ownership in the Bank by the shareholders as suggested by Claimant First Eagle. The methods of valuation proposed by First Eagle are useful to "approximate what fair market value would be in the absence of a functioning market for the property at issue. Where there is such a market, the market price itself furnishes the standard of fair market value."[34]

90. The Bank further contended that the shares of the Bank lack the fundamental characteristics of equity ownership because they lack voting rights, the right to elect members of the Board of Directors, and the right to transfer shares without the consent of the Bank and the central banks of the respective member countries. Further the Bank maintains that shareholders have no right to participate in the profits of the Bank other than the right to receive dividends, and the right to participate in the assets of the Bank is limited to the event of the Bank's liquidation.[35]

91. The Bank also asserted that its shares are traded on recognized stock markets as opposed to the contention by First Eagle that the shares are not traded in a fully efficient market. International law does not require an "efficient market", but simply requires that the market price be freely and fairly determined in a regular market. Therefore, the market price for the Bank's shares furnishes the best and most logical indication of the fair market value at the time the private shareholders were notified of the mandatory redemption. The Bank further submitted that the redemption price satisfied the compensation standards of Human Rights law. The

---

[33] *Id.*, at para. 24.
[34] *Id.*, at para. 27.
[35] *Id.*, at para. 104.

Bank relied on the Convention for the Protection of Human Rights and Fundamental Freedoms,[36] which the Bank contends does not confer on the expropriated owner an unqualified right to compensation of the full value of the expropriated property. The Bank also relied on the American Convention on Human Rights,[37] which provides for "just" as opposed to "full" compensation (Article 21(2) of the Convention). The Bank, therefore, asserts that the standard is one of appropriate, reasonable, fair or equitable compensation.

92. While the Bank accepted that public international law applies to the dispute, it contended that the share redemption should be evaluated under the standards of Human Rights law. The Bank rejected First Eagle's contention that the redemption by the Bank of its own shares is subject to the rules governing the taking of "alien" property by a state. The Bank argued that there is no reason to conclude that private shareholders should be treated as having been aliens in their legal relations to the Bank. The relations between the Bank and its shareholders are subject to the Bank's exclusive organic jurisdiction, *i.e.* the jurisdiction of an organization over its constituents. The shareholders are part of the internal order of the Bank; Human Rights law is the correct standard for a decision concerning any alleged interference with property rights due to the exercise of legislative and administrative powers over the privately held shares. The share redemption was not discriminatory under the Human Rights standard; there was no differential treatment without an objective and reasonable justification and without a relationship of proportionality between the means employed and the aim sought to be realized. The repurchase did not constitute a fundamental change in the Bank that would have required Article 58 procedures. Rather "the existence of the private shareholders just arises out of a tolerance that was granted to central banks initially."[38] "Article 57 was chosen [because] it was not believed to be a change which would affect the basic character of the Bank."[39]

---

[36] 4 November 1950, 213 UNTS, p. 222 (Bank's LA-130).
[37] 22 November 1969, 123 UNTS, p. 1144 (Bank's LA-132).
[38] Transcript, at p. 78.
[39] *Id.*, at p. 79.

93. The Bank asserted that First Eagle wrote to the Bank on 23 June 2000 requesting that the Bank should "consider a public share repurchase on terms similar to the recent share issuances." The Bank concluded that First Eagle's allusion to recent share issuances "presumably refers to the 1999 subscription of new central banks at 30 per cent off net asset value."[40]

94. The Bank indicated it agreed to the use of the J.P. Morgan Report calculations (Exhibit 43) for any finding regarding NAV.[41]

95. The Bank counterclaimed against First Eagle requesting damages for breach by First Eagle of Article 54 of the Statutes in wrongfully ignoring that jurisdictional commitment and suing the Bank in the United States to avoid the jurisdiction of the Tribunal, and for the costs of the arbitration.

b. APPLICABLE LAW

96. The Bank stated that its internal governance, *i.e.* the relation of the Bank to its shareholders, and acts such as the compulsory redemption of the privately held shares performed by the Bank *jure imperii*, are governed by its Constituent Instruments, supplemented by applicable general public international law.[42]

97. The Bank contested Mr. Mathieu's assertion that the Tribunal should take into account Dutch and Swiss public policy. The Bank argued that the Tribunal's Award is governed solely by public international law and that national courts lack jurisdiction *ratione materiae* to annul or invalidate an award of an international court or Tribunal under international law, particularly when it involves a sovereign party acting *jure imperii*.[43]

---

[40] Exhibit 22, Transcript, at p. 325.
[41] Transcript, at p. 331.
[42] Counter-Memorial, at paras. 48-51.
[43] *Id.*, at paras. 53-54.

98. The Bank argued that the share redemption is also subject to the rules of Human Rights law when property is taken for public purposes. "While international organizations usually do not exercise personal or organic jurisdiction over private parties other than their own officials, such jurisdiction may be conferred on an organization by its member states or by the private parties' voluntary acceptance of the organization's internal law" excluding their relations from the state's legislative, administrative, and adjudicative competence.[44] The Bank analogized the present case where it alleged the private party has chosen to become a part of an international organization to the bond between a state and its nationals or residents. The Bank's jurisdiction over private parties with whom it has this special relationship is "parallel to the jurisdiction of states over their nationals."[45] " . . . [T]he European Court of Justice has relied

---

[44] See, *e.g. Weiss v. Institute for Intellectual Cooperation*, 81 Journal de droit international, pp. 744, 745 (Fr. Conseil d'Etat, 20 February 1953) ("[The claimant is] an official of a body with an international character; consequently the Conseil d'Etat has no jurisdiction, in the matter of a claim, in respect of difficulties arising between said international body and one of its officials.") (Bank's LA-101); *ICEM v. Chiti*, II Italian Y.B. of Int'l L., pp. 348, 350-351 (1976) (It. Cass., 7 November 1973) ("Case law has also upheld that acts of self-organisation and the regulation of organisational relations, amongst which are those of public employment, are an expression of the sovereign power of the international law subject in the same way that they are, in Italy, the expression of the sovereign power of the Italian State and are governed by public law . . . . [These acts] should be governed by the international organisation's own rules and are consequently exempted from the Italian legal system as well as from Italian jurisdiction, because of the said immunity.") (Bank's LA-102); *In re Dame Adrien*, 6 Ann. Dig., p. 33 (Fr. Conseil d'Etat, 17 July 1931) (Conseil d'Etat stating it had no competence because: "[t]he petitioners [French officials of the Reparations Commission] belonged to an international organisation and their position was determinable only by international public law") (Bank's LA-103); Finn Seyersted, *Jurisdiction over Organs and Officials of States, the Holy See and Intergovernmental Organisations (2)*, 14 ICLQ, pp. 493, 505 (1965) (Bank's LA-104); Hans-Peter Kunz-Hallstein, *Die Beteiligung Internationaler Organisationen am Rechts und Wirtschaftsverkehr*, Gewerblicher Rechtsschutz und Urheberrecht, Internationaler Teil, pp. 819, 824 (1987) ("Aufgrund der Organisationsgewalt der Internationalen Organisationen [comprising personal jurisdiction] sind ihre inneren Angelegenheiten der Legislationsgewalt der Staaten und deren Gerichtsbarkeit der Sache nach (*ratione materiae*) unmittelbar entzogen.") (Bank's LA-105), *id.*, at p. 73, fn. 90.

[45] Counter-Memorial, at para. 124. First Eagle relies on the International Court of Justice's Advisory Opinion in *Reparations for Injuries Suffered in the Service of the United Nations* as support for its suggestion that the present organic dispute should nonetheless be subject to the rules governing the taking of alien property. FE Memorial, at para. 263. That case is not instructive here. There, the International Court of Justice ("ICJ") had to determine whether the

exclusively on Human Rights law to decide any alleged interferences with property rights by the European Community in the exercise of its legislative or administrative powers over private parties."[46] "*A fortiori*," the Bank asserted, "human rights law applies to the organic relations between the BIS and its shareholders . . . . "[47]

c. RELIEF REQUESTED

99. In response to the request of the Tribunal for final written submissions, the Bank stated:

> The Bank requests that the Tribunal issue an award:
>
> 1. declaring that the Bank is an international organization and that its relations with its shareholders are governed by its constituent instruments and applicable general public international law;
>
> 2. declaring that the mandatory redemption of the Bank's privately held shares was lawful;
>
> 3. declaring that the standard of compensation for the redeemed shares is fair market value;
>
> 4. declaring that the Bank paid fair market value for its shares by compensating the former private shareholders at roughly twice the market price of its shares on 8

United Nations had the capacity to bring a claim in respect of injury caused by a third party to an agent of the United Nations in the performance of his duties. When the ICJ stated that the legal bond between the United Nations and its staff cannot be assimilated to that of a state and its nationals it was considering the external relations between the United Nations and a third party, involving the concurrent jurisdiction of the official's national state, rather than internal relations. Nonetheless the ICJ held that the United Nations possesses a right of functional protection in respect to its agents, recognizing the existence of some system of attribution even in external relations. *Reparations for Injuries Suffered in the Service of the United Nations*, ICJ Reports 1949, at pp. 184-185 (Bank's LA-59), Counter-Memorial, para. 124, at fn. 92.

[46] See, *e.g.* Case 4/73, *Nold v. Commission*, ECR I, pp. 491, 508, at para. 14 (1974) (Bank's LA-108); Case 44/79, *Hauer v. Rheinland-Pfalz*, ECR, pp. 3727, 3745-3746 (1979) (Bank's LA-109), *id.*, at p. 75, fn. 94.

[47] Counter-Memorial, at para. 125.

September 2000, the last trading day before the mandatory redemption was announced;

5. granting the Bank damages for First Eagle's breach of Article 54(1) of the Statutes;

6. granting the Bank the costs of the arbitration; and

7. granting the Bank further relief as the Tribunal deems just and proper.

CHAPTER IV – QUESTION 1 OF PROCEDURAL ORDER NO. 3

100. Procedural Order No. 3 (Terms of Submission) of 5 March 2002, it will be recalled, identified the first of the three matters at issue between all or a number of the Parties as:

> 1. The lawfulness of the compulsory recall of the shares, including the procedures by which it was accomplished and the possible scope of the consequences of a finding of unlawfulness for all those who are private shareholders as of 8 January 2001.

In Section C of Procedural Order No. 3, the Tribunal said:

> 1. Although only Mr. Mathieu and the Bank have raised Issue 1 above, both contend that a finding of unlawfulness would affect the recall program and all those who were shareholders as of 8 January 2001. A finding of unlawfulness of the compulsory recall of shares could therefore affect all the Claimants in these cases.

Accordingly, the Tribunal stated in Section C.1 and C.2:

> 1. The Tribunal requests Mr. Mathieu and the Bank to address all matters they deem relevant to their contentions with respect to the lawfulness of the recall program including its consequences for those who were shareholders as of 8 January 2001;
>
> 2. The Tribunal requests Dr. Reineccius and First Eagle to address all matters they deem relevant to the scope of the possible consequences of a finding of unlawfulness of the recall program for those who were shareholders as of 8 January 2001.

101. It will be recalled that Claimant No. 1, Dr. Reineccius, indicated that he did not believe that there was substance to the claim raised by Claimant No. 3 and, accordingly, would not make a written submission on this matter. However, he reserved his right to make comments on this matter at the Hearings. He later notified the Secretary of the Tribunal that he

would not attend the Hearing on the day that this particular issue was examined.

102. Similarly, First Eagle, in its Memorial of 6 May 2002, stated that "The Bank's authority under its Statutes to effect a mandatory repurchase or partial liquidation upon payment of full compensation is not at issue in the proceeding between First Eagle and the Bank."[48] Nonetheless, First Eagle did avail itself of the opportunity to inform the Tribunal, in its Memorial and at the Hearing, of its view of the scope of possible consequences of a finding of unlawfulness of the recall program.

103. The Tribunal will consider first Mr. Mathieu's arguments with respect to the lawfulness of the recall program. Depending upon its decision about the lawfulness of the recall program, the Tribunal will then turn to the arguments of Mr. Mathieu and First Eagle with respect to the possible consequences of a finding of unlawfulness.

A. First Preliminary Issue: The Character and Status of the Bank

104. The first preliminary issue in the context of question 1 which the Tribunal must address is the legal character and status of the Bank.

105. The Tribunal notes that the rather complicated manner in which the Bank was established must be seen in light of the stage of development of international law in 1930. Apparently, at that time some of the parties to the treaty had doubts as to whether a treaty could establish under public international law a company limited by shares and whether such a company could be generally recognized.

106. For these reasons the parties to the treaty chose to adopt a model whereby pursuant to the treaty obligation Switzerland undertook to grant the Constituent Charter of the Bank and thereby create the company. At the same time, however, the parties made clear that, even though the Charter, as an Annex to the treaty, was also issued under Swiss law, the

[48] FE Memorial, at para. 362.

company could not be subjected to Swiss law. This complicated system does not exclude the applicability of Swiss law for formalities, for instance as to the procedure for general meetings of the Bank, where this is not in conflict with the relevant instruments of international law.

107. Switzerland, however, which takes a monist approach, considers that international law is automatically valid in the Swiss legal order, *i.e.* without needing any act of transformation or incorporation. Accordingly, the Swiss Government granted the Charter by merely ratifying the Convention, after it had been approved by the Swiss Parliament, without enacting any additional legislation. This practice has been followed for all amendments that fell under Article 58 of the Statutes when a "reserved" article was being amended. The Government of Switzerland, by approving this amendment, "sanctioned [the amendment] by a law supplementing the Charter of the Bank" in the sense of Article 58 of the Statutes.

108. The Constituent Instruments confirm that the Bank was established under international law in conformity with a treaty between the Governments of Germany, Belgium, France, the United Kingdom, Italy, Japan[49] and Switzerland, which was concluded on 20 January 1930. Under Article 1 of the Convention, Switzerland undertook "to grant to the Bank for International Settlements, without delay, the following Constituent Charter having force of law . . . . " By approving the Convention, the Swiss Parliament gave the Swiss Government the competence to ratify this treaty and to grant the Constituent Charter, which is an integral part of the Convention. Article 1 of the Charter stated "[t]he Bank for International Settlements . . . is hereby incorporated". Article 2 of the said Charter added that the constitution, the operations and the activities of the Bank were "defined and governed by the annexed Statutes". The Statutes of the Bank and its Constituent Charter were thus determined by an intergovernmental agreement and were annexed to the Convention. The granting of the Charter by Switzerland did not thereby subordinate the Bank to Swiss law. Paragraph 5 of the Charter provided that

[49] See *supra* fn. 3.

> The said Statutes and any amendments which may be made thereto in accordance with Paragraphs 3 or 4 hereof respectively shall be valid and operative notwithstanding any inconsistency therewith in the provisions of any present or future Swiss law.[50]

Thus, the sequence of steps by which the Bank was established demonstrates its international treaty origin. The Bank was created by Governments, through an international instrument, which instrument obligated Switzerland to provide a venue and local status, as well as prescribed immunities. The Bank is chartered as a company limited by shares under Swiss law, while it is registered as an "Internationale Organisation mit eigenem Rechtsstatus" in the "Handelsregister des Kantons Basel-Stadt Hauptregister".[51]

109. The declaration of the Swiss Federal Council (Swiss Federal Government) to the Swiss Federal Parliament of 7 February 1930 makes the sequence of steps of establishment and the preeminence and independence of the international character of the Bank clear:

> La convention concernant la banque des règlements internationaux distingue entre les dispositions conventionnelles proprement dites et la charte constitutive de la banque, qui est réputée constituer un acte de droit interne suisse . . . . Par les premières, la Suisse s'engage à promulguer la charte constitutive et à ne pas la modifier sans le consentement des Etats signataires; en outre, la mise en vigueur et la durée du traité s'y trouvent réglées; enfin, il est prévu, pour le règlement de tous différends survenant entre les Etats contractants, une instance arbitrale . . . . Le contenu de la charte, qui doit être accordée par la Suisse, se trouve intégralement dans la convention. La charte octroie à la banque la personnalité juridique du droit suisse, sanctionne ses statuts nonobstant toute contradiction avec les dispositions impératives de ce droit, et énonce ses privilèges fiscaux et administratifs . . . .[52]

---

[50] See also Constituent Charter, at para. 5.
[51] See Counter-Memorial, at para. 36, fn. 22.
[52] Feuille fédérale de la Confédération suisse, Vol. 1, p. 87 (1930).

110. By the same token, the Swiss commitment not to apply Swiss law in particular to the operations and activities of the Bank was matched by a commitment by the treaty partners establishing the Bank not to change the Statutes in ways that would impose upon Switzerland a different regime, without Swiss concurrence:

> Dans la charte, la Suisse reconnaît, en outre, les statuts de la banque, ainsi que leurs modifications éventuelles, même si les statuts portent atteinte aux dispositions impératives du droit suisse actuel ou futur . . . . Il y a lieu de noter, en particulier, que les dispositions statutaires essentielles ne peuvent être modifiées que par une loi additionnelle à la charte de la banque . . . . Le caractère de la banque – c'est une des conditions de la conclusion de la convention par la Suisse – ne peut donc être modifié sans l'assentiment de notre pays.[53]

111. And, indeed, the Statutes, which were part of the Convention, specify, in Article 60 (currently Article 58), those provisions of the Statutes which, in addition to the adoption by the Bank's amendment procedure also required the enactment of a law "supplementing the Charter of the Bank." The same condition is inserted in Paragraph 4 of the Charter of the Bank, which was also part of the Convention.

112. While the internal structure of the Bank was, according to Article 1 of the Statutes, "a Company limited by Shares," and the Board of the Bank was comprised, on a permanent basis, of the governors of the central banks of the seven founding States and their nominees, the essential international character of the Bank is apparent from its treaty origin.

113. Moreover, the functions of the Bank were quintessentially public international in their character. Auboin, one of the first managing directors of the BIS, has written:

> After the first world war, however, and especially during the currency stabilizations of the period 1922-1930, the principal central banks frequently joined forces for the purpose of granting special "stabilization credits" either in connection with the

---

[53] *Id.*, at pp. 92 and 93.

> reconstruction work undertaken by the Financial Committee of the League of Nations or independently of these schemes. It was therefore natural enough that the monetary and political authorities soon became interested in the idea of substituting for such ad hoc and temporary associations a more permanent system of cooperation.[54]

114. From its inception, the Bank was charged with the performance of a particularly urgent international task. Article 3 of the original Statutes (which is unchanged in the current Statutes) sets out the objects of the Bank in general terms:

> The objects of the Bank are: to promote the co-operation of central banks and to provide additional facilities for international financial operations; and to act as trustee or agent in regard to international financial settlements entrusted to it under agreements with the parties concerned.

Article 4 of the original Statutes, which was abrogated in 1969 (long after it ceased to be relevant to the work of the Bank), makes clear that the principal reason for the creation of the Bank was the management of the so-called "New Plan" or "Young Plan," as it has come to be known, for the settlement of German reparations, a major international and intergovernmental problem at that time.

115. The Bank has cited a number of international instruments that explicitly recognize the Bank as an international organization:[55] the Headquarters Agreement with Switzerland of 1987,[56] the Host Country Agreement

---

[54] R. Auboin, The Bank for International Settlements, 1930-1955, Essays in International Finance, No. 22, Map 1955, at pp. 1-2 (Bank's LA-25).

[55] Counter-Memorial, at para. 40.

[56] Accord entre le Conseil fédéral suisse et la Banque des Règlements internationaux en vue de déterminer le statut juridique de la Banque en Suisse (Agreement between the Swiss Federal Council and the Bank for International Settlements to determine the Bank's legal status in Switzerland), 10 February 1987, SR 0.192.122.971.3 (Bank's LA-16).

Between the Bank and the People's Republic of China of 1998,[57] and the Host Country Agreement with Mexico of 2002.[58]

116. Dr. Reineccius and Mr. Mathieu accept the identity of the Bank as an international organization. First Eagle raises questions about the Bank's identity.[59] First Eagle is incorrect in stating that the above cited Headquarters Agreements do not recognize the Bank as an international organization. Such recognition clearly flows from the provisions of the Agreements. First Eagle begs the question when it contends that, unlike the World Bank and the International Monetary Fund, the Bank for International Settlements has private shareholders and thus cannot be an international organization. That is precisely the question being considered.

117. Nor is First Eagle correct in stating that because the Bank performs some commercial activities common to private sector banks, it cannot be an international organization. Any international organization may have to engage in some private sector activities in pursuit of its public functions and does not automatically and *pro tanto* lose its public international legal character because of them. The fact that international organizations use many of the same accounting techniques as private entities tells us nothing, for these are methods for control and efficiency which are required, in one form or another, in any large scale collaboration. Nor is the Bank the only international organization that shows a profit. But even if the Bank were singular in this regard, or its profits far exceeded those of other international organizations, First Eagle itself acknowledges that

---

57 Art. 1 (Legal Personality and Capacity) reads: "The Government acknowledges the international legal personality and the legal capacity of the Bank within the People's Republic of China, including the HKSAR." Host Country Agreement between the Bank for International Settlements and the People's Republic of China Relating to the Establishment and Status of a Representative Office for the Bank of International Settlements in the Hong Kong Special Administrative Region of the People's Republic of China, 11 May 1998 (Bank's LA-17).

58 Art. 2, para. 1 (Legal Personality and Capacity) reads: "The State acknowledges the international legal personality and the legal capacity of the Bank with the State." Host Country Agreement between the Bank for International Settlements and the United Mexican States Relating to the Establishment and Status of a Representative Office of the Bank for International Settlements in Mexico, Diario Oficial de la Federación, 20 June 2002, at 3 (Bank's LA-18).

59 See FE Memorial, at paras. 229-239.

there is a difference between a profit-making and a profit-maximizing entity. In the declaration by the Swiss Federal Council (Swiss Federal Government), which was considered earlier,[60] it was noted that

> La banque n'a pas pour but principal de faire des bénéfices. Sans doute, les statuts prévoient-ils la possibilité de gains considérables, mais ceux-ci reviendront, en première ligne, aux banques d'émission qui ont le droit de souscrire les actions. La banque des règlements internationaux tend à des buts d'intérêt général . . . .[61]

The issue was not that the Bank might make profits, the possibility of which was taken for granted. It was the purpose for which the Bank was created, to which such profits had to be applied.

118. For the above reasons, the Tribunal finds that the Bank for International Settlements is a *sui generis* creation which is an international organization.

B. SECOND PRELIMINARY ISSUE: THE APPLICABLE LAW WITH RESPECT TO QUESTION 1

119. The Tribunal turns now to the second preliminary issue in the context of question 1, *viz.*, which law applies to the question of the legality of the Bank's recall of 8 January 2001. The question of the applicable law with respect to the valuation of the recalled shares, if the Tribunal reaches it, must be treated separately, as will be explained below.

120. As will be recalled, neither Dr. Reineccius nor First Eagle challenged the legality of the recall or contended that it was *ultra vires* the Statutes. Mr. Mathieu, in contrast, did raise this argument, contending that the amendments of the Statutes of 8 January 2001 were void *ab initio* and asking for a *restitutio in integrum*, reinstating the private shareholders.[62]

---

[60] See *supra* para. 109.
[61] Feuille fédérale de la Confédération suisse, *supra* fn. 52, at p. 95.
[62] Mémoire en Demande, at pp. 5-6; Transcript, at p. 89, lines 18-27.

121. Mr. Mathieu framed his argument in terms of the constituent instruments of the Bank, averring that only if there were *lacunae* or inclarities in the constituent instruments should there be a reference to international law. He also submitted that there was a contingent role for Dutch and Swiss *ordre public international.*

122. The Bank agreed on the role of the Constituent Instruments, but it was particularly concerned that municipal law not be applied and submitted that

> Because the Bank is an international organization, issues implicating its organic principles or internal governance (such as the relation of the Bank to its shareholders) are necessarily governed by public international law.[63]
>
> Claims arising out of an international organization's acts or omissions in the exercise of its sovereign powers can only be governed by public international law. In amending its Statutes to withdraw its privately held shares, the BIS did not act as a private party. Rather, it exercised its legislative authority under Article 57 of the Statutes, which authorizes the BIS to amend its Statutes, including private shareholders' statutory rights. The resolution of the EGM of 8 January 2001 which enacted the amendments effecting the redemption of the privately held shares therefore constitutes a *jure imperii* act which is governed by the BIS's constituent instruments and applicable general public international law.[64]
>
> In sum, the rights of shareholders in the BIS are governed by the BIS's constituent instruments and applicable general public international law, which likewise determine the validity and legality of the redemption of their shares and its legal consequences.[65]

[63] Counter-Memorial, at para. 48.
[64] *Id.*, at para. 50.
[65] *Id.*, at para. 51.

123. The Bank is correct in asserting that "issues implicating its organic principles or internal governance" are governed by international law. But the Bank is wrong in assuming that this statement means that it has "sovereign powers" or that acts, such as the recall of shares, fall in the category of *acta jure imperii*. While states have sovereign powers, an international actor does not, *qua* international actor and by virtue of that status, have sovereignty. As for the distinction between *acta jure imperii* and *acta jure gestionis*, it is used in municipal courts in order to determine whether a foreign state or its agency or instrumentality that has not consented to the local jurisdiction will benefit from immunity from its judicial jurisdiction and execution. The distinction has no relevance in a public international forum, with respect to a state or to any other international actor which is subject to its jurisdiction.

124. Mr. Mathieu errs in contending that Dutch and Swiss *ordre public international* apply.[66] The clear intention of the Agreement between The Netherlands and the Permanent Court of Arbitration of 30 March 1999,[67] as well as of the Headquarters Agreement between the Bank for International Settlements and Switzerland of 10 February 1987[68] was to exclude the application, respectively, of Dutch and Swiss legislative jurisdiction. Moreover, the purpose of paragraph 5 of the Constituent Charter of the Bank, which is part of the 1930 Hague Agreement, would be frustrated if, its terms notwithstanding, Swiss *ordre public* principles applied.

125. The Constituent Instruments of the Bank[69] are assumed, by both Mr. Mathieu and the Bank, to resolve definitively the particular issue of the legality of the recall of the private shares by the amendment of the Statutes on 8 January 2001. Neither of these Parties adduced other legal instruments that might govern this issue, with the exception of the Vienna Convention on the Law of Treaties of 1969, which was invoked

---

[66] Mémoire en Demande, at pp. 7-8.

[67] Agreement Concerning the Headquarters of the Permanent Court of Arbitration between the Kingdom of the Netherlands and the Permanent Court of Arbitration, 30 March 1999, Art. 3.

[68] *Supra* fn. 56.

[69] The Statutes were concluded on 20 January 1930; the text currently in force is as amended on 8 November 1999.

only to provide authoritative guidance on interpretation. Mr. Mathieu did, however, submit that the Tribunal should go beyond the Statutes, by contending that even if the recall amendments were *intra vires* and valid under the Statutes, they still were invalid under general international law. This contention will be considered below.

126. In the light of the above, the Tribunal will turn to an examination of the legality of the Bank's actions.

C. The Amendment of the Bank's Statutes

127. The Statutes of the Bank, in their current version, are comprised of fifty-eight articles. Article 57 (the substance of which has not changed since 1930) provides:

> Amendments of any Articles of these Statutes other than those enumerated in Article 58 may be proposed by a two-thirds majority of the Board to the General Meeting and if adopted by a majority of the General Meeting shall come into force, provided that such amendments are not inconsistent with the provisions of the articles enumerated in Article 58.

Article 58 provides:

> Articles 2, 3, 8, 14, 19, 24, 27, 44, 51, 54, 57 and 58 cannot be amended except subject to the following conditions: the amendment must be adopted by a two-thirds majority of the Board, approved by a majority of the General Meeting and sanctioned by a law supplementing the Charter of the Bank.

The above provisions, as well, have not changed, in substance, since 1930, although the numeration of the reserved articles in Article 58 has changed, due to other additions and deletions from the Statutes over the years.

128. Despite the fact that Article 57 speaks of amendments being proposed to the General Meeting, Article 47 of the Statutes provides:

> Extraordinary General Meetings shall be summoned to decide upon any proposals of the Board
>
> (a) to amend the Statutes;
>
> . . . .

The Statutes do not prescribe a special notice provision for Extraordinary General Meetings; it would appear that the requirement of three weeks' notice for General Meetings, as stated in Article 44, applies, as well, to Extraordinary General Meetings. Nor is there a significant difference in the voting requirements of General Meetings and Extraordinary General Meetings with respect to amending the Statutes.

129. Amendment of any articles of the Statutes, other than the twelve enumerated, reserved articles, requires a proposal by a two-thirds majority of the Board to the General Meeting and adoption by a simple majority of the General Meeting. Amendment of any of the twelve reserved articles, specified in Article 58 of the Statutes, requires *adoption* by a two-thirds majority of the Board and approval by a majority of the General Meeting. There would appear to be no substantial difference between the Board proposing by a two-thirds majority (Article 57 of the Statutes) or adopting by a two-thirds majority (Article 58 thereof). The only significant difference between amendment of the articles, except for the twelve reserved articles, is that Article 58 requires the sanction of Swiss law supplementing the Charter of the Bank after approval by a majority of the General Meeting, for reasons that were explained above. In contrast, amendment of the unreserved articles of the Statutes does not require the enactment of such a law.

130. The reserved articles enumerated in Article 58, for which the special amendment procedure is to be applied, relate to the following items:

> (i) Moving the registered office of the Bank from Basle (Article 2);
>
> (ii) Amending the objects of the Bank (Article 3);

(iii) Increasing or reducing the capital of the Bank and the prescribed distribution of an increase in the Bank's capital (Article 8);

(iv) Changing the regime which would assign voting or representation to shareholders as such (Article 14);

(v) Changing the principle that the operations of the Bank must conform to the monetary policies of the central banks of the countries concerned (Article 19);

(vi) Deciding to permit the Bank to do any of the six explicitly prohibited activities (Article 24);

(vii) Changing the statutory composition of the Board of Governors (Article 27);

(viii) Varying the rights of attendance and voting rights at General Meetings (Article 44);

(ix) Changing the regime for allocation and disbursement of annual profits (Article 51);

(x) Changing the amendment procedures for unreserved articles in the Statutes (Article 57);

(xi) Changing the amendment procedure of any of the reserved articles just considered (Article 58).

The reserved articles of the Statutes concern the special interests of the central banks and of Switzerland and were manifestly designed to protect them. It is only amendments to the Statutes that involve an increase or decrease of the capital of the Bank which require adoption by a two-thirds majority of the General Meeting. As stated above, except for Article 8, the voting procedures for amendment of both reserved and unreserved articles are essentially the same in both the Board of Governors and General Meeting phases. But amendment of the enumerated reserved articles also requires an adjustment of the Charter of the Bank by an act of Swiss legislation, as explained above.

D. Mr. Mathieu's Allegations of Illegality and the Bank's Response Thereto

131. When the Bank decided to recall all of the shares held by private shareholders at its Extraordinary General Meeting on 8 January 2001, the procedure was that of amendment of unreserved articles of the Statutes in accordance with Article 57 of the Statutes. Mr. Mathieu contended that the amendment of the Statutes was illegal because it was not in compliance with the Constituent Instruments of the Bank. In his Memorial, Mr. Mathieu argued:

> La Résolution amendant les Statuts est illégale, ayant été adoptée en violation de la Charte et des Statuts. En effet, la Résolution a prévu l'ajout d'un nouvel article (1.1) ce que ne permettent pas les Instruments constitutifs de la Banque (1.2). Subsidairement, quand bien même il serait possible d'ajouter un nouvel article, il aurait à tout le moins fallu le faire en application de la procédure renforcée (1.3).

Thus, Mr. Mathieu contended that Article 18A was not an amendment of an existing article but the addition of a new article and, as such, a type of modification of the Statutes that, he contended, is not permitted by Article 57 and is, as a result, null and void. As a subsidiary argument, he contended that even if it were possible to add a new article, it would have had to be accomplished under the special procedure set out in Article 58, rather than the general procedure set out in Article 57.

132. With respect to Mr. Mathieu's first argument, he contended that Article 18A is not an amendment, within the meaning of the Statutes, but a new article, which neither the Statutes nor the Charter authorized. He contended that the interpretation of the Charter and the Statutes must be accomplished in conformity with the rules of international law, specifically, Article 31 of the Vienna Convention on the Law of Treaties. On the basis of Article 31, Mr. Mathieu argued that a literal interpretation seeking the "ordinary meaning" demonstrates that Articles 57 and 58 of the Statutes refer to "amendments of any Articles of these Statutes." The reference is to *amendments*, or *modifications* in French, of existing articles, but not to *additions* or the introduction of new articles. Mr. Mathieu's core contention, then, was that the language of

the text refers only to amendments of specific articles and not to the addition of new articles.

133. Mr. Mathieu contended that his reading of what he believes to be the plain and natural meaning of the Statutes is reinforced by an interpretation that looks to context, as that term is used in the Vienna Convention on the Law of Treaties. The Charter and the Statutes distinguish between ordinary articles, which may be amended in the ordinary fashion, and reserved articles which require, in addition to the ordinary amendment procedure, the enactment of an additional law. The specification of articles indicated, according to Mr. Mathieu, that the Statutes contemplated amendment of specific articles but not the Statutes as a whole.

134. Interpretation in the light of the object and purpose of the instrument being construed would further reinforce, according to Mr. Mathieu, the construction that he proposed. In his view, the precision with which the amendment provision was drafted manifested an intention on the part of the drafters to confine within strict limits the exercise of the activities and, in particular, the discretion of the Bank. This showed, in Mr. Mathieu's view, that the States that had created an entity with strictly limited powers did not want that entity to escape their control and to take any liberties with the powers that had been granted to it. Given the delicacy of the political assignments to the Bank at the time of its founding, Mr. Mathieu submitted that the founding States were particularly concerned to carefully delimit the discretionary power of the Bank. Moreover, he contended, no new article has been added to the Statutes since the establishment of the Bank and the only case of suppression of an article concerned the expiration of the Young Plan. The fact that the Bank's activities had evolved, Mr. Mathieu argued, does not permit the Bank to make adjustments in the Statutes, for, citing Judge Bedjaoui, in his individual opinion in the *Gabcíkovo-Nagymaros* case, the law that should govern the interpretation of a treaty is the law that was contemporary at its conclusion rather than law that has subsequently

evolved.[70] Mr. Mathieu also cited the *Namibia* Opinion of the International Court of Justice in this regard.[71]

135. Furthermore, Mr. Mathieu contended that even if the new article is not deemed illegal on the ground that it is an addition rather than a modification or amendment, the Bank should have followed the reserved amendment procedure of Article 58 of the Statutes instead of the less rigorous procedure of Article 57. Mr. Mathieu submitted that authorizing the Bank to introduce new articles through the ordinary procedure would enable the Bank not simply to introduce articles that are objectively contrary to the enumerated reserved articles but even to create new elements and to develop the Statutes in ways that might conform to the letter of the enumerated reserved articles but be incompatible with the original purposes of the States Parties to the 1930 Hague Agreement. To avoid this, Mr. Mathieu contended, it would be reasonable to demand that the additional articles become the object of an additional law, under the procedure of Article 58 of the Statutes. This, according to Mr. Mathieu, would preserve the interest of Switzerland, under Paragraph 6(c)[72] of the Charter, as well as the interests of the States which had concluded the 1930 Convention.

136. In its Counter-Memorial of 22 July 2002, the Bank contended that the ordinary meaning of the word "amendment" is "[a] change made by addition, deletion or correction."[73] Thus the Bank contended that the plain and natural meaning of the language of the Statutes contemplated amendments that would *add* articles and not simply amendments that

---

[70] *Gabcíkovo-Nagymaros Project (Hungary/Slovakia)*, Separate Opinion of Judge Bedjaoui, ICJ Reports 1997, at para. 8.

[71] *Legal Consequences for States of the Continued Presence of South Africa in Namibia (South West Africa) Notwithstanding Security Council Resolution 276 (1970)*, Advisory Opinion of 21 June 1971, ICJ Reports 1971, p. 16, at para. 53.

[72] Para. 6(c) provides: "The Bank shall be exempt and immune from all taxation included in the following categories: all taxes on the Bank's capital, reserves or profits, whether distributed or not, and whether assessed on the profits of the Bank before distribution or imposed at the time of distribution under the form of a coupon tax payable or deductible by the Bank. This provision is without prejudice to the State's right to tax the residents of Switzerland other than the Bank as it thinks fit."

[73] Counter-Memorial, at para. 63, quoting Black's Law Dictionary.

would *change* existing articles. Moreover, the Bank argued that constituent instruments of international organizations have long been interpreted as including the subsequent practice of the organization, a proposition that is supported by Article 31(3)(b) of the Vienna Convention on the Law of Treaties and has been affirmed in a large number of opinions of the International Court of Justice.[74]

137. In this regard, the Bank drew the Tribunal's attention to important amendments of the Statutes which resulted in the addition of new articles through the procedure prescribed by Article 57. In 1969, an Extraordinary General Meeting amended Article 5 (as renumbered) and added the text of Article 6, and a new Article 9 to the Statutes. On two other occasions, Extraordinary General Meetings added new clauses to existing articles.

138. The Bank also contended that a number of other international organizations whose constitutive instruments permit amendment have, in practice, both added and deleted articles of their constituent instruments.[75]

139. With respect to Mr. Mathieu's contention that the intentions of the Bank's founders militated against the addition of new articles through the amendment procedure, the Bank noted the absence of any evidence for the contention and, as a matter of law, relying upon *Certain Expenses of the United Nations*, submitted that speculations about the intentions of the drafters of these instruments, "except such as may be gathered from its terms alone,"[76] are less important in the construction of the constituent instruments of international organizations.

---

[74] *Certain Expenses of the United Nations*, Advisory Opinion of 20 July 1962, ICJ Reports 1962, p. 165; *Reparations for Injuries Suffered in the Service of the United Nations*, *supra* fn. 45, at pp. 174, 180; *Legal Consequences for States of the Continued Presence of South Africa in Namibia (South West Africa)*, *supra* fn. 71, at pp. 16, 22; *Judgments of the Administrative Tribunal of the International Labour Organization Upon Complaints Made Against the United Nations Educational, Scientific and Cultural Organization*, ICJ Reports 1956, pp. 77, 91.

[75] Counter-Memorial, at para. 67, fn. 57, which lists three such constituent instruments.

[76] *Supra* fn. 74, at pp. 184-185.

140. With respect to Mr. Mathieu's submission that the share recall had to comply with the special procedure of Article 58 for the enumerated reserved provisions of the Statutes, the Bank argued that the reserved procedure only applies to the specified provisions. Since there was no inconsistency between the amendments that are at issue here and those provisions, there was no need to comply with the procedures of Article 58. The Bank also contended that, in substance, the amendments in question did not change the Bank's fundamental structure, objectives or purposes and hence would not have required the special procedure of Article 58.

141. With respect to Mr. Mathieu's argument that the amendment was illegal because it was inconsistent with Article 21(g) of the Statutes, restricting the Bank's ability to "buy and sell negotiable securities other than shares for its own account or for the account of central banks," the Bank observed that Article 21(g) is not one of the reserved provisions enumerated in Article 58. So even if there had been, *quod non*, a conflict between the new Article 18A and the preexisting Article 21(g), that conflict would not have required the special amendment procedure prescribed in Article 58.

E. The Tribunal's Consideration Regarding the Alleged Illegality

142. The legality of the repurchase has been contested principally under the Statutes of the Bank and secondarily under principles of international law regarding expropriation. In the first case, the question is whether the modification of the Statutes, assuming conformity with principles of international law, was carried out in accordance with Articles 57 and 58 of the Statutes (see 1 below). If that question is answered in the affirmative, the validity of the modification must still be examined under principles of international law (see 2 below). There is no need to examine this under any municipal law.

1. Conformity of the Recall to the Statutes

143. Given the importance of the text, it will be useful to set out again the language of Articles 57 and 58 of the Statutes. Article 57 provides:

> Amendments of any Articles of these Statutes other than those enumerated in Article 58 may be proposed by a two-thirds majority of the Board to the General Meeting and if adopted by a majority of the General Meeting shall come into force, provided that such amendments are not inconsistent with the provisions of the Articles enumerated in Article 58.

Articles 58 provides:

> Articles 2, 3, 8,14, 19, 24, 27, 44, 51, 54, 57 and 58 cannot be amended except subject to the following conditions: the amendment must be adopted by a two-thirds majority of the Board, approved by a majority of the General Meeting and sanctioned by a law supplementing the Charter of the Bank.

With the exception of the requirement of Swiss legislation to supplement the Charter of the Bank for amendment of the enumerated articles[77] in Article 58, the procedures in Article 57 and Article 58 are actually the same, except that Article 8 specifies that a change of the capital requires a two-thirds majority of the General Meeting rather than a simple majority.

144. The language of Article 57 introduces no substantive limitation on the amendment competence of the General Meeting other than the requirement that those amendments not be inconsistent with the enumerated articles in Article 58. Hence, as a simple textual matter, an amendment to the Statutes accomplished according to the procedures required by Article 57 would be *intra vires* and valid as long as it were not inconsistent with one of the enumerated reserved provisions in Article 58. There is no indication in Article 57 that the mode of

[77] Art. 1 of the Convention stated that Switzerland undertook not to sanction amendments to the Statutes of the Bank referred to in Para. 4 of the Charter without the agreement of the other signatory Governments.

formulation of an amendment, whether as an addition to an existing article or as an entirely new article designated by a new number, has any legal significance. Hence, an interpretation of the Statutes in good faith in accordance with the ordinary meaning to be given to the terms of the Treaty, must find the amendment under discussion as valid and *intra vires* the Statutes.

145. Article 31(3)(b) of the Vienna Convention on the Law of Treaties[78] requires that account be taken of "any subsequent practice in the application of the Treaty which establishes the agreement of the Parties regarding its interpretation." This provision takes on special meaning when applied, in accordance with Article 5 of the Vienna Convention, to the constituent instruments of international organizations. In *Reparations for Injuries Suffered in the Service of the United Nations*, the International Court of Justice held that "the rights and duties of an entity such as the Organization [the United Nations] must depend upon its purposes and functions as specified or implied in its constituent documents and *developed in practice*."[79] The fact that the Bank has, on a number of occasions, amended its Statutes by the introduction of a new article appears to be probative of the authoritative interpretation of the Statutes in this regard.

146. Mr. Mathieu stated that a strict interpretation of the powers of the Bank had been sought by the drafters lest the Bank, once established, escape their control and take liberties with the powers that had been accorded to them.[80] But the decision structure of the Bank, as established in Chapters IV and V of the Statutes, requires two-thirds of the Board to propose amendments and a majority of the General Meeting to approve them. Article 27 of the Statutes, which established the membership of the Board, gave the central banks of the founding States of the Bank a permanent position. Hence it would not appear that Mr. Mathieu's concern is relevant to the interpretation of this part of the Statutes.

---

[78] *Supra* fn. 23.
[79] *Supra* fn. 45, at pp. 174, 180 (emphasis added).
[80] Mémoire en Demande, at p. 12.

147. Article 18A concerning the compulsory repurchase of the privately held shares cannot be plausibly construed as engaging any of the reserved articles in Article 58 or any of the concerns that animated that provision. While the Bank would have been obliged to secure the approval of Switzerland (in agreement with the other signatory Governments; see Article 1 of the Convention) if an amendment of one of the articles enumerated in Article 58 were planned, such approval would only have been required for amendment of a reserved article. In fact, as was reported at the Hearing, the Bank did notify Switzerland of the proposed amendment and Switzerland did not register any demand or objection.[81] Similarly, all the central banks that were members of the Bank were given notice, as required by the Statutes of the Bank, from which fact it is fair to assume that their Governments were also made aware of the pending change. Nor would there appear to be anything implicit in the Statutes or the Charter that would have precluded the change.

148. For the above reasons, the Tribunal finds that the Bank had the authority to add Article 18A to its Statutes and that the compulsory recall of the shares, including the procedures by which it was accomplished, was *intra vires* the Statutes and was, accordingly, a valid exercise of the Bank's powers. The Tribunal would emphasize, however, that a finding that the recall of the private shares was *intra vires* the Constituent Instruments of the Bank, does not address the question of whether the recall by the Bank and the valuation that the Bank set upon the shares held by private parties were lawful for reasons other than compliance with Articles 57 and 58 of the Statutes. The Tribunal now turns to that question.

2. Conformity of the Recall with Substantive Standards of International Law

149. Mr. Mathieu contended that aside from the problem of alleged insufficient compensation, the Bank's action was unlawful because it violated two of international law's cardinal requirements for a lawful expropriation: that the taking be in the public interest and that it be non-discriminatory. The question arises as to whether the Bank's recall of privately held shares in 2001 is to be examined either under the law of

[81] Prof. Giovanoli, Transcript, at p. 79.

State Responsibility, by analogizing the private shareholders to aliens and the Bank to a State engaged in expropriation, or under international Human Rights law, by assimilating the private shareholders to nationals and the Bank to their State engaged in an act of eminent domain. Without entering for the moment into these analogies, or into whether neither is apposite, the Tribunal observes that the Bank's actions of 8 January 2001 would have met the public interest and non-discrimination requirements of international expropriation law which Mr. Mathieu proposed be applied.

a. THE PUBLIC INTEREST REQUIREMENT

150. Now, obviously, the Bank is not a state. If public interest were understood as meaning the public interest of a state, the Bank's actions could not meet the public interest test and would be *eo ipso* unlawful. The reason for this conclusion would not derive from the nature and purpose of the action, but from the fact that the Bank is not a state. That argument, which would be circular and quite sterile, is not the sense in which Mr. Mathieu made his submission. When applied to an actor which is an international entity, but is not a state, public interest must be understood, *mutatis mutandis*, as an action rationally, proportionately and necessarily related to the performance of one of the legitimate international public purposes of the actor undertaking it.

151. With respect to the public interest requirement, the Bank submitted evidence of its conclusion that the presence of private shareholders in an international organization increased certain costs for the Bank and impeded the performance of some of its international public functions. An internal memorandum, prepared by the Bank's Secretariat on 6 November 1998, in presenting the proposal for recalling the privately held shares in the Bank, observed that:

> The need to take into account the interests of private share-holders no doubt limits to some extent the freedom of action of the BIS with regard to its policy of distribution of profits. It should also be mentioned that, on various occasions, the existence of private shareholders negatively affected nego-

> tiations regarding jurisdictional, tax or other immunities of the BIS in a number of other countries.[82]

It is clear that there was a latent conflict between the Bank's responsibilities for discharging its public functions and the Bank's fiduciary responsibilities to its private shareholders. *Prima facie*, the Bank is able to show that, were the international law of expropriation applied, it could meet, *mutatis mutandis*, the public interest requirement.

b. THE REQUIREMENT THAT THE ACTION NOT BE DISCRIMINATORY

152. Nor would the Bank's actions with respect to the private shareholders be characterized as discriminatory under the international law of expropriation. Analytically, one must distinguish between the factual referent of "differentiations" and the legal referent of "discriminations." Not all differentiations are discriminations. A discrimination is an unlawful differentiation. The legal instruments indicate that from 1930 onwards, private shareholders and central banks, although having equal rights as shareholders, had a different status. Only central banks can have voting rights. Although these voting rights are not directly attached to the shares held by the central banks, they are indirectly linked to the shares subscribed to by or through the central banks. This shows that central banks are in a different category from private shareholders.

153. In 1969, it will be recalled, one new share issue was reserved only for sale to central banks. By Resolution III of the Extraordinary General Meeting on 9 June 1969, the Board of Directors was authorized

> (1) to issue, on a single occasion or at intervals, a third tranche of 200,000 shares of 2,500 gold francs each, which will be paid up to the same extent as the shares in circulation on the date of

[82] Secret L-3, Share Capital of the BIS, 6 November 1998, FE Exhibits to Memorial, Tab 26, at p. 2. The same point was made at a restricted meeting of the Members of the Board on 9 November 1998, at p. 1, FE Exhibits to Memorial, Tab 27. First Eagle produced a document from the papers of Thomas H. McKittrick at the Harvard Library, which is dated June 1938, but unsigned. It also comments on the incompatibility of private shareholders in "a true Bank of Banks." FE Exhibits to Memorial, Tab 36, at p. 10.

issue, and which may not be subscribed or purchased by the general public.[83]

154. The very nature of the Bank as an international organization established, *inter alia*, to facilitate relations between the central banks and the functioning of the international monetary system imported a different treatment, for some purposes, of central banks and private shareholders, most dramatically in governance rights, none of which could be acquired by private shareholders.

155. Thus, even were, *arguendo*, the standards of the international law of expropriation to be applied to determine the validity of the Bank's recall of private shares, that transaction would have been lawful in terms of the criteria of public purpose and non-discrimination.

c. COMPENSATION

156. International law also requires that, in order to be lawful, an expropriation should be against payment of compensation. Indeed, the Bank recognized that the recall had the consequence for the private shareholders that they lost their rights. The Bank accepted from the beginning that such a deprivation of property could only be lawful against payment of compensation. The issues concerning the amount of compensation will be addressed separately. However, the Tribunal would underline that a decision by the BIS which has the effect of depriving the private shareholders of their property rights, *i.e.* their shares, cannot be considered lawful without the payment of compensation. This follows from the rules of general international law protecting private property as well as from general principles of law concerning share companies, a point which the Parties did not dispute.

157. Because the Bank has acknowledged that it is subject to the jurisdiction of this Tribunal and has committed itself to paying all the former private shareholders any addition to what it has already paid, if the Tribunal should so order it, this third criterion will, *nunc pro tunc*, meet the

---

[83] Extraordinary General Meeting held in Basle on 9 June 1969, Public Record, FE Exhibits to Memorial, Tab 22.

requirements of international law. The Tribunal will take up this matter below.

158. Accordingly, the Tribunal finds that the decision to recall the privately held shares by the Extraordinary General Meeting of 8 January 2001 was *intra vires* the Statutes and a lawful exercise of the Bank's powers. Nor did this exercise of the Bank's power violate any principles of international law that might apply.

159. Because of the finding of the Tribunal that the amendment of the Statutes by the addition of Article 18A was *intra vires* the Statutes and lawful, the question of the consequences of a finding of unlawfulness for all those who are private shareholders as of 8 January 2001 is moot and, as such, need not be considered.

CHAPTER V – QUESTION 2 OF PROCEDURAL ORDER NO. 3

A. INTRODUCTION

160. A central issue in this case is the adequacy of the amount which the Bank paid for the recalled shares. Whether this question is characterized as one of "reparations," implying that the recall was unlawful, or as "compensation," implying that the recall was expropriatory and that its lawfulness is contingent upon the Bank's paying international law's measure of compensation, or as one of "fair" price, implying, in a more neutral fashion, that the gravamen is simply one of determining the proper value of the recalled shares, all the Claimants and the Bank have agreed that the issue is one of valuation. In this regard, it was the Bank which invoked and relied heavily upon international law's standard.[84] Hence it

---

[84] The Bank also referred to cognate national practice. The Bank adduced a rather extensive state practice with respect to the special phenomenon of central banks recalling, in a compulsory program, the shares of private shareholders. The Bank argued that national practice seems particularly apposite to the case at bar, as the central banks, like the Bank for International Settlements, concluded that the earlier practice of permitting private shareholders in banks that were public institutions had become anachronistic and incompatible with the public functions of the national central banks. Hence the central banks adopted recall programs, not unlike that of the BIS in its decision of 8 January 2001. In virtually all of these compulsory recall programs, the valuation of the shares was based upon an averaging of the market value of the shares prior to the announcement of the recall. There is, however, no indication whether the stock market price approximated net asset value. As the Bank described in its Counter-Memorial, the Bank of Canada was nationalized in 1938 by the Bank of Canada Act Amendment Act (Bank's LA-119). The Bank of Canada was organized as a stock corporation with a capitalization of CAD 5,000,000, with each share carrying a nominal value of CAD 50. Pursuant to the Act, new stock, owned by the Canadian Government, was issued in the amount of CAD 5,100,000, giving the Government a sufficient majority to buy out the private shareholders. Each former private shareholder received CAD 59.20 per share, the market price pertaining at the time (Bank of Canada Act Amendment Act, 1938, Art. 9 (Bank's LA-119)). Similarly the French Government nationalized the Banque de France in 1945 (Loi 45-14 (Bank's LA-115)). At the time the Banque de France had 46,809 shareholders. The price for each share was set at 28,029 francs, an amount equal to the average trading price of the Banque de France shares over a prior twelve-month reference period (Arrêté du juillet 1946, J.O., 21 juillet 1946, at p. 6538 (Bank's LA-115)). Counter-Memorial, at paras. 153-159. In 1949, the Norwegian Government nationalized the Norges Bank. Norway assumed the shares previously owned by private shareholders against the payment of compensation fixed at 180% of the nominal value of the shares (20 Norges Bank Bulletin, No. 4-5, 21 November 1949, at pp. 57, 59 (Bank's LA-121)). This 180% figure was just higher than the market price of 178% of nominal value pertaining at the time. In 1962, Banco de España shareholders received compensation based upon the fair market value of their shares following nationalization. The compensation paid to former shareholders consisted of 5% more

is useful to begin by considering international law on this matter, even though it may not apply where the Parties have established a *lex specialis*.

B. INTERNATIONAL JURISPRUDENCE

161. In situations of expropriation of the shares of foreign investors, the practice of international law rather consistently has valued the shares by reference to their market value, in circumstances in which an efficient market operated.

162. In *American Int'l Group, Inc.*, the claimant sought compensation for its minority shareholding in an Iranian insurance company that was nationalized by the Government of Iran.[85] The claimant requested the "full value" of its interest as of the date of nationalization and the Tribunal concluded that the compensation due was the claimant's share of the fair market value of the property nationalized.[86] In calculating the fair market value, the Tribunal ascertained the "higher and lower limits of the range within which the value of the company could reasonably be assumed to lie," and then arrived at a compensation value by way of an "approxi-

than the greater of either the average price on the stock exchange over the preceding five years, or the maximum price of the previous year (Ley 2/1962, 14 April 1962 (BOE de 16) (Bank's LA-123)). New Zealand nationalized the Reserve Bank of New Zealand in 1936; the buy-out price was set at the share price pertaining on a certain date in the preceding year (New Zealand Parliamentary Debates, Vol. 244, 25 March-6 May 1936, at p. 144 (comments of Hon. Mr. Nash, Minister of Finance) (Bank's LA-114)). Portugal nationalized its central bank, the Banco de Portugal, and the Banco Nacional Ultramarino in 1974, using the average of the year trading price of their stock to set the compensation (Decreto-Lei n° 452/74, 13 Setembro 1974 Art. 5 (Bank's LA-122); see Decreto-Lei n° 451/74, 13 Setembro 1974, Relatório do Conselho de Administração, Art. 5 (Bank's LA-122)). Venezuela nationalized its central bank, the Banco Central de Venezuela, in 1974; the 6,170 private shareholders received a price of the average market value over the preceding six months (Banco Central de Venezuela, 1974 Memoria (Annual Report), p. 14 (Bank's LA-118). Footnote to Counter-Memorial, para. 159).

[85] *American Int'l Group, Inc. v. Islamic Republic of Iran*, Award No. 93-2-3, 4 Iran-U.S. C.T.R. (19 December 1983).

[86] *Id.*, at para. 109.

mation of that value, taking into account all relevant circumstances of that case."[87]

163. In the case of *James Saghi*, the claimants were the majority shareholders of two Iranian companies that were put under management of the Iranian Government. The claimants alleged deprivation of ownership rights in the companies even though there was no formal expropriation. The Tribunal observed that fair market value would be the applicable standard of compensation and summarized the state of customary international law with respect to fair market value as follows:

> Fair market value may be defined as "the amount which a willing buyer would have paid a willing seller for the shares of a going concern, disregarding any diminution of value due to the nationalization itself or the anticipation thereof, and excluding consideration of events thereafter that might have increased or decreased the value of the shares." On the other hand, while any diminution of value caused by the deprivation of property itself should be regarded, "prior changes in the general political, social and economic conditions which might have affected the enterprise's business prospects as of the date the enterprise was taken should be considered."[88]

The Tribunal applied a method of "reasonable approximation" in arriving at the fair market value, taking into account the impact of the Iranian Revolution and currency inflation.[89]

164. International jurisprudence supports finding fair market value by reference to a share trading price when available. In *Faith Lita Khosrowshahi*, the claimant sought compensation for its shareholding in an Iranian company that had been compulsorily acquired by the Government of Iran.[90] The claimant submitted alternative valuations for

---

[87] *Id.*

[88] *James M. Saghi v. Islamic Republic of Iran*, Award No. 544-298-2, 29 Iran-U.S. C.T.R., pp. 20, 46 (22 January 1993).

[89] *Id.*, at para. 103.

[90] *Faith Lita Khosrowshahi v. Islamic Republic of Iran*, Award No. 558-178-2, 30 Iran-U.S. C.T.R., p. 76 (30 June 1994).

its lost shares to the Tribunal, including a valuation based on "a weighted average of three different valuation techniques: an asset accumulation approach, an income capitalization approach, and a market approach" derived from the last traded stock price for the shares which had been publicly traded on the Tehran Stock Exchange.[91] The respondent's valuation relied on a net book value analysis that resulted in a negative value for the shares.[92] Applying a fair market standard of valuation, the Tribunal found that a "contemporaneous market price is clearly the best available evidence" of the value of the expropriated shares.[93] The Tribunal then used the last trading price of the shares as set forth in the Annual Report of the Tehran Stock Exchange "as the basis of the valuation analysis" and applied a 25% discount to account for the negative effect of the Iranian Revolution on the market value of the shares during the eight month period between the last trade and the expropriation of the shares.[94]

165. The *ACSYNGO* case related to shares held by private investors in a French conglomerate that were compulsorily transferred to the French State in 1982.[95] Compensation to the dispossessed shareholders was paid on the basis of the average stock exchange quotation for the shares during a reference period, with adjustments made for the effects of inflation and lost dividends.[96] With respect to the compensation paid by the French State, the Belgian commercial court held that "[t]he fact that the average stock exchange quotation, the effects of inflation and expected dividends were all taken into account, leads to the conclusion that, from the point of view of public international law, the calculation of compensation cannot be criticized."[97]

---

[91] *Id.*, at p. 90.
[92] *Id.*, at p. 91.
[93] *Id.*, at p. 92.
[94] *Id.*, at pp. 93-94.
[95] *"ACSYNGO" and Others v. Compagnie de Saint-Gobain (France) SA and Others*, 82 ILR, p. 127, at p. 130 (1986).
[96] *Id.*, at p. 135.
[97] *Id.*, at p. 137.

166. In *Amoco Int'l Fin. Corp.*, although the Iran-U.S. Claims Tribunal eventually found there to be no "market giving rise to the fixing of an objective market value" for claimant's expropriated interest in an Iranian joint venture, it first stated that market value is the "most commendable standard" and is "regularly referred to in case of nationalization where the nationalized undertaking is a corporation the capital stock of which is freely traded in the stock exchange."[98] The Tribunal further opined that market value is "most easily ascertained when a market exists for identical or similar assets, *i.e.* when the assets are the object of a continuous flow of free transactions."[99]

167. First Eagle contended that the *conditio sine qua non* for the application of the above standard was an efficient market and that such a market did not obtain for the shares of the BIS. The Bank contended that the Zurich and Paris Exchanges were quite efficient and that any problems of comparative illiquidity of the shares in the Bank arose from the nature of those shares and not from the exchanges in which they were traded. It is certainly correct that the shares of the Bank were illiquid, compared to other shares trading on the French or Swiss exchanges. Factors such as (i) the small number of such shares being traded; (ii) the requirement of double-approval by the central bank to which they had been issued as well as by the Bank for International Settlements before shares could be sold; and (iii) the possibility of the Bank calling for payment of the other 75% of the value of the shares all contributed to the comparative illiquidity of these shares on the markets in which they were bought and sold. But the inefficiency derived from the nature of the shares and not from the markets in which they were traded and the market discounted these inefficiencies, as markets do. Arguments about relative efficiency or liquidity aside, the fact remains that the Bank itself never referred to the stock market price when it evaluated the shares prior to this arbitration (see paras. 193 *et seq.* below).

168. Furthermore, the Tribunal is not persuaded by the Bank's conception of the international legal standard of compensation as one of "appropriate"

---

[98] *Amoco Int'l Fin. Corp. v. The Government of the Islamic Republic of Iran and Others*, Partial Award No. 310-56-3, 15 Iran-U.S. C.T.R., pp. 189, 255-256 (14 July 1987).

[99] *Id.*

compensation. While it is true that the jurisprudence of the European Court of Human Rights has adopted a flexible standard, described as one of "appropriate" compensation for takings by a state of the property of its nationals, the analogy of the Bank to a state taking the property of the shareholders, who are to be deemed its "nationals" is unpersuasive. The issue of the general relevance of regional Human Rights law aside, the mainstream of general international law, were it to apply to this case, has required full compensation. While that standard may have been qualified during the Cold War and may have been adjusted in some cases in which certain developing countries, particularly with respect to petroleum, nationalized their single or primary resource,[100] it is clear that it has been reestablished in the recent jurisprudence.

169. Thus, the full compensation standard was applied in an *ad hoc* arbitration carried out under the UNCITRAL Arbitration Rules, where the Government of Ghana was found to have expropriated the claimants' investment in Ghana.[101] There, the Tribunal held that "[u]nder the principles of customary international law, a claimant whose property has been expropriated by a foreign state is entitled to full – *i.e.* to prompt, adequate and effective – compensation."[102]

170. The general trend in the Iran-U.S. Claims Tribunal has also been to apply the full compensation standard in a number of cases. In *Sedco*, when deciding the proper standard of compensation for claimant's expropriated shareholder interest in SEDIRAN Drilling Company, the Tribunal found that full compensation was the applicable standard.[103] The Tribunal stated that while some commentators had voiced support for a lesser standard in cases of nationalization by developing countries, full compensation was still the accepted standard in cases of individual expropriation.[104] In *Sola Tiles*, the Tribunal awarded full compensation for claimant's

---

[100] *Aminoil v. Kuwait*, 66 ILR, p. 518 (1982).

[101] *Biloune and Marine Drive Complex Ltd v. Ghana Investments Centre and the Government of Ghana*, 95 ILR, p. 183 (1993).

[102] *Id.*, at p. 211.

[103] *Sedco, Inc. v. National Iranian Oil Company, et al.*, Award No. 59-129-3, 10 Iran-U.S. C.T.R., pp. 180, 188 (27 March 1986).

[104] *Id.*, at p. 188.

expropriated assets.[105] In deciding whether the Treaty of Amity between the United States and Iran provided a *lex specialis* governing the standard of compensation, the Tribunal found that the treaty's requirement that compensation "shall represent the full equivalent of the property taken" was the same as the standard required by customary law.[106] While the Tribunal recognized that the term "appropriate" had been widely applied to the standard of compensation in cases of expropriation, it found that its meaning could encompass "full compensation".[107]

171. Finally, it is to be noted that on the advice of its consultant, J.P. Morgan, the Bank, using a Dividend Perpetuity Model method, actually paid the private shareholders almost double the market exchange value of the recalled shares. Under the standard of the international law of expropriation, were it to apply, the Bank's level of compensation would have met the international standard. But, in fact the Bank paid twice the stock market value of the recalled shares and only argued for the application of the stock market price in the arbitration. Banks operate under strict rules with respect to the money entrusted to them; they may not give money away without a proper legal basis. Moreover, the record reveals that the internal documents of the Bank indicate that the Bank did not use stock market price for establishing the premium for new tranches. The Bank's behavior raises doubts about its own contemporaneous conviction with respect to the application of the market value standard detailed above, especially in a case that is not an expropriation but rather a forced recall of shares.

C. THE BANK'S CONSTITUENT INSTRUMENTS AND INTERNATIONAL LAW

172. The Tribunal has found that the Bank is an international organization. While the Bank is, thus, subject to international law, all Parties agree that

---

105 *Sola Tiles, Inc. v. Islamic Republic of Iran*, Award No. 298-317-1, 14 Iran-U.S. C.T.R., p. 223 (22 April 1987).

106 *Id.*, at p. 234.

107 *Id.*, at p. 236.

the rights of shareholders are, in the first instance, determined by the Constituent Instruments. Dr. Reineccius, representing himself, did not explicitly address the question of the applicable law, but clearly based his submission on his understanding of the Statutes and, in his view, their necessary implications. First Eagle, in its Memorial, also based its claim, in the first instance, on an interpretation of the Statutes.[108] Mr. Mathieu, in his Memorial, based his argument, also in the first instance, on the Constituent Instruments of the Bank, submitting that only if they failed to provide an answer was the Tribunal to turn to general international law. In its Statement of Defense, the Bank said that "its relations with its shareholders are governed by its constituent instruments . . . supplemented as appropriate by general public international law."[109] In its Counter-Memorial, the Bank stated that "the rights attached to the shares in the BIS must be determined by reference to the terms of the Statutes rather than by recourse to municipal corporate law concepts or dictionary definitions of share ownership."[110]

173. Thus the Parties agree that the issue that falls to be decided here must be resolved by reference to the Bank's Constituent Instruments and only by international law should the Constituent Instruments fail to provide an answer. Because the Parties agree that the questions posed to the Tribunal should be resolved in the first instance by reference to the Constituent Instruments of the Bank, the relationship of the Statutes to international law must be clarified. The Constituent Instruments of the Bank constitute a *lex specialis* as between the Parties. Insofar as the *lex specialis* in this case – the 1930 Agreement, the Charter and the Statutes – provides an answer to the questions arising in this case, the Tribunal would not be permitted to turn to international law – unless the *lex specialis* purported to incorporate an explicit *renvoi* to general international law or would have violated a fundamental principle of international law.

174. In fact, neither the applicable law clause of the 1907 Convention for the Pacific Settlement of International Disputes nor the 1930 Hague

[108] FE Memorial, at para. 205.
[109] Statement of Defense, at para. 85.
[110] Counter-Memorial, at para. 94.

Agreement incorporate a *renvoi* to international law, as such. Article 15 of the 1930 Agreement does not include an explicit applicable law clause. Nor does Annex XII of the 1930 Agreement, entitled, "Arbitration. Rules of Procedure" contain an explicit choice of law clause. But Annex XII does incorporate, by reference, Chapter III of The Hague Convention of 1907 for the Pacific Settlement of International Disputes, whose provisions are to apply, unless and to the extent modified by the provisions of Annex XII or the 1930 Agreement. Article 73 of the 1907 Convention speaks simply of "applying the principles of law." Article 26 of the "Rules for Arbitration between the Bank for International Settlements and Private Parties" provides that "The Tribunal shall apply the instruments relevant to the case as well as other relevant principles of law." In sum, the *lex specialis* of this case – the 1930 Agreement, the Charter and the Statutes – was conceived as self-contained and not incorporating general international law, except insofar as the *lex specialis* failed to provide an answer to a question that might arise or violated a fundamental principle of international law. In that eventuality, a Tribunal seised of the case was to turn to general international law.[111]

175. The right to compensation is part of both general international law and the specific area of Human Rights law and it is quite possible that an action purporting to abrogate such a right might be held to be invalid for violation of international law. If the Statutes had purported to deny shareholders compensation, a general international law problem could have arisen. But in the instant case, the Statutes did require compensation and the fact that the *lex specialis*, because of the specific provisions of the Statutes establishing the equal rights of the shares, might prescribe a higher amount than would general international law cannot be considered a breach of international law. Hence there is no ground for the Tribunal to depart from the *lex specialis* applicable to the Parties and to use the international law standard which would apply market value for the shares.

---

[111] In this respect, the sequential legal regime created by the *lex specialis*, may be compared to Art. 42 of the 1965 Convention on the Settlement of Investment Disputes between States and Nationals of Other States ("1965 Washington Convention").

D. Valuation

176. The Tribunal now turns to the issue of valuation. The Bank has acknowledged, from the first discussions of the recall program, that its recall had to be accompanied by a valuation of the shares and payment to the shareholders. In contrast to Mr. Mathieu, who accused the Bank of suppressing information and relying upon external advisers who lacked independence, Dr. Reineccius stated his belief that the Bank was quite correct in presenting full information about its valuation data and methods. Dr. Reineccius' gravamen related to the method that the Bank adopted on the advice of its consultants: the DPM model. Having considered the record, the Tribunal finds no evidence of bad faith on the part of the Bank.

1. The Earning Power Method

177. Dr. Reineccius submitted that the appropriate model for valuation was not DPM, but either an earning power method ("EPM"), which, he stated, is widely used in Germany for situations in some ways comparable to the one confronting the Tribunal, or, alternatively, a proportionate share of net asset value. The Tribunal should select, he submitted, whichever proved to be higher. First Eagle and Mr. Mathieu also submitted that a proportionate share of NAV was the proper valuation methodology. In fact, Dr. Reineccius' preference for EPM is linked to his assumption (shared by Mr. Mathieu and, with some qualifications, by First Eagle) that each share in the Bank for International Settlements is entitled to a proportionate share of its profits. EPM presumes that a shareholder is entitled to the profits of the company. Dr. Reineccius felt that the DPM "is appropriate when a company distributes the major part of its net profit as a dividend,"[112] but inappropriate when a company follows a policy of husbanding profits and issuing very low dividends.

178. The assumption for Dr. Reineccius' view that DPM is an inappropriate valuation method is that companies should act for the welfare of their shareholders, whose interest is receiving profits in the form of dividends

[112] Transcript, at p. 202, lines 36-37.

and, who, accordingly, expect the company in which they own shares to distribute as much as is consistent with the future productivity of the firm. That is a valid assumption for most domestic and private sector corporations in advanced capitalist systems. But as explained earlier, the Bank for International Settlements is *sui generis*, in that it is an international organization but is organized, in the language of Article 1 of the Statutes, as a "company limited by shares." It has a public international mandate, in the performance of which considerable profits may be generated. The private shareholders wished the profits to be expressed in larger dividends, yet the Bank's public international mandate was, in the view of the Board, best served by a significant reduction in dividends and a corresponding accumulation of profits in the various statutory reserves of the Bank.

179. Thus Dr. Reineccius' implicit analogy of the Bank's profit/dividend practice to that of private municipal corporations' profit/dividend policies is inapposite. Moreover, it does not have a basis in the *lex specialis*. The statutory right of BIS shareholders is not to profits *simpliciter*, but to profits as determined by a decision process specified in Article 51 of the Statutes which deals with the annual net profits. Article 13 of the Statutes provides:

> The shares shall carry equal rights to participate in the profits of the Bank and in any distribution of assets under Articles 51, 52 and 53 of the Statutes.

Dr. Reineccius would read Article 13 as if it said only "The shares shall carry equal rights to participate in the profits of the Bank [.]" without the qualifying language that follows. If Article 13 were, in fact, truncated in the fashion in which Dr. Reineccius understands the provision, with a full-stop after "the Bank," then net profits would perforce be equivalent to dividends, which then would, indeed, have to be distributed equally. But Article 51 qualifies each share's "equal rights to profits" in Article 13, by granting the General Meeting on the recommendation of the Board the power to exercise a wide discretion in setting the dividend (Article 51, paragraphs 2 and 4). Thus, assuming that the proper procedures were followed, the discrepancy between large profits and small dividends, if decided in the proper procedure, would be valid for the Bank under the Statutes.

180. In the Governors' Meeting of 9 April 1936, a decision was taken unanimously to seek to repurchase the privately held shares of the French and Belgian issues and, of particular importance in this context, to amend the dividend policy in Article 53 of the Statutes:

> During the year 1936-1937 steps will be taken in order to change Article 53 sub b and c of the Statutes with the object of abolishing the cumulative character of the dividend . . . and creating provision that any residue of the net profits . . . will be placed to the credit of a dividend reserve fund to be distributed to the shareholders if and when the General Meeting will decide so; the meaning of this being that this fund will only be distributed at a moment when the General Meeting decides (on the advice of the Board) that this fund is no longer needed as a reserve.
>
> In changing Article 53 it will be made clear, that this will also apply to the existing dividend reserve fund, which therefore will not be distributed before the General Meeting decides so; therefore, this meeting will be under no obligation to distribute this fund even if less than 6% dividend is paid from net profits.[113]

In 1975, at an Extraordinary General Meeting, Articles 51 and 52 of the Statutes were amended, in the language of the Chairman of the Board of Directors,

> to remove the concept of a dividend related to the amount of the paid-up capital. As a result, the Board and the General Meeting would have greater discretion then [sic] hitherto when deciding on the application of the net profits either in the form of dividend or of appropriations to the reserves.[114]

---

[113] Draft Minutes, Basle, 9 April 1936, FE Exhibits to Memorial, at Tab 20.

[114] Extract from the speech delivered by the Chairman of the Board of Directors on the occasion of the Extraordinary General Meeting of the Bank for International Settlements held on 8th July 1975, Annex III to Notice to Shareholders (other than the central banks) of the American Issue of the Bank's Capital, in FE Exhibits to Memorial, Tab 8, at p. 7.

The Director added that

> [i]n view of the importance of the proposed reform, however, it seemed appropriate to provide these shareholders, if they so wish, with the opportunity to dispose of their shares on fair term, *viz*. at the price of 3,100 Swiss francs per share.[115]

That price was based on the average share price of the American issue in Basle rounded up to the nearest hundred francs over the previous six weeks. The offer was taken up by only a few shareholders.

181. It is the different and potentially conflicting responsibilities of the Bank to profit and dividend policy for private shareholders, on the one hand, and to its public functions, on the other, that is one of the public interest reasons that may justify the recall of the private shares under international law, as explained above in paragraph 151.

182. For these reasons, the Tribunal concludes that EPM, despite its cogency for private sector domestic corporations, is an inapt method for valuation of the shares of the Bank for International Settlements.

2. The Net Asset Value (NAV) Method

183. All three Claimants have submitted that the appropriate method for valuation, either exclusively or, for Dr. Reineccius, alternatively, is a per share proportionate part of the undiscounted net asset value or NAV of the Bank. As stated earlier, all the Parties concurred that an interpretation of the Constituent Instruments is critical in deciding this issue and that only if it did not yield an answer should the Tribunal turn to general international law.

184. First Eagle based its submission, first, on Articles 1 and 13 of the Statutes and their necessary implications, to wit, that "the shares of the Bank in the aggregate, like those of any other company limited by shares, constitute the entire ownership interest in the company."[116] Unlike Dr.

---

[115] *Id.*, at p. 8.

[116] FE Memorial, at para. 213.

Reineccius, however, First Eagle invoked Article 13 in order to show that all the shares, in the words of the Bank, "carry identical property rights."[117] First Eagle, like Dr. Reineccius, would read Article 13 of the Bank's Statutes as if it were unqualified. But, unlike Dr. Reineccius' principal argument, First Eagle also contends that

> the only way for the shareholders to continue to participate equally in profits of the Bank that are not distributed as dividends in the year they are earned is to carry an equal right to the accumulated assets of the Bank and to its accumulated reserves.[118]

This argument is not affected by the statutory power assigned to the Board and the General Meeting, under Article 51 of the Statutes, to determine how much, if any, of the profits should be distributed as dividends.

185. The Statutes, while carefully drafted to deal with the usual range of corporate events, do not address, either directly or by implication, the right to conduct and the consequences for a compulsory recall of any shares. But, for First Eagle, if a mandatory redemption of shares is permissible

> the equality of property rights in the ongoing profits of the business and its assets on liquidation that the Statutes expressly recognize would apply with no less force in the context of the newly authorized exclusion.[119]

First Eagle contended that the recall of shares was a partial liquidation, because it was financed by the conversion of assets of the Bank to pay for them, which assets were thereby reduced by that amount. By the same token, the shareholders' interests, which were converted to cash,

---

[117] Bank for International Settlements, Note to Private Shareholders: Withdrawal of All Shares of the Bank for International Settlements Held by Its Private Shareholders, 15 September 2000, at p. 2. Cited in FE Memorial, at para. 218.

[118] *Id.*, at para. 221.

[119] *Id.*, at para. 224.

were also liquidated.[120] Hence the contingency for application of Articles 13 and 52, unnumbered paragraph 3, was fulfilled.

186. Mr. Mathieu argued, like First Eagle, that a proper interpretation of Articles 13 and 51 to 53 demonstrates that the equality of shares means an equality with respect to profits and distributions.

187. The Bank agreed that the question falls, in the first instance, to be decided by reference to the Constituent Instruments. The central argument of the Bank was that Article 13:

> does not vest in shareholders unqualified rights to participate in the profits and assets of the BIS, clearly subjecting such rights to, and determining them by, specific reference to Articles 51, 52, and 53.[121]

Because, the Bank continued, (i) sale of shares is subject to approval of both the Bank and the central bank to whose national issue the shares belong; and (ii) shares do not carry any governance rights, the shares lack fundamental characteristics of equity ownership.[122] These various encumbrances, the Bank argued, were taken account of by the markets which discounted the proportionate NAV of the shares by 75%.[123]

188. The interpretation of the Statutes proffered here by the Bank is only partially correct. Given the nature of the shares, the special encumbrances to which they are subjected and their lack of governance rights, the Bank is correct in characterizing its shares as different from the equity of conventional private corporations. The Bank is also correct in its contention that, as explained above, the Statutes do not give shares equal rights to profits *simpliciter*, but to profits as determined by the Board and General Meeting, under Article 51 of the Statutes.[124]

---

[120] *Id.*, at para. 225.
[121] Counter-Memorial, at para. 95.
[122] *Id.*, at paras. 97 and 98.
[123] *Id.*, at para. 102.
[124] *Id.*, at para. 95.

189. But the words "to participate" in the Bank's argument that Article 13:

> does not vest in shareholders unqualified rights to participate in the profits and assets of the BIS, clearly subjecting such rights to, and determining them by, specific reference to Articles 51, 52, and 53[125]

refer indiscriminately to governance rights and rights to participate in the distribution of assets. Article 13 states: "Shares shall carry equal rights . . . to participate in the . . . distribution of assets." The procedural disabilities which the Statutes impose on shareholders, *qua* shareholders, with respect to participating in governance, have nothing to do with the substantive rights of the shareholders to the assets of the Bank upon distribution.

190. The Bank also errs in implying that the clearly qualified rights in Article 13 and Articles 51 and 52 with respect to profits are matched by correspondingly qualified rights with respect to the assets in a liquidation. While the shareholders, *qua* shareholders, have no rights to participate in a liquidation decision, the imperative language of Article 52's unnumbered paragraph 3 makes clear that in a liquidation, the shareholders have equal rights:

> These reserve funds, in the event of liquidation, and after the discharge of the liabilities of the Bank and the costs of liquidation, shall be divided among the shareholders.

The qualifications to a right to profits in the second part of Article 13, which is subjected to the procedures of Articles 51, and which, effectively, transformed a right to participate in profits into a right to such dividends as the governing process of the Bank might decide, do not apply to a liquidation. From this, one infers from the Statutes that shareholders do, indeed, have equal rights to the aggregate assets of the Bank.

---

[125] *Id.*

191. With respect to First Eagle's claim that the Statutes' provisions with respect to liquidation apply to the instant case, the Bank argued that the liquidation provisions apply only to a total dissolution of the Bank and that such an event requires a decision by a three-fourths majority of the General Meeting, which did not occur on 8 January 2001.[126] The Bank likened its share recall to a voluntary share repurchase program which is lawful in a number of municipal systems.[127] But, of course, the predicate of the dispute before the Tribunal is that the recall was involuntary. Given its compulsory character, the closest domestic analogue, were it appropriate to resort to it, would be a "squeeze-out." The Bank, as stated, rejected the notion that any domestic corporation law applies to this case.[128]

192. Neither the Bank nor First Eagle was able to find convincing support in the Statutes for its respective submission. As already noted, the Statutes did not directly contemplate a compulsory recall of the shares held by private parties. Indeed, the Bank's president, in 1936, when considering "getting rid of the private shareholders," was apparently advised that such an operation would be *ultra vires* the Statutes.[129] As for First Eagle's submission, it is true that one of the legal meanings of the word "liquidation" is any transformation of an asset or claim into cash. But it seems apparent that Article 52, unnumbered paragraph 3, was drafted in anticipation of a dissolution of the Bank.

193. For the proper interpretation of the relevant legal instruments, it is clearly of importance to examine how the BIS itself understood the requirements for a recall of the privately held shares. A note from the papers of former Bank President McKittrick dated June 1938, which had considered a buy-out of the private shareholders, proposed, as the method of valuation of the shares, determining "the actual or break-up value of the B.I.S. shares."[130] An internal memorandum prepared by the Secretariat, for the 318th Meeting of the Board of Directors of the Bank on 8 September

---

[126] *Id.*, at paras. 107 and 109. In fact, the decision of 8 January 2001 was passed unanimously.

[127] *Id.*, at para. 113 and see also fn. 83 there.

[128] *Id.*, at para. 153, fn. 61.

[129] 1936 Weiser Memorandum, at pp. 3-4, FE Exhibits to Memorial, Tab 35.

[130] Untitled Document, FE Exhibits to Memorial, Tab 36, at p. 11.

1969, took for granted that the private shareholders had a "potential share of the Bank's provisions and reserves."[131] It is also instructive that the valuation method recommended by the Secretariat for pricing a new issue of shares was based upon a discounted net asset value.[132] The recommendation was adopted by the Board at the 319th Meeting of the Board on 17 November 1969.[133] An internal memorandum of 6 November 1998, prepared by the Bank's Legal Service, noted the need "to respect the principle of equal rights for all shareholders in any distribution of profits or assets, which principle is embodied in Art. 13 of the Statutes."[134] It is to be noted that the exclusion memo specifically refers to the need to pay the full patrimonial value of each share of the Bank. "Patrimonial" value here can only have referred to the real value of the assets of the Bank. In none of the internal deliberations of the Bank about compulsory repurchase was the market value of the shares considered the appropriate standard for the calculation of the value of the shares. The J.P. Morgan Report of 7 September 2000, which will be examined in more detail below, also noted that "[i]n its recent issue of shares to the 4 new members of BIS, the share price has been calculated by BIS based on net asset value."[135] The NAV for that issue was US$ 20,080 per share, which was discounted by 30% to US$ 14,056 or 5,020 gold francs per share. The Report also noted that "for a previous share issue of total [sic] 44,000 shares to 13 member central banks in November 1996 the NAV calculation yielded a value of US$18,772 per share, representing an equivalent of [. . .]3,643 [gold francs]."[136]

194. In sum, from 1936 onwards, the Bank, in its internal deliberations, appears, from the evidence available to the Tribunal, to have assumed that all shares were entitled to an equal proportionate share of the assets of the Bank, to have priced new shares on that basis (with a discount

---

[131] Agenda for the 318th Meeting, Adjustment of the capital of the Bank and amendment of its Statutes, FE Exhibits to Memorial, Tab 23, at p. 2.

[132] *Id.*, at p. 4.

[133] Agenda for the 319th Meeting, Tab 24, at p. 7.

[134] Secret L-3, Share Capital of the BIS, 6 November 1998, *supra* fn. 82, at p. 3.

[135] J.P. Morgan, Project Primus Presentation to the Board of Directors of the Bank for International Settlements (BIS) Valuation Report and Suggested Transaction Price Range, 7 September 2000. FE Exhibits to Memorial, Tab 43, at p. 24; Statement of Defense, Exhibit 23.

[136] *Id.*, at unnumbered note at bottom of page.

which will be considered below) and to have taken for granted that, if it were to compulsorily repurchase its privately held shares, the Statutes would require it to price the shares by using a method of valuation of shares based on some form of the net assets of the Bank. In none of the internal deliberations of the Bank about compulsory repurchase was the stock price considered to be the proper standard for the calculation of the price of the shares.

3. The Question and Scope of a Possible Discount

195. Having determined that a proportionate share of net asset value is the method required by the Constituent Instruments as confirmed by the past practice of the Bank, the Tribunal turns to the question of whether and to what extent the per share proportionate NAV should be discounted. In this regard, the Tribunal has found particularly instructive the internal document, already referred to, entitled AGENDA FOR THE THREE HUNDRED AND EIGHTEENTH MEETING OF THE BOARD OF DIRECTORS OF THE BANK FOR INTERNATIONAL SETTLEMENTS,[137] which was prepared by the Legal Counsel, then approved by the Consultative Committee of the Board of Directors and finally approved by the Board of Directors itself on 17 November 1969.[138] Item 8 of that document, entitled "Adjustment of the capital of the Bank and amendment of its Statutes (318/E(1) & (2))", was prepared to provide background and a recommendation for the Board of Directors on the pricing of a new tranche of 200,000 shares of 2,500 gold francs each, which could be subscribed only by central banks. The document noted that the question of a premium for shares had never arisen before[139] and explored the different considerations that could influence such a determination.

---

[137] *Supra* fn. 131, at Tab 23.
[138] *Supra* fn. 133.
[139] *Supra* fn. 131, at p. 1.

196. The Report continued, "[t]he Board . . . needs to find an objective base on which to calculate a premium . . . ."[140] The Report proceeded to review the "three most generally recognized methods,"[141] which were

(i) future profitability of the enterprise;

(ii) market value of the shares; and

(iii) the mathematical method.

The future profitability method (which is akin to the DPM, used by J.P. Morgan and adopted by the Board in its decision at the Extraordinary General Meeting of 8 January 2001), presented a number of problems. There were wide fluctuations in profits and no predictability as to future price and the Bank's dividend policy was dictated by concern for the objects of the Bank rather than for profit for shareholders. Accordingly, the Report dismissed that method. As for the market value method, the Report opined that, given the nature of the shares of the Bank, the various stock exchanges on which they were bought and sold, and the special position of the Bank itself, it was "an unreliable basis on which to calculate the premium."[142]

197. As for the mathematical method, akin to the NAV, the Report found, in the case of the BIS, this was:

> . . . the only reliable way . . . as it avoids as far as possible the capricious nature of the other methods considered above and is not affected by external circumstances. It also has an additional advantage in that the balance sheet of the BIS offers a more exact picture of the value of the enterprise than the balance sheet of an ordinary commercial enterprise; the BIS has no real hidden reserves and apart from the value attributable to its full-amortised buildings and land, which of course would always be

---

[140] *Id.*, at pp. 2-3.
[141] *Id.*
[142] *Id.*

> open to discussion, the balance sheet gives a fairly accurate picture of the actual worth of the enterprise.[143]

The Report proceeded to calculate the net asset value, if the Bank were to be liquidated forthwith. But because the ordinary net asset value does not take account of a hypothetical liquidation, the Report tried to factor in the impacts that would have occasioned a liquidation, such as:[144]

> (i) heavy losses, leading to substantially reduced reserves;
>
> (ii) reduced value of land and buildings in a liquidation;
>
> (iii) the exhaustion of the Special Dividend Reserve Fund.

The Report concluded

> . . . it appears that the premium should be calculated by the mathematical method, but that it would be equitable to apply a discount to the total of the Bank's own funds in order to take account of all the considerations discussed above. It is suggested that a discount of 30 per cent. would be appropriate.[145]

198. The J.P. Morgan Report of 7 September 2000 also addressed the question of discounting share value in an NAV methodology. Although some of its numerical conclusions roughly parallel those of the 1969 Board of Directors' report, the method it deployed was quite different. For one thing, the J.P. Morgan Report makes no mention of Articles 1 and 13 of the Statutes, which establish the equality of shares. It is worth recalling that Article 1 provides:

> There is constituted under the name of the Bank for International Settlements . . . a Company limited by shares.

---

143 *Id.*, at p. 4.
144 *Id.*, at p. 5.
145 *Id.*, at pp. 5-6.

and Article 13 provides:

> The shares shall carry equal rights to participate in the profits of the Bank and in any distribution of the assets under Articles 51, 52, and 53 of the Statutes.

For another, the Board of Directors' report arrived at its discount largely by introducing the variables of a hypothetical liquidation, which could be expected to lower value; the J.P. Morgan Report makes no reference to an adjusted liquidation price, but discounts for (i) lack of voting rights; (ii) reduced marketability; and (iii) the restriction arising from a double veto over sales of shares.[146]

199. Although the analysis which J.P. Morgan undertakes is rigorous and sophisticated, the Tribunal would note that it confuses two methods of valuation: share price as determined by the market and NAV valuation. The three factors which the J.P. Morgan Report identifies may help to explain the disparity between market price and proportionate NAV price but they are not relevant to an NAV analysis for an entity whose constituent documents establish the essential equality of all the shares with respect to their rights to the assets of the Bank. Thus, much of the data on the basis of which J.P. Morgan reached its 30% discount for lack of voting rights is derived from market trends.[147] Similarly, J.P. Morgan's proposal to apply an additional 15% discount for marketability may be appropriate in determining the proper market value of a traded share, but is inapposite in an NAV analysis in an entity whose constituent instruments establish the equality of the right of all shares to the assets of the company.

200. The Arthur Andersen report, which also recognized the inappropriateness of a stock market value method in view of the Bank's characteristics, reviewed the J.P. Morgan Report and concluded that the price of CHF 16,000 per share "is a fair price."[148] But some of its brief

---

146 *Id.*, at p. 28 *et seq*. The J.P. Morgan Report also creates an additional category of "further considerations" but ultimately concludes that it is not applicable.

147 *Id.*, at p. 29.

148 FE Exhibits to Memorial, Tab 45, at p. 16; Statement of Defense, Exhibit 21, at pp. 7-8.

observations are not entirely consistent with the approach of the J.P. Morgan Report. The Arthur Andersen report, for example, notes that "the value of a listed share cannot be higher than the price paid by central banks at the time of an increase in capital;"[149] in fact, the J.P. Morgan Report fixed the price of the recalled shares at considerably less "than the price paid by central banks at the time of an increase in capital." Although it raises a number of other questions about some of the J.P. Morgan Report's estimations, it too ignores the *lex specialis* of the Statutes and largely shares the major assumptions upon which J.P. Morgan operated.

201. For the reasons stated, the Tribunal does not find the discount analyses in the J.P. Morgan Report or the Arthur Andersen report, legally pertinent to the case at bar. Rather the Tribunal finds that the discount analysis of the Board of Directors in 1969, which has been applied in pricing the various tranches of newly issued shares which were designated for sale to new central banks thereafter, is appropriate for determining a discount of NAV. The use of a hypothetical liquidation value, which was the approach taken by the Board of Directors in 1969 and thereafter is also apposite, in view of the fact that First Eagle has argued that the most fitting analogy in the Statutes is to a liquidation or "partial liquidation;" the Board of Directors' approach was based upon a projected liquidation value. Moreover, the resulting price per share that emerges from this analysis appears to have been what at least one of the Claimants, First Eagle, had thought to be an appropriate price when it approached the Bank on 23 June 2000 and proposed a public share repurchase "on terms similar to the recent share issuances."[150] But the most telling evidence in favor of a discount of 30% is the consistent use of it by the Bank in pricing shares issued to new central banks. Accordingly, the Tribunal finds that the appropriate discount of the NAV is 30%.

202. For the foregoing reasons, the Tribunal finds that the appropriate compensation for the recalled shares, as required by the Statutes, was a proportionate share of the NAV of the Bank, discounted by 30%, subject

---

[149] *Id.*

[150] Statement of Defense, Exhibit 22.

to the additional NAV assessment for real estate. As the Bank paid less than this amount, it is obliged to pay the difference to each private shareholder.

4. The NAV of the Bank as of 8 January 2001

203. The J.P. Morgan Report assessed the NAV of the Bank, averaging it from valuations at three different dates. The J.P. Morgan Report arrived at a figure of US$ 10,072,000,000 or US$ 19,034 (CHF 33,820) per share for the 529,165 shares in the Bank. Dr. Reineccius indicated that he would accept this figure as the NAV. Mr. Mathieu wished an opportunity to litigate the issue of the value of the real estate of the Bank, as it was not included in the J.P. Morgan Report.[151] First Eagle suggested, contingently, that it would accept the NAV in the J.P. Morgan Report if a valuation of real estate were made by an expert.[152] The Tribunal will reserve the question of the Bank's NAV as discounted for the next and final phase of this arbitration.

[151] See para. 84 *supra*; Transcript, at p. 318.
[152] See para. 76 *supra*; Transcript, at p. 329.

CHAPTER VI – OTHER MATTERS

A. Interest

204. In light of the foregoing, a precise sum to be determined in the next phase plus interest is due. With respect to interest, the present state of the record does not enable the Tribunal to determine the amount of interest owing and the rate to be applied, the date from which it should be paid, the amount with respect to which it should be paid and whether simple or compounded interest is owed.

B. Real Estate Valuation

205. Since the agreed net asset value does not include the Bank's real estate, this valuation must also be effected in the next phase of the arbitration. The valuation of real estate will be made by an expert. The choice of the expert, his or her terms of reference, and the timetable for the valuation, will be determined by the Tribunal after consultation with the Parties.

C. The Bank's Counterclaim

206. It is to be recalled that the Bank counterclaimed against First Eagle requesting damages for breach by First Eagle of Article 54 of the Statutes in wrongfully ignoring that jurisdictional commitment and suing the Bank in the United States to avoid the jurisdiction of the Tribunal, and for the costs of the arbitration.

207. In the present state of the record, the Tribunal is insufficiently informed of the contentions of the Bank and First Eagle in regard to that counterclaim, including the quantification thereof. Consequently, the Tribunal determines that the issue of the counterclaim is to be resolved in the next phase of the arbitration according to a schedule to be decided in consultation with the Parties.

D. Costs

208. The Tribunal is insufficiently informed regarding claims for costs in the arbitration. The Tribunal determines that the issue of costs is to be resolved in the next phase of the arbitration according to a schedule to be decided in consultation with the Parties, taking account, insofar as they deem relevant, the Tribunal's *Order In the Matter of Reginald H. Howe v. Bank of International Settlements*.

CHAPTER VII – DECISIONS

209. FOR THE FOREGOING REASONS, the Arbitral Tribunal unanimously renders the following decisions:

1. DETERMINES that the amendment of the Statutes of the Bank for International Settlements of 8 January 2001 to the effect that private shareholders are excluded as shareholders of the Bank was lawful;

2. DETERMINES that Claimants Nos. 1, 2 and 3 are entitled to a compensation for each of their recalled shares in the Bank for International Settlements corresponding to a proportionate share of the Net Asset Value of the Bank, discounted by 30%;

3. NOTES that, for the purposes of the compensation referred to in Decision No. (2), Claimants Nos. 1, 2 and 3 accept that the Net Asset Value of the Bank for International Settlements is US$ 10,072,000,000, being US$ 19,034 (equivalent to CHF 33,820) per share, not counting the value of the real estate of the Bank;

4. GRANTS the relief sought by Claimants Nos. 1, 2 and 3 to the extent that it is consistent with the foregoing Decisions and DISMISSES all other relief sought by Claimants Nos. 1, 2 and 3 inconsistent therewith as well as the relief sought by the Bank for International Settlements relating to those Decisions;

5. RETAINS jurisdiction with respect to the valuation of the real estate of the Bank for International Settlements, the determination of the exact amount owing by the Bank per share including interest thereon to Claimants Nos. 1, 2 and 3, the counterclaim of the Bank for International Settlements against Claimant No. 2 (First Eagle), and the costs of the arbitration, as well as any relief requested by any of the Parties relating to those matters;

6. DETERMINES that it will issue one or more Procedural Orders with respect to the conduct of the next phase of the arbitration concerning the matters mentioned in Decision No. (5) after consultation with the Parties.

Done at the Peace Palace, The Hague, this 22nd day of November 2002,

Professor W. Michael Reisman

Professor Dr. Jochen A. Frowein

Professor Dr. Mathias Krafft

Professor Dr. Paul Lagarde

Professor Dr. Albert Jan van den Berg

Phyllis P. Hamilton, Secretary

APPENDIX A

Agreement regarding the Complete and Final Settlement of the Question of Reparations (signed at The Hague on 20 January 1930)

ANNEX XII

ARBITRATION. RULES OF PROCEDURE

1. The proceedings in any arbitration shall be governed by the dispositions of Chapter III of The Hague Convention of 1907 for the Pacific Settlement of International Disputes, except in so far as the same are modified by the following provisions or by those of the Agreement of The Hague of January, 1930:

   In particular Article 85 of The Hague Convention shall apply to these proceedings, and each Party shall pay its own expenses and an equal share of those of the Tribunal.

2. The Tribunal shall sit at The Hague or such other place as may be fixed by the Tribunal.

   The date of sitting shall be determined by the Chairman and at least fourteen days' previous notice shall be given to the Parties.

3. Each Party shall appoint a representative.

   Any communication between the Parties and the Tribunal or between the Parties themselves shall be conducted through these representatives.

   The Tribunal shall appoint a Secretary to whom communications shall be addressed.

4. The procedure shall consist of two stages:

   (1) Written cases or pleadings; and

(2) Oral debates.

The oral discussion shall be public.

5. The Party which is in the position of plaintiff shall deliver its case within six weeks from the date of the special agreement or a date to be fixed by the Chairman or by the Tribunal, and the other Party shall present its counter-case within six weeks from the date on which it receives the case of the first Party.

If any dispute shall arise as to which Party is in the position of Plaintiff in any particular case, the matter shall be decided summarily by the President of the Tribunal or any Member thereof appointed for this purpose by the President.

6. Cases shall contain: –

(1) a statement of the facts on which the claim is based;

(2) a statement of law;

(3) a statement of conclusions;

(4) a list of the documents in support; these documents shall be attached to the Case.

Counter-Cases shall contain:

(1) the affirmation or contestation of the facts stated in the Case;

(2) a statement of additional facts, if any;

(3) a statement of law;

(4) conclusions based on the facts stated; these conclusions may include counter-claims, in so far as the latter come within the jurisdiction of the Tribunal;

(5) a list of the documents in support; these documents shall be attached to the Counter-Case.

7. The Parties shall also respectively have the right to deliver a reply and rejoinder within three weeks after the receipt of the last preceding pleading.

All cases shall be printed, six copies at least to be delivered to the opposing Party and twelve at least to the Tribunal. Each Party shall acknowledge the receipt of any document to the Party which has delivered it, and shall inform the Tribunal of the date of receipt.

Certified copies of any documents on which reliance is placed shall be annexed to the pleading in which they are referred to.

8. The periods above fixed may be extended either by the agreement of the Parties or by a decision of the Chairman or of the Tribunal.

9. The written proceedings may be in English, French or (where Germany is a Party) in German. It shall, however, be open to any member of the Tribunal to require that any pleading or other document (including any translation) delivered in one of those three languages should be translated into another and, if necessary, duly certified.

10. Not more than two advocates may appear on behalf of each Party for each separate question submitted to arbitration.

11. The advocates may address the Tribunal in their own language, subject to the right of any member of the Tribunal or an opposing Party to require a translation into English or French.

12. Shorthand minutes shall be taken on behalf of the Tribunal of all oral arguments, and transcripts shall be supplied with all possible despatch to the members of the Tribunal and to the Parties. The Secretary of the Tribunal shall be responsible for the execution of this clause and for the preparation of the necessary minutes.

13. For all the purposes of the arbitration up to the commencement of the oral proceedings, the President or any two members of the Tribunal

appointed by him shall be qualified to take in the name and on behalf of the Tribunal any decisions which the Tribunal is authorised to take.

14. No Party may, without the consent of the other Party, make use in the course of the discussion of any document which has not been previously communicated to the other Party.

15. Any member of the Tribunal may put to the Parties during the discussion any questions which he thinks proper. The Tribunal may at any time before reaching a decision employ any means of information which it considers necessary, and may ask for any supplementary notes, memoirs or documents which it thinks desirable. Should, however, the Tribunal resort to other means of information than those supplied by the Parties, it will allow them to submit arguments on the additional information.

16. No oral explanation will be received from either Party unless the other Party is present or has been duly summoned.

17. Any request or communication addressed to the Tribunal by one of the Parties will be communicated at the same time to the other.

18. The Secretary of the Tribunal shall notify all proceedings instituted before the Tribunal to all Parties to The Hague Agreement of January 1930.

19. When any signatory Power or the Bank for International Settlements considers that it has an interest of a legal nature which may be affected by the decision in a case, it may submit a request to the Tribunal to be permitted to intervene as a third Party.

In the absence of an agreement between the Parties, the Chairman or any member of the Tribunal appointed by him for that purpose shall fix the time within which the Party intervening is to deliver his case.

Subject to any contrary decision of the Tribunal, the foregoing rules and the provisions as to Arbitration of the Agreement of The Hague of January 1930, and in particular those relating to the appointment of an additional member in certain cases, shall apply to a Party intervening in the same manner as to the original Parties.

APPENDIX B

Agreement regarding the Complete and Final Settlement of the Question of Reparations (signed at The Hague on 20 January 1930)

Article XV

1. Any dispute, whether between the Governments signatory to the present Agreement or between one or more of those Governments and the Bank for International Settlements, as to the interpretation or application of the New Plan shall, subject to the special provisions of Annexes I, Va, VIa and IX be submitted for final decision to an arbitration Tribunal of five members appointed for five years, of whom one, who will be the Chairman, shall be a citizen of the United States of America, two shall be nationals of States which were neutral during the late war; the two other shall be respectively a national of Germany and a national of one of the Powers which are creditors of Germany.

   For the first period of five years from the date when the New Plan takes effect this Tribunal shall consist of the five members who at present constitute the Arbitration Tribunal established by the Agreement of London of 30 August, 1924.

2. Vacancies on the Tribunal, whether they result from the expiration of the five-yearly periods or occur during the course of any such period, shall be filled, in the case of a member who is a national of one of the Powers which are creditors of Germany, by the French Government, which will first reach an understanding for this purpose with the Belgian, British, Italian and Japanese Governments; in the case of the member of German nationality, by the German Government; and in the cases of the three other members by the six Governments previously mentioned acting in agreement, or in default of their agreement, by the President for the time being of the Permanent Court of International Justice.

3. In any case in which either Germany or the Bank is plaintiff or defendant, if the Chairman of the Tribunal considers, at the request of one or more of the Creditor Governments parties to the proceedings, that

the said Government or Governments are principally concerned, he will invite the said Government or Governments to appoint – and in the case of more Governments than one by agreement – a member, who will take the place on the Tribunal of the member appointed by the French Government.

In any case in which, on the occasion of a dispute between two or more Creditor Governments, there is no national of one or more of those Governments among the Members of the Tribunal, that Government or those Governments shall have the right to appoint each a Member who will sit on that occasion. If the Chairman considers that some of the said Governments have a common interest in the dispute, he will invite them to appoint a single member. Whenever, as a result of this provision, the Tribunal is composed of an even number of members, the Chairman shall have a casting vote.

4. Before and without prejudice to a final decision, the Chairman of the Tribunal, or, if he is not available in any case, any other Member appointed by him, shall be entitled, on the request of any Party who makes the application, to make any interlocutory order with a view to preventing any violation of the rights of the Parties.

5. In any proceedings before the Tribunal the Parties shall always be at liberty to agree to submit the point at issue to the Chairman or any one of the Members of the Tribunal chosen as a single arbitrator.

6. Subject to any special provisions which may be made in the Submission – provisions which may not in any event affect the right of intervention of a Third Party – the procedure before the Tribunal or a single arbitrator shall be governed by the rules laid down in Annex XII.

   The same rules, subject to the same reservation, shall also apply to any proceedings before this Tribunal for which the Annexes to the present Agreement provide.

7. In the absence of an understanding on the terms of Submission, any Party may seize the Tribunal directly by a proceeding *ex parte*, and the Tribunal may decide, even in default of appearance, any question of which it is thus seized.

8. The Tribunal, or the single arbitrator, may decide the question of their own jurisdiction, provided always that, if the dispute is one between Governments and a question of jurisdiction is raised, it shall, at the request of either Party, be referred to the Permanent Court of International Justice.

9. The present provisions shall be duly accepted by the Bank for the settlement of any dispute which may arise between it and one or more of the signatory Governments as to the interpretation or application of its Statutes or the New Plan.

PERMANENT COURT OF ARBITRATION

ARBITRATION TRIBUNAL ESTABLISHED PURSUANT
TO ARTICLE XV OF THE AGREEMENT SIGNED AT
THE HAGUE ON 20 JANUARY 1930

Prof. W. Michael Reisman
Prof. Dr. Jochen A. Frowein
Prof. Dr. Mathias Krafft
Prof. Dr. Paul Lagarde
Prof. Dr. Albert Jan van den Berg

Phyllis Hamilton, Secretary
Permanent Court of Arbitration, Registry

DR. HORST REINECCIUS, CLAIMANT (CLAIM NO. 1)
FIRST EAGLE SOGEN FUNDS, INC., CLAIMANT (CLAIM NO. 2)
MR. PIERRE MATHIEU AND LA SOCIÉTÉ DE CONCOURS HIPPIQUE
DE LA CHÂTRE, CLAIMANTS (CLAIM NO. 3)
-VERSUS-
BANK FOR INTERNATIONAL SETTLEMENTS, RESPONDENT

FINAL AWARD
ON THE CLAIMS FOR COMPENSATION FOR THE SHARES FORMERLY HELD BY THE CLAIMANTS, INTEREST DUE THEREON AND COSTS OF THE ARBITRATION AND ON THE COUNTERCLAIM OF THE BANK AGAINST FIRST EAGLE SOGEN FUNDS, INC.

The Hague, 19 September 2003

Table of Contents

CHAPTER I – INTRODUCTION

1. On 22 November 2002, the Tribunal Concerning the Bank for International Settlements (hereafter the "Tribunal") unanimously rendered a Partial Award (hereafter "Partial Award") in the cases concerning Dr. Horst Reineccius (hereafter "Dr. Reineccius" or "Claimant No. 1"), First Eagle SoGen Funds, Inc. (hereafter "First Eagle" or "Claimant No. 2") and Mr. Pierre Mathieu and the Société de Concours Hippique de La Châtre (hereafter collectively "Mr. Mathieu" or "Claimant No. 3") against the Bank for International Settlements (hereafter the "Bank" or "BIS"). In that Partial Award, the Tribunal rendered the following decisions:

> 1. DETERMINES that the amendment of the Statutes of the Bank for International Settlements of 8 January 2001 to the effect that private shareholders are excluded as shareholders of the Bank was lawful;
>
> 2. DETERMINES that Claimants Nos. 1, 2 and 3 are entitled to a compensation for each of their recalled shares in the Bank for International Settlements corresponding to a proportionate share of the Net Asset Value of the Bank, discounted by 30%;
>
> 3. NOTES that, for the purposes of the compensation referred to in Decision No. (2), Claimants Nos. 1, 2 and 3 accept that the Net Asset Value of the Bank for International Settlements is US$ 10,072,000,000, being US$ 19,034 (equivalent to CHF 33,820) per share, not counting the value of the real estate of the Bank;
>
> 4. GRANTS the relief sought by Claimants Nos. 1, 2 and 3 to the extent that it is consistent with the foregoing Decisions and DISMISSES all other relief sought by Claimants Nos. 1, 2 and 3 inconsistent therewith as well as the relief sought by the Bank for International Settlements relating to those Decisions;
>
> 5. RETAINS jurisdiction with respect to the valuation of the real estate of the Bank for International Settlements, the determination of the exact amount owing by the Bank per share including interest thereon to Claimants Nos. 1, 2 and 3, the counterclaim of the Bank for International

Settlements against Claimant No. 2 (First Eagle), and the costs of the arbitration, as well as any relief requested by any of the Parties relating to those matters;

6. DETERMINES that it will issue one or more Procedural Orders with respect to the conduct of the next phase of the arbitration concerning the matters mentioned in Decision No. (5) after consultation with the Parties.[1]

[1] Partial Award, at para. 209.

CHAPTER II – PROCEDURAL HISTORY

2. Upon receipt of the Partial Award, the Parties agreed upon an exchange of documents and a schedule of written submissions addressed to the matters still before the Tribunal: the Counterclaim of the Bank against First Eagle, the value of the Bank's buildings and their contents (hereafter the "real estate"), the amount still owed to each private shareholder, the issues of interest, costs and expenses of the Arbitration,[2] and any related matters.[3] In the second phase of the Arbitration, Dr. Reineccius, First Eagle and the Bank agreed that, if the Tribunal used the 7 September 2000 exchange rate, the proper NAV per share was CHF 33,936.[4]

3. The Parties notified the Tribunal of their agreement regarding the procedural schedule for the second phase of the Arbitration which the Tribunal confirmed on 31 January 2003 in Procedural Order No. 9 (Order on Consent with Respect to the Schedule for Documents, and Appointment of An Expert in the Second Phase) (hereafter "Procedural Order No. 9 (On Consent)").

4. Pursuant to the terms of the Partial Award, the Tribunal received: (1) an Application dated 17 January 2003 from First Eagle for the Production of Documents from the Bank, (2) an Application dated 17 January 2003 from the Bank for the Production of Documents from First Eagle, (3) a Revised Application dated 21 January 2003 from First Eagle for Documents from the Bank, (4) First Eagle's Objections to the Bank's

---

[2] See also, Order on Costs (5 October 2001). The full text of all of the referenced Procedural Orders can be found at www.pca-cpa.org.

[3] Partial Award, at para. 209(5).

[4] The Tribunal noted in para. 203 of the Partial Award that the J.P. Morgan Report arrived at a Net Asset Value ("NAV") of the Bank of US$ 10,072,000,000 or US$ 19,034 (CHF 33,820) per share. As both the Bank and First Eagle agree (see First Eagle's Memorial Pursuant to Partial Award ("FE Memorial Part. Award"), at para. 59), "this was presumably a clerical error, as it actually reflects the data from only one of the three months from which J.P. Morgan calculated an average NAV amount. The conclusion in the report is that: 'J.P. Morgan has derived the net asset value of BIS of US$19,099 (CHF 33,936) per share . . . .' J.P. Morgan Valuation Report 21 (7 Sept. 2000) (the J.P. Morgan Report (Ex. 54))." Counter-Memorial Pursuant to Partial Award ("BIS Counter-Memorial Part. Award"), at para. 2, fn. 2. Claimant No. 1 also used this value in his prayer for relief. Transcript, at p. 386, ln. 29; see also *infra* para. 19. Claimant No. 3 used the CHF 33,936 figure in his Reply Memorial. Mathieu Mémoire en Duplique sur la Seconde Phase de l'Arbitrage ("Mathieu Mémoire en Duplique Seconde Phase"), at p. 5.

Application dated 28 January 2003, (5) the Bank's Response and Objections to First Eagle's Application dated 28 January 2003, (6) a Reply of the Bank dated 30 January 2003 to First Eagle's Objections, and (7) First Eagle's Reply dated 4 February 2003 to the Objections of the Bank. The Bank and First Eagle were unable to agree on:

(i) First Eagle's request for documents relating to the formation of the Tribunal,

(ii) First Eagle's request for documents which would permit the calculation of the Bank's NAV on 8 January 2001, and

(iii) the Bank's request for documents relating to First Eagle's decision to sue the Bank and documents relating to communications between First Eagle and its shareholders or public officials concerning the exclusion transaction.[5]

5. The Tribunal considered the submissions of the Parties and issued Procedural Order No. 10 deciding that

> First Eagle's Application in (i) above disregards the schedule agreed between the Parties for a phase within which jurisdictional or lack of independence objections were to be lodged. Requesting documents relating to the formation of the Tribunal in this phase of the arbitration, after the Parties' explicit acceptance[6] of the jurisdiction and independence of the Tribunal, is untimely.

The Tribunal deferred a decision upon First Eagle's request in (ii) above to a later date "should the Tribunal hold that the 8 January 2001 date be used to calculate the U.S. dollar/Swiss franc exchange rate in determining the amount to be paid to claimants."[7]

---

[5] Procedural Order No. 10 (9 March 2003) ("Procedural Order No. 10").

[6] Procedural Order No. 3 (Terms of Submission) (5 March 2002), at para. 1, recorded the Parties' statements at the 26 February 2002 meeting of the Parties with the Tribunal to establish the Terms of Reference that "they have no jurisdictional objections."

[7] Procedural Order No. 10, at para. B.

6. The Tribunal granted the Bank's Application in (iii) above, for documents relating to the Bank's claim that First Eagle violated Article 54(1) of the Statutes of the Bank for International Settlements of 20 January 1930; text as amended on 8 January 2001 (hereafter "Statutes of the Bank" or "Bank's Statutes"). First Eagle was ordered to produce to the Bank:

   a. All non-privileged documents relating to First Eagle's decision to sue the Bank in the United States and the conduct of such suit ("First Eagle's United States Litigation"), other than briefs, affidavits and other materials filed by First Eagle with the United States courts;

   b. All documents created on or after 11 September 2000 (the public announcement of the Bank's intention to amend its Statutes to exclude private shareholders) and before 31 August 2001 (the date of First Eagle's Notice of Arbitration) reflecting communications among First Eagle and any shareholder (or purported shareholder) of the Bank (including any advisor of such shareholder) regarding (i) the transaction by which the Bank withdrew its shares held by persons other than central banks (the "exclusion transaction") and (ii) First Eagle's United States Litigation;

   c. All communications among First Eagle and its own shareholders concerning (i) the exclusion transaction and (ii) First Eagle's United States Litigation; and

   d. All documents reflecting First Eagle's communications with public officials in the United States (other than courts) seeking to block the exclusion transaction.[8]

7. Further, the Tribunal confirmed the appointment of the Zurich office of C.B. Richard Ellis, the firm proposed by the Parties, to appraise the Bank's buildings in Basle and their contents pursuant to the Parties'

[8] *Id.*, at para. C.

stipulation of their selection of the Ellis firm subject to the requirement that the appraiser provide a statement of its independence in the matter.[9] The Secretary requested a proposal and fee estimate for the appraisal from the Ellis firm that was provided and circulated to the Parties on 5 April 2003. The Parties confirmed their acceptance of the Ellis firm's proposal.

8. The Parties exchanged documents pursuant to Procedural Order No. 9 (On Consent) and the rulings in Procedural Order No. 10. The Tribunal received from Dr. Reineccius a letter, dated 24 January 2003, stating his arguments and the relief he requested, referencing his letters of 27 November 2002 and 3 January 2003. The Tribunal received from Claimants Nos. 2 and 3: (1) a Memorial dated 28 February 2003 from First Eagle, (2) a Memorial on its Counterclaim dated 28 February 2003 from the Bank, (3) a Memorial dated 3 March 2003 from Mr. Mathieu, (4) a Counter-Memorial dated 21 April 2003 from First Eagle, (5) a Counter-Memorial dated 21 April 2003 from the Bank, (6) a Reply from First Eagle dated 16 May 2003, (7) a Reply from Mr. Mathieu dated 16 May 2003, and (8) a Reply from the Bank dated 16 May 2003.

9. The Tribunal issued Procedural Order No. 11 (On Consent) on 16 May 2003 (hereafter "Procedural Order No. 11") which recorded that:

> [T]he Tribunal received from the expert its statement of independence in this matter as required by the Parties on 7 April 2003, and the expert, accompanied by the Secretary of the Tribunal, inspected all of the properties on 16 April 2003, and then provided on 28 April 2003 a Certificate of Valuation and underlying Valuation Reports which were circulated to, and accepted by, the Parties . . . .
>
> . . . .
>
> B. The Tribunal will use the value of CHF 168,094,000 (One hundred and sixty-eight million, ninety-four thousand Swiss Francs), as determined by the expert, for the purpose of valuing as of 7 September 2000 the Bank's

[9] *Id.*, at para. D.

buildings and their contents as required by the 22 November 2002 Partial Award.[10]

In addition, the Tribunal confirmed the agenda for oral argument.

10. On 25 May 2003 the Tribunal issued Procedural Order No. 12 (On Consent) (Re: Proposed New Exhibit 104) granting First Eagle's application to file new Exhibit 104.

11. The Tribunal issued Procedural Order No. 13 (On Consent) on 27 May 2003 granting Dr. Reineccius' application to file a one-page bank statement as Exhibit 1.

12. Public Hearings in the final phase of the Arbitration pursuant to Article XV of the Agreement regarding the Complete and Final Settlement of the Question of Reparations, signed at The Hague on 20 January 1930 (hereafter the "1930 Hague Agreement") and Article 20 of the Rules for Arbitration were held in the Great Hall of Justice at the Peace Palace in The Hague from 28–29 May 2003. At the request of the Parties, their separate claims were heard in parallel with some integration for efficiency and the convenience of the Parties. First Eagle was represented, throughout the Hearings, by Mr. Donald Francis Donovan and Mr. Dietmar W. Prager of the Debevoise & Plimpton firm. Mr. Mathieu was represented by Mr. Elie Kleiman and Mr. Guillaume Tattevin of the Freshfields Bruckhaus Deringer firm. The Bank was represented by Mr. Jonathan I. Blackman, Mr. Laurent Cohen-Tanugi and Ms. Claudia Annacker of the Cleary, Gottlieb, Steen & Hamilton firm. Prof. Dr. Mario Giovanoli and Dr. James Freis were also present on behalf of the BIS Secretariat. Dr. Reineccius appeared *pro se* on 28 May.

---

[10] Claimants Nos. 1 and 2 objected during the 28 May 2003 Hearings to the value that the expert determined. See also *supra* paras. 7 and 9, and *infra* fn. 17 and paras. 18, 19(ii), and 32. The Bank requested that the Tribunal abide by the determination in the Partial Award that one expert would determine the value of the real estate and the Parties' explicit selection of the Ellis firm to determine the value. Transcript, at pp. 604–605.

13. In accordance with the Convention respecting the Bank for International Settlements of 20 January 1930 (hereafter the "1930 Hague Convention"), simultaneous translations in English, French and German were provided for the Hearings.

CHAPTER III – THE PARTIES' CLAIMS

A. CLAIMANT NO. 1, DR. REINECCIUS

1. Arguments

a. CALCULATION OF COMPENSATION

14. In his 27 November 2002 letter, Dr. Reineccius requested that the Tribunal decide that CHF 33,820[11] plus the proportional amount of the Bank's real estate be paid to him in Swiss francs. Dr. Reineccius had indicated at the Hearings in August of 2002[12] that he would stipulate that the J.P. Morgan calculations of the NAV were correct for the purpose of calculating the additional payment to private shareholders. In his letter of 24 January 2003, Dr. Reineccius again requested that the Tribunal award him CHF 33,820 pursuant to paragraph 209(5) of the Partial Award plus the amount determined by the expert for the buildings' value.

b. INTEREST

15. He requested interest on that amount at a minimum of 3¼% per annum which he analogized to the CHF-*Geldmarktzins* prior to 17 September 2001. He noted that the rate was lower after September 2001 but maintained that valuation prior to that time was appropriate.[13]

c. COSTS OF THE ARBITRATION

16. In his 3 January 2003 letter, Dr. Reineccius requested that the Tribunal direct reimbursement by the Bank of his deposits for the costs of the Arbitration.

d. SUBMISSIONS

17. Dr. Reineccius, in his letter of 24 January 2003, notified the Tribunal of his intention to participate in the Hearings on 28–29 May 2003. He approved the schedule of submissions in Procedural Order No. 9 (On

---

11 See *supra* fn. 4, but see *infra* para. 19(i).
12 Transcript, at p. 331.
13 *Id.*, at p. 388.

Consent) and requested that copies be sent to him of: (1) documents exchanged by the Parties pursuant to Procedural Order No. 9, paragraphs 5–8, and (2) the written submissions set forth in the Order.

e. STIPULATIONS

18. Dr. Reineccius indicated his willingness to stipulate to the J.P. Morgan calculation of the NAV of the Bank as described in paragraph 2 *supra*. Regarding the valuation of the real estate pursuant to paragraph 205 of the Partial Award, Dr. Reineccius wrote on 27 November 2002:

> Ich überlasse es First Eagle, in ihrem und in meinem Namen einen Vorschlag für die Benennung eines Immobilien-Experten und seinen Zeitplan für die Bewertung zu machen.[14]

First Eagle stipulated to the appointment of an expert.[15]

2. Relief Requested

19. Dr. Reineccius requested the Tribunal to find that:

(i) as decided by the Tribunal in para. 209(3) of the Partial Award, he should be paid a proportion of the J. P. Morgan Report NAV of the Bank which he calculated to be CHF 33,936 per share compensation for his compulsorily recalled shares;[16]

(ii) the proportionate value of the Bank's buildings and their contents to be paid to him should be CHF 767 per share;[17]

(iii) the Bank must pay him interest at a minimum of 3¼% per annum

---

[14] I leave it up to First Eagle to make a proposal in their and my name as to the nomination of a real estate expert and the schedule for the valuation. [Translation provided by the Tribunal.]

[15] See *infra* para. 32.

[16] Transcript, at p. 386.

[17] *Id.*, at p. 387. At the Hearings on 28 May 2003, Dr. Reineccius requested that the Tribunal substitute the value for which the Bank's real estate was insured for the value determined by the expert. See also *supra* paras. 7, 9, and fn.10, and *infra* para. 32.

from 8 January 2001 to the date of payment on the above compensation;[18]

(iv) his costs of the Arbitration (the deposits he made to the BIS Tribunal Account), *i.e.* EUR 1,852.64 should be reimbursed and compensation should be paid to him for his expense and his efforts (*Bemühungen*) in bringing his case to the Tribunal;[19]

(v) a specific date for payment of this compensation including interest is ordered;[20]

(vi) the Tribunal should "expressly forbid the Bank from making upcoming payments dependent on signing a waiver".[21]

B. CLAIMANT NO. 2, FIRST EAGLE

1. Arguments

a. CALCULATION OF COMPENSATION

20. First Eagle maintained that, pursuant to the Partial Award, it is entitled to an award of CHF 7,755.20 (excluding the real estate value) on each of the 9,110 shares it owned,[22] with "interest at a rate of at least 7%[23] compounded monthly[24] . . . from 8 January 2001 through the date of payment,"[25] plus the costs, fees, and expenses it incurred in this proceeding.[26]

---

[18] Transcript, at p. 388.
[19] Letter from Dr. Reineccius to Secretary to the Tribunal (27 November 2002).
[20] Transcript, at p. 387.
[21] *Id.*, at p. 388.
[22] First Eagle's Reply Memorial Pursuant to Partial Award ("FE Reply Memorial Part. Award"), at para. 186(a).
[23] *Id.*, at para. 154.
[24] *Id.*, at para. 162.
[25] *Id.*, at paras. 151 and 186(e).
[26] *Id.*, at para. 186(d) and (e).

21. First Eagle argued in its submissions of 28 February 2003 and 16 May 2003 that the Bank's NAV for the purposes of determining the base award of First Eagle's damages must be set at CHF 33,936 per share, the value calculated by J.P. Morgan in its report of 7 September 2000.[27]

> [T]his result is compelled by the parties' stipulation at the August 2002 hearing accepting J.P. Morgan's calculation of the Bank's NAV. By so stipulating, the parties agreed to accept as conclusive a September 2000 valuation analysis . . . in the event that the January 2001 exchange rate were to be used, the NAV would have to be recalculated as of that date as well.[28]

Without such a recalculation, First Eagle would be forced to "bear the downside effect of changing currency conversion rates . . . without calculating the offsetting increase in the Bank's NAV as of the later date."[29]

22. First Eagle characterized the Bank's argument that the date of Swiss franc to U.S. dollar exchange should be 8 January 2001, not 7 September 2000, as "an attempt to deny First Eagle the compensation to which the Partial Award entitles it."[30] First Eagle asserted that the Bank's actual use of the J.P. Morgan Report in the exclusion transaction relied upon J.P. Morgan's Swiss franc calculations.

> In the exclusion transaction out of which First Eagle's claim arises, the Bank first, on 10 September 2000, fixed a redemption price in Swiss francs. It did so in reliance on the J.P. Morgan Report, which used exchange rates prevailing in September 2000 . . . . The Bank then, on 8 January 2001, committed to pay (and subsequently did pay) that same redemption price in Swiss francs.[31]

---

27 FE Memorial Part. Award, at para. 10; FE Reply Memorial Part. Award, at para. 4.
28 FE Reply Memorial Part. Award, at para. 5.
29 FE Memorial Part. Award, at para. 70.
30 FE Reply Memorial Part. Award, at para. 3.
31 FE Memorial Part. Award, at para. 76.

23. First Eagle argued that the Bank's past share issuance practice was irrelevant but nonetheless supported reliance on J.P. Morgan's September 2000 Swiss franc NAV:[32]

> [P]ast share practices were of little or no significance compared to the Bank's actual practice in the exclusion transaction, which was to set a purchase price in Swiss francs in September 2000, based on the then-prevailing exchange rates, and to hold that price constant over the entire period of the share repurchase.[33]

24. First Eagle dismissed the Bank's argument[34] that three documents proved it had been monitoring post-September 2000 exchange rate fluctuations as irrelevant, because the Bank did not take any action as a result.[35] Further, First Eagle observed, when J.P. Morgan updated its entire valuation analysis, the documents "show that the Bank itself did not apply post September 2000 exchange rates to the September 2000 NAV . . . . [T]he Bank recalculated the NAV at the same time it recalculated the exchange rate, rather than apply new exchange rates to the September NAV. . . ."[36]

b. COSTS OF THE ARBITRATION AND EXPENSES

25. First Eagle asserted:

> First Eagle is also entitled to reimbursement from the Bank of the costs of the arbitration and its legal fees and expenses. *First*, as the prevailing party, First Eagle is entitled to its costs and fees in order to be fully compensated for the Bank's refusal to pay lawful compensation at the time it was due. *Second*, because this proceeding was necessary to correct the otherwise unlawful compensation paid by the Bank, and hence to ensure that the transaction met the requirements of international law, First Eagle's costs, fees, and expenses constitute a component of the

[32] FE Reply Memorial Part. Award, at para. 83.
[33] *Id.*
[34] The Bank "actively monitored movements in the market exchange rate of Swiss francs and U.S. dollars up until the EGM decision." BIS Counter-Memorial Part. Award, at para. 77.
[35] FE Reply Memorial Part. Award, at para. 79.
[36] *Id.*, at para. 80.

> transaction costs necessary to put into effect the exclusion transaction. *Finally*, at a minimum, because First Eagle's efforts have substantially benefitted all the Bank's excluded shareholders, those shareholders should share, pro rata, in First Eagle's expenses.[37]

c. INTEREST

26. First Eagle maintained it was entitled to interest from 8 January 2001 "on the outstanding compensation payment, as well as [on] its costs, fees, and expenses, at a rate of at least 7% compounded monthly."[38] First Eagle reasoned that 7% interest

> reflects the minimum return First Eagle would have expected to earn on alternative investments of the same risk had it received full compensation when it was due. If First Eagle were paid less than 7% interest, the Bank would earn a windfall . . . and thereby be unjustly enriched.[39]

Interest should be compounded monthly, First Eagle stated, "in accordance with the current international law and financial practice, including that of the Bank itself".[40]

d. DECLARATORY JUDGMENTS

27. First Eagle opposed the Bank's request for a final Award declaring that "the Tribunal has exclusive jurisdiction over any claims against the Bank arising out of or in connection with the validity, procedures and amount of compensation provided in the 8 January 2001 [compulsory repurchase]".[41] First Eagle argued that the Tribunal cannot render "an advisory opinion on matters outside its jurisdiction."[42]

---

[37] *Id.*, at para. 9.
[38] *Id.*, at para. 12.
[39] *Id.*, at para. 13.
[40] *Id.*
[41] Memorial ("BIS Memorial"), at para. 70.
[42] FE Reply Memorial Part. Award, at para. 14.

28. First Eagle further argued it was entitled to an award ordering the Bank to pay compensation and interest due on all 9,110 shares claimed by First Eagle, both those registered to First Eagle and those held by a custodian. On 8 January 2001, First Eagle was the registered owner of 5,250 shares in the Bank.[43] However, First Eagle claimed compensation for 9,110 shares of the Bank. First Eagle indicated that the 3,860 shares for which First Eagle claims compensation, but is not the registered owner,

> were held by two custodians in whose names the shares were registered . . . . Serving as the Swiss subcustodian for the Bank of New York, Credit Suisse First Boston . . . held 3655 shares, and serving as the Swiss subcustodian for J.P. Morgan Chase, UBS held 205 shares . . . . For purposes of this proceeding, each of the Bank of New York and J.P. Morgan Chase has confirmed that, if any compensation is paid to them rather than First Eagle on the shares they held as custodian, they will pay that compensation over to First Eagle.[44]

First Eagle further explained that it had

> earlier claimed in this proceeding for 9085 shares, or 25 shares less than the total for which it now claims . . . in January 2001, a prospective trade was pending . . . [which] was cancelled after the exclusion transaction prevented it from settling . . . . It now seeks the additional compensation due on those shares as well.[45]

e. FIRST EAGLE'S DEFENSE TO THE BANK'S COUNTERCLAIM

29. First Eagle asserted it had the right to litigate in the U.S. District Court on both its securities law claims and the dispute over arbitral jurisdiction; it requested the Tribunal to deny the Bank's claim for damages for breach of Article 54(1) of the Bank's Statutes since those claims did not fall within the agreement to arbitrate.

---

[43] FE Memorial Part. Award, at paras. 28–29.
[44] *Id.*, at paras. 30–31.
[45] *Id.*, at paras. 32–33.

30. First Eagle alleged that the bulk of the litigation in the United States concerned the securities law claims[46] and "arose from First Eagle's application for interim measures."[47] First Eagle defended its recourse to the District Court as action that did not breach Article 54(1) because municipal jurisdictions in general do not give the arbitrator the right to rule first on jurisdiction.[48] Therefore, First Eagle asserted, it had the right to litigate "both the securities law claims and the dispute over arbitral jurisdiction, and because the fees the Bank incurred . . . resulted only from litigating those two matters, the Bank's claim for breach of Article 54(1) must be denied."[49]

31. First Eagle also argued that Article 54 was unenforceable. When First Eagle filed suit in the United States, the Tribunal did not yet exist and "the appointment of each of the members after the dispute arose by governments with an interest in the dispute – did not comport with basic principles of public policy."[50]

f. STIPULATIONS

32. First Eagle stated during the Hearings that it was prepared to stipulate, if the Bank also so stipulated, that the NAV of the Bank is as determined by J.P. Morgan in Exhibits in Support of First Eagle's Memorial (hereafter "FE Ex.") 43. Regarding a stipulation concerning the value of the Bank's real estate, First Eagle stated:

> In their 7 January 2003 stipulation the parties agreed that they would "attempt to resolve by agreement the value of the real estate of the Bank and, failing agreement on the value, seek to propose an agreed process and schedule by which the question might be determined." The parties have since agreed to the Tribunal's retention of an appraiser to value the real estate.[51]

---

[46] Transcript, at pp. 533–534.
[47] First Eagle's Counter-Memorial in Opposition to Counterclaim ("FE Counter-Memorial Counterclaim"), at para. 77.
[48] *Id.*, at para. 89.
[49] *Id.*, at para. 97.
[50] *Id.*, at para. 118.
[51] FE Memorial Part. Award, at para. 58.

First Eagle, with the other Parties, proposed that the Zurich office of the firm of C.B. Richard Ellis be appointed by the Tribunal to determine the value of the Bank's buildings and their contents whose valuation would be final and would be added to the NAV.[52]

2. *Applicable Law*

33. In its Memorial, First Eagle stated that general principles of international law govern this dispute and that it, as well as the Bank, agrees that "the rules of general public international law apply to the interpretation of the Statutes and hence to the determination of the excluded shareholders' property interest in the Bank."[53]

34. First Eagle challenged the *lex specialis* basis for the Tribunal's jurisdiction. First Eagle stated that while it had clearly submitted to the Tribunal's jurisdiction, that consent formed the basis for the jurisdiction, not the *lex specialis*. It cited *Siemens AG v. Dutco Constr. Co.*[54] in support of its claim that it was entitled to seek a ruling on the validity of the arbitration agreement in a domestic court. As further support for its argument that Article 54 was unenforceable, First Eagle relied[55] upon the New York Convention because "the composition of the arbitral authority . . . was not in accordance with the agreement of the parties."[56]

---

52 See also Procedural Order No. 9 (On Consent); Partial Award, at para. 205; Mémoire en Demande sur la Seconde Phase de l'Arbitrage ("Mathieu Mémoire en Demande Seconde Phase"), at p. 4; Transcript, at pp. 329–331.

53 First Eagle's Memorial ("FE Memorial"), at para. 205.

54 Cour de Cassation (France), 7 January 1992, reprinted in XVIII Y.B. Comm. Arb. p. 140, at pp. 141–142 (1993).

55 Transcript, at p. 520.

56 United Nations Convention on the Recognition and Enforcement of Foreign Arbitral Awards, New York, 10 June 1958, Art. V(1)(d), 21 UST p. 2517, 330 UNTS p. 38 ("New York Convention").

3. Relief Requested

35. First Eagle requested in its Reply Memorial that the Tribunal issue a final award ordering the Bank to:

a) pay First Eagle additional compensation of CHF 7755.20 per share (equal to 70% of NAV of CHF 33,936 per share less the CHF 16,000 per share compensation already received) for each of the 9110 shares held by First Eagle, or a total of CHF 70,649,872;

b) pay First Eagle its share of the value of the Bank's real estate;

c) pay First Eagle its costs of the arbitration, which currently amount to $546,913.40, or, at a minimum, the share of such costs in excess of First Eagle's share of the total amount of the shares subject to the exclusion transaction;

d) pay First Eagle its legal fees and expenses in an amount to be fixed after the May 2000 [sic] hearing in this matter in a manner to be directed by the Tribunal or, at a minimum, the share of such legal fees and expenses in excess of First Eagle's share of the total amount of the shares subject to the exclusion transaction;

e) pay First Eagle interest at a rate of at least 7% compounded monthly and running, as to the additional compensation, from 8 January 2001 through the date of payment of such compensation and, as to First Eagle's costs and fees, from the date of payment by First Eagle through the date of reimbursement by the Bank;

f) deny all relief requested by the Bank, BIS CM2 p. 91; and

g) provide First Eagle such other and further relief as the Tribunal may deem just and proper.[57]

---

[57] FE Reply Memorial Part. Award, at para. 186; on 22 May 2003, First Eagle made a further deposit in respect of the costs of arbitration of US$ 259,173.00, bringing its total contribution to the costs of the arbitration to US$ 806,086.40

C. CLAIMANT NO. 3, MR. MATHIEU

1. Arguments

a. CALCULATION OF COMPENSATION

36. Mr. Mathieu asked the Tribunal to calculate the additional compensation owed to the former private shareholders pursuant to the 22 November 2002 Partial Award utilizing the 6 September 2000 rate of exchange:

> Dire que la date devant être retenue pour déterminer le taux de change applicable en vue de la conversion en francs suisses de l'actif net réévalué de la BRI libellé en dollars américains a d'ores et déjà été fixée par le Tribunal au 6 septembre 2000.[58]

37. Mr. Mathieu argued that the Bank's proposed substitution of the 8 January 2001 date contradicted the Parties' stipulation to the NAV in the J.P. Morgan Report.[59] Further, Mr. Mathieu argued, the Bank's claims that its past practice justified the use of the 8 January exchange rate were irrelevant to the compulsory repurchase:

> [L]a BRI a en effet soutenu dans son Contre-mémoire que le calcul de l'indemnité doit se faire sur la base de son procédé habituel de calcul des montants en matière d'émission d'actions nouvelles. Cependant, cet usage n'a aucun titre à être appliqué à l'instance. La BRI fait en réalité une interprétation contestable du raisonnement du Tribunal dans la Sentence partielle. Qui plus est, la méthode proposée n'est pas adaptée à la situation du retrait forcé.[60]

38. If the Tribunal were to use the 8 January 2001 date proposed by the Bank, the NAV of the Bank must be recalculated, by an expert of the Tribunal's choosing, at the Bank's expense:

---

[58] Mathieu Mémoire en Duplique Seconde Phase, at p. 15.
[59] *Id.*, at p. 5.
[60] *Id.*, at p. 3.

> A titre subsidiaire, si le Tribunal devait décider qu'il convient de retenir le taux de change applicable au 8 janvier 2001, dire que l'actif net de la BRI devra être réévalué à cette même date et désigner à cette fin, aux frais de la BRI, tel expert indépendant qu'il plaira au Tribunal de nommer . . . .[61]

b. DATE UPON WHICH EXCHANGE RATE IS SET

39. Mr. Mathieu argued that 6 September 2000 is the date, consistent with the Partial Award and the J.P. Morgan valuation, to set the exchange rate for the additional compensation to be paid to the former shareholders:

> La différence est en effet significative : en appliquant le taux de change ayant cours au 6 septembre 2000, à savoir 0,5628 dollar américain pour un franc suisse, une action de la banque évaluée à 19.034 dollars américains se convertit à la somme de 33.820 francs suisses. Si, comme le soutient la Banque, le taux de change devant être retenu était celui applicable au 8 janvier 2001, à savoir 0,6256 dollar américain pour un franc suisse, la contre-valeur en francs suisses de cette même action ne serait plus que de 30.425,80. La controverse porte donc sur un enjeu d'un montant de 3.394,20 francs suisses par action. Ce montant correspond, pour la Banque, à l'économie qu'elle espère réaliser sur l'indemnisation que le droit international lui impose de verser en contrepartie des actions, dont elle conserve pour l'avenir la propriété et les espérances de plus values qui leur sont attachées – ne serait-ce qu'en considération de la décote de 30% sur la valeur d'actif net retenue aux termes de la Sentence.[62]

c. INTEREST

40. Mr. Mathieu requested that interest should be paid on the additional amount to be paid to the private shareholders from 8 January 2001.[63]

---

[61] *Id.*, at p. 15.
[62] Mathieu Mémoire en Demande Seconde Phase, at p. 5 (internal citations omitted).
[63] Mathieu Mémoire en Duplique Seconde Phase, at pp. 11–12.

41. Mr. Mathieu further requested that he be paid interest on the CHF 16,000 which the Bank had offered as compensation but which Mr. Mathieu had declined to accept until after the Tribunal's 22 November 2002 Partial Award.

> Le Demandeur, dans son Mémoire en demande du 13 mai 2002, développe ainsi trois moyens: (i) l'illégalité de la résolution amendant les statuts, (ii) l'illicéité de l'opération de rachat forcé des actions et (iii) l'insuffisance de l'indemnité accordée aux actionnaires privés.
>
> Le Demandeur aura par conséquent, du premier jour du litige jusqu'à la Sentence du 22 novembre 2002, toujours soutenu que l'opération de rachat forcée était illégale et qu'en raison de cette illégalité, il possédait toujours sa qualité d'actionnaire de la Banque. Il n'est dès lors pas surprenant que ce dernier se soit toujours opposé à percevoir l'indemnité qui lui était proposée, afin de rester cohérent dans sa démarche à l'encontre de la Banque. L'on ne saurait, en effet, demander une chose et son contraire.[64]

42. Mr. Mathieu requested that the Tribunal award 7% compound interest by reference to the J.P. Morgan Report that stated the Bank's cost of capital to be in the 6.7–7% range.[65] Compound interest should be paid in keeping with the requirements of international law and modern commercial practice:

> Le principe de réparation intégrale exige enfin que les intérêts soient capitalisés. En effet les intérêts à percevoir contribuent à former un capital et doivent donc eux-mêmes être porteurs d'intérêts, ainsi que l'exige une jurisprudence établie en droit international. Conformément aux usages du commerce international, ces intérêts seront capitalisés sur une base mensuelle.[66]

---

[64] Mathieu Mémoire en Demande Seconde Phase, at p. 14.
[65] *Id.*, at p. 15.
[66] *Id.*, at p. 16.

d. COSTS OF THE ARBITRATION AND EXPENSES

43. Mr. Mathieu argued that the Bank as the losing Party should pay the costs of the Arbitration including their legal expenses. However, if the Tribunal does not decide to have the Bank bear the cost of the Arbitration, then the expenses of the Arbitration and Claimants' legal fees should be apportioned among all the private shareholders. Such apportionment is equitable because the expenses were incurred in actions that conferred a benefit upon the entire group of former private shareholders. Mr. Mathieu stated that his costs and expenses should be paid by the Bank and interest paid thereon equal to the rate of interest awarded for the additional payment. Mr. Mathieu further requested payment of the expenses and disbursements he and his lawyers incurred during the course of the Arbitration, EUR 4,321.67.[67]

e. DECLARATORY JUDGMENT

44. Further, Mr. Mathieu argued that the Tribunal should not grant the Bank's request for a ruling that the Award in this Arbitration be final and binding upon all Parties and dispositive of any potential claims.[68]

f. STIPULATIONS

45. Mr. Mathieu indicated that he joined the other Claimants in the stipulations described in paragraph 32 *supra* regarding the use of the NAV as determined in the J.P. Morgan Report (FE Ex. 43) with the addition of the value of the Bank's real estate.[69]

2. Applicable Law

46. Mr. Mathieu argued that the constituent instruments of the Bank and general international law were applicable in deciding the rights of the shareholders. Further, Mr. Mathieu argued that the international public

---

[67] *Id.*, at p. 18; see *infra* para. 48.
[68] Mathieu Mémoire en Duplique Seconde Phase, at p. 13.
[69] Transcript, at p. 330; see *supra* para. 18 and *infra* para. 67; Mathieu Mémoire en Demande Seconde Phase, at p. 4.

policy of both Switzerland and The Netherlands should be respected as the place of Arbitration and the place of potential enforcement.[70]

3. Relief Requested

47. Mr. Mathieu, in his submission of 16 May 2003, requested the following relief:

> Le Demandeur requiert qu'il plaise au Tribunal Arbitral de:
>
> Dire que la date devant être retenue pour déterminer le taux de change applicable en vue de la conversion en francs suisses de l'actif net réévalué de la BRI libellé en dollars américains a d'ores et déjà été fixée par le Tribunal au 6 septembre 2000;
>
> A titre subsidiaire, si le Tribunal devait décider qu'il convient de retenir le taux de change applicable au 8 janvier 2001, dire que l'actif net de la BRI devra être réévalué à cette même date et désigner à cette fin, aux frais de la BRI, tel expert indépendant qu'il plaira au Tribunal de nommer;
>
> Dire que les intérêts dus par la BRI au Demandeur ont couru, à compter du 8 janvier 2001, et à titre subsidiaire à compter du 14 février 2001, tant sur le complément d'indemnité en cours de détermination et ce jusqu'à parfait paiement, que sur la somme de 16.000 francs suisses entre le 8 janvier 2001 et le 9 janvier 2003 par la BRI, au taux minimum de 7%; ordonner la capitalisation des intérêts sur une base mensuelle;
>
> Dire que la BRI supportera seule l'intégralité des frais liés au présent arbitrage; à titre subsidiaire, dans l'hypothèse où le Tribunal déciderait du contraire, donner acte au Demandeur de l'engagement de la BRI de supporter en toute hypothèse la moitié des frais d'arbitrage, et dire que toute partie de ces frais qui ne sera pas mise à la charge de la BRI sera répartie entre la totalité des actionnaires privés de celle-ci proportionnellement au nombre d'actions dont chacun de ces actionnaires était propriétaire au 8 janvier 2001 rapporté au nombre total de 74.952 [sic] actions; réserver la justification des frais (pour mémoire);

---

[70] Mémoire en Demande ("Mathieu Mémoire"), at pp. 7–8.

> Dire que des intérêts sont dus par la BRI sur les frais d'arbitrage à compter de la date du déboursement effectif de ces sommes jusqu'à parfait paiement par la BRI, au taux minimum de 7% avec capitalisation sur une base mensuelle;
>
> Condamner, en toute hypothèse, la BRI à régler au Demandeur la totalité des honoraires d'avocat encourus dans le cadre du présent arbitrage (pour mémoire);
>
> Enfin, rectifier dans la sentence finale le nom de la Société de Concours hippique de La Châtre.[71]

48. Mr. Mathieu further requested reimbursement of his expenses, EUR 4,436.75, and reimbursement of the amounts he deposited for the costs of the Arbitration, EUR 760.25.[72]

D. RESPONDENT, THE BANK FOR INTERNATIONAL SETTLEMENTS

1. Arguments

a. COUNTERCLAIM

49. The Bank argued that First Eagle's suit in the United States[73] which challenged (1) the Bank's right to carry out the redemption and (2) the amount of compensation provided by Article 18A of the Bank's Statutes, seeking money damages "in the amount of the full value of plaintiffs' proportionate interest in the Bank,"[74] breached Article 54. "As a result of this breach, the Bank incurred direct economic damages in excess of US$ 587,000 defending First Eagle's lawsuit, as well as wasted internal legal and management resources."[75]

---

[71] Mathieu Mémoire en Duplique Seconde Phase, at pp. 15–16.

[72] Mathieu Mémoire en Demande Seconde Phase, at p. 18; Letter from Mr. Mathieu to the Tribunal and the Bank (27 August 2003).

[73] *First Eagle SoGen Funds, Inc. v. Bank for Int'l Settlements*, No. 01 Civ. 0087(RO), 2001 WL 1150323 (S.D.N.Y., 28 September 2001).

[74] Reply Memorial Pursuant to Partial Award ("BIS Reply Memorial Part. Award"), at para. 4 (internal citations omitted).

[75] *Id.*, at para. 2.

50. The Bank challenged First Eagle's representation that it intended to obtain disclosure,[76] and "to determine the validity" of its "agreement" to arbitrate under Article 54.[77] The Bank argued that even if the "securities claims had been independent of First Eagle's claims for conversion, breach of contract and breach of fiduciary duty . . . that would not somehow excuse First Eagle from its obligation to arbitrate the latter under Article 54."[78]

51. The Bank cited the text of Article 54(1):

> If any dispute shall arise between the Bank, on the one side, and any central bank, financial institution, or other bank referred to in the present Statutes, on the other side, or between the Bank and its shareholders, with regard to the interpretation or application of the Statutes of the Bank, the same shall be referred for final decision to the Tribunal provided for by the Hague Agreement of January, 1930.[79]

The Bank alleged:[80]

> First Eagle tried to avoid its duty to arbitrate these issues under Article 54 by pretending that the shares recall was a voluntary tender offer rather than a mandatory redemption. But this did not fool the District Court, which found that "[p]laintiff's only real issue is with the price and method of valuation."[81] . . . Nor did it fool the Court of Appeals, which recognized that "[i]ndeed, the primary complaint advanced by First Eagle appears to be that the valuation methods employed by J.P. Morgan and Arthur Andersen undervalued the privately held shares."[82]

---

76 FE Counter-Memorial Counterclaim, at para. 38.

77 *Id.*, at para. 5.

78 BIS Reply Memorial Part. Award, at para. 5.

79 *Id.*, at para. 10.

80 *Id.*, at para. 14.

81 Exhibits to Memorial ("BIS Ex.") 25 (*First Eagle SoGen Funds, Inc. v. Bank for Int'l Settlements*, No. 01 Civ. 0087 (RO), 2001 WL 66321, at p. *3 n. 6 (S.D.N.Y., 26 January 2001)).

82 BIS Ex. 50 (*First Eagle SoGen Funds, Inc. v. Bank for Int'l Settlements*, 252 F.3d p. 604, at p. 607 (2d. Cir. 2001)).

> Article 54(2) specifically provides that the Tribunal has "power to decide all questions [concerning the terms of submission under Article 54(1)] (including the question of its own jurisdiction)" . . . [and] Article 16(1) of the Tribunal's Rules of Procedure, which provides that "[t]he Tribunal shall have the power to decide the question as to its own jurisdiction . . . ."[83] All questions of jurisdiction in disputes between the Bank and its shareholders with regard to the interpretation or the application of the Statutes must therefore be raised exclusively before the Tribunal.[84]

52. The Bank distinguished the legal authorities cited by First Eagle as assuming the existence of "an agreement to arbitrate entered into upon the election of the parties, or a specific arbitral regime that explicitly or implicitly provides for recourse to national judiciaries."[85]

53. The Bank argued that the rules which bind it, including those concerning its dispute-resolution forum, are not the subject of private agreement.

> The obligation of the Bank and its shareholders to refer questions of arbitrability exclusively to the Tribunal is . . . an obligation created by the treaty mechanism establishing the Bank, which provides its own exclusive mechanism for resolving internal disputes over "the interpretation or application of the Statutes of the Bank." Such disputes implicating an international organization's internal law are excluded from municipal legislative, administrative, and adjudicative competence.[86]

54. The Bank denied "First Eagle's assertion that there is a universal principle that parties to an arbitration may seek interim measures from a court".[87] The Bank quoted the United Nations Commission on International Trade Law ("UNCITRAL") Working Group for Arbitration and Conciliation, in paragraph 22 of its Note on Preparation of Uniform Provisions on Interim Measures of Protection of January 2002:

---

83 BIS Legal Authorities, at 39.
84 BIS Reply Memorial Part. Award, at para. 21.
85 *Id.*, at para. 22.
86 *Id.*, at para. 23 (internal citations omitted).
87 *Id.*, at para. 34.

> Other laws provide that the authority to issue interim relief is vested exclusively in the arbitral tribunal and the courts do not have the power to issue interim measures in support of arbitration. The court's lack of jurisdiction may be the result of provisions that oust the jurisdiction of the court where there is an arbitration agreement.[88]

55. The Bank further distinguished the legal authorities cited by First Eagle as indicating that in the context of a commercial arbitration agreement, the right of a party to seek interim measures from a court exists where the rules governing the arbitration or the parties' agreement reserve that option. The Bank argued that the Convention on the Settlement of Investment Disputes between States and Nationals of Other States ("ICSID")[89] treaty regime provides a closer analogy.

> [T]he Rules of Procedure for Arbitration Proceedings, Arbitration Rules under the 1965 Convention on the Settlement of Investment Disputes provides that a party can apply to a non-ICSID forum for provisional relief only if the arbitration agreement permits such applications.[90]

56. The Bank argued that First Eagle's arguments regarding the validity of Article 54 were raised unsuccessfully in the United States and were abandoned by First Eagle in the proceedings before the Tribunal.[91]

57. The Bank pointed out that:

> [M]embers of international courts and tribunals, including courts and tribunals that decide disputes between the states concerned and private parties, are usually appointed by governments. The role of national governments in appointing members of international courts and tribunals has never been considered incompatible with the independence of members of international courts and tribunals. As regards internal disputes of international organizations, such disputes are typically referred to internal

---

[88] *Id.*, at para. 35.
[89] Washington, 18 March 1965, TIAS p. 6090, 575 UNTS p. 159.
[90] BIS Reply Memorial Part. Award, at para. 35.
[91] *Id.*, at para. 54.

> courts or arbitration. From an organizational point of view, the courts or tribunals established by or within the framework of an international organization are organs of the organization concerned. As a result, the organization or the governments of its member states, rather than the parties to the dispute, exercise rights in respect of the tribunal's composition, competence and procedure that are not reserved to the tribunal itself. The European Court of Human Rights confirmed in *Waite and Kennedy v. Germany* that the dispute settlement procedure provided for in the European Space Agency (the "ESA") Convention, which subjects disputes between the Agency and its staff members and former staff members to the ESA's Appeals Board, satisfies the standards of the European Convention on Human Rights.[92]

58. First Eagle did not, the Bank observed, complain that the appointment procedures in any way led to bias or prejudice with respect to any party.[93]

59. The Bank stated that its expenses in litigating arbitrable claims in the U.S. court are compensable and that it should receive the full measure of the costs and legal fees it claimed.[94]

b. THE BANK'S POSITION REGARDING THE CALCULATION OF COMPENSATION

60. The Bank answered the Claimants' arguments regarding the calculation of the sum owed the former private shareholders:

> The Bank believed [its stipulation at the August Hearings regarding the J.P.Morgan NAV calculation] this to be an agreement to the accuracy of the J.P. Morgan-calculated NAV of U.S. $19,099 and nothing more . . . . Consistent with the Tribunal reasoning in adopting the NAV minus 30% formula and the underlying principle of equal treatment of all shareholders (both central bank and former private shareholders), that formula should

---

[92] *Id.*, at para. 58 (internal citations omitted).
[93] *Id.*, at para. 59.
[94] *Id.*, at para. 47.

> be applied to the NAV calculated by J.P. Morgan in the same manner as the Bank has consistently applied it to the pricing of shares for central bank subscriptions. Under a consistent application of the NAV minus 30% formula to the withdrawn shares, as illustrated in Part III.A.2 *infra*, the total amount of additional compensation would be CHF 4,494 per share.
>
> Alternatively, if instead of following past practice the Tribunal were simply to take the J.P. Morgan-calculated NAV and apply it to the statutory obligation that arose on the 8 January 2001 share withdrawal under Article 18A to pay compensation in Swiss francs for the private shareholders interest in that NAV, the most straightforward method of converting the discounted U.S. dollar NAV to the amount of Swiss franc compensation would be to use the 8 January 2001 exchange rate. This would result in additional compensation of CHF 5,458 per share.[95]

c. DATE UPON WHICH EXCHANGE RATE IS SET

61. The Bank argued that the J.P. Morgan-calculated NAV should be adjusted by reference to the January 2001 Swiss franc/U.S. dollar exchange rate. The Bank maintained

> that its balance sheet is effectively in US dollars (its official unit of account for the period at issue was the gold franc, which had a fixed parity of US$ 1.94149) and that its consistent past practice in applying the discounted NAV formula has been for the board of directors to decide on a share issuance, at a fixed gold franc price, with payments in hard currencies to be made applying the exchange rate of the date of payment; hence, the discounted NAV stated in US dollars in the J.P. Morgan report should be converted to Swiss francs as of the 8 January 2001 date of withdrawal of the privately owned shares, rather than applying the 6 September 2000 exchange rate stated in the J.P. Morgan report . . . .[96]

---

[95] BIS Counter-Memorial Part. Award, at paras. 2–3 (internal citations omitted).
[96] Procedural Order No. 9 (On Consent).

d. THE BANK'S REQUEST FOR A DECLARATORY JUDGMENT

62. The Bank requested, and First Eagle opposed, a ruling from the Tribunal that it has "exclusive jurisdiction over any claims against the Bank arising out of or in connection with the validity, procedures and amount of compensation provided in the 8 January 2001 redemption of the Bank's privately held shares".[97]

e. INTEREST

63. The Bank contended:

1. neither international law nor special rules applicable to the BIS require the Tribunal to award interest to the Claimants in these proceedings;

2. should the Tribunal nevertheless determine to award interest on the additional amount of the compensation, it should be at no more than the Swiss franc market rate for the period between 8 January 2001 and the date of the final award;

3. there is no basis for awarding compound interest; and

4. in the case of First Eagle and M. Mathieu, no interest should be awarded at all.[98]

64. The Bank offered to pay interest, if the Tribunal were to decide "that interest is due on the additional compensation to be awarded to former private shareholders . . . from the date when the right to initial compensation arose, *i.e.* 8 January 2001, to the date on which the Tribunal renders its final award."[99] The Bank justified the choice of the date of the final Award by analogy to the payments decided 8 January

---

[97] FE Counter-Memorial Counterclaim, at para. 140; BIS Reply Memorial Part. Award, at para. 70(a).

[98] BIS Counter-Memorial Part. Award, at para. 114.

[99] *Id.*, at para. 138.

2001. Interest had not been paid then on the time between 8 January and the actual payment to shareholders.

65. The Bank argued[100] further that First Eagle's claim for interest on its costs and legal fees from the date on which those costs and fees were paid[101] was without legal authority. The Bank reasoned that any liability to pay costs or expenses incurred by First Eagle, if such existed, would not accrue until the date of the Tribunal's decision.

f. COSTS OF THE ARBITRATION AND EXPENSES

66. The Bank asserted that the *lex specialis* of the Bank precludes an award of costs and fees.

> These claims have no basis in the *lex specialis* of the Bank, which the Tribunal determined to be the governing law of these proceedings. Under the *lex specialis*, consisting of the Bank's Statutes and the treaties under which they were enacted, the costs of the Tribunal are required to be divided equally between Claimants and the Bank; the Tribunal has the power to allocate the Claimants' portion of these costs among the various Claimants, but not to impose that portion on the Bank. The *lex specialis* also expressly requires each party to bear its own expenses, which includes legal expenses.[102]

g. STIPULATIONS

67. The Bank indicated it agreed to the use of the J.P. Morgan Report calculations for any finding regarding NAV.[103] The Bank joined the other Parties in proposing that the Tribunal appoint the Zurich Office of the C.B. Richard Ellis firm to value the Bank's real estate.

---

100 *Id.*, at para. 147.
101 FE Memorial Part. Award, at para. 163.
102 BIS Counter-Memorial Part. Award, at para. 6.
103 Transcript, at p. 331.

h. IDENTITY OF RECIPIENTS OF PAYMENT

68. The Bank resisted First Eagle's demand that First Eagle be paid for 9,110 shares.

> The BIS does not register shares in the name of a "nominee" acting as holder of record for an unidentified beneficial owner . . . . Article 18 [of the Bank's Statutes] conclusively establishes that First Eagle has a valid and enforceable interest in only those shares registered in the Bank's books under its name. The Bank share register shows that on 8 January 2001 First Eagle owned 5,250 shares, and not the 9,110 shares First Eagle has claimed to have owned . . . . Any beneficial interest First Eagle may purport to have had in the shares as a result of contractual relations with third parties is invalid, irrelevant to and unenforceable against the Bank.[104]

2. Applicable Law

69. In its Counter-Memorial Pursuant to Partial Award, the Bank argued that "the rights of shareholders in the BIS are governed by the BIS's constituent instruments and applicable general public international law".[105] In doing so, the Bank countered First Eagle's assertion that the Bank is a private organization, and asserted the importance of an international organization being governed by public international law. Relying on its status as an international organization, the Bank also objected to First Eagle's argument that municipal law should apply, stating that "[t]here is no basis to apply municipal corporate law to these issues, and attempts to impose municipal law . . . on the significantly different legal regime established by the Statutes of the Bank should be rejected."[106]

---

[104] BIS Counter-Memorial Part. Award, at paras. 159–161.
[105] Counter-Memorial ("BIS Counter-Memorial"), at para. 51.
[106] *Id.*

3. Relief Requested

70. The Bank requested that the Tribunal render an award:

(a) declaring that the Tribunal has exclusive jurisdiction over any claims against the Bank arising out of or in connection with the validity, procedures and amount of compensation provided in the 8 January 2001 redemption of the Bank's privately held shares;

(b) finding that First Eagle violated Article 54(1) of the Statutes by suing the Bank in the United States courts on claims committed to the Tribunal's exclusive jurisdiction;

(c) granting the Bank damages from First Eagle in an amount of US$ 587,413.49 in reimbursement of direct legal expenses and additional relief the Tribunal deems appropriate for First Eagle's breach of Article 54(1) of the Statutes[;][107]

[d] declaring that the Tribunal's award is final and binding on the parties and that payment of additional compensation of CHF 4,494 per share to Claimants for each share registered in their own names on the books of the Bank on 8 January 2001 discharges the Bank from any obligation towards Claimants in connection with the compulsory recall of its former privately held shares;

[e] dismissing Claimants' requests for legal fees and costs;

[f] dismissing Claimants' requests for interest, or alternatively awarding interest at the Swiss franc market rate from 8 January 2001 to the date of the final award; and

[g] granting the Bank further relief as the Tribunal deems just and proper.[108]

---

[107] BIS Memorial Part. Award, at para. 70.
[108] BIS Counter-Memorial Part. Award, at Relief Requested.

CHAPTER IV – THE AWARD

A. DETERMINATION OF THE EXACT AMOUNT OWED BY THE BANK FOR INTERNATIONAL SETTLEMENTS PER SHARE

71. The J.P. Morgan Report (7 September 2000) stated its view of the amount to be paid to the shareholders in the Bank's compulsory repurchase of private shares.[109] The Report indicated the amount in U.S. dollars, followed parenthetically by the equivalent amount, as of the date of the Report, in Swiss francs. Claimants pray for the value of the supplementary payment—which the Partial Award determined was owed by the Bank—in Swiss francs at the U.S. dollar/Swiss franc exchange rate that obtained on 7 September 2000. The Bank prays for a calculation of the amount of the supplementary payment at the U.S. dollar/Swiss franc exchange rate that obtained on 8 January 2001, the date of the implementation of the compulsory share repurchase or, in the alternative, for a calculation at the U.S. dollar/Swiss franc exchange rate that obtains on the date of payment set in the final award. Because the value of the Swiss franc in relation to the U.S. dollar increased approximately 10% between 7 September 2000 and 8 January 2001, the disposition of this matter by the Tribunal will have an appreciable effect on the amount owed by the Bank.

72. Procedural Order No. 9 (On Consent) provided in pertinent part:

> Whereas the Parties are agreed that the Bank's net asset value (NAV) in US dollars for purposes of the final award shall be as stated in the J.P. Morgan report (with the addition of the value of the real estate), but
>
> (a) the Bank takes the position that its balance sheet is effectively in US dollars (its official unit of account for the period at issue was the gold franc, which had a fixed parity of US $1.94149) and that its consistent past practice in applying the discounted NAV formula has been for the board of directors to decide on a share issuance, at a fixed gold franc price, with payments in hard currencies to be made applying the exchange rate of the date of payment; hence, the discounted NAV stated in US dollars in the J.P.

[109] See *supra* fn. 4.

Morgan report should be converted to Swiss francs as of the 8 January 2001 date of withdrawal of the privately owned shares, rather than applying the 6 September 2000 exchange rate stated in the J.P. Morgan report, while

(b) [First Eagle takes] the position that the Tribunal should award the net asset value in Swiss francs stated in the J.P. Morgan report (as noted in paragraph 209(3) of the Partial Award), but that if the US dollar value were converted as of 8 January 2001 (which it should not be) instead of as in the J.P. Morgan report, the Bank's net asset value should be reassessed as of that date to take account of the impact of the change in the conversion rate on the Bank's non-dollar denominated assets, and hence on its net asset value, as well as of any retained earnings since the J.P. Morgan valuation date.

73. While the parties argued extensively over the meaning of the stipulation in the Procedural Order No. 9 (On Consent), the Tribunal does not find it dispositive, as the Order merely states, in pertinent part, that "the Parties are agreed that the Bank's net asset value (NAV) in US dollars for purposes of the final award shall be as stated in J.P. Morgan Report . . . ." That agreement does not resolve the question before the Tribunal and, indeed, the rest of the quoted section of Procedural Order No. 9 proceeds to state precisely the issue in controversy here. Nor does the Tribunal find dispositive the Bank's submission that:

> Consistent with the Tribunal's reasoning in adopting the NAV minus 30% formula and the underlying principle of equal treatment of all shareholders (both central bank and former private shareholders), that formula should be applied to the NAV calculated by J.P. Morgan in the same manner as the Bank has consistently applied it to the pricing of shares for central bank subscriptions. Under a consistent application of the NAV minus 30% formula to the withdrawn shares, as illustrated in Part III.A.2 *infra*, the total amount of additional compensation would be CHF 4,494 per share.
>
> Alternatively, if instead of following past practice the Tribunal were simply to take the J.P. Morgan-calculated NAV and apply it to the statutory obligation that arose on the 8 January 2001

> share withdrawal under Article 18A to pay compensation in Swiss francs for the private shareholders' interest in that NAV, the most straightforward method of converting the discounted U.S. dollar NAV to the amount of Swiss franc compensation would be to use the 8 January 2001 exchange rate. This would result in additional compensation of CHF 5,458 per share.[110]

Nor is assistance to be found in the dividend payment practice of the Bank, as the transaction under review here is not a dividend payment, but a compulsory repurchase of shares.

74. In its Partial Award, the Tribunal found the Bank's practice in pricing tranches of newly issued shares indicative of the Bank's and the new shareholders' valuation of each share in the Bank, *i.e.* what the Bank and the central banks deemed the shares to be worth.[111] But the Tribunal finds no comparable assistance in the procedures by which the central bank purchasers could pay for the newly issued shares, for that involved an entirely consensual transaction in which, moreover, the times of payment for the purchase could, within certain limits, be decided by the purchaser. That consensual transaction is quite different from the compulsory repurchase procedure of Article 18A of the Statutes.

75. That said, the Tribunal finds the practice of the Bank with respect to the pricing and exchange rate mechanism which the Bank itself put in place for the compulsory repurchase program dispositive of this issue. As will be recalled, the Bank adopted a valuation method on 7 September 2000 which it implemented in its decision on 8 January 2001; the amount which had been determined in Swiss francs on 7 September 2000, was paid in Swiss francs on 8 January 2001, without regard to the change in value relative to other convertible currencies. In its Partial Award, the Tribunal held that the recall itself was a valid exercise of the Bank's power and that the procedures followed in the recall of the privately held shares were lawful.[112] It was only the valuation method for the compulsorily repurchased shares which the Bank applied that was

---

[110] BIS Counter-Memorial Part. Award, at paras. 2–3.
[111] Partial Award, at para. 201.
[112] *Id.*, at paras. 142–158.

incorrect. But the fact is that the Bank paid on 8 January 2001 the amount it had determined in Swiss francs at the U.S. dollar/Swiss franc conversion rate that had obtained on 7 September 2000. As noted above, in the interval between 7 September 2000 and 8 January 2001, the value of the Swiss franc had increased relative to the U.S. dollar, such that if the Bank had applied the payment theory it now proposes to the Tribunal, it would have recalculated the conversion rate of dollars to francs on 8 January 2001 and paid the private shareholders approximately 10% less than they would have received on 7 September 2000. In fact, the Bank did not do this. Rather than taking advantage of the decline of the U.S. dollar in the exchange rate and obtaining benefits from a currency exchange, the Bank paid the shareholders the per share Swiss franc amount that had been determined in the 7 September 2000 report. The Bank is not a for-profit institution,[113] but it is by its very character a profit-maximizer with, moreover, fiduciary duties to all of its shareholders. If the Bank had believed that it was legally entitled to benefit from a change in currency values, it would have been legally obliged to do so and would have done so.

76. As stated, the Partial Award held that the Bank's compulsory share repurchase program was lawful, but that an incorrect valuation method was applied: the Bank should have paid per share a proportionate amount of the Bank's NAV, discounted by 30%, and the Tribunal has ordered the Bank to do so. But the Tribunal found no fault with the rest of the payment structure and procedure which the Bank had established and followed. Accordingly, the per share valuation of 7 September 2000 must now be replaced by a per share valuation of NAV (as determined by the J.P. Morgan Report and stipulated by the parties) discounted by 30%, and the difference between what was paid on 8 January 2001 and what was lawfully required must now be paid. In these circumstances, the same procedure which the Bank followed on 8 January 2001 should, *mutatis mutandis,* be replicated.

---

[113] This is not to say that it may not realize profits, as was observed by the Swiss Federal Council in 1930. See Partial Award, at para. 117.

77. In this regard, the Tribunal notes the fact that the Bank itself took for granted that this would be the exchange rate for fulfilling the Partial Award. On 25 November 2002, *i.e.* three days after the publication of the Partial Award, the Bank issued a press release in which it summarized the Tribunal's principal holding and then stated, "[a]s a consequence, the Bank will be called upon to make an additional payment of about half of the amount already paid . . . ."[114] The Bank's projection on 25 November of what was owing was clearly based on the assumption that the U.S. dollar/Swiss franc conversion date was 7 September 2000.

78. Hence, the amount which was owed in Swiss francs to the private shareholders for the compulsory purchase of their shares is the per share value of the Bank's NAV, as calculated by the J.P. Morgan Report, discounted by 30%, plus the per share value of the Bank's real estate, discounted by 30%. As noted, Dr. Reineccius, First Eagle and the Bank agreed that, if the Tribunal were to use the 7 September 2000 exchange rate, the value, per share, was CHF 33,936.[115] That sum must be discounted by 30%, as determined in the Partial Award, producing a remainder of CHF 23,755. As the Bank had paid each private shareholder CHF 16,000, the Bank owes each of the Claimants (subject to certain qualifications which are set out below), a supplementary payment of CHF 7,755.20 per share. To this sum must be added 70% of the per share value of the real estate, a matter to which the Tribunal will return below.

B. IDENTITY OF RECIPIENTS

79. First Eagle requested[116] that the Tribunal order the Bank to pay the additional compensation due under the Partial Award to First Eagle in accord with First Eagle's records that it owns 9,110 shares, either outright or through a custodian.[117] The Bank prefers to make the payment

---

[114] BIS Press Release, *Hague Arbitral Tribunal decision regarding the repurchase of privately held shares of the Bank for International Settlements* (25 November 2002).
[115] See *supra* fn. 4.
[116] FE Memorial Part. Award, at paras. 28–33; Transcript, at p. 371.
[117] See *supra* para. 19.

from the Bank's books recording share ownership, as it did with the payment of the compensation approved at the 8 January 2001 Extraordinary General Meeting.[118] Because Article 18 of the Statutes of the Bank provides that "[t]he registration of the name of a shareholder in the books of the Bank establishes the title to ownership of the shares so registered" (which, moreover, First Eagle recognized),[119] the Tribunal holds that the Bank is entitled to pay only the shareowners of record as they are inscribed in the Bank's share register.

C. Interest: Applicability and Rate

80. Dr. Reineccius claimed interest on the additional compensation due under the Partial Award, reasoning that on 8 January 2001 he had become "a creditor of the Bank. Therefore, the compensation due to me has to carry interest . . . the money market interest in Swiss francs on that particular date . . ."[120] which he quantified as no less than 3¼% per annum.[121] First Eagle maintained it was entitled to interest from 8 January 2001 on the outstanding compensation payment, as well as on its costs, fees, and expenses, at a rate of at least 7% compounded monthly. Mr. Mathieu also requested a minimum of 7% interest with "la capitalisation des intérêts sur une base mensuelle".[122] First Eagle and Mr. Mathieu base their claim for interest on the principle of full compensation. As Mr. Mathieu contended:

> En tout état de cause, les intérêts ayant pour fonction d' "*(. . .) indemniser un créancier de l'absence, pendant un certain temps, des fonds qui lui sont dus (. . .)*", le Demandeur a droit aux intérêts portant sur la somme qui *aurait dû* être versée le 8 janvier 2001.[123]

---

[118] BIS Counter-Memorial Part. Award, at paras. 159–161.
[119] Transcript, at p. 371.
[120] *Id.*, at p. 387.
[121] *Id.*
[122] Mathieu Mémoire en Demande Seconde Phase, at p. 19.
[123] *Id.*, at p. 10 (internal citations omitted).

81. First Eagle and Mr. Mathieu argued that the measure of interest should be the return the Bank would have received on the retained funds. First Eagle also reasoned that 7% interest reflects the minimum return First Eagle would have expected to earn on alternative investments of the same risk had it received full compensation when it was due. First Eagle argued that were it paid less than 7% interest, the Bank would earn a windfall from the compensation withheld and thereby be unjustly enriched. First Eagle asserted:

> A reasonable rate of interest should first and foremost reflect the fact that the Bank retained part of the compensation payment due the private shareholders and had the funds available for its own use as equity.[124]

82. Similarly, Mr. Mathieu stated:

> Le Tribunal tiendra également compte du fait que la Banque a réalisé une économie substantielle en retenant le complément d'indemnité dû aux actionnaires évincés et qu'elle a pu faire libre usage de ce capital obtenu sans rien débourser entre la date de rachat forcé et la date où elle devra effectivement verser le complément d'indemnité.[125]

83. First Eagle and Mr. Mathieu claimed alternatively that the interest rate should be the rate used by J.P. Morgan to discount future dividend payments in its Dividend Perpetuity Model[126] analysis, because payment of interest is analogous in this case to a dividend payment.[127]

84. Mr. Mathieu also claimed interest on the original payment of compensation from 8 January 2001.[128]

---

[124] FE Memorial Part. Award, at para. 166.
[125] Mathieu Mémoire en Demande Seconde Phase, at p. 15.
[126] Partial Award, at para. 171.
[127] FE Memorial Part. Award, at para. 170; Mathieu Mémoire, at pp. 14–15.
[128] Mathieu Mémoire en Demande Seconde Phase, at p. 10.

85. The Bank responded at the May 2003 Hearings[129] that an award of interest was not provided for by the Bank's Statutes, the *lex specialis* of the Arbitration, nor, argued the Bank, was it mandated under international law. However, if the Tribunal should award interest on the additional compensation due under the Award, the Bank took the view that it should pay simple interest at the three-month Swiss franc LIBOR (London Interbank Offered Rate) on the additional compensation the Bank has agreed to pay to all the former private shareholders.

86. The Bank argued:

> [T]he Bank's *lex specialis* does not speak directly to the question of interest. However, Article 18A of the Statutes clearly provides that compensation after the 8 January 2001 share recall will be paid to former private shareholders only after they present their share certificates to the Bank and does not provide for the accrual or payment of interest during the open-ended period for presentation of share certificates, verification by the Bank and payment of the recall price. Nor is an award of interest required under general principles of international law. Should the Tribunal nonetheless make such an award with respect to the additional amount of compensation, it should be made at the Swiss (non-compounded) market rate, since the compensation is payable in Swiss francs and Switzerland is the place where payment is due.[130]

87. Further, the Bank addressed the Claimants' argument that interest should be determined by reference to the rate of return on its investments stated in the Morgan Report:

> [A]ny other argument that the former private shareholders should receive interest that is in any way linked to the profits or returns of the Bank, is fundamentally inconsistent with the Tribunal's decision upholding the lawfulness of the shares withdrawal. While shareholders, they did have a claim on the profits of the Bank (in the attenuated form of dividends, as declared by the

---

[129] Transcript, at p. 427.
[130] BIS Counter-Memorial Part. Award, at para. 7.

Board of Directors under Article 51), but on 8 January 2001 that property right was transformed into something different, i.e., a statutory claim for compensation not in any way related to the earnings or profits of the Bank.[131]

88. With respect to Mr. Mathieu's claim for interest on the original offer of compensation from the Bank, the Bank contended that no interest at all should be due. The Bank pointed out that receipt of the original compensation had been within the control of Mr. Mathieu. His refusal to tender his shares should not make the Bank liable for interest.

89. As indicated above, the Claimants have proposed rates of interest varying from 3¼% to 7%, based upon different theories of public international law (including theories of unjust enrichment), international commercial law and Swiss practice. The Tribunal also heard extensive arguments on recent international arbitral decisions awarding compound interest and on the extent to which it may or may not have become customary international law.

90. Neither the 1930 Hague Agreement, nor the 1907 Hague Convention,[132] nor the Statutes of the Bank prescribes, *expressis verbis*, a rate of interest for any purpose, let alone for a compulsory repurchase of privately held shares. Yet, as it stated in the Partial Award, the Tribunal is of the opinion that interest is due,[133] for it is a general rule that interest is owed where payments are to be made on a specific date but are not made. The Tribunal has found that this rule also applies to the Bank as far as its relations with its shareholders are concerned. The question is the proper rate of interest.

91. International law does not prescribe a specific rate of interest, but several other legal systems, which do so, could be relevant. In circumstances in which the laws of several different legal systems could be applied to a particular transaction or event, it is a frequent practice to select the law

---

[131] *Id.*, at para. 133.

[132] Convention (II) for the Pacific Settlement of International Disputes, The Hague, 18 October 1907 ("1907 Hague Convention").

[133] Partial Award, at para. 204.

of the legal system with which the question to be decided has, in the specific case, the closest contacts. In this regard, the Tribunal notes that Article 2 of the Statutes of the Bank designates Basle, Switzerland, as the place where the registered office of the Bank shall be situated and that Switzerland has consistently been the *siège* and operational center of the activities of the Bank. In addition, the Bank has made dividend payments in Swiss francs, and the currency in which interest must be paid is the Swiss franc. Moreover, the private shareholders dealt with the Bank in Switzerland, and their dividends were paid in Swiss francs. These reciprocal relationships between the Bank and its shareholders constitute elements of practice. All of these facts, extending over more than seven decades of continuous operation of the Bank, indicate that the Swiss legal system is the one having the closest contacts with this question.

92. In the view of the Tribunal, these facts make it appropriate to refer to Swiss law[134] for guidance on the rate of interest. Article 73 of the Code of Obligations provides:

> 1. Celui qui doit des intérêts dont le taux n'est fixé ni par la convention, ni par la loi ou l'usage, les acquitte au taux annuel de 5 pour cent.
>
> 2. La répression des abus en matière d'intérêt conventionnel est réservée au droit public.

Article 104 (*intérêt moratoire*) of the Code provides:

> 1. Le débiteur qui est en demeure pour le paiement d'une somme d'argent doit l'intérêt moratoire à 5 pour cent l'an, même si un taux inférieur avait été fixé pour l'intérêt conventionnel.
>
> 2. Si le contrat stipule, directement ou sous la forme d'une provision de banque périodique, un intérêt supérieur à 5 pour cent, cet intérêt plus élevé peut également être exigé

[134] Code des obligations (Loi fédérale complétant le Code civil suisse, Livre cinquième: Droit des obligations du 30 mars 1911).

du débiteur en demeure.

3. Entre commerçants, tant que l'escompte dans le lieu de paiement est d'un taux supérieur à 5 pour cent, l'intérêt moratoire peut être calculé au taux de l'escompte.

Swiss law thus applies a 5% simple rate for moratory interest.

93. As is apparent, the decision to apply Swiss moratory interest is the result of the application of a number of factors with respect to the practice of the Bank and the preponderance of contacts with Swiss law. It is not based upon any assumption of subjection of the Bank to Swiss law. Nor should the Tribunal's decision be taken as indicating any position for or against recent trends with respect to the application of compound interest in contemporary international law; that is a question that does not arise in this case, in view of the dispositive effect of the Bank's practice and the preponderance of contacts with the Swiss legal system insofar as interest in the present case is concerned.

94. Accordingly, the Tribunal decides that the rate of interest to be paid by the Bank is 5% simple interest.

D. Time from Which Interest is to be Paid

95. First Eagle argued that interest be calculated for the period between the date payment should have been made, or 8 January 2001, and the date it is actually made.[135] Dr. Reineccius[136] and Mr. Mathieu[137] also requested interest from 8 January 2001 until the date payment is made. Mr. Mathieu further requested interest on the CHF 16,000 payment for the time between 8 January 2001 and 9 January 2003 when he presented his shares for payment.[138]

---

135 Transcript, at pp. 373–375.
136 *Id.*, at p. 388.
137 Mathieu Mémoire en Demande Seconde Phase, at p. 19.
138 Transcript, at pp. 395–396.

96. The Bank proposed that interest be paid, if the Tribunal should find interest due on the additional compensation, from 8 January 2001 until the date of the final Award. The Bank further proposed that the Bank should not pay post-Award interest unless it failed to make payment of the additional compensation within a reasonable time period that could be established by the Tribunal.[139]

97. Moratory interest under Swiss law is to be paid from the time at which the debt becomes due until the time the debtor tenders payment. With respect to the Bank's compulsory repurchase of private shares, the word "debt" has a number of component references. For all Claimants, there is a debt owing from the Bank for the supplementary payment which results from the difference between what the Bank paid on 8 January 2001 and the application of the formula of NAV minus 30% which the Tribunal determined in its Partial Award to be the lawful standard for valuing individual shares. Accordingly, 5% simple interest is calculated for all Claimants with respect to that supplement from 8 January 2001 until the date of this Award.

98. In contrast to Claimant No. 1, Dr. Reineccius, who presented his shares to the Bank in accordance with the decision of the Extraordinary General Meeting (reserving his right to the additional payment to which he was entitled) and was paid, Claimants Nos. 2 and 3 did not present their shares until later dates, whereupon the Bank paid them the amount fixed on 8 January 2001. Claimant No. 3 has claimed interest on this amount from 8 January 2001 until the date upon which he presented his shares for payment.

99. The predicate of moratory interest is that the debtor has withheld payment; moratory interest is not owing in circumstances in which the debtor indicates willingness and capacity to pay, but delay in payment is due solely to refusal or failure of the creditor to take the steps necessary to receive payment. With respect to Claimant No. 3, the debtor in this context, the Bank, was prepared to make payment from 8 January 2001 and, moreover, to respect any reservations of rights concerning the

---

139 *Id.*, at pp. 432–433.

valuation of shares. Hence moratory interest is not owing to Claimant No. 3 for the period from 8 January 2001 until the shares were presented for payment and timely paid.

E. VALUATION OF THE REAL ESTATE

100. The NAV computation in the J.P. Morgan Report to which all the parties, as noted in paragraphs 18, 32, 45, and 67 *supra*, stipulated their agreement did not include a current valuation of the real estate of the Bank. In paragraph 205 of the Partial Award, the Tribunal stated that the valuation of the real estate would be made by an expert, whose identity, terms of reference and timetable would be determined by the Tribunal after consultation with the Parties. As the Parties could not resolve by agreement the value of the real estate, in accordance with paragraph 209(5) of the Partial Award, the Parties notified the Tribunal of their selection of the Zurich office of C.B. Richard Ellis to determine the value of the real estate. The Tribunal confirmed to the Parties its appointment of the Ellis firm in Procedural Order No. 10. The Tribunal received from the expert the statement of independence as required by the Parties, and the expert, accompanied by the Secretary of the Tribunal, inspected all of the properties and provided a Valuation Report on 28 April 2003, whereupon the Secretary of the Tribunal circulated copies of the Report to the Parties, with an invitation for comments. None were forthcoming. On 16 May 2003, in Procedural Order No. 11 (On Consent), the Tribunal stated:

> The Tribunal will use the value of CHF 168,094,000 (...), as determined by the expert, for the purpose of valuing as of 7 September 2000 the Bank's buildings and their contents as required by the 22 November 2002 Partial Award.

101. At the Hearings in May 2003, Dr. Reineccius and First Eagle raised, for the first time, certain objections to the Ellis Report.[140] As agreement to the Report had been stipulated by the Parties and, that notwithstanding, a further and ample opportunity had been afforded to the Parties to

[140] See *supra* para. 31.

comment upon the Report before the Procedural Order No. 11 (On Consent) of 16 May 2003 was issued, the Tribunal holds the objections raised at the hearing out of time and inadmissible and confirms the Ellis Report as final.

102. The per share value of CHF 168,094,000 is CHF 317.66 which when discounted by 30%[141] results in an additional payment to the Claimants of CHF 222.36 per share. This amount will be added to the sum set out in paragraph 78 *supra*, CHF 7,755.20 per share.

F. Conclusions with Respect to Computations

103. The Tribunal concludes that the Bank must pay each claimant an additional CHF 7,977.56 per share. That sum represents 70% of the comprehensive per share NAV of the Bank, *i.e.* the sum of CHF 33,936 per share (J.P. Morgan Report calculation of per share NAV[142]) and CHF 317.66 per share (the value of the Bank's real estate[143]), discounted by 30%, minus the CHF 16,000 per share already paid by the Bank to each private shareholder. Moratory interest is to be paid on this sum from 8 January 2001 until the date of this Award at 5% simple interest.

G. Counterclaim

104. The Bank claimed that First Eagle's suit in the United States[144] which (1) challenged the Bank's right to carry out the redemption and the amount of compensation provided by Article 18A of the Bank's Statutes, and (2) sought money damages "in the amount of the full value of plaintiffs' proportionate interest in the Bank," breached Article 54 of the Statutes of the Bank.[145]

---

141 Partial Award, at para. 209(2) and (3).
142 See *supra* fn. 4.
143 See *supra* paras. 99–101.
144 *First Eagle SoGen Funds, Inc. v. Bank for Int'l Settlements*, No. 01 Civ. 0087(RO), 2001 WL 1150323 (S.D.N.Y., 28 September 2001).
145 BIS Reply Memorial Part. Award, at para. 1.

> As a result of this breach, the Bank incurred direct economic damages in excess of U.S. $587,000 defending First Eagle's lawsuit, as well as wasted internal legal and management resources.[146]

105. The Bank challenged First Eagle's representation that First Eagle's "attempt to enjoin the shares recall"[147] was intended to obtain disclosure,[148] and its refusal to arbitrate was intended "to determine the validity" of its "agreement" to arbitrate under Article 54.[149] Instead, the Bank argued, First Eagle had "disregarded Article 54, and sued the Bank in the United States for a judgment [and] . . . money damages in the amount of the full value of plaintiff's proportionate interest in the Bank, together with interest thereon".[150] The Bank argued that even if the "securities claims had been independent of First Eagle's claims for conversion, breach of contract and breach of fiduciary duty . . . that would not somehow excuse First Eagle from its obligation to arbitrate the latter under Article 54."[151]

106. The Bank argued that First Eagle's second defense (that it had invoked the jurisdiction of the U.S. courts "to determine the validity and applicability of [its] agreement to arbitrate"[152] was "doubly false":

> [L]egally, because Article 54 is not a private commercial "agreement to arbitrate," but an integral part of a self-contained legal regime that excludes the competence of national courts with respect to the "interpretation or application of the Statutes of the Bank," including issues of the Tribunal's jurisdiction; and factually, because First Eagle in any case did not seek a declaration regarding the validity of Article 54, but sued the Bank for damages in breach of that Article.[153]

---

[146] *Id.*, at para. 2.
[147] *Id.*, at para. 3.
[148] FE Counter-Memorial Counterclaim, at para. 38.
[149] *Id.*, at para 5.
[150] BIS Reply Memorial Part. Award, at para. 4 (internal citations omitted).
[151] *Id.*, at para. 5.
[152] FE Counter-Memorial Counterclaim, at para. 59.
[153] BIS Reply Memorial Part. Award, at para. 17.

The Bank pointed out that it is an international organization:[154]

> governed . . . by a self-contained statutory legal regime, created by the 1930 Hague Agreement, the Convention and the Constituent Charter of the Bank. Under that regime, the rights and duties of its shareholders *vis à vis* the Bank, including their rights and duties under Article 54, must be resolved by reference to the Bank's constituent instruments. *See* Partial Award ¶¶173–74 . . . . National courts do not have the competence to adjudicate the organic disputes of an international organization, unless that competence is specifically and affirmatively provided for in the organization's governing instruments . . . . Article 55(1) of the Statutes confirms the Bank's *immunity* from national court jurisdiction, subject only to the narrow (and inapplicable) exceptions provided therein. [155]
>
> Article 54(2) specifically provides that the Tribunal has "power to decide all questions [concerning the terms of submission under Article 54(1)] (including the question of its own jurisdiction)" . . . [and] Article 16(1) of the Tribunal's Rules of Procedure, which provides that "[t]he Tribunal shall have the power to decide the question as to its own jurisdiction". All questions of jurisdiction in disputes between the Bank and its shareholders with regard to the interpretation or the application of the Statutes must therefore be raised exclusively before the Tribunal.[156]

107. The Bank reasoned that "the nature of the Bank as an international organization" requires that issues "be determined on a uniform and consistent basis." The probability of inconsistencies inherent in decision-making by individual national courts requires "that disputes implicating an international organization's internal law are entrusted to internal courts or tribunals or arbitration."[157]

---

[154] *Id.*, at para. 19.
[155] *Id.*, at paras. 19–20 (some internal citations omitted).
[156] *Id.*, at para. 21 (internal citations omitted).
[157] *Id.*, at para. 24.

108. As to First Eagle's assertion that it was free to seek interim measures from a municipal court, the Bank argued that the *lex specialis* of the Bank's Statutes provides for interim measures of protection:

> Before giving a final decision and without prejudice to the questions at issue, the President of the Tribunal, or, if he is unable to act in any case, a member of the Tribunal to be designated by him forthwith, may, on the request of the first party applying therefor, order any appropriate provisional measures in order to safeguard the respective rights of the parties.[158]

109. The Bank continued that this power to grant provisional measures is not "concurrent with the jurisdiction of municipal courts. On the contrary, Article 55 confirms the Bank's immunity from municipal jurisdiction, subject to very narrow and specific exceptions."[159] The Bank stated that Article 54 does not contain any exception to this immunity although, as Article 55 demonstrates, the States Parties to the 1930 Hague Agreement could have provided for such an exception.

110. First Eagle asserted that it had the right to litigate in the U.S. District Court on both its securities law claims and the dispute over arbitral jurisdiction; it requested the Tribunal to deny the Bank's claim for damages for breach of Article 54(1) of the Bank's Statutes. First Eagle sought to distinguish its claims under U.S. securities law arguing that both the Bank and the U.S. District Court acknowledged that those claims did not fall within the agreement to arbitrate. First Eagle argued that when the Bank asked the District Court to rule on the merits of the securities law claims, it "confirmed that First Eagle's securities law claims did not fall within the scope of Article 54(1)."[160]

111. First Eagle alleged that the bulk of the litigation in the United States concerned the securities law claims and "arose from First Eagle's application for interim measures."[161] In addition, First Eagle cited a

---

158 *Id.*, at para. 31 (quoting Bank's Statutes, Art. 54(3)).
159 *Id.*, at para. 32.
160 FE Counter-Memorial Counterclaim, at para. 64.
161 *Id.*, at para. 77.

number of authorities[162] to support its contention that "[u]nder all arbitration laws the parties to an arbitration agreement may apply to the court for provisional relief without getting in conflict with the arbitration agreement."[163] Further, First Eagle provided citations to authorities examining the relation of the New York Convention to suits before national courts.[164]

112. First Eagle defended its recourse to the District Court as action that did not breach Article 54(1) because "courts are entitled to review the existence and validity of the arbitration agreement on which the arbitrators' jurisdiction is based . . . ."[165] Thus, First Eagle asserted, it had the right to litigate "both the securities law claims and the dispute over arbitral jurisdiction, and because the fees the Bank incurred . . . resulted only from litigating those two matters, the Bank's claim for breach of Article 54(1) must be denied."[166]

113. The Tribunal notes at the outset that the *lex specialis* of the Bank for International Settlements is comprised of the 1930 Hague Convention, the Constituent Charter of the Bank for International Settlements (20 January 1930) (hereafter "Constituent Charter"), and the Statutes of the Bank. These are international instruments, a characteristic that is particularly important when assessing the relation between them and municipal law. Article 54(1) of the Statutes provides:

> If any dispute shall arise between the Bank, on the one side, and any central bank, financial institution, or other bank referred to in the present Statutes, on the other side, or between the Bank and its shareholders, with regard to the interpretation or application of the Statutes of the Bank, the same shall be referred for final decision to the Tribunal provided for by the Hague Agreement of January, 1930.

---

162 *Id.*, at paras. 85–88.
163 Klaus Peter Berger, INTERNATIONAL ECONOMIC ARBITRATION 331 (1993).
164 FE Counter-Memorial Counterclaim, at paras. 91–93.
165 FOUCHARD, GAILLARD & GOLDMAN ON INTERNATIONAL COMMERCIAL ARBITRATION, ¶667 (E. Gaillard & J. Savage eds., 1999).
166 FE Counter-Memorial Counterclaim, at para. 97.

Article 55(1) of the Statutes provides:

> The Bank shall enjoy immunity from jurisdiction, save:
>
> a) to the extent that such immunity is formally waived in individual cases by the President, the General Manager of the Bank, or their duly authorized representatives; or
>
> b) in civil or commercial suits, arising from banking or financial transactions, initiated by contractual counterparties of the Bank, except in those cases in which provision for arbitration has been or shall have been made.

114. The regime that emerges is quite unique. Article 55 of the Statutes is, besides being part of the international legal structure of the Bank, a bilateral commitment that operates parallel to Article 54 and Article 17. By accepting the Statutes pursuant to Article 17, shareholders also accept Article 54 and thus the jurisdiction of a Tribunal established under the 1930 Agreement, and agree not to pursue actions within the jurisdiction of such a Tribunal before national courts. The regime that emerges from these provisions makes clear that disputes between, *inter alia*, the Bank and its shareholders with regard to the interpretation or application of the Statutes were to be referred to a Tribunal established in accordance with the 1930 Hague Agreement. Such a Tribunal was empowered to decide "all questions (including the question of its own jurisdiction)" and, in addition, to "order any appropriate provisional measures in order to safeguard the respective rights of the parties."[167] Article 55 underlines the exclusive character of a Tribunal's jurisdiction by establishing the immunity of the Bank from other national jurisdictions, with two explicit exceptions, neither of which is relevant to the case at bar.

115. A private shareholder of the Bank could not be a formal party to the 1930 Hague Agreement. But a private shareholder, purchasing shares, acquired a special and equally binding type of privity with respect to the dispute resolution regime described above. Article 17 of the Bank's Statutes states that "[o]wnership of shares of the Bank implies acceptance of the

---

[167] Bank's Statutes, Art. 54(2) and (3).

Statutes of the Bank." Each share certificate carried the same notice. The Prospectus for shares stated the exclusive jurisdictional regime. A Declaration of Acceptance of Shares included an agreement to accept the dispute resolution regime. In sum, private actors, purchasing shares, accepted, through manifold instruments whose multiplicity and reiteration belie any possibility of misunderstanding, the dispute resolution regime, including the immunity of the Bank from national courts and the competence of a Tribunal formed under the 1930 Hague Agreement and the Statutes to decide its own jurisdiction and to issue provisional measures. The Tribunal would emphasize the critical factor of *acceptance* of the regime. With respect to the question of the competent jurisdiction, private shareholders accepted the international legal status of the Bank unconditionally.

116. Much attention was directed to national practice with respect to the application of Article II of the New York Convention. The Tribunal need not enter into the question of whether, the explicit language of Article II of that instrument notwithstanding, there is a general right under that treaty to test in the national courts of States Parties the validity of an agreement to arbitrate beyond confirmation of whether the agreement "is null and void, inoperative or incapable of being performed."[168] Nor, indeed, need the Tribunal take up the question of whether an arbitration award under the 1930 Hague Agreement even falls under the purview of the New York Convention. The question before the Tribunal is much more narrowly focused. A procedure to test the validity of an arbitral agreement may be available in the United States to putative parties to that agreement. But even if it is, it is not a legal imperative, which requires resort to that procedure. It is a power or option, but not an obligation. A power or option provided by U.S. law cannot be used to justify violation of a commitment that operates on the level of international law. In trying to exercise an option that may have been available to it under U.S. law, First Eagle violated the obligations it had assumed in the Statutes of the Bank and, in particular, with respect to Article 54.

---

[168] *Supra* fn. 56, at Art. II.

117. Nor does the Tribunal find persuasive the contention that the Tribunal did not exist at the time of First Eagle's attempt to divert its dispute into a U.S. court. Many arbitration tribunals are not standing, but have to be constituted after a dispute arises. As long as there was a workable mechanism for establishing the Tribunal, the action by First Eagle violated its obligations under the Bank's Statutes. The *Siemens AG v. Dutco Constr. Co.* case,[169] relied upon by Claimants Nos. 2 and 3, does not teach otherwise. *Dutco* concerned parties disputing a private contractual agreement to arbitrate. This Tribunal's jurisdiction arises from the 1930 Hague Agreement, the Constituent Charter and the Statutes of the Bank, an international framework accepted by the private shareholders when they purchased shares.

118. First Eagle has contended that some of its claims before a U.S. court were not within the jurisdiction of this Tribunal and were only available in an appropriate U.S. court. The Bank argued that those claims were only pretexts, a conclusion to which the U.S. courts in question appear to have come. In any case, both parties acknowledged that the issues were intertwined. What is beyond doubt is that key critical issues were within the exclusive jurisdiction of the Tribunal.

119. For the above reasons, the Tribunal finds that in pursuing its claims against the Bank in a U.S. court, First Eagle violated its obligations under the Bank's Statutes and unlawfully required the Bank to expend a considerable amount in defending its rights under the Statutes, giving the Bank a right to reparation. Accordingly, First Eagle must reimburse the Bank for the Bank's expenses in the U.S. litigation. The US$ 587,413.49 claimed by the Bank, which the Tribunal finds to be reasonable, may be set off by the Bank at the U.S. dollar/Swiss franc exchange rate obtaining on the date of this award against sums owing to First Eagle as a consequence of this award.

---

[169] *Supra* fn. 55.

H. REQUEST FOR DECLARATORY RELIEF

120. As part of its Counterclaim, the Bank has requested the following declaratory relief.

> For all of the foregoing reasons, the Bank requests that the Tribunal render an award:
>
> a. declaring that the Tribunal has exclusive jurisdiction over any claims against the Bank arising out of or in connection with the validity, procedures and amount of compensation provided in the 8 January 2001 redemption of the Bank's privately held shares . . .[170]

121. Dr. Reineccius requested in his prayer for relief that the Tribunal "expressly forbid the Bank from making upcoming payments dependent on signing a waiver" of rights to resort to ordinary courts to obtain a more favorable judgment.[171]

122. First Eagle opposed the Bank's request for the declaratory Award proposed above.[172] First Eagle argued that the Tribunal cannot render an advisory opinion "on matters outside its jurisdiction." Further, First Eagle continued, the Tribunal should not impose any conditions on the excluded shareholders' receipt of their rightful payments.[173]

123. The Tribunal is confronted with a request for a declaratory judgment and must ascertain if the Bank has demonstrated a specific interest that the Tribunal must address. Because Claimant No. 2 has clearly contemplated return to another forum,[174] and Claimant No. 1 has apparently not excluded such a possibility,[175] that requirement is satisfied.

---

[170] BIS Memorial, at para. 70.
[171] Transcript, at p. 388.
[172] FE Reply Memorial Part. Award, at paras. 170–175.
[173] *Id.*, at para. 173.
[174] Transcript, at pp. 590–600.
[175] *Id.*, at p. 388.

124. It is in the nature of an award, as a *res judicata* between the parties, that it declares the law that obtains with respect to the matter being arbitrated as between the parties to an arbitration. As between the Parties to this Arbitration, this decision is final and binding; no other remedy is available to the Parties *inter se* with respect to the issues determined in the present Arbitration. Moreover, a tribunal must interpret the instruments invoked by the parties in the exercise of its jurisdiction. By virtue of the exclusive jurisdiction which this Tribunal has concerning the interpretation and application of the Statutes of the Bank, its holdings with respect to the meaning of the Statutes in regard to the issues before it represent the authoritative interpretation of the Statutes. Therefore, the holdings of the Tribunal interpreting the Statutes with respect to jurisdiction in this matter, with respect to the validity of the procedures followed by the Bank in the compulsory recall of privately held shares in its decision of 8 January 2001, and with respect to the proper standard for valuation of the recalled shares represent the authoritative interpretation of the Statutes of the Bank applicable to all those who are subject thereto.

I. EXPENSES OF THE PARTIES

125. The Tribunal now turns to the expenses of the Parties. The Tribunal notes that Claimants Nos. 1, 2, and 3 have requested that they be paid their expenses, and Claimant No. 2 has requested payment of its legal fees. The Tribunal notes that the Arbitration Annex XII to the 1930 Hague Agreement provides that each party shall pay "its own expenses". The Tribunal is of the view that this provision must be interpreted and applied in light of the principle of effective access to justice, as outlined earlier in the specific context of a suit between private shareholders and the Bank.

126. In the *Waite* case,[176] the European Court of Human Rights held that a correlative of the immunity of international organizations is an obligation to provide for fair access to justice. In the view of the Tribunal, that

[176] *Waite & Kennedy v. Germany*, App. No. 26083/94, 30 ECHR p. 261 (1999).

holding is consonant with a general principle of law. The Bank indicated its appreciation of the fact that the costs of access to justice must be regulated in such a way that access to justice is not effectively rendered impossible for single shareholders who lack the resources of major corporate bodies. Claimants Nos. 1 and 3 are individual claimants with limited financial resources. Claimant No. 1 was not represented by counsel. Claimant No. 3 was represented *pro bono* by the Paris office of the Freshfields Bruckhaus Deringer law firm.[177] Therefore, it is only necessary for the Bank to pay the expenses, EUR 4,436.75, incurred by Claimant No. 3.[178] The Tribunal notes with satisfaction that the Bank, fully recognizing the principle of effective access to justice, has from the beginning made clear its willingness to accept the competence of the Tribunal to allocate the costs of access to justice for individual claimants in such a way as not to chill their formal procedural opportunities. Therefore, the expenses (EUR 4,436.75) of Claimant No. 3 will be borne by the Bank and reimbursed by it directly to Claimant No. 3.

127. Claimant No. 2 is a corporate entity with substantial financial resources, and has, moreover, been assured of substantial additional payments of compensation by the Bank through its success in these proceedings. The Tribunal also notes that the Bank, for its part, has prevailed in the Counterclaim procedure. As to the question whether expenses and legal fees should be paid by the Bank to Claimant No. 2, the Tribunal first notes that effective access to justice was not at issue for First Eagle in defending its claims. Indeed, First Eagle first brought costly proceedings in the United States before turning to this Tribunal.

128. The Tribunal is of the opinion that it is within its discretion to award expenses and fees also to Claimant No. 2 where either the principle of effective access to justice or any other principle concerning the fairness of the Arbitration procedure would so require. The Tribunal is not of the view that any such principle applies here. The Tribunal has noted the argument by Claimant No. 2 that this procedure has been beneficial to

---

[177] Transcript, at p. 477.

[178] Mathieu Mémoire en Demande Seconde Phase, at p. 18; letter from Mr. Mathieu to the Secretary to the Tribunal, copy to the Bank (27 August 2003).

many other shareholders. However, Claimant No. 2, being the former owner of one of the largest private shareholdings, was defending its own rights and interests. First Eagle should therefore pay its own expenses.

129. As to the expenses of the Bank, the Tribunal is of the view that there are no reasons to depart from the rule according to which each party bears its own expenses. Therefore, the Bank shall pay its expenses and legal fees.

130. Subject to the special circumstances set out in *supra* paragraph 126, each Party will accordingly bear its own attorney's fees.

J. Costs of the Arbitration

131. The Tribunal now turns to the costs of the Arbitration.[179] The Tribunal notes that Annex XII ("Arbitration. Rules of Procedure") of the 1930 Hague Agreement[180] provides: "In particular Article 85 of the Hague Convention shall apply to these proceedings, and each Party shall pay its own expenses and an equal share of those of the Tribunal." Article 85 of the 1907 Hague Convention reads: "Each Party pays its own expenses and an equal share of the expenses of the Tribunal."

132. The provisions referred to above are clearly binding on the Tribunal for interstate proceedings or proceedings between a State and the Bank as envisaged in Article XV of the 1930 Hague Agreement. The question arises, however, whether the rules for governmental entities enshrined in the cited Articles are fully applicable for disputes between the Bank and other private shareholders. All shareholders are covered by the arbitration provision in Article 54 of the Statutes of the Bank, but proceedings

---

[179] Article 33 of the Rules of Procedure provides that:

> The Tribunal shall fix the costs of arbitration in its award. The term 'costs' includes: (a) The fees of the Tribunal to be fixed by the Tribunal itself; (b) The travel and other expenses incurred by the arbitrators; (c) The costs of expert advice and of other assistance required by the Tribunal; (d) [T]he fees and expenses of the Secretary of the Tribunal and the International Bureau.

[180] 1930 Hague Agreement, Annex XII, at para. 1.

involving non-State shareholders are not distinguished in the Arbitration Annex or in the 1907 Hague Convention.

133. In applying the obligations of Article 54(1) to private shareholders as well as central banks, the drafters clearly intended to establish a regime that would enable, rather than prevent, private shareholders to exercise that right. Hence, the Tribunal is of the view that Article 54 of the Bank's Statutes[181] providing for Arbitration between shareholders and the Bank must be interpreted in a way which makes access to justice for every shareholder not only theoretically possible but, in reality, feasible. This has been recognized by the Bank from the very beginning of these proceedings.[182] The reference to Article 85 of the 1907 Hague Convention must be applied in the light of this principle of effective access to justice which is fully recognized in present-day human rights law. Even if this rule was not fully developed in 1930, international law has evolved and the Tribunal must apply the law in its contemporary acceptance.

134. In its 31 August 2001 Procedural Order Concerning R. Howe, the Tribunal stated:

> H. With respect to the allocation of deposits and costs: does the Tribunal have the legal competence or "equitable discretion" to allocate deposits and costs to take account of the circumstances of any particular claimant?
>
> H.1. The 1930 Agreement and the 1907 Convention contemplated an equal division of the costs of an arbitration between the parties. As the context of those instruments was inter-state arbitration and not arbitration

---

[181] Under Article 54(1):

> If any dispute shall arise between the Bank, on the one side, and any central bank, financial institution, or other bank referred to in the present Statutes, on the other side, or between the Bank and its shareholders, with regard to the interpretation or application of the Statutes of the Bank, the same shall be referred for final decision to the Tribunal provided for by the Hague Agreement of January, 1930.

[182] See *infra* para. 134, H.5.

between a state or an international organization, on the one hand, and individual claimants on the other, that system of equal allocation was consistent with the notion of the sovereign equality of states and may have provided a formula that was likely to achieve equity in specific cases.

H.2. Article 54 of the Statutes of the Bank extended the jurisdiction of the Tribunal to disputes between the Bank and individual shareholders. In this form of privity, the equal division of costs that was, not unreasonably, prescribed for inter-state arbitration could create inequities and even restrain or "chill" the access of individuals to arbitration. In this regard, the Tribunal takes note of the statement of the Bank in its letter of August 23, 2001, that "[t]he Bank does not wish that costs alone should serve to prohibit individual former private shareholders from arbitrating a claim." Wholly aside from the Bank's expression of its wish, an interpretation of a provision in one of the instruments of the Tribunal's regime that had the effect of prohibiting individuals entitled to arbitrate from doing so could hardly be lawful. As will be recalled, Article 9(1) of the Tribunal's Rules provides that

> Subject to these Rules and the Agreement and Convention under which it operates, the Tribunal may conduct the arbitration in such manner as it considers appropriate, provided that the parties are treated with equality and that at any stage of the proceedings each party is given a full opportunity of presenting its case.

An allocation of deposits and costs that had the effect of not providing a party with a "full opportunity of presenting its case" would not meet the test of Article 9(1).

H.3. The "Rules for Arbitration Between the Bank for International Settlements and Private Parties," which were adapted on the basis of the authority in the 1930 Agreement to regulate arbitrations between the Bank and private shareholders, empower the Tribunal in Article 33 to "fix" the costs, a term which, in the context of this form of arbitration, includes the competence to allocate the costs in ways that further the shared objectives of the parties to the arbitration in order to achieve a fair process and a just outcome, consistent with law.

H.4. Hence, the Tribunal has the competence with respect to arbitrations under Article 54 of the Statutes of the Bank to allocate costs in ways that conduce to the optimum use of the arbitration as contemplated by the Article 54 and justice and fairness in the process of each arbitration.

H.5. The Tribunal takes note of the statement of the Bank in its letter of August 23, 2001 which says in relevant part that:

> [I]t is the Bank's understanding of Article 33 of the Tribunal's Rules that the Tribunal has equitable discretion to apportion costs as it sees fit, including awarding them to a successful claimant. We also understand that any advance deposit of costs under Article 34 could be subject to similar equitable allocation, which could appropriately take account of the circumstances of any particular claimant . . . . It remains, however, for the Tribunal to determine how any advance deposits should be apportioned based on the total number of claims ultimately filed and all the other facts and circumstances regarding such claims.

H.6. Given the case-by-case and contextual imperative of any equitable allocation, the Tribunal cannot decide, in advance, the allocation of costs, all the more insofar as such an allocation is to "appropriately take account of the circumstances of any particular claimant." But even without knowing those circumstances in cases that have yet to advance or even to be filed, the Tribunal takes note of the Bank's statement that "[i]t is certainly not the Bank's understanding that multiple claimants, collectively, must bear more than half the Tribunal's costs . . . ."

H.7. The foregoing observations also apply *mutatis mutandis* to the deposits for the arbitration as provided for by Articles 33 and 34 of the Rules of the Tribunal.

> H.8. Accordingly, the Tribunal has the legal competence and equitable discretion to allocate costs in ways that contribute to access to the arbitral procedure provided for in Article 54 of the Statutes, that ensure the fairness of the procedure and that secure a meaningful award.

It will be recalled that the Bank, for its part, stated in H.5. *supra*: "it is the Bank's understanding of Article 33 of the Tribunal's Rules that the Tribunal has equitable discretion to apportion costs as it sees fit, including awarding them to a successful claimant."

135. For a case between two States, or a State and the Bank, the quoted Articles provide for an equal distribution between the parties. For the Bank, an international organization with significant financial assets, such a distribution would cause no impediment to justice. In contrast, were this provision applied to individual claimants, requiring them to pay half of the costs of the Tribunal, it would make their access to justice illusory. Considering all of these circumstances, including the fact that the Bank lost in important parts of the dispute, though successful in some others, and including the agreement between the parties with respect to the Tribunal's competence to exercise an equitable discretion to apportion costs as its sees fit, the Tribunal holds that the Bank will bear the full costs of the Arbitration.

136. The costs of the Arbitration, as defined by Article 33 of the Rules of Arbitration, shall be fully borne by the Bank as follows: the Bank shall reimburse directly to Claimant No. 1 EUR 1,852.64; the Bank shall reimburse directly to Claimant No. 2 US$ 806,086.40; the Bank shall reimburse directly to Claimant No. 3 EUR 760.25.

137. In its discretion, the Tribunal denies the Claimants' requests[183] for interest on the sums paid for the costs of the Arbitration.

---

[183] See *supra* paras. 26, 35(e), 43, and 47.

CHAPTER V – DECISIONS

138. FOR THE FOREGOING REASONS, the Arbitral Tribunal unanimously renders the following decisions:

1. DETERMINES that the amount now to be paid to each Claimant is CHF 7,977.56 per share.

2. DETERMINES that with respect to the shares claimed by Claimant No. 2 (First Eagle) that are not registered in its name, the Bank is entitled to pay the above amount only to the share owners of record as they are inscribed in the Bank's share register.

3. DETERMINES that Claimant No. 2 (First Eagle) must reimburse the Bank US$ 587,413.49, the Bank's costs in defending the law suit brought by Claimant No. 2 (First Eagle) in the United States, which the Bank may set off against the sums owing to Claimant No. 2 (First Eagle) as a consequence of this Award.

4. DETERMINES that 5% simple interest is to be paid to all of the Claimants on the amount in paragraph 138(1) *supra* from 8 January 2001 until the date of this Award.

5. REJECTS the claim of Claimant No. 3 (Mr. Mathieu) for interest on the amount set by the Extraordinary General Meeting on 8 January 2001 under Article 18A of the Statutes of the Bank.

6. DETERMINES that the Bank shall reimburse directly to Claimant No. 3 (Mr. Mathieu) EUR 4,436.75 for expenses. The Tribunal also determines that Claimant No. 2 (First Eagle) shall bear its own attorneys' fees and other expenses.

7. DETERMINES that the costs of the Arbitration shall be fully borne by the Bank as follows: the Bank shall reimburse directly to Claimant No. 1 (Dr. Reineccius) EUR 1,852.64; the Bank shall reimburse directly to Claimant No. 2 (First Eagle) US$ 806,086.40; the Bank shall reimburse directly to Claimant No. 3 (Mr. Mathieu) EUR 760.25.

8. REJECTS the Claimants' requests for interest on the sums paid for the costs of the Arbitration.

9. DETERMINES that all of the above amounts are to be paid within 90 days.

10. DETERMINES that no other remedy is available to the Parties *inter se* with respect to the issues determined in the present Arbitration.

11. DISMISSES all other relief inconsistent with the foregoing Decisions.

Done at the Peace Palace, The Hague, this 19th day of September 2003,

Professor W. Michael Reisman

Professor Dr. Jochen A. Frowein

Professor Dr. Mathias Krafft

Professor Dr. Paul Lagarde

Professor Dr. Albert Jan van den Berg

Phyllis P. Hamilton, Secretary

L'ARBITRAGE RELATIF A LA BANQUE DES RÈGLEMENTS INTERNATIONAUX

Sa contribution au droit international

par

V.V.Veeder*

Les lois de la nature veulent que les banques soient demanderesses et créancières, et non défenderesses. Les banques n'aiment être attaquées en justice par personne, et les banques centrales encore moins, comme fait plus que le confirmer la récente affaire londonienne des réclamations portées contre la Banque d'Angleterre par des milliers de déposants de la Bank of Credit and Commerce International (BCCI), en faillite.[1] Il est donc difficile d'imaginer ce qu'a pu ressentir la banque centrale des banques centrales, la Banque des Règlements Internationaux de Bâle, lorsqu'elle fut assignée en justice par l'un de ses actionnaires privés, en janvier 2001. Ce mois-là, First Eagle (un fonds d'investissement de droit américain) saisit le tribunal de district de New York pour demander des mesures conservatoires en vue d'empêcher la reprise forcée par la Banque de l'ensemble de ses actions détenues par des actionnaires privés.

La Banque fut fondée en tant qu'établissement financier en 1930, dans le prolongement de l'Accord relatif au règlement complet et définitif du problème des réparations, signé à La Haye le 20 janvier 1930 (l'« Accord de La Haye de 1930 »). La Convention concernant la Banque des Règlements Internationaux[2]

---

* *Queen's Counsel*, *Essex Court Chambers*, Londres, Professeur extraordinaire d'arbitrage international au King's College de l'Université de Londres.

[1] Le litige relatif à la BCCI porté devant le tribunal de commerce de Londres, dans l'affaire *Three Rivers et al v. The Bank of England*, prit fin au milieu de l'année 2006, un jugement définitif ayant été rendu après près de deux ans de procès (provoquant le mécontentement général, y compris du juge du fond, quoique pour d'autres raisons). La procédure s'étala globalement sur plus de douze ans, donnant lieu à plus de vingt-cinq décisions publiées des juridictions anglaises (dont de nombreuses excursions du tribunal de commerce à la cour d'appel et à la Chambre des Lords), ce qui aurait coûté aux parties plus de 130 millions de livres.

[2] Société des Nations, Recueil des Traités, vol. 104, p. 441.

fut conclue le même jour entre la Belgique, l'Allemagne, la France, le Royaume-Uni, l'Italie, le Japon et la Suisse . Cette Convention comprenait les instruments constitutifs de la Banque, c'est-à-dire sa Charte constitutive et ses Statuts, la mission de la Banque étant de faciliter le recouvrement et la répartition des réparations de guerre dues par l'Allemagne à l'issue de la Première Guerre Mondiale. Il s'agissait d'une vaste initiative menée dans le cadre du Plan Young,[3] ayant des répercussions économiques sur le plan mondial. Avant la création de la Banque, aux termes du Plan Dawes, les réparations de l'Allemagne étaient administrées à Berlin par J.P. Morgan, qui perçut de l'Allemagne plus d'un milliard de marks en 1924–1925, plus de 1,22 milliard de marks en 1926–1927, 2 milliards de marks en 1927–1928 et 2,5 milliards de marks en 1928–1929. Ces sommes furent déposées par J.P. Morgan dans une banque berlinoise, l'Allemagne ayant été autorisée en contrepartie à emprunter, à long terme et dans l'intérêt mutuel du débiteur et des créanciers, une somme d'un montant supérieur à celle qu'elle avait versée.[4] Heureusement, pour nos besoins actuels, la Banque fut aussi mise en avant comme organe général de coopération entre les banques centrales pour la conduite de leurs opérations financières, un rôle qui revêt toujours une grande importance dans l'économie mondiale du XXIe siècle. La Banque est un établissement financier de droit suisse siégeant à Bâle, mais ses instruments constitutifs précisent qu'elle n'est régie par le droit d'aucun des Etats signataires, ni par celui du pays de son siège social: elle doit au contraire être considérée comme une personne morale internationale régie par ses propres instruments constitutifs. Il convient de noter, aux présentes fins, que l'article 55, paragraphe 1, alinéa b, des Statuts de la Banque de 1930 confère à celle-ci une immunité de juridiction à l'égard des actions civiles ou commerciales découlant de transactions bancaires ou financières intentées par des cocontractants de la Banque « sous réserve des cas pour lesquels des dispositions d'arbitrage ont ou auront été prises ».

Au mois de septembre 2000, la Banque annonça que, le 8 janvier 2001, elle réunirait ses banques centrales actionnaires pour voter une modification de ses Statuts permettant la reprise forcée de l'ensemble de ses actions sans droit de vote en circulation, celles détenues par des actionnaires privés. Ces actions en mains privées représentaient à l'époque 14% du total des actions de la Banque, dont 12,5% étaient détenues par First Eagle. Par le passé, il n'était pas inhabituel

---

[3] Le Plan Young (1930) portait sur la question du paiement des réparations imposées à l'Allemagne par le Traité de Versailles à l'issue de la Première Guerre Mondiale.

[4] Louis Fischer, Men and Politics p. 103 (New York 1941).

que même des banques centrales aient des actionnaires privés, mais ce n'était plus le cas en l'an 2000 et de nombreux pays, notamment le Canada, la France, la Norvège, l'Espagne, la Nouvelle-Zélande, le Portugal et le Vénézuela, avaient procédé au rachat obligatoire des actions en mains privées de leurs banques centrales. De la même manière, le plan de reprise forcée de la Banque avait été mis sur pied pour remédier à la tension croissante entre la mission d'intérêt public assumée par la Banque, consistant à promouvoir la coopération financière internationale entre les banques centrales et ce qui pouvait être considéré, notamment par ses actionnaires privés, comme une obligation de nature intéressée et commerciale consistant à maximaliser ses propres bénéfices sociaux. C'est pourquoi la Banque souhaitait annuler l'inscription de toutes ses actions en mains privées (qui devaient ensuite être redistribuées entre les banques centrales actionnaires de la Banque) puis, à titre d'indemnité, accorder à chaque actionnaire privé le droit au paiement d'une somme de 16 000 francs suisses par action (environ 10 000 dollars américains courants), une évaluation établie à la suite d'une expertise menée par J.P. Morgan, en sa qualité de conseiller financier de la Banque.

First Eagle porta l'affaire devant le tribunal fédéral de district de New York le 5 janvier 2001 avant de modifier sa requête le 8 janvier 2001, immédiatement après l'approbation par les banques centrales du plan de reprise de la Banque, pour demander que le juge statue en urgence et prononce parallèlement des mesures conservatoires. Dans sa requête modifiée, First Eagle affirmait que la Banque, en modifiant ses Statuts, avait outrepassé ses pouvoirs, que l'évaluation de J.P. Morgan était incorrecte et enfin que la Banque avait violé les obligations d'ordre public prévues par droit boursier fédéral en matière de communication d'informations. Ce tribunal examina la demande de mesures conservatoires le jour même de son dépôt avant de la rejeter le 24 janvier 2001, au motif que First Eagle n'avait pas établi l'existence d'un risque de préjudice irréparable. First Eagle interjeta ensuite appel devant la cour d'appel fédérale pour le deuxième circuit, qui l'examina le 5 mars 2001. Cette cour débouta l'appelant le 7 juin 2001, au motif que la décision du juge était avant dire droit (donc en principe non susceptible d'appel) et que First Eagle n'aurait subi aucun préjudice grave ou irréparable ne pouvant être dûment réparé au moyen de dommages et intérêts.[5]

---

[5] *First Eagle SoGen Funds, Inc. v. Bank for Int'l Settlements*, 252 F.3d 604 (2d Cir. 2001).

Avant que l'appel soit interjeté, le tribunal de district avait également motivé sa décision par le fait qu'une voie de recours adéquate était ouverte à First Eagle, l'arbitrage en application de la clause compromissoire énoncée dans les Statuts de la Banque. En réaction, la Banque présenta au tribunal de district une demande de renvoi à l'arbitrage au titre de la loi fédérale sur l'arbitrage. Laissant de côté ses demandes distinctes en droit boursier (*securities claims*), First Eagle décida alors de porter ses autres demandes contre la Banque à l'arbitrage, déposant à cette fin une notification le 31 août 2001. Il y eut néanmoins d'autres escarmouches de procédure au mois de septembre 2001, devant le tribunal de district. Ce dernier jugea que la demande de renvoi à l'arbitrage présentée par la Banque était désormais sans objet (étant donné qu'à ce stade, First Eagle avait déjà introduit l'instance arbitrale), que le sursis à statuer serait prononcé concernant la procédure de droit boursier (*securities claim*) engagée par First Eagle en attendant l'issue de la procédure d'arbitrage et que la demande présentée par First Eagle tendant à ce que sa plainte soit modifiée en vue d'y ajouter des demandes au titre d'une action de groupe était rejetée.[6]

C'est ainsi que le théâtre du litige changea, du contentieux judiciaire à New York au contentieux arbitral à La Haye. La clause compromissoire en cause était énoncée à l'article 54, paragraphe 1, des Statuts de la Banque, une clause que tous les actionnaires étaient censés avoir acceptée en vertu de l'article 17 de ces mêmes Statuts. Cette clause précisait que si un différend venait à s'élever entre la Banque et, notamment, l'un de ses actionnaires quant à l'interprétation ou à l'application de ses Statuts, ce différend serait soumis, pour décision définitive, au Tribunal prévu par l'article XV de l'Accord de La Haye de janvier 1930 (reproduit en annexe B de la sentence partielle). La procédure arbitrale était décrite dans l'annexe XII de l'Accord de 1930 (reproduite en annexe A de la sentence partielle) qui englobe, par référence, la convention de La Haye de 1907 pour le règlement pacifique des conflits internationaux (l'une des deux conventions ayant fondé la Cour permanente d'arbitrage). En outre, le Tribunal adopta un Règlement d'arbitrage entre la Banque des règlements internationaux et des parties privées, dont l'apparition au mois de mars 2001 coïncidait manifestement avec le différend opposant la Banque et ses actionnaires privés.[7] Pour le cas d'espèce, l'article XV

[6] Ce jugement est publié sous la référence suivante: 2001 U.S. Dist. LEXIS 15574.

[7] Ces règles spéciales de procédure, le Règlement d'arbitrage entre la Banque des règlements internationaux et des parties privées du 23 mars 2001 (ci-après le « Règlement de procédure »), peuvent être consultées sur le site Internet de la Cour permanente d'arbitrage (CPA) à l'adresse suivante: <http://www.pca-cpa.org>.

de l'Accord de La Haye de 1930 prévoyait un tribunal arbitral composé de cinq membres ayant la nationalité des pays suivants: États-Unis d'Amérique, Allemagne, Suisse, France et Pays-Bas, et nommés par les gouvernements de la Belgique, de la France, de l'Allemagne, de l'Italie et du Royaume-Uni (le Japon ayant renoncé à son droit de nomination en 1951). Aucun des arbitres ne fut désigné par les actionnaires privés de la Banque, ni même par les trois demandeurs à l'instance, et les cinq arbitres avaient donc tous été nommés par des Etats dont les banques centrales étaient à la fois actionnaires de la Banque et bénéficiaires indirects du plan de reprise des actions des demandeurs. L'annexe XII imposait expressément à chaque partie à la procédure d'arbitrage de « supporter . . . ses propres frais et une fraction égale des frais du tribunal » (article 1). Elle prévoyait également que les débats oraux seraient « publics » (article 4). Aucune des parties ne pouvait avoir, « pour chaque question distincte soumise à l'arbitrage », plus de deux avocats (article 10). Les Etats parties à l'Accord de 1930 bénéficiaient d'un droit d'intervention (article 19).

Au bout du compte, à l'issue de cette procédure d'arbitrage, deux sentences arbitrales ont été rendues: la première, la sentence partielle du 22 novembre 2002, et la seconde, la sentence définitive du 19 septembre 2003. Il s'agit de deux documents très longs qui méritent un examen approfondi pour plusieurs raisons. Premièrement, le raisonnement est particulièrement limpide, compréhensible et concis. Les motifs pour lesquels le Tribunal arbitral a statué sur les questions qui se posaient apparaissent clairement aux yeux des parties au litige (mais aussi des lecteurs moins au fait du différend), sans qu'il faille deviner lequel des arguments des parties aurait pu être retenu ou écarté par le Tribunal et pourquoi. Il s'agit donc d'une leçon salutaire en matière de rédaction des sentences pour tous les arbitres qui emploient soit trop peu de mots, soit trop mais pas ceux qu'il faut.

Deuxièmement, le Tribunal, dans son raisonnement, a également examiné plusieurs questions importantes de procédure, qui auront probablement un plus grand intérêt à long terme que les questions de fond tranchées dans les deux sentences. Parmi ces questions de procédure, il y avait les demandes multiples formulées par différentes parties, leur jonction (*de facto*), l'égalité des armes quant à la désignation des membres du tribunal arbitral (la question de la jurisprudence *Dutco*[8]), la segmentation de l'instance en deux phases, la

---

[8] *Siemens AG & BKMI Industrienlagen GmbH v. Dutco Consortium Construction Co.*, Cour de cassation (France), 7 janvier 1992, reproduite *in* XVIII Y.B. COMM. ARB. p. 140 et Article 6 de la Convention européenne des Droits de l'homme: voir FOUCHARD, GAILLARD & GOLDMAN ON INTERNATIONAL COMMERCIAL ARBITRATION pp. 468–470 (E. Gaillard & J. Savage, dir. de publ., 1999).

confidentialité, la production de documents (notamment l'invocation des *Rules on the Taking of Evidence in International Commercial Arbitration* de l'Association internationale du barreau et du droit à la confidentialité des communications entre l'avocat et son client, ainsi que la renonciation tacite à ce droit), les expertises, les supports visuels, les parties comparaissant sans avocat et celles représentées par des avocats *pro bono*, la contestation de la nomination d'un arbitre compte tenu de ses liens antérieurs avec un cabinet d'avocats représentant une partie à l'arbitrage et le trilinguisme.

Troisièmement, sur le fond, le raisonnement du Tribunal constitue une addition notable à la jurisprudence en vigueur concernant l'évaluation des avoirs expropriés (y compris concernant le rôle des droits de l'homme, en tant que branche distincte du droit international), l'octroi d'intérêts composés, la répartition des frais de procédure et notamment le droit pour une partie d'obtenir de la partie adverse un remboursement de ces frais si cette dernière a violé la convention d'arbitrage en saisissant une juridiction nationale sur le fond. Toutefois, la question principale qui se posait devant les juridictions des États-Unis et devant le Tribunal arbitral était la nature de la convention multipartite imposant à la Banque et à ses anciens actionnaires privés de soumettre leurs différends à l'arbitrage.

Depuis toujours, en droit anglais des sociétés (comme dans de nombreux pays de *common law*), les actes constitutifs d'une société (c'est-à-dire ses statuts) lient la société et ses actionnaires comme si ces instruments avaient chacun été signés en bonne et due forme par chaque actionnaire et prenaient acte de leur engagement de respecter l'ensemble des dispositions de ces instruments.[9] Lors des débuts de l'arbitrage en Angleterre, il n'était pas rare d'insérer une clause compromissoire dans le règlement d'une association professionnelle puis, ultérieurement, dans les statuts d'une société, pour obliger ses actionnaires à soumettre leurs différends à l'arbitrage privé plutôt qu'au juge. Sur le plan des principes juridiques, la formation de conventions d'arbitrage multipartites au moyen d'actes individuels d'acceptation *a posteriori*, sans recourir au processus formel d'offre et d'acceptation par toutes les parties contractantes, ne posait aucun problème, et l'inverse eût été en effet tragique car ces conventions d'arbitrage multipartites eussent été impossibles à conclure en pratique.[10]

---

[9] Il s'agit aujourd'hui de l'article 14 de la loi de 1985 sur les sociétés, qui reprend l'article 16 de la loi de 1862 sur les sociétés.

[10] Pour un aperçu général, voir *Clarke v. Dunraven* (l'affaire dite du « Satanita ») [1897] A.C. 59 et, pour l'application de cette jurisprudence à une clause compromissoire multipartite, *Walkinshaw*

Pourtant, la question de la validité de ce type de clause compromissoire au regard du droit et de la pratique anglais de l'arbitrage se posa. L'actionnaire d'une société pouvait acquérir ses titres à la bourse sans signer ni accepter la clause compromissoire, voire sans même la connaître, et les statuts de la société pouvaient être modifiés une fois les actions acquises par l'actionnaire de manière à insérer ou supprimer le renvoi à l'arbitrage alors même que cette personne s'y opposait ou manifestait énergiquement son désaccord. En outre, par cette fiction juridique, la législation anglaise sur les sociétés considérait que les actionnaires, mais pas (expressément) la société elle-même, avaient signé les statuts en bonne et due forme, et cette fiction ne concernait absolument pas le cas des dirigeants et des administrateurs de la société, ni des autres tiers. Ces difficultés, ajoutées à d'autres, firent l'objet de vives controverses devant les juridictions anglaises, aboutissant à la décision rendue par la Cour d'appel d'Angleterre en l'affaire *London Sack & Bag Company* (1943),[11] qui précisait qu'une telle clause compromissoire ne pouvait en principe satisfaire aux critères d'une convention d'arbitrage écrite exigés par l'article 4 de la loi anglaise de 1889 sur l'arbitrage. Dans l'opinion majoritaire de la Cour dont il donna lecture, le *Lord Justice* Scott (un juge expérimenté qui connaissait bien le droit commercial) raillait ouvertement l'idée qu'« un accord purement verbal donné à l'insertion d'une clause compromissoire écrite sur un mur pût satisfaire aux dispositions de la loi [de 1889] ».[12] L'éminent magistrat était toutefois disposé à reconnaître que la clause compromissoire pouvait produire ses effets entre les actionnaires, en leur qualité d'actionnaires, mais pas pour des questions entièrement étrangères à cette relation. L'image employée par le juge était prémonitoire car la loi anglaise de 1996 sur l'arbitrage reconnaîtrait aujourd'hui la validité de l'exemple de la clause compromissoire sous la forme d'un graffiti mural incorporée par renvoi à un contrat oral (articles 5 et 6). En

---

v. Pedro Diniz (1999), publié *in* 17(2) ARB. INT'L p. 193 (2001). Voir également Gabrielle Kaufmann-Kohler & Henry Peter, *Formula 1 Racing and Arbitration: The FIA Tailor-Made System for Fast Track Dispute Resolution*, 17(2) ARB. INT'L p. 173 (2001). En droit suisse, le tribunal fédéral, dans sa décision *Andersen Consulting c. Arthur Andersen* (8 déc. 1989), publié *in* 18 ASA BULLETIN p. 546 (2000, No. 3), a adopté une approche similaire concernant les sociétés multipartites et les différends relatifs aux sociétés.

[11] *London Sack & Bag Company Limited v. Dixon & Lugton Limited* (1944) 170 L.T. 70; [1943] 2 All E.R. 763 (Court of Appeal). D'autres affaires sont évoquées *in* MUSTILL & BOYD, THE LAW AND PRACTICE OF COMMERCIAL ARBITRATION p. 75, n.2 (1ère éd. 1982), notamment *Hickman v. Kent & Romney Marsh Sheepbreeders' Association* [1915] 1 Ch. 881.

[12] P. 72. Avant d'être nommé juge, Sir Leslie Scott (1869–1950) avait été l'arbitre anglais désigné par le demandeur dans l'affaire *Lena Goldfields Co. Ltd. v. U.S.S.R.* (1930), sentence arbitrale du 2 septembre 1930, *in* LAUTERPACHT, ANNUAL DIGEST OF PUBLIC INTERNATIONAL LAW CASES p. 426 (1929/30) et 47 INT'L COMP. L.Q. p. 747 (1998).

effet, les exigences du commerce veulent que les conventions d'arbitrage soient efficaces, aussi l'attitude du juge et du législateur a-t-elle notablement changé.

De la même manière, une application uniforme des clauses compromissoires est nécessaire pour qu'elles puissent être utilisées efficacement dans le commerce transnational, comme le montrent l'article II de la Convention de New York sur l'arbitrage[13] et l'article 7 de la loi type de la CNUDCI sur l'arbitrage commercial international. Pour ce qui est des conventions d'arbitrage prévues dans les statuts d'une société, le traitement comparable accordé au sein de l'Union européenne aux clauses attributives de compétence en matière de commerce transnational constitue un bon exemple. Dans l'arrêt *Powell Duffryn c. Wolfgang Petereit* (1992),[14] la Cour de justice des Communautés européennes a jugé qu'une clause attributive de compétence figurant dans les statuts d'une société allemande, auxquels les actions étaient soumises en droit allemand, était opposable à la société et à un actionnaire étranger en vertu de l'article 17 de la Convention de Bruxelles (aujourd'hui l'article 23 du Règlement n° 44/2001 concernant la compétence judiciaire). La Cour s'est prononcée ainsi alors même que la clause aurait pu ne pas être reconnue en droit allemand comme une clause attributive de compétence, au motif que cette notion devait être appréciée à l'aune des dispositions de la Convention de Bruxelles en tant que notion autonome et (au regard des faits de l'espèce) alors même que les actionnaires, au cours de l'assemblée générale de la société, s'étaient opposés à l'insertion d'une clause compromissoire et avaient voté contre celle-ci. L'efficacité tant des clauses attributives de compétence que des clauses d'arbitrage, à l'égard des statuts d'une société, peut donc désormais dépendre non seulement des lois nationales, mais aussi des traités et accords internationaux.

Il est significatif qu'aucune de ces difficultés anciennes n'ait constitué d'obstacle majeur en la présente espèce, ni devant les juridictions new-yorkaises aux États-Unis, ni devant le Tribunal arbitral à La Haye: les juges et les parties ont tous interprété la clause compromissoire entre les actionnaires privés et la Banque comme étant régie par le droit international. Le chien de garde des droits nationaux ne s'est pas réveillé. First Eagle soutenait que les principes généraux du droit international trouvaient à s'appliquer au différend, notamment en ce qui

---

[13] Convention des Nations Unies pour la reconnaissance et l'exécution des sentences arbitrales étrangères, New York, 10 juin 1958, *Journal officiel de la République française*, 6 juin 1959 ; Nations Unies, *Recueil des traités*, vol. 330, p. 38.

[14] Affaire C-214/89, *Powell Duffryn plc c. Wolfgang Petereit*, 1992 R.E.C. 1-1745.

concerne l'interprétation des Statuts de la Banque. Les autres demandeurs, bien qu'ayant avancé d'autres arguments, n'étaient pas matériellement en désaccord sur ce point (celui-ci étant moins important pour eux que pour First Eagle, le seul défendeur dans le cadre de la demande reconventionnelle formulée par la Banque). En ce qui concerne cette demande reconventionnelle, la Banque soutenait devant le Tribunal que la clause compromissoire était non pas régie par un accord privé, mais directement stipulée dans l'Accord de La Haye de 1930, sans renvoi au droit d'un pays quelconque. Le Tribunal a retenu cet argument, considérant la convention d'arbitrage comme une *lex specialis* établie par les instruments constitutifs de la Banque en vertu des seules règles du droit international. Après avoir examiné les dispositions des articles 17, 54 et 55 des Statuts de la Banque, voici ce qu'a conclu le Tribunal:

> Le régime qui en découle est tout à fait unique. Outre le fait qu'il fasse partie de la structure juridique internationale de la Banque, l'article 55 des Statuts constitue un engagement bilatéral applicable parallèlement aux articles 54 et 17. En acceptant les Statuts conformément à l'article 17, les actionnaires acceptent aussi l'article 54 et par conséquent, la compétence d'un tribunal établi en vertu de l'Accord de 1930 et conviennent de ne pas porter devant les tribunaux nationaux toute affaire relevant de la compétence de tel tribunal. Il ressort clairement du régime institué par ces dispositions que les litiges entre notamment la Banque et ses actionnaires quant à l'interprétation ou à l'application des Statuts doivent être portés devant un tribunal établi en conformité avec l'Accord de La Haye de 1930. Un tel tribunal a le pouvoir de « statuer sur toute question, y compris celles relatives à l'étendue de sa compétence » et, en plus, d'« ordonner des mesures conservatoires provisoires pour sauvegarder les droits respectifs des parties ». L'article 55 met en lumière le caractère exclusif de la compétence du tribunal, puisqu'il établit l'immunité de la Banque à l'égard d'autres juridictions nationales, sous réserve de deux exceptions expresses, dont aucune n'est pertinente dans le cas d'espèce.
>
> Un actionnaire privé de la Banque ne pouvait pas être officiellement partie à l'Accord de La Haye de 1930. Cependant, un actionnaire privé achetant des actions était tenu à un type particulier et également contraignant d'obligation à l'égard du régime de règlement des conflits décrit ci-dessus. L'article 17 des Statuts de la Banque dispose que « la propriété d'actions de la Banque emporte adhésion aux Statuts de la Banque. » Tous les certificats d'action portaient la même mention. Les brochures présentant les actions signalaient le régime de la compétence exclusive. Une déclaration d'acceptation des actions impliquait l'accord de se soumettre au régime de règlement des litiges. En somme, les acteurs privés qui achetaient des actions acceptaient, au moyen de divers instruments dont la multiplicité et la réitération excluaient toute possibilité de malentendu, le régime de règlement des litiges, y compris l'immunité de la Banque à l'égard des tribunaux nationaux et la compétence d'un tribunal créé en

vertu de l'Accord de 1930 et des Statuts afin de décider de sa propre compétence et de prendre des mesures conservatoires. Le Tribunal insiste sur le facteur déterminant de l'*acceptation* du régime. S'agissant de la question de la juridiction compétente, les actionnaires privés ont accepté sans réserve le statut juridique international de la Banque.[15]

Ce mode de raisonnement montre clairement que l'arbitrage opposant les personnes privées aux personnes internationales ou aux Etats a atteint le stade de la maturité, établissant pour les personnes privées le droit indépendant de recourir à l'arbitrage selon les règles du droit international, sans soumission au droit d'un pays quelconque ni subrogation opérée par le biais de la protection diplomatique que peut exercer l'État dont la personne privée est ressortissante. Par conséquent, pour reprendre la terminologie du Professeur Rosalyn Higgins, la personne privée n'est désormais ni un sujet ni un objet du droit international, mais un « participant ».[16] Il s'agit d'une entorse fondamentale à l'orthodoxie qui veut que si une personne privée doit un jour jouir de ce statut, ce ne peut être que par l'application d'une règle de droit national prévoyant ce résultat précis.[17] Le raisonnement du Tribunal a depuis lors été confirmé par la décision récente rendue par la Cour d'appel d'Angleterre en l'affaire *Ecuador v. Occidental* (2006), dans le cadre d'une procédure accessoire à un arbitrage entre un investisseur américain privé à un État, régi par un traité d'investissement bilatéral (BIT) et s'étant déroulé à Londres. La Cour, dans cette affaire, a reconnu que c'étaient les règles du droit international qui s'appliquaient directement à la convention d'arbitrage résultant d'une clause compromissoire figurant dans le BIT entre les États-Unis et l'Équateur et accepté que l'investisseur invoque cette clause, rejetant ainsi catégoriquement le système classique selon lequel un investisseur ne peut exercer les droits procéduraux énoncés dans un traité que s'il est subrogé par un État partie à ce traité.[18] En la présente espèce, cependant, la clause compromissoire figurant dans

---

[15] Voir sentence définitive, paras. 114–115.

[16] ROSALYN HIGGINS, PROBLEMS & PROCESS: INTERNATIONAL LAW AND HOW WE USE IT p. 50 (1994); voir également Stephen Schwebel, *The Law Applicable in International Arbitration: Application of Public International Law*, ICCA Series No. 7, pp. 562–564 (1994).

[17] Pour le cas particulier du Tribunal des réclamations Iran/Etats-Unis établi en vertu des déclarations d'Alger, voir *Dallal v. Bank Mellat* [1986] Q.B. p. 441; XI Y.B. COM. ARB. p. 547 (1986). Pour un aperçu plus général, voir Francis Mann QC, *State Contracts and International Arbitration*, 42 BRITISH Y.B. OF INT'L L. pp. 1, 8 (1967).

[18] *Ecuador v. Occidental* [2006] 2 W.L.R. p. 70 (CA); voir également Zachary Douglas, *Nothing if Not Critical for Investment Treaty Arbitration*: *Occidental, Eureko and Methanex*, 22(1) ARB. INT'L pp. 27, 30 et s. (2006).

les Statuts de la Banque, en tant que *lex specialis*, s'imposait à First Eagle avant même que cette société n'engage la procédure d'arbitrage à La Haye.

A La Haye, le Tribunal avait en face de lui deux autres demandeurs privés qui contestaient aux aussi, pour des motifs différents, le montant de l'indemnité accordée au titre de leurs actions reprises: le Dr Reineccius (de nationalité allemande) et M. Mathieu (de nationalité française) en son nom en en celui de la *Société de concours hippique de La Châtre*. M. Mathieu était le seul des trois demandeurs à avoir contesté la licéité de la reprise des actions par la Banque. Le Dr Reineccius, qui n'est pas juriste, a comparu sans avocat tout au long de la procédure d'arbitrage, tout en se distinguant par la qualité de ses arguments, tandis que M. Mathieu était représenté, *pro bono*, par d'éminents avocats parisiens. La Banque était représentée par des avocats tout aussi éminents, de même que First Eagle. Pour des raisons pratiques, le Tribunal a joint ces différentes instances en arbitrages « parallèles » et décidé, par sa troisième ordonnance de procédure, de statuer dans une première sentence partielle, à l'issue d'une première phase, sur la licéité de la reprise et sur les normes applicables à l'évaluation des actions ayant fait l'objet de cette reprise puis, dans une sentence définitive, à l'issue d'une seconde phase, si cela s'avérait nécessaire (ce qui fut finalement le cas), sur l'application de ces normes.

Une réunion préparatoire, le 7 septembre 2001, puis une réunion sur des questions de procédure, le 26 février 2002, furent tenues à La Haye. Aux fins de la première phase de l'arbitrage, la CPA organisa des audiences publiques dans la Grande Salle de Justice du Palais de la Paix, à La Haye, du 26 au 28 août 2002, puis d'autres audiences publiques, les 28 et 29 mai 2003, aux fins de la seconde phase. Conformément aux exigences de l'Accord de La Haye de 1930, les plaidoiries furent traduites simultanément en anglais, en français et en allemand. Parmi toutes les ordonnances de procédure d'importance secondaire rendues par le Tribunal, la plus intéressante du point de vue pratique était celle portant sur la technologie électronique utilisée par les avocats des parties lors des audiences. Depuis de nombreuses années, tels des empereurs romains au Colisée, les arbitres se frottaient les mains par avance à l'idée que les avocats des parties allaient braver les périls du logiciel PowerPoint, tout cela pour les voir chuter lorsque le logiciel tombait en panne, qu'il y avait une coupure de courant, que l'ordre des diapositives était modifié par des mains inconnues – ou pire. Il se trouvait en outre toujours un arbitre pour exiger, sans penser à mal, au beau milieu de l'audience, que le représentant d'une partie modifie l'ordre des questions qu'il allait examiner, avec des résultats tout aussi désastreux. Aujourd'hui, les technologies électroniques se sont nettement améliorées, de même que, globalement, les moyens techniques employés dans le cadre des arbitrages, c'est pourquoi le recours accru aux supports visuels a donné lieu à de nouvelles difficultés sur le plan procédural. La huitième ordonnance procédurale constitue donc un modèle à suivre. Voici ce qu'elle prévoit:

> 1. L'utilisation d'écrans permettant de visionner des preuves et autres supports visuels, qu'ils soient assistés par ordinateur ou pas, n'est pas inhabituelle dans les audiences arbitrales internationales. De tels supports visuels peuvent être employés par les parties, si la documentation concernée est fondée uniquement sur des moyens de preuve déjà versés au dossier et si elle a été communiquée préalablement aux audiences, à la partie opposée, aux fins de vérification.
> 2. L'introduction de nouveaux moyens de preuve ne sera pas permise, à moins qu'une requête en ce sens ait été adressée au tribunal, que celui-ci y ait fait droit et que la partie adverse ait eu la possibilité de présenter ses commentaires dans un délai raisonnable.[19]

Comme il est indiqué ici, dès lors que des supports visuels sont utilisés lors de plaidoiries, le tribunal doit exiger au préalable qu'une version papier soit distribuée au tribunal et à toutes les parties (les arbitres se servent de cette version papier pour prendre des notes) et, pour facilement s'y rapporter par la suite, les parties doivent indiquer des numéros de référence précis sur tous leurs supports visuels, afin notamment d'en rendre intelligible la transcription écrite ultérieure. Dans la plupart des cas, toutefois, il ne sera pas possible, comme cela s'est produit en l'espèce, de limiter les supports visuels aux « moyens de preuve déjà versés au dossier »: peut-être sera-t-il utile de présenter visuellement certains arguments, d'autres documents juridiques ou des supports de démonstration ne constituant pas des moyens de preuve. Dans ce cas, des problèmes de procédure risquent de se poser pour ce qui est de fixer les limites précises entre les arguments déjà présentés par écrit, les nouveaux arguments oraux venant étayer une thèse déjà exposée et les thèses entièrement nouvelles. Les premiers sont permis, les troisièmes en principe interdits et les deuxièmes pourraient être permis ou non, mais même s'ils le sont, ils peuvent être interdits si le support visuel contrevient à une ordonnance de procédure antérieure rendue par le Tribunal fixant les délais pour l'échange des écritures ou conclusions précédant la procédure orale.

---

[19] Ordonnance de procédure n° 8 (Projections faites par ordinateur, conditions relatives au dépôt tardif de moyens de preuve ou de documents juridiques), 23 août 2002. Voir le site Internet de la CPA, *supra*, note 7 et la première sentence partielle, para. 49.

Au cours de la première phase, le Tribunal a examiné les deux premières questions. En ce qui concerne la première, soulevée par M. Mathieu, le Tribunal a jugé que la modification des Statuts de la Banque le 8 janvier 2001 était licite, justifiant ainsi l'exclusion de tous les actionnaires privés du capital de la Banque. En ce qui concerne la deuxième question, le Tribunal a dit que les trois demandeurs avaient droit à ce que la Banque leur verse, pour chacune de leurs actions reprises, une indemnité égale à une part proportionnelle de l'actif net réévalué (« ANR ») de la Banque avec application d'une décote de 30%. Le Tribunal a également constaté l'acceptation par les demandeurs du montant de cet ANR, qui s'élevait à 10 072 000 000 de dollars américains, soit 19 034 dollars américains (équivalant à 33 820 francs suisses) par action, compte non tenu de la valeur des biens immobiliers de la Banque. Pour se prononcer ainsi, il a fallu que le Tribunal examine plusieurs questions, notamment la nature et le statut juridique de la Banque, le droit applicable sur ce point, la modification par celle-ci de ses Statuts et l'illicéité alléguée par M. Mathieu.

Pour ce qui est de la deuxième question, le Tribunal a dû examiner les principes juridiques s'appliquant à l'évaluation des actions reprises, pour savoir d'abord s'il s'agissait de « réparations », laissant supposer que la reprise était illicite, ou d'« indemnités », laissant supposer que la reprise valait expropriation et que sa licéité dépendait du versement par la Banque d'une indemnité d'un montant suffisant et du caractère complet, juste, équitable ou approprié de cette indemnité, pour reprendre les diverses formules de rigueur. C'est dans ce passage de la sentence partielle que l'on peut lire l'analyse fort utile de la jurisprudence internationale faite par le Tribunal sur l'évaluation de la valeur de marché des actions d'investisseurs privés ayant fait l'objet d'une expropriation.[20] Le cas d'espèce était compliqué car il n'existait pas de valeur de marché fiable établie à partie d'opérations effectuées dans un marché efficient en raison de la faible liquidité des actions privées de la Banque, de l'absence de droit de vote caractérisant ces actions et de la sous-évaluation notoire de leur valeur sur le marché compte tenu du faible montant des dividendes payés par la Banque, ainsi que d'autres caractéristiques juridiques de ces actions.

---

[20] L'intérêt croissant porté aux questions de calcul dans ce domaine est remarquable, comme en témoigne le site Internet récemment créé du *British Institute for International and Comparative Law* consacré notamment aux dommages et intérêts accordés dans le cadre d'arbitrages entre les investisseurs et les États: voir <http://www.biicl.org/damages_investment_law>. Voir également Wilson, Cain & Gray, *ICSID Arbitration Awards and Cost*, Transnational Dispute Management (2006). Voir également Irmgard Marboe, *Compensation and Damages in International Law*, 7(5) J. World Investment & Trade (2006).

La Banque, reprenant le rapport de J.P. Morgan, avait employé une méthode d'évaluation fondée sur le modèle des dividendes à perpétuité (« MDP »), parvenant à un prix des actions double du cours effectif sur certains marchés. Le Dr Reineccius soutenait que la méthode d'évaluation appropriée était non pas la MDP, au motif que la Banque ne distribuait généralement à ses actionnaires, à titre de dividendes, qu'une petite part de ses bénéfices réels, mais la méthode de la valeur de rentabilité (« MVR »). Les deux autres demandeurs (auxquels le Dr Reineccius se joignait sur ce point à titre subsidiaire) soutenaient que la méthode d'évaluation était une part proportionnelle par action de l'ANR de la Banque, sans décote. Le Tribunal s'est prononcé pour la méthode de l'ANR, avant de chercher à savoir si et dans quelle mesure cet ANR proportionnel devait faire l'objet d'une décote compte tenu de la nature juridique des actions privées. Le Tribunal a finalement jugé que la décote appropriée, compte tenu des caractéristiques juridiques des actions, serait de 30%, sous réserve d'une nouvelle évaluation de l'ANR supplémentaire constitué par les biens immobiliers (dont le rapport de J.-P. Morgan n'avait pas tenu compte). L'évaluation par la Banque des actions des demandeurs établie par la Banque étant inférieure à ce montant, quelles que soient les modalités de calcul, le Tribunal a jugé que la Banque était tenue de verser la différence à chacun des demandeurs, le montant de cette différence devant être déterminé dans la sentence définitive.

C'est ainsi que, au cours de la seconde phase de la procédure, le Tribunal s'est attaché à déterminer le montant de l'indemnité à verser aux demandeurs, concluant que la Banque devait à chacun d'eux la somme de 7 977,56 francs suisses par action, ainsi que des intérêts au taux simple de 5% à compter du 8 janvier 2001 et jusqu'à la date de la sentence définitive. Pour le calcul du montant de l'indemnité, le Tribunal reçut de l'expert qu'il avait désigné une évaluation de la valeur des biens immobiliers de la Banque. En ce qui concerne la demande reconventionnelle présentée par la Banque contre First Eagle fondée sur la violation de la convention d'arbitrage, le Tribunal a ordonné à First Eagle de rembourser à la Banque la somme de 587 413,49 dollars américains (représentant le montant raisonnable des frais de justice encourus dans le cadre de la procédure judiciaire à New York). Quant aux frais de procédure des parties elles-mêmes, le Tribunal a ordonné à la Banque de ne prendre en charge que ceux, modestes, de M. Mathieu (en tant que client représenté *pro bono*). Enfin, quant aux frais de l'arbitrage, par une interprétation ingénieuse, quoique rationnelle, de l'Annexe XII, le Tribunal a jugé que la Banque les supporterait en totalité (bien qu'il se soit refusé, comme les demandeurs en avaient fait la demande, à imposer des intérêts sur les sommes qu'ils avaient consignées à titre d'avance sur ces frais). D'autres questions ont été soulevées concernant la devise utilisée dans la sentence, les intérêts composés et les dates à compter desquelles les intérêts devaient être calculés.

Pour ce qui est des intérêts réclamés par les demandeurs sur le montant du complément d'indemnité qui, selon la sentence, devait leur être versé, leur taux variait de 3¼% – le taux du marché du franc suisse – pour des intérêts simples, à 7% pour des intérêts composés. Leurs demandes étaient fondées sur les principes généraux de l'enrichissement sans cause (la Banque ayant perçu des revenus sur les indemnités qu'elle n'avait pas versées), du droit commercial comparé et de la pratique bancaire suisse. En ce qui concerne les intérêts composés, il était soutenu que, en vertu de « récentes décisions rendues par des instances d'arbitrage international », l'octroi d'intérêts de ce type était imposé par le droit international coutumier. En réponse, la Banque a fait valoir que ni l'Accord de La Haye de 1930, ni la Convention de La Haye de 1907, ni les Statuts de la Banque (y compris la clause compromissoire) ne prévoyaient l'octroi d'intérêts quelconques, et que celui-ci n'était pas non plus « requis » par les principes généraux du droit international, mais que si le Tribunal devait octroyer des intérêts, il ne devrait s'agir que d'intérêts simples au taux LIBOR à trois mois pour le franc suisse au motif que l'indemnité devait être versée dans cette monnaie et dans ce pays, à Bâle, là où siège la Banque.

Le Tribunal a jugé dans la sentence partielle, confirmée par sa sentence définitive, que des intérêts étaient dus par la Banque au motif qu'« il est habituel que des intérêts soient versés, lorsque des paiements doivent être effectués à une date précise et qu'ils ne le sont pas ».[21] Cette règle du droit international était considérée par le Tribunal comme trop évidente pour justifier la citation de références faisant autorité, c'est pourquoi il s'est attaché dans sa sentence définitive à déterminer le taux d'intérêt approprié. Ayant reconnu que le droit international ne prévoyait aucun taux particulier, le Tribunal a constaté que le droit suisse était celui de l'ordre juridique auquel la question à trancher était « le plus étroitement lié », compte tenu notamment du lieu du siège social de la Banque et du rôle joué la monnaie suisse tant dans le cadre du versement des dividendes dans le passé qu'à l'égard des indemnités à verser par la Banque. Appliquant les articles 73 et 104 du code suisse des obligations, le Tribunal a opté pour un intérêt simple de 5 % par an jusqu'à la date de la sentence, sans rien prévoir après cette date.

---

[21] Sentence partielle, para. 204 ; sentence définitive, para. 90.

Au vu des circonstances de l'espèce, ce résultat était sans risque et ne prêtait pas à controverse. Comme il est constaté dans le commentaire de l'article 38 des Articles de la Commission du droit international sur la responsabilité de l'État, « [l]es cours et tribunaux ont généralement pris position contre l'allocation d'intérêts composés ».[22] Dans tous les pays, les anciennes lois relatives à l'usure peuvent influencer encore aujourd'hui le contentieux commercial judiciaire et arbitral, et la différence concrète entre intérêts simples et intérêts composés sur une courte période ne peut toujours justifier la fureur jurisprudentielle suscitée par l'octroi d'intérêts composés. A titre incident, si un juriste de *common law* peut avoir des réserves sur une règle de conflit fondée sur l'idée qu'une dette puisse être quérable, au lieu d'établissement du débiteur(plutôt que portable, au lieu d'établissement du créancier), le seul pays potentiel dont le droit pouvait s'appliquer en l'espèce était sans conteste la Suisse, et on pouvait certainement s'attendre à ce que la Banque honore la sentence dans les meilleurs délais, rendant inutile en pratique l'octroi d'intérêts postérieurement à la date de la sentence. Toutefois, le Tribunal a également émis une réserve importante, laissant supposer que les arbitres ont peut-être eu quelques difficultés à s'entendre unanimement sur les raisons concrètes de ce résultat pourtant logique:

> [L]a décision d'appliquer l'intérêt moratoire suisse est le résultat de l'application de plusieurs facteurs liés à la pratique de la Banque et à la prépondérance des liens avec le droit suisse. Ladite décision ne se fonde pas sur l'hypothèse que la Banque est soumise au droit suisse. Il ne faut pas non plus voir dans la décision du Tribunal une prise de position en faveur ou contre les tendances récentes en matière d'application d'intérêts composés en droit international contemporain ; cette question ne se pose pas en l'espèce compte tenu de l'effet déterminant de la pratique de la Banque et de la prépondérance des liens avec l'ordre juridique suisse en ce qui concerne les intérêts dans la présente affaire.[23]

Voilà donc un commandement judiciaire mettant fermement en garde les praticiens à l'avenir contre toute citation de cette affaire pour justifier l'octroi ou le refus d'intérêts composés devant d'autres tribunaux internationaux, notamment dans le cadre des arbitrages soumis au CIRDI régis par l'article 42, paragraphe 1,

---

[22] JAMES CRAWFORD, ARTICLES DE LA COMMISSION DU DROIT INTERNATIONAL SUR LA RESPONSABILITÉ DE L'ÉTAT p. 237 (Cambridge University Press 2002); voir également CHRISTOPH SCHREUER, THE ICSID CONVENTION pp. 733–734 (Cambridge University Press 2001); et en français: <http://untreaty.un.org/ilc/texts/instruments/francais/commentaires/9_6_2001_francais.pdf>.

[23] Sentence définitive, para. 93.

de la Convention de Washington.[24] Il n'empêchera cependant pas une reprise du débat, notamment dans le prolongement de la sentence analogue rendue dans l'affaire *Wena Hotels c. Egypte*[25] (qui, à l'inverse, a ordonné le versement d'intérêts composés malgré les lois égyptiennes en sens contraire). Ce débat, qui a eu lieu parallèlement aux délibérations du Tribunal et à la rédaction de sa sentence définitive, se poursuit encore.[26] Cet attendu ne renversera pas non plus le consensus de plus en plus marqué depuis une décennie, selon lequel, dans presque tous les cas, seuls des intérêts composés permettent de réparer adéquatement le préjudice financier subi par le demandeur. C'est cette idée qui fut finalement retenue dans l'article 49, paragraphe 3, de la loi anglaise de 1996 sur l'arbitrage.[27] Quant aux tribunaux internationaux, une tendance de plus en plus nette se dégage, érigeant en principe de droit international l'octroi d'intérêts composés, surtout lorsque le comportement du défendeur est répréhensible.[28] Cette règle n'a rien d'injuste sur le plan économique et les banques n'auront certainement pas à s'en plaindre. Il ne fait aucun doute que si les trois demandeurs avaient dû de l'argent à la Banque, celle-ci aurait ajouté à cette dette des intérêts non pas simples, mais composés, conformément aux usages bancaires.[29] Il s'agit là aussi d'une loi de la

---

[24] Convention pour le règlement des différends relatifs aux investissements entre États et ressortissants d'autres États, Washington, 14 octobre 1966, Nations Unies, *Recueil des traités*, vol. 575, p. 159.

[25] *Wena Hotels c. la République arabe d'Égypte*, sentence CIRDI, 8 décembre 2000 (Ibrahim Fadlallah; Don Wallace et Monroe Leigh); et décision du Comité *ad hoc* du CIRDI, 28 janvier 2002 (K.D. Kerameus; Andreas Bucher et Francisco Orrego Vicuòa), 41 I.L.M. pp. 896 & 933 (2002).

[26] Voir notamment Emmanuel Gaillard & Yas Banifatemi, *The Meaning of "and" in Article 42(1), Second Sentence, of the Washington Convention: The Role of International Law in the ICSID Choice of Law Process*, 18 ICSID REV. – FOREIGN INVESTMENT LAW JOURNAL p. 375 (2003); et Eric Schwartz, *Finality at What Cost? The Decision of the Ad Hoc Committee in Wena Hotels v. Egypt*, *in* ANNULMENT OF ICSID AWARDS p. 68 et s. (E. Gaillard & Y. Banifatemi, dir. De publ., International Arbitration Institute, 2004).

[27] La *Law Commission* d'Angleterre et du Pays de Galles a proposé d'élargir les pouvoirs des arbitres pour leur permettre d'ordonner aux juridictions anglaises d'octroyer des intérêts composés ; voir sa note de consultation n° 167 (2002) et son rapport n° 287 (2004). Sur la genèse de ce texte au regard du droit et de la pratique de l'arbitrage commercial en Angleterre, voir l'article rédigé par l'auteur, intitulé *Whose Arbitration Is It Anyway: The Parties or the Arbitration Tribunal – An Interesting Question?*, *in* THE LEADING ARBITRATORS' GUIDE TO INTERNATIONAL ARBITRATION pp. 354–367 (Newman & Hill, dir. de publ., 2004).

[28] Stephen Schwebel, *Compound Interest in International Law*, Vol. 2, numéro 5 TRANSNATIONAL DISPUTE MANAGEMENT p. 1 (2005); et RAYMOND DOAK BISHOP, JAMES CRAWFORD & MICHAEL REISMAN, FOREIGN INVESTMENT DISPUTES p. 1373 et s. (2005). Ce n'est pas le fruit du hasard si, au cours des cinq dernières années, la doctrine est de plus en plus abondante en ce qui concerne les intérêts composés.

[29] En droit anglais, un tel usage bancaire est reconnu depuis longtemps: voir *National Bank of Greece v. Pinios Shipping Co. (No. 1)* [1990] 1 AC 637.

nature, et ce qui est bon pour l'un devrait être bon pour l'autre – pas en l'espèce, cependant.

Toutefois, l'élément le plus intéressant de cette sentence définitive est le raisonnement du Tribunal concernant la demande reconventionnelle fondée sur la violation par First Eagle de la convention d'arbitrage lorsque celui-ci a saisi le juge à New York. Le Tribunal a reconnu que les juridictions new-yorkaises pouvaient constituer pour First Eagle une voie de recours lui permettant de contester la validité de la clause compromissoire, mais qu'« aucun impératif juridique n'impos[ait] le recours à ladite procédure ».[30] Il s'agissait pour First Eagle d'un simple droit ou d'une simple option, mais pas d'une obligation et, comme le prévoit le droit national, ce droit ou cette option ne pouvait être utilisé pour justifier la violation d'une obligation qui relevait du droit international. En vertu de la convention d'arbitrage qui s'imposait à First Eagle, le Tribunal jouissait d'une compétence exclusive pour se prononcer sur sa propre compétence, et une décision contraire des juridictions new-yorkaises ne pouvait préjuger la décision du Tribunal sur l'existence ou l'étendue de sa compétence. Le Tribunal a également écarté le moyen tiré par la Banque de l'inexistence du Tribunal à l'époque où les procédures judiciaires avaient été engagées, au motif qu'un « mécanisme praticable était prévu pour la constitution du tribunal ». Sur ce point, le fait que la demande de mesures conservatoires formulée par First Eagle ait si piteusement échoué n'est sans doute pas sans importance au vu des éléments du dossier. Si les juridictions fédérales de New York avaient prononcé ces mesures, à une époque où le Tribunal n'existait pas et ne pouvait statuer en urgence sur cette demande,[31] le Tribunal aurait-il encore jugé que cette demande constituait une violation de la convention d'arbitrage ? Au vu du raisonnement du Tribunal, la réponse n'est pas tout à fait évidente (car la question ne s'était pas posée), mais on peut vraisemblablement penser que oui.

---

[30] Sentence définitive, para. 116.

[31] L'article 21 du Règlement de procédure (voir *supra*, note 7) prévoyait que le président du Tribunal ou tout autre arbitre désigné par le président pouvait prononcer des mesures conservatoires, et avait notamment le pouvoir d'exiger du demandeur des garanties relatives aux coûts de telles mesures. Ce pouvoir impliquait la désignation préalable du président du Tribunal et, quoi qu'il en soit, ces règles étaient postérieures à la demande de mesures conservatoires formulée par First Eagle à New York le 8 janvier 2001. Toutefois, ce problème pratique ne se posera plus: le Tribunal a été reconstitué en tant qu'organe permanent (pour une durée de cinq ans), comme l'a confirmé la lettre datée du 19 septembre 2006 adressée à la CPA par le ministre français des affaires étrangères au nom de l'ensemble des Etats intéressés.

Ayant pris fin à La Haye en 2003, ces procédures d'arbitrage trouvèrent leur épilogue en France en 2004, lorsque la Cour d'appel de Paris, infirmant un jugement du tribunal de commerce de Paris, reconnut elle aussi la validité de la convention d'arbitrage énoncée dans les Statuts de la Banque.[32] La juridiction de première instance avait jugé que plus de 200 anciens actionnaires privés de la Banque pouvaient assigner la Banque devant les juridictions françaises au motif que, n'étant plus désormais actionnaires de celle-ci, aucun d'eux ne demeurait lié par l'article 54 des Statuts de la Banque, dans lequel était énoncée la convention d'arbitrage. La Cour d'appel, en application du principe de validité de la convention d'arbitrage (qui avait été initialement acceptée par ces anciens actionnaires et n'avait pas été modifiée par la suite) et écartant les autres moyens fondés sur l'ordre public international, a déclaré que les juridictions françaises n'avaient pas compétence sur le fond et a invité les demandeurs à utiliser la voie de l'arbitrage qui leur était ouverte à La Haye.

*

En conclusion, on peut voir, par ces deux sentences, que l'arbitrage international permet de gagner sur tous les tableaux. Bien que parsemé d'embûches sur le plan procédural et sur le fond, cet arbitrage parvint à terme assez rapidement (deux années de procédure en tout, avec seulement cinq jours d'audiences), les frais étaient relativement peu élevés (ceux de l'arbitrage s'élevaient à environ 810 000 euros, somme à laquelle il faut ajouter les propres frais des parties) mais, avant tout, la décision rendue était équitable, comme le montrent à l'évidence la qualité, la minutie et la limpidité du raisonnement du Tribunal. En outre, l'autre solution qui consistait à saisir le juge national de ce différend, surtout si elle avait donné lieu à une action collective, eût été bien moins efficace à presque tous les égards, sans même qu'il faille rappeler les procédures multipartites avortées devant les juridictions de New York et de Paris, et encore moins les difficultés posées récemment par le litige relatif à la BCCI devant les juridictions anglaises.

---

[32] *Madame Alhinc et al c/ S.A. Banque de France & S.A. Banque des Règlements Internationaux:* arrêt de la Cour d'appel de Paris daté du 25 février 2004, infirmant le jugement du tribunal de commerce de Paris daté du 17 mars 2003. Sur la question de la jurisprudence *Dutco*, la Cour d'appel a souligné que les cinq arbitres avaient tous été nommés par des Etats et non par leur banque centrale en qualité d'actionnaire de la Banque, ni par la Banque elle-même. Pourvoi rejeté par la Cour de cassation (Cass. 1re civ., 23 mai 2006, pourvoi n° 04-13800).

COUR PERMANENTE D'ARBITRAGE

TRIBUNAL ARBITRAL ÉTABLI CONFORMÉMENT
À L'ARTICLE XV DE L'ACCORD SIGNÉ À
LA HAYE LE 20 JANVIER 1930

Prof. W. Michael Reisman
Prof. Dr. Jochen A. Frowein
Prof. Dr. Mathias Krafft
Prof. Dr. Paul Lagarde
Prof. Dr. Albert Jan van den Berg

Phyllis Hamilton, Secrétaire
Cour Permanente d'Arbitrage, Greffe

DR. HORST REINECCIUS, DEMANDEUR (DEMANDE N°1)
FIRST EAGLE SOGEN FUNDS, INC., DEMANDERESSE (DEMANDE N° 2)
M. PIERRE MATHIEU ET LA SOCIÉTÉ DE CONCOURS HIPPIQUE
DE LA CHÂTRE, DEMANDEURS (DEMANDE N° 3)
-CONTRE-
BANQUE DES RÈGLEMENTS INTERNATIONAUX, DÉFENDERESSE

SENTENCE PARTIELLE
CONCERNANT LA LICÉITÉ DE LA REPRISE DES ACTIONS DÉTENUES PAR DES PERSONNES PRIVÉES DÉCIDÉE LE 8 JANVIER 2001 ET LES NORMES APPLICABLES POUR L'ÉVALUATION DESDITES ACTIONS

La Haye, le 22 novembre 2002

Table des matières

CHAPITRE I – INTRODUCTION

1. Le 20 janvier 1930, les gouvernements de l'Allemagne, de la Belgique, de la Grande-Bretagne, de l'Italie, du Japon et de la Suisse ont conclu à La Haye la Convention concernant la Banque des Règlements Internationaux. La Convention comprend la Charte constitutive et les Statuts de la Banque (ci-après, la Convention, la Charte constitutive et les Statuts de la Banque sont désignés collectivement par les termes "Instruments constitutifs"). La Banque des Règlements Internationaux (ci-après la "Banque" ou la "BRI") est constituée, en vertu de l'article 1 des Statuts, sous la forme d'une "société anonyme par actions" et a pour objet, en vertu de l'article 3,

> de favoriser la coopération des banques centrales et de fournir des facilités additionnelles pour les opérations financières internationales; et d'agir comme mandataire (trustee) ou comme agent en ce qui concerne les règlements financiers internationaux qui lui sont confiés en vertu d'accords passés avec les Parties intéressées.

2. L'article 10 des Statuts stipule que, en prenant les dispositions nécessaires pour les souscriptions du capital de la Banque, "le Conseil [d'administration de la Banque] doit tenir compte de l'intérêt qui s'attache à faire participer à la Banque le plus grand nombre possible de banques centrales."

3. Les actions ne confèrent pas de droit dans la conduite des affaires de la Banque. L'article 15 des Statuts stipule notamment que:

> La propriété d'une action de la Banque ne comporte aucun droit de vote ni de représentation aux Assemblées générales. Les droits de représentation et de vote sont exercés, en proportion du nombre des actions souscrites dans chaque pays, par la banque centrale de ce pays ou par la personne désignée par elle.

4. Étant donné que certaines banques centrales n'étaient pas en mesure, à l'époque de la constitution de la Banque, de souscrire et de détenir des actions et que d'autres auraient trouvé lourde la charge financière liée à l'acquisition et à la détention d'actions, l'article 16 des Statuts dispose que "[t]out établissement ou tout groupe de banques ayant souscrit des actions peut émettre ou faire émettre dans le public les actions souscrites

par lui." En vertu de cette possibilité, la Federal Reserve des États-Unis, la Banque centrale française et la Banque centrale belge ont émis la totalité ou une partie des actions qu'elles avaient souscrites pour les vendre à des personnes privées. À l'époque de la constitution de la Banque, "une part importante des actions"[1] était détenue par des personnes privées. Les actions de l'émission française ont été négociées sur le marché au comptant de Paris; les actions belges et américaines ont été négociées sur le Nebensegment/marché annexe de Zurich.[2]

5. En 2000, 529.165 actions de la Banque étaient émises, dont 72.648 étaient détenues par des actionnaires privés, c'est-à-dire 13,73% des actions de la Banque. Le 11 septembre 2000, le Conseil d'administration de la Banque a proposé de réserver à l'avenir aux banques centrales le droit de détenir des actions de la Banque et, à cet effet, de convoquer une Assemblée générale extraordinaire à la date du 8 janvier 2001 pour modifier les Statuts, de manière à exclure les actionnaires privés contre paiement d'une indemnité de 16.000 francs suisse, indemnité qui, selon le Conseil, représentait une prime de 95% pour les actions américaines, 105% pour les actions belges et 155% pour les actions françaises. Le montant de l'indemnité a été fixé sur recommandation de J.P. Morgan, qui avait préparé un rapport pour la Banque.

6. Trois demandeurs qui ont contesté le montant de l'indemnité, dont un a également contesté la licéité de la reprise par la Banque des actions détenues par des personnes privées, ont saisi le Tribunal arbitral établi conformément à l'article XV de l'Accord concernant le règlement complet et définitif de la question des réparations, signé à La Haye le 20 janvier 1930 (voir annexe B à la présente sentence).

---

[1] Henry H. Schloss, The Bank for International Settlements, p. 40 (North-Holland Publishing Company, Amsterdam, 1958).

[2] "En février 1956, les cours moyens à la Bourse de Paris des actions de la Banque des Règlements Internationaux de l'émission française s'élevaient à 88.140 francs français; les cours non-officiels de la Bourse de Bruxelles en février 1956 étaient de 10.050 et 10.100 francs belges pour les émissions américaine et belge respectivement. Source: Banque des Règlements Internationaux," *Id.*, note de bas de page. 7.

CHAPITRE II – HISTORIQUE DE LA PROCÉDURE

7. Le présent Tribunal concernant la Banque des Règlements Internationaux (ci-après le "Tribunal") a été établi conformément à l'article XV de l'Accord concernant le règlement complet et définitif de la question des réparations, signé à La Haye le 20 janvier 1930 (ci-après l'"Accord de La Haye de 1930").

8. L'article XV de l'Accord de La Haye de 1930 stipule que:

> 1. Tout différend, soit entre les gouvernements signataires du présent accord, soit entre un ou plusieurs d'entre eux, et la banque des règlements internationaux au sujet de l'interprétation et de l'application du nouveau plan, sera soumis, sous réserve des dispositions spéciales prévues aux annexes I, V*bis*, VI*bis* et IX, pour décision définitive, à un tribunal arbitral de cinq membres nommés pour 5 ans, dont un, qui remplira les fonctions de président, devra être citoyen des États-Unis d'Amérique, dont deux devront être ressortissants d'États ayant été neutres pendant la dernière guerre, et dont les deux derniers seront respectivement ressortissants de l'Allemagne et de l'une des puissances créancières de l'Allemagne.
>
> Pour la première période de cinq ans, à dater de la mise en exécution du nouveau plan, ce tribunal sera composé des cinq membres qui constituent actuellement le tribunal arbitral institué par l'accord de Londres du 30 août 1924.
>
> 2. Il sera pourvu, soit au renouvellement des membres du tribunal à l'expiration de chaque période, soit à toute vacance qui pourrait se produire en cours de période: en ce qui concerne le membre ayant la nationalité de l'une des puissances créancières de l'Allemagne, par le gouvernement français qui s'entendra préalablement à cet effet avec les gouvernements belge, britannique, italien, japonais; en ce qui concerne le membre ayant la nationalité allemande, par le gouvernement allemand, et, en ce qui concerne les trois autres membres, par les six gouvernements précédemment mentionnés agissant d'un commun accord, ou, faute de cet accord, par le président en exercice de la cour permanente de justice internationale.

3. Dans tous les cas où, soit l'Allemagne, soit la banque sera partie demanderesse ou défenderesse, si le président du tribunal estimait, à la requête d'un ou plusieurs d'entre les gouvernements créanciers parties au litige, que ce ou ces gouvernements sont principalement intéressés, il invitera ce ou ces gouvernements à désigner, d'un commun accord, si plusieurs gouvernements sont en cause, un membre qui remplacera dans le tribunal le membre nommé par le gouvernement français.

   Au cas où, lors d'un différend entre deux ou plusieurs gouvernements créanciers, le tribunal ne compterait pas sur le siège un ressortissant d'un ou de plusieurs d'entre ces gouvernements, ce ou ces gouvernements auraient le droit de désigner chacun un membre qui siégera à cette occasion. Le président, s'il estime que certains de ces gouvernements ont un intérêt commun au litige, les invitera à désigner un seul membre; toutes les fois que, par l'effet de cette disposition, le tribunal sera composé d'un nombre pair de membres, le président aura voix prépondérante.

4. Avant toute décision finale et sans préjudice du fond, le président du tribunal ou, en cas d'empêchement de sa part, dans un cas quelconque, tout autre membre désigné par lui, pourra, sur requête de la partie la plus diligente, ordonner des mesures conservatoires destinées à garantir les droits des parties.

5. En recourant au tribunal, les parties peuvent toujours se mettre d'accord pour soumettre leur différend au président ou à un des membres choisi comme arbitre unique.

6. Sauf dispositions spéciales prévues au compromis qui ne sauraient en aucun cas porter atteinte au droit d'intervention d'une tierce partie, la procédure du tribunal ou celle de l'arbitre unique sera réglée conformément à l'annexe XII.

   Ces règles de procédure s'appliquent également, sous la même réserve, à toute instance devant le tribunal prévue aux annexes du présent accord.

> 7. Faute d'entente sur les termes du compromis, toute partie pourra saisir directement et par simple requête le tribunal qui statuera, fût-ce par défaut, sur toute question dont il sera de la sorte saisi.
>
> 8. Le tribunal et l'arbitre unique sont juges de leur compétence. Toutefois, au cas où, dans un conflit s'élevant entre gouvernements, la question de la compétence serait soulevée, elle sera, à la demande de l'une des parties, déférée à la cour permanente de justice internationale.
>
> 9. Les présentes dispositions seront dûment acceptées par la banque en vue du règlement de tout différend pouvant surgir entre elle et un ou plusieurs des gouvernements signataires en ce qui concerne l'interprétation ou l'application de ses statuts ou du nouveau plan.

9. En conformité avec les procédures décrites à l'article XV de l'Accord de La Haye de 1930, les gouvernements belge, français, allemand, italien et britannique ont désigné les cinq membres du Tribunal pour une durée de cinq ans. Le gouvernement français, en accord avec les gouvernements belge, italien et britannique, a désigné le Président du Tribunal.[3] Les procédures du Tribunal sont décrites à l'annexe XII de l'Accord de La Haye de 1930 (le texte intégral est joint à l'annexe A de la présente sentence), qui comprend les dispositions du chapitre III de la Convention de la Haye de 1907 pour le règlement pacifique des conflits internationaux, dans la mesure où elles ne sont pas modifiées par l'Accord de La Haye de 1930.

10. Les membres du Tribunal, désignés conformément à l'article XV de l'Accord de La Haye de 1930, sont Prof. W. Michael Reisman (États-Unis d'Amérique), président, Prof. Dr. Jochen A. Frowein (Allemagne), Prof. Dr. Mathias Krafft (Suisse), Prof. Dr. Paul Lagarde (France) et Prof. Dr. Albert Jan van den Berg (Pays-Bas). Le 17 janvier 2001, le Tribunal a désigné Mme Phyllis Hamilton de la Cour permanente

---

[3] Le Japon a renoncé à tous ses droits en vertu de l'Accord avec l'Allemagne du 20 janvier 1930, y compris les annexes audit accord, voir article 8, point c, du Traité de Paix du 8 septembre 1951.

d'Arbitrage (ci-après la "CPA") en tant que Secrétaire et le Bureau international de la CPA en tant que Greffe.

11. Le présent différend entre les demandeurs susnommés et la Banque concerne les Statuts de la Banque des Règlements Internationaux du 20 janvier 1930, modifiés au 8 janvier 2001 (ci-après les "Statuts").

12. L'article 54, paragraphe 1, des Statuts stipule que:

> Si un différend vient à s'élever quant à l'interprétation ou à l'application des Statuts de la Banque, soit entre la Banque, d'une part, et telle banque centrale, établissement financier ou autre banque visé aux Statuts, d'autre part, soit entre la Banque et ses actionnaires, ce différend sera soumis, pour décision définitive, au Tribunal prévu par l'Accord de La Haye de janvier 1930.

13. Par une notification d'arbitrage et une requête du 7 mars 2001, Dr. Horst Reineccius (ci-après "Dr. Reineccius") a porté à la connaissance du Tribunal son différend avec la Banque. Dr. Reineccius a fait valoir que le montant de l'indemnité versée pour ses actions de la Banque, qui avaient été annulées lorsque la Banque avait modifié ses Statuts lors de l'Assemblée générale extraordinaire du 8 janvier 2001, était inférieur au montant auquel il avait droit (demande n° 1).

14. Le 23 mars 2001, le Tribunal, conformément à l'article 54 des Statuts, à l'article XV et à l'annexe XII de l'Accord de La Haye de 1930 (qui comprend les dispositions du chapitre III de la Convention de La Haye de 1907 pour le règlement pacifique des conflits internationaux, dans la mesure où elles ne sont pas modifiées par l'accord de La Haye de 1930), a adopté le règlement d'arbitrage entre la Banque et des Parties privées (ci-après "règlement d'arbitrage"). Conformément à l'article 10, paragraphe 1, du règlement d'arbitrage, le Tribunal siège à La Haye.

15. Le 25 juillet 2001, M. Reginald Howe, ancien actionnaire privé de la Banque, a demandé au Greffe des informations concernant les anciens actionnaires privés de la Banque. Par lettre du 30 juillet 2001, le Greffe a invité la Banque à commenter la demande de M. Howe. Par lettre du 2 août 2001, le conseil de la Banque a répondu que le type d'informations

demandées par M. Howe serait examiné lors de la réunion préparatoire des Parties. Le conseil de la Banque a ajouté qu'en vertu du règlement d'arbitrage, M. Howe ne pourrait participer à la réunion préparatoire et obtenir le type d'informations qu'il souhaite que s'il introduisait une notification d'arbitrage et une requête contre la Banque. Par lettre du 2 août 2001, le Greffe a invité M. Howe à commenter la lettre de la Banque.

16. Par lettre du 17 août 2001 adressée à la Secrétaire du Tribunal, M. Howe a répondu en demandant au Tribunal "des conseils, éclaircissements ou informations". M. Howe a fait observer qu'il était informé de la procédure pour participer à l'arbitrage, mais qu'il n'avait pas l'intention à cette date de soumettre une notification d'arbitrage. Le 21 août 2001, le Greffe a invité la Banque à faire connaître son opinion sur les nouvelles demandes formulées par M. Howe dans la lettre. Le 23 août 2001, la Banque a répondu qu'il n'était pas correct que M. Howe demande une mesure exceptionnelle *ex parte* et l'accès à des informations, alors qu'il ne se soumettait pas à la juridiction du Tribunal par la présentation d'une notification d'arbitrage.

17. Le 31 août 2001, le Tribunal a rendu une ordonnance de procédure par laquelle il a rejeté la demande de M. Howe tendant à être autorisé à participer à la réunion préparatoire des Parties sans soumettre, comme il se doit, une notification d'arbitrage. Cependant, l'ordonnance a chargé la Secrétaire du Tribunal de rendre accessible sur le site Internet de la CPA certaines informations concernant les réclamations formulées par d'anciens actionnaires privés contre la Banque, ainsi que le calendrier des procédures actuellement pendantes devant le Tribunal.

18. Par une notification d'arbitrage du 31 août 2001, le demandeur First Eagle SoGen Funds, Inc. (ci-après "First Eagle") a initié une procédure contre la Banque, faisant valoir que le montant de l'indemnité perçue pour ses actions de la Banque, qui avaient été reprises par décision de l'Assemblée générale extraordinaire du 8 janvier 2001, était inférieur au montant auquel elle avait droit (demande n° 2).

19. Le 7 septembre 2001, conformément à l'article 12 du règlement d'arbitrage, le Tribunal a organisé une réunion préparatoire, au cours de

laquelle il a invité les Parties à se consulter à propos du calendrier de la procédure, des conditions d'une ordonnance homologuant un accord de confidentialité et de la production des pièces requises pertinentes pour les questions à soumettre à l'arbitrage et à remettre un rapport sur ces discussions au plus tard le 21 septembre 2001.

20. Le 10 octobre 2001, M. Pierre Mathieu a soumis au Tribunal une notification d'arbitrage, alléguant que la Banque avait agi de façon illicite en procédant au rachat forcé de ses actions et de l'action détenue par la Société Hippique de La Châtre (tous deux ci-après dénommés "M. Mathieu") (demande n° 3).

21. Le 11 octobre 2001, le Tribunal, après avoir examiné les lettres des Parties concernant la répartition des frais et des sommes à consigner pour l'arbitrage, a rendu une ordonnance concernant les frais, stipulant:

> 1. La Banque déposera sans attendre la moitié des frais estimés de la procédure arbitrale tels que détaillés dans le tableau soumis aux Parties lors de la première réunion préparatoire.
>
> 2. Chacun des demandeurs déposera sans attendre une somme calculée en proportion de sa part respective (sur la base du nombre de parts détenues par chaque demandeur) dans la moitié restante des frais estimés de la procédure arbitrale. En outre, la même formule fondée sur le nombre d'actions détenues par des actionnaires privés sera utilisée pour procéder à la répartition des frais devant être pris en charge par tout nouveau demandeur dans la procédure arbitrale, tout en prenant en considération la possibilité que la participation à la procédure de Parties supplémentaires entraîne une augmentation des frais de la procédure arbitrale.

22. Dans son ordonnance concernant les frais, le Tribunal a pris note du fait que le 5 octobre 2001, la Banque avait fait état de sa position à l'égard de la répartition des frais entre l'ensemble des actionnaires privés dans le cas où ceux-ci bénéficieraient des effets d'une sentence rendue en faveur des demandeurs dans la présente procédure. Dans ce cas, les frais à prendre en charge par les premier et deuxième demandeurs pourraient

être réduits proportionnellement. Le Tribunal s'est également réservé le droit d'ordonner le dépôt de sommes supplémentaires si les circonstances entraînaient une augmentation des frais d'arbitrage (les circonstances envisagées sont notamment, mais non exclusivement, la complexité des questions soulevées dans la requête ou le mémoire en défense, le temps nécessaire pour procéder aux dépositions de témoins ou à l'analyse de rapports d'experts entendus comme témoins, l'augmentation de la durée des audiences ou la nécessité d'organiser davantage de réunions qu'il n'en est prévu actuellement).

23. Le 17 octobre 2001, le Tribunal a rendu l'ordonnance de procédure n° 1 homologuant un accord entre les Parties, qui comprend un calendrier pour le dépôt des conclusions, mentionnant notamment les conditions de date et de fondement de la requête de chaque demandeur, une demande de production de pièces et une proposition d'ordonnance relative au calendrier de la procédure, comprenant la soumission de mémoires, préalables aux audiences, concernant le droit, les faits et les moyens de preuve invoqués à l'appui des demandes. L'ordonnance enjoint à la Banque de soumettre une défense, une réponse à la demande de production de pièces et une réponse à la proposition d'ordonnance relative au calendrier. L'ordonnance prévoit par ailleurs que le Tribunal organisera une réunion ou une réunion par téléphone aux fins d'entendre les Parties sur les points litigieux découlant de la demande de production de pièces et de la proposition d'ordonnance relative au calendrier et afin d'ordonner ou programmer d'autres étapes de procédure comme il le jugera approprié.

24. En outre, l'ordonnance de procédure n° 1 charge la Secrétaire de mettre sur le site Internet du Greffe un avis invitant les demandeurs potentiels désireux de voir leurs demandes soumises à une procédure se déroulant en coordination avec celles déjà engagées à la date du 17 octobre 2001 (date de la présente ordonnance), à soumettre leurs requêtes pour le 15 novembre 2001. L'ordonnance précise que cette disposition ne vaut pas consentement à toute forme de consolidation ou de coordination avec des requêtes qui seraient soumises à la date de la présente ordonnance ou des requêtes qui pourraient être soumises avant le 15 novembre 2001. L'ordonnance relève que dans le cas de requêtes additionnelles, la Banque se réserve le droit de demander un délai supplémentaire pour

soumettre sa défense. Le demandeur First Eagle se réserve le droit de s'opposer à une telle demande de prorogation de délais.

25. Le 17 octobre 2001, les Parties ont soumis conjointement un accord de confidentialité applicable à la production des pièces. Sous réserve de cet accord de confidentialité, la Banque a remis à First Eagle le rapport établi par J.P. Morgan, décrit dans la note adressée aux actionnaires privés datée du 15 septembre 2000.

26. Le 7 février 2002, le Tribunal a rendu l'ordonnance de procédure n° 2 homologuant un accord entre les Parties, faisant savoir que First Eagle avait soumis à la date du 12 novembre 2001, conformément à l'ordonnance de procédure n° 1, une requête contre la Banque et une demande de production de pièces; en vertu de ladite ordonnance, la Banque a soumis sa défense et une réponse à la demande de production de pièces à la date du 14 janvier 2002, ainsi qu'une demande de production de documents à fournir par First Eagle. First Eagle et la Banque ont convenu par ailleurs que pour le 11 février 2002 au plus tard, First Eagle présenterait une note en réponse à la demande de production de pièces formulée par la Banque et que pour le 20 février 2002 au plus tard, la Banque présenterait une note concernant la réponse de First Eagle à la demande de production de pièces formulée par la Banque. Les Parties ont convenu que le Tribunal se réunirait avec les Parties le 26 février 2002 aux fins d'établir l'acte de mission; lors de cette réunion, le Tribunal entendrait également les Parties concernant les questions de procédure non réglées.

27. Le Tribunal s'est réuni avec les Parties et leurs conseils le 26 février 2002 à La Haye aux fins d'établir l'acte de mission conformément à l'article 12 du règlement d'arbitrage entre la Banque et des parties privées (entré en vigueur le 23 mars 2001).

28. À la réunion du 26 février, le Président a mentionné une lettre de la Banque du 22 février 2002 et une réponse du cabinet juridique Freshfields à Paris du 25 février 2002 concernant des questions ayant trait à un possible conflit d'intérêts, dans le cas où le conseil du cabinet Freshfields de Paris représenterait M. Mathieu. Le conseil de M. Mathieu s'est entretenu avec le conseil de la Banque et le Tribunal au sujet de la

représentation de la Banque d'Angleterre par le cabinet Freshfields et de l'association antérieure du professeur van den Berg avec le cabinet Freshfields à Amsterdam. Le professeur van den Berg a fait savoir que l'association avait pris fin. Le conseil de la Banque a alors signalé que la Banque se réjouissait de ce qu'il n'existait aucun conflit d'intérêts.

29. Le 5 mars 2002, le Tribunal a rendu une ordonnance de procédure n° 3 concernant l'acte de mission. Dans ladite ordonnance, le Tribunal a indiqué que les Parties avaient déclaré ne pas soulever d'exceptions d'incompétence, mais que les questions suivantes continuaient à opposer toutes les Parties ou certaines d'entre elles:

(i) la licéité de la reprise forcée des actions, y compris les procédures selon lesquelles elle a été effectuée et l'étendue possible des conséquences d'une constatation d'illicéité pour tous ceux qui étaient actionnaires privés au 8 janvier 2001;

(ii) la détermination des normes applicables à l'évaluation des actions ayant fait l'objet d'une reprise forcée;

(iii) l'application aux actions ayant fait l'objet d'une reprise forcée, des normes visées au point (ii) ci-dessus.

Le Tribunal a estimé qu'il était plus expédient d'examiner dans une première phase les deux premières questions et de différer l'examen de la troisième question à une deuxième et dernière phase, si cela s'avérait nécessaire.

30. Bien que la question (i) ci-dessus ait été soulevée uniquement par M. Mathieu et la Banque, tous deux ont affirmé qu'une constatation d'illicéité compromettrait l'opération de reprise des actions et aurait des conséquences pour tous ceux qui étaient actionnaires au 8 janvier 2001. Une constatation d'illicéité de la reprise forcée des actions pourrait donc avoir des conséquences pour tous les demandeurs. Partant,

(i) le Tribunal a invité M. Mathieu et la Banque à traiter de toutes les questions qu'ils estimaient pertinentes au regard de leurs allégations concernant la licéité de l'opération de reprise, y compris ses conséquences pour ceux qui étaient actionnaires au 8 janvier 2001;

(ii) le Tribunal a invité Dr. Reineccius et First Eagle à traiter de toutes les questions qu'ils estimaient pertinentes au regard de l'étendue des conséquences éventuelles d'une constatation d'illicéité de l'opération de reprise pour ceux qui étaient actionnaires au 8 janvier 2001;

(iii) toutes les Parties ont été invitées à traiter de toutes les questions qu'elles estimaient pertinentes au regard de la nature et de l'étendue des droits des actionnaires privés et des normes applicables à l'évaluation des actions ayant fait l'objet d'une reprise forcée.

31. L'ordonnance de procédure n° 3 ordonne en outre (1) que M. Mathieu soumette une requête consolidée au plus tard le 12 mars 2002; (2) que les trois demandeurs soumettent leurs mémoires au plus tard le 20 avril 2002; (3) que la défenderesse soumette un contre-mémoire au plus tard le 15 juillet 2002; et (4) que les audiences dans la présente phase d'arbitrage aient lieu au Palais de la Paix à La Haye durant la semaine du 26 août 2002.

32. Le Tribunal a fait droit aux demandes suivantes, formulées par First Eagle, de communication de pièces par la Banque pour le 15 mars 2002:

(i) pièces concernant l'offre faite par la Banque d'acheter les actions détenues par des actionnaires privés en 1975 ou aux environs de cette même année, y compris les notes d'information relatives à cette offre et autres communications aux actionnaires, et les évaluations et autres méthodes ou analyses envisagées par la Banque pour fixer le prix à payer pour ces actions;

(ii) tous les accords de souscription relatifs à l'émission par la Banque de nouvelles actions depuis 1969;

(iii) toutes les pièces relatives à la fixation par la Banque des prix de souscription pour des actions émises depuis 1969, y compris toutes évaluations;

(iv) toutes les pièces communiquées aux souscripteurs d'actions depuis 1969, dans la mesure où il s'agit de notes d'information, de prospectus, d'offres de souscription et d'états financiers;

(v) toutes les pièces, depuis 1990, ayant trait à l'évaluation par la Banque des actions de la Banque;

(vi) toutes les pièces, depuis 1990, ayant trait à d'éventuels transferts de ses actions par la Banque, y compris le prix desdits transferts;

(vii) toutes les versions des Statuts de la Banque, tels que modifiés, depuis et y compris la version originale adoptée en 1930 ou autour de cette date.

33. Le Tribunal a constaté que Dr. Reineccius, M. Mathieu et la Banque avaient déclaré ne pas soumettre de demandes de communication de pièces à cette phase de la procédure.

34. Conformément au point D.5 de l'ordonnance de procédure n° 3 (acte de mission) du 5 mars 2002, les Parties ont convenu de modifier le calendrier pour le dépôt de leurs conclusions, visé aux points D.2 et D.3 de ladite ordonnance. C'est pourquoi le 1er avril 2002, le Tribunal a rendu l'ordonnance de procédure n° 4 homologuant un accord entre les Parties, qui stipule:

(i) First Eagle doit soumettre son mémoire au plus tard le 6 mai 2002;

(ii) M. Mathieu doit soumettre son mémoire au plus tard le 13 mai 2002;

(iii) Dr. Reineccius doit soumettre son mémoire ou des suppléments au mémoire de First Eagle au plus tard le 13 mai 2002;

(iv) la défenderesse (la Banque) doit soumettre son contre-mémoire au plus tard le 22 juillet 2002.

35. Le Tribunal a par ailleurs fait savoir qu'après avoir reçu, conformément aux points D.1 à E.3 de l'ordonnance de procédure n° 3, la requête consolidée de M. Mathieu à la date du 12 mars 2002 et sa demande de production de pièces du 20 mars 2002, ainsi que la réponse de la Banque à la date du 26 mars 2002, le Tribunal ferait droit aux demandes suivantes, formulées par M. Mathieu, de communication de pièces par la Banque pour le 5 avril 2002 au plus tard:

(i) pièces concernant l'offre faite par la Banque d'acheter les actions détenues par des actionnaires privés en 1975 ou aux environs de cette même année, y compris les notes d'information relatives à cette offre et autres communications aux actionnaires, et les évaluations et autres méthodes ou analyses envisagées par la Banque pour fixer le prix à payer pour ces actions;

(ii) tous les accords de souscription relatifs à l'émission par la Banque de nouvelles actions depuis 1969;

(iii) toutes les pièces relatives à la fixation par la Banque des prix de souscription pour des actions émises depuis 1969, y compris toutes évaluations;

(iv) toutes les pièces communiquées aux souscripteurs d'actions depuis 1969, dans la mesure où il s'agit de notes d'information, de prospectus, d'offres de souscription et d'états financiers;

(v) toutes les pièces, depuis 1990, ayant trait à l'évaluation par la Banque des actions de la Banque;

(vi) toutes les pièces, depuis 1990, ayant trait à d'éventuels transferts de ses actions par la Banque, y compris le prix desdits transferts;

(vii) toutes les versions des Statuts de la Banque, tels que modifiés, depuis et y compris la version originale adoptée en 1930 ou autour de cette date;

(viii) les pièces décrites au paragraphe 2, point h, de la requête de M. Mathieu du 20 mars 2002.

36. Le Tribunal a reçu en avril 2002 des lettres des Parties concernant la production de pièces au cours de la procédure d'arbitrage. Le 3 mai 2002, le Tribunal a rendu une ordonnance de procédure n° 5 (Communication de pièces entre les demandeurs, accès aux archives de la BRI, confidentialité des documents), faisant savoir que les Parties avaient convenu que les demandeurs se communiqueraient mutuellement les pièces et enverraient des copies à la Banque. Néanmoins, toutes les communications demeuraient régies par les dispositions des Accords de Confidentialité conclus conformément aux dispositions du paragraphe 4 de l'ordonnance de procédure n° 1 (homologuant un accord entre les Parties) entre la Banque, d'une part, et Dr. Reineccius, First Eagle et M. Mathieu, d'autre part.

37. S'agissant de la demande datée du 5 avril 2002 émanant de First Eagle tendant à ce que le Tribunal rende une ordonnance enjoignant à la Banque d'autoriser l'accès à ses archives, ainsi que la réponse de la Banque à cette demande datée du 11 avril 2002 tendant au prononcé du rejet de ladite demande, le Tribunal a estimé que la demande de First Eagle n'était pas conforme au calendrier de la procédure, décrit dans l'ordonnance de procédure n° 1 et accepté d'un commun accord par les Parties, ni au calendrier de production de pièces visé au paragraphe E de l'ordonnance n° 3 et ne pouvait, par conséquent, pas être prise en considération. La demande a donc été rejetée.

38. L'ordonnance de procédure n° 5 fait droit à la demande de production de pièces, formulée par First Eagle, selon les modalités suivantes:

> 1. La Banque consignera par écrit la liste des documents tombant sous le coup des dispositions du paragraphe E de l'ordonnance n° 3 et n'ayant pas fait l'objet de communication ou ayant été caviardés, pour des motifs tirés du caractère confidentiel de la relation entre l'avocat et son client, ou d'une "sensibilité politique ou institutionnelle particulière" ou pour d'autres motifs correspondant à ceux énumérés à l'article 9, paragraphe 2, des *Rules on the Taking of Evidence in International Commercial Arbitration* de l'Association internationale du barreau (International Bar Association – IBA) (1999). Ladite liste sera transmise à First Eagle le 8 mai 2002 au plus tard.

2. Cette liste identifiera: (i) le numéro du document, son auteur et son ou ses destinataire(s), (ii) la partie du document non communiquée ou caviardée, et (iii) le motif particulier invoqué pour refuser la communication ou caviarder le document, et le fondement allégué à l'appui de ce motif. Il sera également fait mention de toute partie d'un document dont la communication est refusée au motif que cette partie est réputée non pertinente, alors que sans cette partie, ce document serait pertinent.

3. First Eagle fera parvenir le 10 mai 2002 au plus tard ses objections aux motifs visés au paragraphe 1.

4. Le Tribunal enverra, le 13 mai 2002, sa secrétaire à l'endroit où les documents sont retenus par la Banque pour trouver une solution aux objections soulevées, en concertation avec First Eagle et la Banque. Les questions ayant trait à la communication de pièces aux termes du paragraphe E de l'ordonnance n° 3, qui seraient demeurées en suspens au terme de l'examen et de la consultation susmentionnés seront soumises au Tribunal le 17 mai au plus tard.

39. Conformément à l'ordonnance de procédure n° 5, First Eagle et la Banque se sont entendues sur certaines questions concernant la production de pièces aux termes de l'ordonnance de procédure n° 3. Elles ont ensuite pris contact avec la Secrétaire du Tribunal et lui ont demandé d'organiser une conférence téléphonique au cours de laquelle il serait discuté des dernières objections de First Eagle. Lors de la conférence téléphonique qui a eu lieu le 13 mai 2002 et à laquelle ont participé les conseils de First Eagle et de la Banque, ainsi que la Secrétaire du Tribunal, First Eagle a indiqué que la pertinence de neuf (9) documents était encore en litige, des parties de ces documents n'ayant pas été communiquées par la Banque pour des motifs tirés soit de leur défaut de pertinence au regard de l'ordonnance n° 3, soit de la règle de la confidentialité des communications entre l'avocat et son client. Les conseils de First Eagle et de la Banque ont demandé à la Secrétaire d'examiner les neufs documents (tels que numérotés dans la liste datée du 8 mai 2002 établie par la Banque et ayant donné lieu aux Objections de First Eagle soumises le 10 mai 2002) qui se trouvaient au siège de la

Banque, à Bâle en Suisse, et de soumettre à discussion ses recommandations concernant la pertinence des parties caviardées, lors d'une conférence téléphonique à laquelle participeraient les conseils de la Banque et de First Eagle. Les conseils se sont entendus pour soumettre au Tribunal des mémoires traitant des allégations de la Banque relatives à la confidentialité des communications entre l'avocat et son client.

40. Les 15 et 16 mai 2002, la Secrétaire a examiné les neuf documents litigieux au siège de la Banque et a discuté avec les conseils de la pertinence éventuelle de certaines parties de cinq documents au regard du paragraphe E.1.f. de l'ordonnance n° 5; le conseil de la Banque a accepté de communiquer des parties de ces cinq documents qui avaient d'abord été caviardées en raison de leur défaut de pertinence. Lors d'une conférence téléphonique avec le conseil de First Eagle et la Secrétaire qui a eu lieu le 16 mai 2002, la Banque a informé First Eagle qu'elle communiquerait aussitôt lesdites parties de ces cinq documents. Les Parties sont convenues que les quatre autres documents avaient été caviardés à juste titre. Le 22 mai 2002, la Banque a soumis au Tribunal son mémoire consacré aux questions soulevées dans ses objections du 10 mai 2002 concernant la confidentialité des communications entre l'avocat et son conseil. First Eagle a, à son tour, soumis le 29 mai 2002 un mémoire à l'appui de ses objections.

41. Dix-sept documents tombant sous le coup des dispositions du paragraphe E de l'ordonnance de procédure n° 3 (Acte de mission) ont été énumérés par la Banque; cinq documents ont été caviardés en partie et douze documents n'ont pas été communiqués au motif qu'ils tombaient sous le coup de la règle de la confidentialité des communications entre l'avocat et son client. Les documents ont été décrits dans la liste préparée par la Banque en exécution de l'ordonnance de procédure n° 5 et sont accompagnés de résumés des objections de First Eagle.

42. Dans ses objections déposées le 10 mai 2002, First Eagle a affirmé que la Banque n'avait pas le droit d'invoquer le motif de la confidentialité des communications entre l'avocat et son client, parce qu'une société n'était pas autorisée à invoquer ladite confidentialité à l'égard de ses propres actionnaires.

43. Le 22 mai 2002, la Banque a fait valoir dans son mémoire que la confidentialité des communications entre la Banque et son conseil était protégée dans des litiges entre la Banque et ses actionnaires privés en vertu des principes de droit bien établis.

44. Dans son mémoire du 29 mai 2002, First Eagle a affirmé que la différence de traitement réservée par la Banque à ses actionnaires privés en ce qui concerne les communications dont First Eagle cherchait à obtenir la production était incompatible avec les principes de droit international sur lesquels First Eagle s'était fondée. Six des documents que la Banque a refusé de communiquer ne pouvaient, selon First Eagle, bénéficier de la règle de la confidentialité, car ils avaient été rédigés avant l'annonce par le Conseil de l'opération de rachat forcé. First Eagle a aussi fait valoir que la Banque ne pouvait unilatéralement refuser de communiquer des documents qu'elle avait divulgués "par inadvertance".

45. Le 11 juin 2002, le Tribunal a rendu l'ordonnance de procédure n° 6 (Ordonnance relative à la communication de certains documents pour lesquels le caractère confidentiel des communications entre l'avocat et son client a été invoqué), enjoignant à la Banque de communiquer le document n° 34, dans la mesure où il avait été divulgué à une conférence de presse, à chacun des demandeurs conformément aux dispositions de l'ordonnance de procédure n° 5. Le Tribunal a décidé que seize documents étaient régis par la règle de la confidentialité des communications entre l'avocat et son client.

46. Par lettre datée du 28 mai 2002 adressée au Tribunal et dont copie a été envoyée aux conseils de First Eagle et de la défenderesse, à savoir la Banque, Dr. Reineccius a demandé la nomination d'un expert en matière bancaire. En réponse à la lettre de Dr. Reineccius, le Tribunal a reçu le 4 juin 2002 des commentaires de First Eagle, le 10 juin 2002 des commentaires de M. Mathieu, le 10 juin 2002 des commentaires de la Banque, ainsi qu'une communication additionnelle de Dr. Reineccius datée du 11 juin 2002. First Eagle et M. Mathieu, ainsi que la Banque, ont indiqué qu'ils considéraient comme étant prématurée la nomination d'un expert en matière bancaire à ce stade de l'arbitrage, étant donné que les questions que Dr. Reineccius proposait de soumettre à un expert en matière bancaire ne se posaient pas dans la présente phase de l'arbitrage.

47. Le Tribunal a examiné les communications des Parties et, le 17 juin 2002, a rendu l'ordonnance de procédure n° 7 (Ordonnance relative à la demande de Dr. Horst Reineccius, demandeur n° 1, tendant à ce que le Tribunal nomme un expert), considérant que la demande de nomination d'un expert, soumise par Dr. Reineccius, était prématurée.

48. Après s'être entretenu avec les Parties et avoir reçu de chacune d'elles son approbation au calendrier proposé, la Secrétaire, conformément à l'article 20 du règlement d'arbitrage, a transmis au Tribunal et aux Parties le 10 août 2002 les dates des audiences, soit du 26 au 29 août 2002, et a diffusé ledit calendrier sur le site Internet du Greffe.

49. Le 23 août 2002, le Tribunal a rendu une ordonnance de procédure n° 8 (Projections faites par ordinateur, conditions relatives au dépôt tardif des moyens de preuve ou de documents juridiques) en réponse à: (1) une lettre de la Banque datée du 19 août 2002; (2) une lettre de First Eagle du 20 août 2002 et (3) une lettre de la Banque datée du 21 août 2002. Ces lettres faisaient savoir que la Banque et First Eagle n'étaient pas en mesure de s'entendre sur les conditions de procédure relatives à (1) l'utilisation des moyens informatiques pour la projection de preuves et l'illustration du débat oral lors des audiences et (2) le dépôt de moyens de preuve ou de documents juridiques après les délais établis en accord avec les Parties et énoncés dans les ordonnances n° 3 et 4. Le Tribunal a décidé comme suit:

(i) L'utilisation d'écrans permettant de visionner des preuves et autres supports visuels, qu'ils soient assistés par ordinateur ou pas, n'est pas inhabituelle dans les audiences arbitrales internationales. De tels supports visuels peuvent être employés par les Parties, si la documentation concernée est fondée uniquement sur des moyens de preuve déjà versés au dossier et si elle a été communiquée préalablement aux audiences, à la partie adverse, aux fins de vérification.

(ii) L'introduction de nouveaux moyens de preuve ne sera pas permise, à moins qu'une requête en ce sens ait été adressée au Tribunal, que celui-ci y ait fait droit et que la partie adverse ait eu la possibilité de présenter ses commentaires dans un délai raisonnable.

(iii) Il peut être fait référence durant les audiences à de nouveaux documents juridiques, pour réfuter ou compléter d'autres documents juridiques, à condition que leur nombre ne soit pas excessif.

(iv) Les questions concernant les copies de documents juridiques prétendus écourtés doivent au préalable être résolues entre avocats. La partie alléguant que des documents juridiques sont incomplets a la charge d'identifier ces derniers auprès de la Partie qui les a soumis.

50. Le texte intégral de toutes les ordonnances de procédure mentionnées cidessus peut être consulté sur le site Internet www.pca-cpa.org.

51. Conformément à l'article XV de l'Accord de La Haye de 1930 et à l'article 20 du règlement d'arbitrage, les audiences publiques ont eu lieu du 26 au 28 août 2002 dans la Grande Salle de Justice du Palais de la Paix à La Haye. À la demande des Parties, les demandes séparées ont été entendues en parallèle mais avec une certaine intégration pour l'efficacité et la commodité des Parties. Pendant les audiences, First Eagle était représentée par M. Donald Francis Donovan et M. Dietmar W. Prager du cabinet Debevoise & Plimpton. M. Mathieu était représenté par M. Elie Kleiman et M. Guillaume Tattevin du cabinet Freshfields Bruckhaus Deringer. La Banque était représentée par M. Jonathan I. Blackman, M. Laurent Cohen-Tanugi et Mlle Claudia Annacker du cabinet Cleary, Gottlieb, Steen & Hamilton. Le professeur Mario Giovanoli et M. James Freis étaient également présents pour le compte du Secrétariat de la BRI et le professeur Giovanoli est intervenu pour répondre à une question posée par le Tribunal le premier jour des audiences.[4] Dr. Reineccius a comparu sans avocat les 27 et 28 août; il a renoncé à exercer son droit d'assister aux plaidoiries du 26 août concernant la licéité des actions entreprises par la Banque, car sa demande ne visait pas le droit de la Banque de racheter les actions.

52. En conformité avec l'Accord de La Haye de 1930, des traductions simultanées en anglais, français et allemand ont été fournies pendant les audiences.

---

[4] Compte rendu, p. 79.

53. Le premier jour des audiences, conformément à l'ordonnance de procédure n° 8, First Eagle a demandé la permission de soumettre un classeur contenant de nouveaux documents juridiques et la Banque a demandé au Tribunal la permission de soumettre, à titre de nouveaux moyens de preuve, trois rapports annuels de First Eagle. Le Tribunal a autorisé le dépôt tardif desdites pièces, à condition que les conseils ne mentionnent pas les pièces déposées à titre de nouveaux éléments de preuve avant les plaidoiries du jour suivant, lorsque la seconde question formulée dans l'ordonnance de procédure n° 3 aurait été discutée, de manière à donner au conseil de la partie adverse le temps d'examiner les pièces déposées tardivement.[5]

[5] *Id.*, p. 83.

CHAPITRE III – LES PARTIES ET LEURS DEMANDES

A. IDENTITÉ DES PARTIES

54. Le demandeur n° 1, Dr. Horst Reineccius, est domicilié à Hanovre (Allemagne) et détenait 20 actions de la Banque.

55. Le demandeur n° 2, First Eagle SoGen Funds, Inc., est un organisme de placement collectif inscrit aux États-Unis et régi par les lois de l'État de Maryland (États-Unis d'Amérique). First Eagle est dirigée par Arnhold and S. Bleichroeder Advisers, Inc., conseiller en valeurs, inscrit aux États-Unis. First Eagle est domiciliée et a son siège d'exploitation principal à 1345 Avenue of the Americas, New York, New York 10105. First Eagle détenait 9.085 actions de la Banque.

56. Le demandeur n° 3, M. Pierre Mathieu, est domicilié à Urmont, F-36400 Montgivray (France) et détenait 8 actions de la Banque; la Société Hippique de La Châtre est une association à but non lucratif qui détenait une action et est domiciliée aux fins de la présente procédure d'arbitrage à la même adresse que M. Mathieu.

57. La défenderesse, la Banque, a été constituée, comme expliqué ci-dessus, conformément à l'Accord de La Haye de 1930, en tant que société anonyme par actions. Le siège social de la Banque est établi à Bâle (Suisse).

B. ACTE DE MISSION

58. L'article 3, paragraphe g, du règlement d'arbitrage contient la définition suivante: "'acte de mission': tel qu'entendu dans l'Accord de 1930, la question ou les questions soumises au Tribunal et les procédures particulières devant être suivies."

59. Dans l'ordonnance de procédure n° 3 (Acte de mission) du 5 mars 2002, le Tribunal a fait observer que bien que les Parties aient déclaré ne pas soulever d'exceptions d'incompétence, les questions suivantes continuent à opposer toutes les Parties ou certaines d'entre elles:

(i) la licéité de la reprise forcée des actions, y compris les procédures selon lesquelles elle a été effectuée et l'étendue possible des conséquences d'une constatation d'illicéité pour tous ceux qui étaient actionnaires privés au 8 janvier 2001;

(ii) la détermination des normes applicables à l'évaluation des actions ayant fait l'objet d'une reprise forcée;

(iii) l'application aux actions ayant fait l'objet d'une reprise forcée, des normes visées au point (ii) ci-dessus.

Le Tribunal a estimé qu'il était plus expédient d'examiner dans une première phase les deux premières questions et de différer l'examen de la troisième question à une deuxième et dernière phase, si cela s'avérait nécessaire.

C. CONCLUSIONS DES PARTIES

1. Dr. Reineccius, demandeur n° 1

a. ARGUMENTS

60. "[L'usage par la Banque] du modèle des dividendes à perpétuité pour l'évaluation des actions, lequel modèle a été appliqué par les experts mandatés par la Banque, . . . est justifié, si la société distribue entièrement la majeure partie de ses bénéfices nets . . . . Au cours des deux derniers exercices financiers, la Banque des Règlements Internationaux a distribué moins d'un cinquième des bénéfices nets, le modèle des dividendes à perpétuité n'est dès lors pas acceptable."

61. "À titre d'arguments supplémentaires, . . . la Banque invoque la faiblesse des cours de bourse et le fait que les actionnaires privés n'avaient pas le droit de vote. L'extrême sous-évaluation des actions de la BRI était principalement due aux faibles dividendes et donc à la Banque elle-même. La politique générale de la Banque est décidée par les membres fondateurs en leur qualité d'actionnaires principaux. Le vote lors des assemblées générales de la BRI n'est pas une source de division et

l'exclusion des actionnaires privés a été décidée à l'unanimité. Dès lors, il ne faut pas accorder d'importance particulière au fait que les actionnaires privés n'avaient pas le droit de vote."

62. "La méthode de la valeur de rentabilité permet de calculer la valeur d'une action en divisant le bénéfice net par action par le rendement . . . . De même, la méthode de l'actif net réévalué pour l'évaluation de l'action de la BRI est appropriée – toutefois, la décote de 45% "estimée" par les experts de J.P. Morgan & Cie SA ne l'est pas. Au contraire, dans le cas d'une banque dont la rentabilité est bonne, il convient d'appliquer une prime, car l'actif net de la banque augmentera grâce à ses bénéfices futurs."

63. Dr. Reineccius a signalé lors des audiences[6] qu'il convenait expressément que les calculs de l'actif net réévalué présentés par J.P. Morgan étaient corrects.

b. DÉCISION DEMANDÉE

64. Dr. Reineccius requiert qu'il plaise au Tribunal de dire que:

(i) l'indemnité doit être basée sur la valeur totale des actions (la valeur la plus élevée obtenue par une analyse de l'actif net réévalué ou par une analyse de la méthode de la valeur de rentabilité), y compris un intérêt de 3¼% l'an à compter du 8 janvier 2001;

(ii) la valeur de ces actions ne peut pas être moindre ou inférieure à l'actif net réévalué;

(iii) un premier montant de 17.000 francs suisses par action doit lui être versé;

(iv) un expert doit être nommé pour calculer la rentabilité et l'actif net réévalué des actions de la Banque à la date du 8 janvier 2001 et expliquer lequel des deux résultats tient correctement compte de la valeur des actions.

[6] *Id.*, p. 331.

2. *First Eagle, demandeur n° 2*

a. ARGUMENTS

65. Dans son mémoire, First Eagle affirme ce qui suit:

> En vertu des Statuts, de même qu'en vertu du droit international, First Eagle a droit à une indemnité égale à la valeur totale de sa participation dans la Banque par rapport à l'ensemble des participations . . . . Pour calculer le montant de l'indemnité due à First Eagle, la Banque a utilisé le modèle des dividendes à perpétuité, une variante de la méthode de la valeur actualisée des flux de trésorerie. Cependant, la Banque a utilisé le modèle pour évaluer uniquement le flux des dividendes, bien qu'elle affecte régulièrement la majeure partie de ses bénéfices à l'augmentation de l'actif. Étant donné qu'elle a évalué uniquement les dividendes, la Banque a violé le droit des actionnaires exclus à participer de façon égale aux "bénéfices" de la Banque – à l'ensemble des bénéfices.[7]

> La Banque a également calculé l'actif net réévalué par action, qui était égale au double de l'indemnité payée. Plutôt que de verser aux actionnaires exclus leur part proportionnelle de l'actif net réévalué au moment où ils ont été exclus de la société, la Banque a appliqué une décote de 45% au titre de l'absence de droit de vote et du manque de liquidité du titre, ce qui a ramené l'actif net réévalué par action approximativement au montant de l'indemnité déterminée par l'évaluation du flux des dividendes . . . [l]es actions de la Banque sont identiques et par conséquent, l'application d'une décote constitue une violation de la garantie de l'égalité des droits visée à l'article 13 des Statuts.[8]

66. La pièce jointe n° 23, préparée par la Banque en 1969 pour le Conseil d'administration, constitue "un exemple antérieur d'une répartition des bénéfices et des actifs pour laquelle tous les actionnaires étaient traités sur un pied d'égalité."[9] First Eagle a fait valoir que le but de cette note

---

[7] Mémoire de First Eagle, par. 15-16.
[8] *Id.*, par. 17-18.
[9] Compte rendu, p. 170.

était de déterminer la prime pour la troisième tranche . . . la valeur des actions au-delà de leur valeur nominale. Dans la note, la Banque envisage trois méthodes d'évaluation: (1) une analyse de la valeur actualisée des flux de trésorerie; (2) le prix du marché; (3) "la méthode mathématique". First Eagle soutient que d'après la note, la Banque a rejeté les méthodes (1) et (2), parce qu'elles étaient imparfaites et a recommandé la méthode mathématique qui, de l'avis de First Eagle, est la méthode de l'actif net réévalué.[10] Selon First Eagle, la méthode mise au point en 1969 "a été appliquée à chacune des émissions d'actions réalisées par les banques centrales actionnaires et la Banque a renoncé à cette méthode uniquement pour l'opération visant à exclure [les actionnaires privés] . . . . Dans chacun de ces cas [antérieurs], la Banque s'est basée sur l'actif net réévalué diminué de 30 pour cent."[11]

67. La pièce jointe n° 15, une note interne de la BRI rédigée en 1998, informe que dans l'éventualité d'un rachat, le prix offert "ne doit pas être considéré comme étant inférieur à la valeur patrimoniale de chaque action."[12]

68. L'application de décotes aurait constitué une violation du droit international même en l'absence de la garantie visée à l'article 13. Les tribunaux internationaux reconnaissent que dans le cadre d'une expropriation, le caractère coercitif de la cession exclut l'application de décotes au titre d'absence de droit de vote ou de manque de liquidité des titres dans le but de réduire l'indemnité à payer.[13]

69. First Eagle déclare que la Banque n'a pas préconisé l'usage du modèle des dividendes à perpétuité en vertu duquel elle a fixé l'indemnité des actionnaires exclus ni de la méthode, également applicable, de l'actif net réévalué. "Au lieu de cela, [la Banque] affirme qu'[elle] s'est acquittée de ses obligations envers les actionnaires exclus en leur versant une indemnité supérieure aux prix auxquels les actions sont négociées en Bourse . . . . [É]tant donné que le marché pour ses actions comporte des

---

[10] *Id.*, p. 171.
[11] *Id.*, p. 172.
[12] *Id.*
[13] *Id.*, p. 199.

défauts structurels, les cours de bourse ne peuvent constituer une preuve fiable de leur valeur."

70. Selon First Eagle, le prix du marché correspond au montant offert par la Banque en 1936 et 1975 pour un rachat volontaire; dans les deux cas, ces opérations "ont complètement échoué."[14]

71. First Eagle a fait valoir que le transfert des actions était illégal, car la reprise de ces titres "n'était pas accompagnée de l'indemnité complète correspondant à la participation cédée."[15]

> L'indemnité complète en contrepartie de la reprise . . . doit être supérieure à l'actif net réévalué de la Banque par action.[16]
>
> Les tribunaux, qui reconnaissent que l'actif net réévalué est une valeur tant fiable que modérée, ont fréquemment accordé une indemnité calculée à partir de l'actif net réévalué, lorsque le demandeur leur en faisait la demande. La Banque, qui s'est basée sur ses propres chiffres, a donc privé First Eagle de quelque 84 millions de dollars.[17]

72. Par ailleurs, First Eagle a fait valoir ce qui suit:

> Tous les actionnaires de la Banque avaient un droit égal, protégé par le droit international, de participer au produit de l'entreprise provenant du capital auquel ils ont contribué. Si l'exclusion des actionnaires autres que les banques centrales est à présent possible, leur droit égal à participer ne peut être défendu que par le paiement d'une indemnité égale à leur part proportionnelle de la valeur totale de la Banque, compte tenu de l'actif net, du fonds commercial et des perspectives futures. Les actionnaires exclus, étaient propriétaires de la Banque avec les autres actionnaires et ce droit de propriété ne peut pas être bafoué par l'opération d'exclusion.[18]

---

[14] *Id.*, p. 141.
[15] *Id.*, p. 29.
[16] Mémoire de First Eagle, par. 22.
[17] *Id.*, par. 25.
[18] *Id.*, par. 30.

b. DROIT APPLICABLE

73. Dans son mémoire, First Eagle déclare que "les principes généraux du droit international sont applicables au présent différend" et que, comme la Banque, elle est d'avis que "les règles du droit international public général président à l'interprétation des Statuts et donc à l'appréciation de la participation des actionnaires exclus dans la Banque."[19] First Eagle ajoute que "les dispositions pertinentes des Statuts de la Banque, en particulier, doivent être interprétées en conformité avec les principes généraux du droit international qui régissent l'interprétation des traités, formulés aux articles 31, 32 et 33 de la Convention de Vienne sur le droit des traités de 1969."[20]

74. En outre, First Eagle cite et s'appuie sur une déclaration de la Banque selon laquelle les relations entre la Banque et "ses actionnaires sont régies par ses Instruments constitutifs . . . complétés, le cas échéant, par le droit international public général."[21]

c. DÉCISION DEMANDÉE

75. En réponse à la demande formulée par le Tribunal lors des audiences en vue du dépôt de conclusions écrites finales, First Eagle a conclu à ce qu'il plaise au Tribunal de prononcer une sentence tendant à ce que:

(i) la Banque soit tenue de payer à First Eagle la valeur totale sans décote de sa participation proportionnelle dans la Banque considérée dans son ensemble;

(ii) la valeur totale de la participation proportionnelle de First Eagle dans la Banque doit, au regard du droit, être au moins égale à la part proportionnelle, revenant à First Eagle, de l'actif net réévalué sans décote de la Banque;

(iii) l'actif net réévalué sans décote de la Banque doit être au moins égal à l'actif net réévalué sans décote calculé par la

---

[19] *Id.*, par. 205.
[20] *Id.*, par. 206.
[21] *Id.*, par. 205.

Banque en concertation avec J.P. Morgan (c'est-à-dire 32.846 francs suisses au 30 novembre 2000) et First Eagle aura la possibilité d'apporter des preuves ayant trait au calcul correct de l'actif net réévalué de la Banque au cours de la phase suivante de cette procédure;

(iv) First Eagle a droit à une indemnité supplémentaire correspondant à la différence entre sa participation proportionnelle dans la valeur de la Banque, qui est une entreprise en pleine activité, et sa part proportionnelle de l'actif net réévalué sans décote de la Banque;

(v) à la lumière des preuves présentées au Tribunal et au regard du droit, les cours des actions négociées en Bourse ne peuvent pas être pris en compte dans le calcul de la valeur totale de la participation proportionnelle de First Eagle dans la Banque considérée dans son ensemble;

(vi) au regard du droit, le modèle des dividendes à perpétuité ne peut pas être utilisé pour calculer la valeur totale de la participation proportionnelle de First Eagle dans la Banque considérée dans son ensemble et si une variante de la méthode de la valeur actualisée des flux de trésorerie est utilisée, elle doit tenir compte de la rentabilité totale de la Banque;

(vii) si le modèle des dividendes à perpétuité devait être utilisé pour déterminer la valeur de la participation de First Eagle dans la Banque, First Eagle aura la possibilité de produire des éléments de preuve concernant l'application adéquate de ce modèle au cours de la phase suivante de la présente procédure;

(viii) First Eagle aura le droit de percevoir des intérêts appropriés sur les sommes attribuées;

(ix) First Eagle sera remboursée des frais exposés aux fins de la procédure.

d. PRÉCISIONS CONCERNANT LE CALCUL DE L'ACTIF NET RÉÉVALUÉ

76. First Eagle a déclaré au cours des audiences[22] qu'elle était disposée à ne pas contester, si la Banque en faisait de même, que l'actif net réévalué correspondait à la valeur déterminée par J.P. Morgan, telle qu'elle est mentionnée dans la pièce jointe 43 de son rapport. Cependant, étant donné que le rapport de J.P. Morgan ne contient pas de calcul de la valeur des biens immobiliers de la Banque, First Eagle a proposé que le Tribunal nomme un expert pour déterminer la valeur des biens immobiliers dont l'évaluation serait définitive et serait ajoutée à l'actif net réévalué.

3. M. Mathieu, demandeur n° 3

a. ARGUMENTS

77. La résolution du 8 janvier 2001 portant modification des Statuts (modification des articles 6, 12, 15, 16, 17, 18, ajout de l'article 18A) est illicite, car elle n'est pas conforme aux Instruments constitutifs de la Banque. "Une analyse des Statuts et de la Charte de la Banque en conformité avec les principes établis du droit international en matière d'interprétation des traités[23] n'autorise pas l'ajout d'un article. Même si cet ajout avait été autorisé, il n'aurait pas dû être mis en oeuvre en vertu de l'article 57 des Statuts de la Banque, qui dispose que les modifications peuvent être 'adoptées par la majorité de l'Assemblée générale', mais plutôt en vertu de l'article 58 des Statuts qui stipule que 'la modification doit être adoptée par une majorité des deux tiers du Conseil, approuvée par la majorité de l'Assemblée générale et sanctionnée par une loi additionnelle à la Charte de la Banque'."[24]

78. M. Mathieu conclut que la résolution portant modification des Statuts, en tant qu'acte d'une organisation internationale contraire aux Instruments constitutifs, est nulle et non avenue. Par conséquent, la reprise des

---

[22] Compte rendu, p. 329.
[23] Convention de Vienne sur le droit des traités, 23 mai 1969, Nations Unies, *Recueil des traités* n° 1155, vol. 331, art. 31(3)(c).
[24] Compte rendu, p. 17-19, 25-26.

actions détenues par des personnes privées est nulle et non avenue à l'égard de tous les actionnaires privés. Pour prouver que la Banque n'avait pas le pouvoir d'exclure les actionnaires privés, M. Mathieu a cité une note interne rédigée par M. Weiser en 1936, qui affirmait: "une chose que l'Assemblée générale ne peut pas faire est de priver les actionnaires de leur qualité de membres de l'entreprise commune."[25]

79. L'illicéité de la résolution de la Banque constitue aussi un acte illicite au regard du droit international, qui a pour effet de soumettre la Banque à une obligation de réparation des dommages causés.

80. Par ailleurs, même si le Tribunal ne devait pas retenir l'illicéité de la résolution de la Banque, le retrait forcé des actions constituerait une expropriation illicite. Le retrait forcé a été effectué par un sujet de droit international, a privé le demandeur de son titre de propriété, c'est-à-dire de ses actions, et était motivé par des considérations économiques et financières plutôt que politiques. De surcroît, la Banque a violé les principes généraux du droit international, car les conditions nécessaires pour réaliser une expropriation licite – à savoir, existence d'un fondement légal, satisfaction de l'intérêt public, respect du principe de non-discrimination et indemnisation juste et équitable – n'étaient pas remplies.

b. DROIT APPLICABLE

81. M. Mathieu a fait valoir que le présent différend était régi par les Instruments constitutifs de la Banque. Il a déclaré en outre qu'"en l'absence de précision ou dispositions contraires des Instruments constitutifs de la BRI, le droit international général [était] également applicable".

82. De surcroît, M. Mathieu a soutenu que puisque la sentence serait rendue aux Pays-Bas et qu'elle était susceptible d'exécution en Suisse, où la Banque a son siège, le Tribunal devait tenir compte de la politique publique internationale de ces deux États.

---

[25] Pièce jointe 35, compte rendu p. 12.

c. DÉCISION DEMANDÉE

83. Dans ses conclusions modificatives du 28 août 2002, M. Mathieu a demandé ce qui suit:

> M. Mathieu et la Société de Concours Hippique de La Châtre (ci après, *"le Demandeur"*) requièrent qu'il plaise au Tribunal Arbitral recevoir les présentes conclusions modificatives qui annulent et remplacent les conclusions figurant en pages 56 à 58 du Mémoire en demande en date du 13 mai 2002 et, y faisant droit, statuer comme suit:
>
> 1. A titre principal:
>
> 1.1. Dire et juger que la résolution du 8 janvier 2001 est illégale;
>
> 1.2. La dire en conséquence nulle;
>
> 1.3. Constater le caractère irréversible des opérations de mise en œuvre de ladite résolution et, en particulier, l'impossibilité de réinscrire les actions de la Banque des Règlements Internationaux (ci-après *"la BRI"*) à la cote des marchés boursiers réglementés de Paris et de Zurich; dire que cette impossibilité fait dès lors obstacle à toute restitution à l'identique;
>
> 1.4. Ordonner, en conséquence de l'illégalité de la résolution du 8 janvier 2001 et de la nullité l'invalidant, une restitution intégrale par équivalent, et en conséquence condamner la BRI au paiement au Demandeur d'une compensation financière correspondant: (i) à la valeur patrimoniale des actions dont le Demandeur a été privé, estimée au 8 janvier 2001, date de la résolution invalidée, augmentée des intérêts capitalisés ayant couru depuis cette date jusqu'à la date du parfait paiement au Demandeur; et (ii) au montant des dividendes dont le Demandeur a été privé depuis le 8 janvier 2001, avec intérêts capitalisés depuis la date de leur mise en versement jusqu'à la date de parfait paiement au Demandeur;

2. En outre:

   2.1. Dire et juger qu'en adoptant une résolution illégale, la BRI a engagé sa responsabilité internationale;

   2.2. Dire et juger que l'opération de retrait forcé constitue une expropriation illicite de nature à engager la responsabilité de la BRI;

   2.3. Dire et juger que le Demandeur a subi un dommage du fait des actes illicites de la BRI;

   2.4. En conséquence, condamner la BRI au paiement au Demandeur d'une compensation financière correspondant: (i) dans l'hypothèse où le Tribunal ne ferait pas droit aux demandes sollicitées au point 1. ci-dessus, à la valeur patrimoniale des actions dont le Demandeur a été privé, estimée au 8 janvier 2001, date de la résolution querellée, augmentée des intérêts capitalisés ayant couru depuis cette date jusqu'à la date du parfait paiement au Demandeur; et en toute hypothèse (ii) au préjudice matériel et moral subi par le Demandeur;

3. Dans tous les cas, aux fins de calcul de la réparation par équivalent pour la privation de la propriété des actions:

   3.1. Rejeter les estimations de la BRI; et:

   3.2. Ordonner, le cas échéant par une sentence intérimaire, qu'il soit fait application de la méthode de l'actif net réévalué pour estimer à la date du 8 janvier 2001 la valeur des actions reprises;

   3.3. Dire qu'aucune décote ne viendra diminuer les estimations retenues;

   3.4. Dire en conséquence que le montant du supplément d'indemnisation que devra verser la BRI au Demandeur, venant s'ajouter aux sommes que la BRI a d'ores et déjà reconnu devoir, correspondra à la différence entre le montant de l'indemnisation reconnue et celui qui sera établi par application de la méthode de l'actif net réévalué;

4. Subsidiairement:

4.1. Dire et juger qu'en tout état de cause la BRI doit aux actionnaires évincés la valeur de leurs actions;

4.2. Constater que cet engagement n'a pas été rempli;

4.3. Retenir en conséquence une méthode plus appropriée pour évaluer la valeur des actions reprises;

4.4. Dire que cette valeur doit être déterminée par la méthode de l'actif net réévalué;

5. Dans l'hypothèse où la Sentence du Tribunal serait définitive, dire et juger que la BRI paiera au Demandeur les frais de toute nature exposés dans le cadre de la procédure arbitrale, et en particulier mettre à sa charge les honoraires des Conseils du Demandeur.

84. M. Mathieu a indiqué qu'il se joignait aux autres demandeurs quant à la déclaration visée au paragraphe 76 ci-dessus concernant l'utilisation de l'actif net réévalué, telle qu'il est déterminé dans la pièce jointe n° 43 du rapport de J.P. Morgan avec ajout de la valeur des biens immobiliers de la Banque.[26]

4. La Banque des Règlements Internationaux, défenderesse

a. ARGUMENTS

(i) Licéité du rachat des actions

85. La Banque a déposé son mémoire en défense et sa demande reconventionnelle le 14 janvier 2002 et son contre-mémoire le 22 juillet 2002.

---

[26] Compte rendu, p. 318.

Conformément à l'ordonnance de procédure n° 3, la Banque a d'abord examiné la licéité du rachat forcé des actions détenues par des personnes privées. La Banque a soutenu qu'elle avait compétence pour modifier les Statuts de la Banque en vertu de l'article 57 desdits Statuts. La Banque a fait valoir que "tout article des Statuts", autre que les articles "réservés" énumérés à l'article 58, pouvait être modifié par une majorité des deux tiers du Conseil d'administration et après approbation de ladite proposition par la majorité de l'Assemblée générale, "pourvu que ces modifications ne soient pas incompatibles avec les dispositions des articles énumérés à l'article 58."[27]

86. La Banque a contesté qu'il existait une distinction valable entre l'"ajout" d'un article et la "modification" d'un article, comme M. Mathieu l'a fait valoir. "Le terme "modification" englobe tout changement, notamment dû à l'ajout de nouveaux termes à un instrument ou à un accord existant."[28] En outre, l'argument de M. Mathieu selon lequel la procédure, décrite à l'article 58, relative à la modification des articles réservés, qui requiert une disposition supplémentaire à la Charte de la Banque et son approbation par une loi suisse, doit être appliquée aux articles non réservés n'est pas fondé. Les Statuts font explicitement la distinction entre la modification des articles non réservés selon les procédures définies à l'article 57 et la modification des articles réservés en vertu de l'article 58. La Banque n'a pas modifié les articles réservés.[29]

(ii) Conséquences d'une constatation d'illicéité

87. La Banque a fait valoir que si le Tribunal constatait l'illicéité de l'opération, (1) la Banque devrait restituer les actions retirées aux actionnaires privés ou (2) les actionnaires privés n'auraient d'autre choix que de garder l'indemnité qu'ils avaient reçue pour leurs actions sur la base d'un accord volontaire avec la Banque. La Banque a affirmé qu'une constatation d'illicéité ne permettrait pas d'augmenter l'indemnité versée pour les actions retirées, comme le demande First Eagle.[30]

---

27 Contre-mémoire, par. 8.
28 *Id.*, par. 9.
29 *Id.*, par. 11.
30 *Id.*, par. 90.

(iii) Normes d'évaluation

88. La Banque conteste l'affirmation de First Eagle selon laquelle les actionnaires privés détenaient "une participation proportionnelle dans la Banque considérée dans son ensemble".[31] La Banque fait valoir que les actionnaires ne possédaient pas les caractéristiques fondamentales attachées à une participation: ils ne jouissaient pas du droit de vote (article 14 des Statuts), du droit de "choisir les membres du Conseil (id)", ni du droit de "transférer des actions sans l'approbation de la Banque et de la banque centrale de l'État qui avait émis lesdites actions (article 12 des Statuts)."[32] Les nouvelles banques centrales ont payé plus que le prix du marché pour les actions correspondant à leur nouvelle émission nationale, car "ces actions pouvaient leur donner ce qu'aucun autre actionnaire n'a jamais pu obtenir, à savoir la participation dans la conduite des affaires de la Banque et la surveillance de celle-ci grâce au droit de vote que seule leur procurait l'existence de ces nouvelles actions."[33]

89. S'agissant de la méthode d'évaluation appliquée par la Banque pour le calcul de l'indemnité correspondant aux actions rachetées, la Banque a soutenu que la norme d'évaluation à appliquer était celle de la juste valeur du marché, à savoir le prix du marché des actions négociées en Bourse plutôt que la valeur de la participation proportionnelle des actionnaires dans la Banque, comme le demandeur First Eagle l'a suggéré. Les méthodes d'évaluation proposées par First Eagle sont utiles pour "déterminer de façon approximative ce que serait la juste valeur de marché de la participation considérée, en l'absence d'un marché opérationnel. Si un tel marché existe, le prix du marché fournit lui-même la norme de la juste valeur du marché."[34]

90. Par ailleurs, la Banque a déclaré que les actions de la Banque étaient dépourvues des propriétés fondamentales attachées aux participations, parce qu'elles ne conféraient pas le droit de vote, ni le droit de choisir les

---

[31] Mémoire First Eagle, par. 15.
[32] Contre-mémoire, par. 20.
[33] *Id.*, par. 24.
[34] *Id.*, par. 27.

membres du Conseil d'administration ni le droit de céder des actions sans l'autorisation de la Banque et des banques centrales des États membres respectifs. En outre, la Banque soutient que les actionnaires n'ont pas le droit de participer aux bénéfices de la Banque, hormis le droit de percevoir des dividendes, et que leur droit de participer à l'actif de la Banque ne peut être exercé qu'en cas de liquidation de la Banque.[35]

91. La Banque a également déclaré que ses actions étaient négociées sur des marchés boursiers reconnus, contrairement à l'affirmation de First Eagle selon laquelle les actions n'étaient pas négociées sur un marché pleinement efficient. Le droit international n'exige pas un "marché efficient" mais requiert simplement que le prix du marché soit librement et équitablement fixé sur un marché ordinaire. C'est pourquoi le prix du marché pour les actions de la Banque constitue la meilleure indication et la plus logique de la juste valeur du marché à la date où les actionnaires privés ont été informés du rachat forcé. Par ailleurs, la Banque a fait valoir que le prix de rachat satisfaisait aux critères d'indemnisation prévus par la législation des droits de l'homme. La Banque s'est référée à la Convention de sauvegarde des Droits de l'Homme et des Libertés fondamentales,[36] qui, de l'avis de la Banque, ne confère pas au propriétaire exproprié un droit inconditionnel d'indemnisation pour la valeur totale de la propriété expropriée. La Banque s'est également fondée sur la Convention américaine relative aux droits de l'homme,[37] qui prévoit le paiement d'une "juste" indemnité et non d'une indemnité "complète" (article 21, paragraphe 2, de ladite convention). C'est pourquoi la Banque affirme que la norme correspond à une indemnité appropriée, raisonnable, juste ou équitable.

92. Bien que la Banque ait admis que le droit international public était applicable au différend, elle a déclaré que le rachat des actions devait être évalué en conformité avec les principes de la législation des droits de l'homme. La Banque a rejeté l'affirmation de First Eagle selon laquelle

[35] *Id.*, par. 104.
[36] 4 novembre 1950, Nations Unies, *Recueil des traités*, vol. 213, p. 222 (Documents juridiques de la Banque n° 130).
[37] 22 novembre 1969, Nations Unies, *Recueil des traités*, vol. 123, p. 1144 (Documents juridiques de la Banque n° 132).

le rachat par la Banque de ses propres actions était régi par les règles applicables à la reprise d'un bien "étranger" par un État. La Banque a fait valoir qu'il n'y avait pas lieu de conclure que les actionnaires privés devaient être considérés comme des étrangers dans leurs relations juridiques avec la Banque. Les relations entre la Banque et ses actionnaires relèvent de la compétence organique exclusive de la Banque, c'est-à-dire de la compétence d'une organisation à l'égard de ses éléments constitutifs. Les actionnaires font partie de l'ordre interne de la Banque; la législation des droits de l'homme constitue la norme correcte à appliquer pour une décision ayant trait à une ingérence alléguée dans les droits patrimoniaux, due à l'exercice de pouvoirs législatifs et administratifs sur des actions détenues par des personnes privées. Le rachat des actions n'était pas discriminatoire au regard des normes de la législation des droits de l'homme; il n'y a pas eu de différence de traitement sans une justification objective et raisonnable et sans une relation de proportionnalité entre les moyens employés et l'objectif recherché. Le rachat n'a pas représenté un changement fondamental dans la Banque qui aurait nécessité la mise en oeuvre des procédures prévues à l'article 58. Au contraire, "l'existence d'actionnaires privés découle simplement d'une tolérance qui a été initialement accordée aux banques centrales."[38] "L'article 57 a été choisi [parce que] le changement engendré n'était pas censé porter atteinte au caractère fondamental de la Banque."[39]

93. La Banque a déclaré que First Eagle lui avait écrit à la date du 23 juin 2000 pour lui demander d'"envisager un rachat public d'actions dans des conditions similaires à celles des récentes émissions d'actions." La Banque a conclu que l'allusion de First Eagle aux récentes émissions d'actions "se rapport[ait] sans doute à la souscription faite en 1999 par de nouvelles banques centrales à 30 pour cent en dessous de l'actif net réévalué."[40]

---

[38] Compte rendu, p. 78.
[39] *Id.*, p. 79.
[40] Pièce 22, compte rendu, p. 325.

94. La Banque a fait savoir qu'elle acceptait l'utilisation des calculs présentés dans le rapport de J.P. Morgan (pièce n° 43) pour toute constatation relative à l'actif net réévalué.[41]

95. La Banque a déposé une demande reconventionnelle contre First Eagle, par laquelle elle réclame des dommages et intérêts pour violation de l'article 54 des Statuts, en ce que First Eagle a ignoré à tort cet engagement relatif à la juridiction et a intenté une action contre la Banque aux États-Unis, pour éviter la juridiction du Tribunal, et pour les frais d'arbitrage.

b. DROIT APPLICABLE

96. La Banque a déclaré que la conduite interne de ses affaires, c'est-à-dire les relations entre la banque et ses actionnaires, et les actes, tels que le rachat forcé des actions détenues par des personnes privées, accomplis par la Banque *jure imperii*, sont régis par ses Instruments constitutifs, complétés par le droit international public général applicable.[42]

97. La Banque a répondu à l'affirmation de M. Mathieu selon laquelle le Tribunal devait tenir compte de l'intérêt public néerlandais et suisse. La Banque a fait valoir que la sentence du Tribunal était uniquement guidée par le droit international public et que les tribunaux nationaux ne jouissaient pas de la compétence *ratione materiae* pour annuler ou infirmer une sentence rendue par une cour ou un tribunal international en vertu du droit international, en particulier lorsque ladite sentence concernait une partie souveraine agissant *jure imperii*.[43]

98. La Banque a soutenu que le rachat d'actions était également régi par les dispositions de la législation des droits de l'homme applicables lorsqu'un titre de propriété est enlevé à des fins publiques. "Alors que les organisations internationales n'exercent habituellement pas de compétence personnelle ou organique à l'égard des parties privées autres que leurs propres agents, cette compétence peut être accordée à une

---

[41] Compte rendu, p. 331.
[42] Contre-mémoire, par. 48-51.
[43] *Id.*, par. 53-54.

organisation par ses États membres ou du fait de l'acceptation volontaire du droit interne de l'organisation par les parties privées", qui soustraient ainsi leurs relations à la compétence législative, administrative et adjudicative de l'État.[44] La Banque a assimilé la présente affaire, dans laquelle elle a allégué que la partie privée avait choisi de faire partie d'une organisation internationale, au lien qui unit un État et ses ressortissants ou ses résidents. La compétence de la Banque à l'égard des parties privées avec lesquelles elle a cette relation particulière est "parallèle à la compétence des États à l'égard de leurs ressortissants."[45]

---

[44] Voir, par exemple, *Weiss c. Institute for Intellectual Cooperation*, Journal de droit international, n° 81, p. 744, 745 (Conseil d'État français, 20 février 1953) ("[Le plaignant] ayant la qualité de fonctionnaire d'un organisme à caractère international; qu'il n'appartient pas au Conseil d'État statuant au contentieux de connaître des difficultés pouvant exister entre ledit organisme international et l'un de ses agents.") (Documents juridiques de la Banque n° 101); *ICEM v. Chiti*, Italian Yearbook of International Law, 1976, vol. II, p. 348, 350-351 (Cass. it., 7 novembre 1973) ("La jurisprudence a également confirmé que les actes d'auto-organisation et la réglementation des relations organisationnelles, dont celles de l'emploi public, sont l'expression du pouvoir souverain du sujet de droit international de la même manière qu'ils sont, en Italie, l'expression du pouvoir souverain de l'État italien et sont régis par le droit public . . . [Ces actes] doivent être régis par les règles propres à l'organisation internationale et ne relèvent donc pas du système juridique italien ni de la juridiction italienne en raison de ladite immunité.") (Documents juridiques de la Banque n° 102); *In re Dame Adrien*, Ann. Dig., n° 6, p. 33 (Conseil d'Etat français, 17 juillet 1931) (Le Conseil d'État a déclaré qu'il n'était pas compétent, parce que "[l]es demandeurs [agents français de la Commission des réparations] appartenaient à une organisation internationale et leur position ne pouvait être déterminée qu'en vertu du droit international public") (Documents juridiques de la Banque n° 103); Finn Seyersted, *Jurisdiction over Organs and Officials of States, the Holy See and Intergovernmental Organisations (2)*, International and Comparative Law Quaterly, 1965, vol. 14, p. 493, 505 (Documents juridiques de la Banque n° 104); Hans-Peter Kunz-Hallstein, *Die Beteiligung Internationaler Organisationen am Rechts und Wirtschaftsverkehr*, Gewerblicher Rechtsschutz und Urheberrecht, Internationaler Teil, 1987, p. 819, 824 ("Aufgrund der Organisationsgewalt der Internationalen Organisationen [comprenant la compétence personnelle] sind ihre inneren Angelegenheiten der Legislationsgewalt der Staaten und deren Gerichtsbarkeit der Sache nach (*ratione materiae*) unmittelbar entzogen.") (Documents juridiques de la Banque n° 105), *id.*, p. 73, note de bas de page 90.

[45] Contre-mémoire, par. 124. First Eagle s'appuie sur l'avis consultatif rendu par la Cour internationale de Justice dans l'affaire *Réparation des dommages subis au service des Nations Unies* pour étayer son argument selon lequel le présent différend organique doit néanmoins être régi par les règles applicables à la reprise d'une propriété étrangère. Mémoire de First Eagle, par. 263. Cette affaire apporte peu d'éléments au cas d'espèce. Dans ladite affaire, la Cour internationale de Justice ("CIJ") devait déterminer si les Nations Unies avaient qualité pour présenter une réclamation en vue d'obtenir la réparation des dommages causés par un tiers à un

". . . [L]a Cour de Justice des Communautés européennes s'est exclusivement fondée sur la législation des droits de l'homme, lorsqu'elle s'est prononcée sur des ingérences alléguées de la Communauté européenne dans les droits patrimoniaux dans l'exercice de ses pouvoirs législatifs ou administratifs à l'égard de parties privées."[46] Selon la Banque, "la législation des droits de l'homme est *a fortiori* applicable aux relations organiques entre la BRI et ses actionnaires . . . . "[47]

c. DÉCISION DEMANDÉE

99. En réponse à la demande du Tribunal en vue du dépôt de conclusions écrites finales, la Banque a déclaré ce qui suit:

> La Banque conclut à ce qu'il plaise au Tribunal de rendre une sentence:
>
> 1. déclarant que la Banque est une organisation internationale et que ses relations avec ses actionnaires sont régies par ses Instruments constitutifs et par le droit international public général applicable;
>
> 2. déclarant que le rachat forcé des actions de la Banque détenues par des personnes privées est licite;
>
> 3. déclarant que la norme d'indemnisation pour les actions rachetées est la juste valeur du marché;

agent des Nations Unies dans l'exercice de ses fonctions. Lorsqu'elle a déclaré que le lien juridique entre les Nations Unies et son personnel ne pouvait pas être assimilé à celui qui unit un État et ses ressortissants, la CIJ examinait les relations extérieures entre les Nations Unies et un tiers, qui intéressaient la compétence concurrente de l'État national de l'agent, plutôt que les relations intérieures. Cela étant, la CIJ a estimé que les Nations Unies jouissaient d'un droit de protection fonctionnelle à l'égard de ses agents, reconnaissant l'existence d'un système d'attribution même en matière de relations extérieures. *Réparation des dommages subis au service des Nations Unies*, Recueil CIJ 1949, p. 184-185 (Documents juridiques de la Banque n° 59), contre-mémoire, par. 124, note de bas de page 92.

[46] Voir, par exemple, affaire 4/73, *Nold c. Commission*, Rec. I 1974, p. 491, 508, par. 14 (Documents juridiques de la Banque n° 108); affaire 44/79, *Hauer c. Rheinland-Pfalz*, Rec. 1979, p. 3727, 3745-3746 (Documents juridiques de la Banque n° 109), *id.*, p. 75, note de bas de page 94.

[47] Contre-mémoire, par. 125.

4. déclarant que la Banque a payé la juste valeur du marché pour ses actions, puisqu'elle a versé aux anciens actionnaires privés une indemnité égale à environ le double du prix du marché de ses actions à la date du 8 septembre 2000, soit le dernier jour de négociation avant l'annonce du rachat forcé;

5. accordant à la Banque des dommages et intérêts pour la violation de l'article 54, paragraphe 1, des Statuts par First Eagle;

6. accordant à la Banque les frais d'arbitrage;

7. accordant à la Banque d'autres mesures de réparation, si le Tribunal l'estime juste et approprié.

CHAPITRE IV – PREMIÈRE QUESTION DE L'ORDONNANCE DE PROCÉDURE N° 3

100. On rappellera que l'ordonnance de procédure n° 3 (Acte de mission) du 5 mars 2002 définit de la façon suivante la première des trois questions qui continuent à opposer toutes les Parties ou certaines d'entre elles:

> 1. La licéité de la reprise forcée des actions, y compris les procédures selon lesquelles elle a été effectuée et l'étendue possible des conséquences d'une constatation d'illicéité pour tous ceux qui étaient actionnaires privés au 8 janvier 2001.

À la section C de l'ordonnance de procédure n° 3, le Tribunal déclare:

> 1. Bien que la première question ait été soulevée uniquement par M. Mathieu et la Banque, tous deux affirment qu'une constatation d'illicéité compromettrait l'opération de reprise des actions et aurait des conséquences pour tous ceux qui étaient actionnaires au 8 janvier 2001. Une constatation d'illicéité de l'opération de reprise forcée des actions pourrait donc avoir des conséquences pour tous les demandeurs dans ces affaires.

En conséquence, le Tribunal déclare aux sections C.1 et C.2:

> 1. Le Tribunal invite M. Mathieu et la Banque à traiter de toutes les questions qu'ils estiment pertinentes au regard de leurs allégations concernant la licéité de l'opération de reprise, y compris ses conséquences pour ceux qui étaient actionnaires au 8 janvier 2001.
>
> 2. Le Tribunal invite Dr. Reineccius et First Eagle à traiter de toutes les questions qu'ils estiment pertinentes au regard de l'étendue possible des conséquences éventuelles d'une constatation d'illicéité de l'opération de reprise pour ceux qui étaient actionnaires au 8 janvier 2001.

101. On rappellera que le demandeur n° 1, Dr. Reineccius, a fait savoir que selon lui, la demande formée par le demandeur n° 3 n'était pas fondée et que, par conséquent, il ne déposerait pas de conclusions écrites à ce sujet. Cependant, il s'est réservé le droit de présenter des observations à cet

égard lors des audiences. Il a, par la suite, informé la Secrétaire du Tribunal qu'il ne serait pas présent à l'audience le jour où cette question précise serait examinée.

102. De même, First Eagle, dans son mémoire du 6 mai 2002, a affirmé que "le pouvoir, conféré à la Banque par les Statuts, d'effectuer un rachat forcé ou une liquidation partielle contre paiement d'une indemnité complète n'est pas en cause dans la procédure qui oppose First Eagle à la Banque."[48] Néanmoins, First Eagle a saisi l'occasion d'exposer au Tribunal, dans son mémoire et à l'audience, son point de vue à l'égard de l'étendue des conséquences éventuelles d'une constatation d'illicéité de l'opération de reprise.

103. Le Tribunal examinera tout d'abord les arguments de M. Mathieu concernant la licéité de l'opération de reprise. Compte tenu de sa décision à l'égard de la licéité de l'opération de reprise, le Tribunal considérera ensuite les arguments de M. Mathieu et de First Eagle concernant les conséquences éventuelles d'une constatation d'illicéité.

A. Première question préliminaire: caractère juridique et statut de la Banque

104. La première question préliminaire au regard de la première question que le Tribunal doit examiner est le caractère juridique et le statut de la Banque.

105. Le Tribunal fait observer que le processus plutôt compliqué par lequel la Banque a été constituée doit être analysé à la lumière de l'état de développement qui caractérisait le droit international en 1930. Il semble qu'à cette époque, certaines des Parties signataires de la Convention doutaient qu'un traité puisse constituer, en vertu du droit international public, une société anonyme par actions et que cette société puisse être généralement reconnue.

---

[48] Mémoire de First Eagle, par. 362.

106. C'est pourquoi les Parties à la Convention ont choisi d'adopter un modèle en vertu duquel la Suisse, conformément à l'obligation conventionnelle, s'est engagée à accorder la Charte constitutive de la Banque et donc à créer la société. Dans le même temps, cependant, les parties ont clairement indiqué que, bien que la Charte, en tant qu'annexe à la Convention, ait également été établie en vertu du droit suisse, la société ne pouvait pas être régie par le droit suisse. Ce système compliqué n'exclut pas la possibilité d'appliquer le droit suisse pour certaines formalités, comme par exemple la procédure à suivre pour les assemblées générales de la Banque, si cette application n'est pas incompatible avec les instruments pertinents de droit international.

107. Cela étant, la Suisse, qui adopte une approche moniste, considère que le droit international est automatiquement valable dans l'ordre juridique suisse, sans qu'il soit besoin d'aucun acte de transformation ou d'incorporation. Par conséquent, le gouvernement suisse a accordé la Charte par la simple ratification de la Convention, après que celle-ci eut été approuvée par le Parlement suisse, sans avoir promulgué de dispositions législatives additionnelles. Cette pratique a été suivie pour toutes les modifications relevant de l'article 58 des Statuts, lorsqu'un article "réservé" était modifié. Le gouvernement suisse, dès lors qu'il approuvait la modification, "a sanctionné [ladite modification] par une loi additionnelle à la Charte de la Banque" au sens de l'article 58 des Statuts.

108. Les Instruments constitutifs confirment que la Banque a été constituée en vertu du droit international conformément à un traité entre les gouvernements de l'Allemagne, de la Belgique, de la France, du Royaume-Uni, de l'Italie, du Japon[49] et de la Suisse, qui a été signé le 20 janvier 1930. En vertu de l'article 1 de la Convention, la Suisse s'est engagée à "accorder sans délai à la Banque des Règlements Internationaux la Charte constitutive ayant force de loi . . . ." En approuvant la Convention, le Parlement suisse a conféré au gouvernement suisse la compétence de ratifier ledit traité et d'accorder la Charte constitutive, qui fait partie intégrante de la Convention. L'article 1 de la Charte dispose que "[l]a personnalité juridique est conférée par la présente Charte à la Banque des Règlements Internationaux . . . ." L'article 2 de ladite Charte

---

[49] Voir *supra* note de bas de page 3.

ajoute que la constitution, les opérations et le domaine d'activité de la Banque sont "définis et régis par les Statuts annexés". Les Statuts de la Banque et sa Charte constitutive ont donc été déterminés par un accord intergouvernemental et ont été annexés à la Convention. Le fait que la Charte ait été accordée par la Suisse n'entraîne pas la subordination de la Banque au droit suisse. Le paragraphe 5 de la Charte dispose que

> Les Statuts et toute modification qui leur serait apportée conformément aux dispositions des paragraphes 3 et 4 ci-dessus seront valables et auront effet nonobstant toute contradiction avec toutes dispositions actuelles ou futures du droit suisse.[50]

Dès lors, la séquence des étapes par lesquelles la Banque a été constituée démontre qu'elle tire son origine d'un traité international. La Banque a été créée par des gouvernements au moyen d'un instrument international, qui a obligé la Suisse à lui accorder un siège et un statut local, ainsi que les immunités prescrites. La Banque est constituée en tant que société anonyme par actions de droit suisse, alors qu'elle est enregistrée en tant que "Internationale Organisation mit eigenem Rechtsstatus" au "Handelsregister des Kantons Basel-Stadt Hauptregister".[51]

109. La déclaration du Conseil fédéral suisse (gouvernement fédéral suisse) au Parlement fédéral suisse à la date du 7 février 1930 expose clairement la séquence des étapes de la constitution, ainsi que la prééminence et l'indépendance du caractère international de la Banque:

> La convention concernant la banque des règlements internationaux distingue entre les dispositions conventionnelles proprement dites et la charte constitutive de la banque, qui est réputée constituer un acte de droit interne suisse . . . . Par les premières, la Suisse s'engage à promulguer la charte constitutive et à ne pas la modifier sans le consentement des Etats signataires; en outre, la mise en vigueur et la durée du traité s'y trouvent réglées; enfin, il est prévu, pour le règlement de tous différends survenant entre les Etats contractants, une instance arbitrale . . . . Le contenu de la charte, qui doit être accordée par

[50] Voir également la Charte constitutive, par. 5.
[51] Voir contre-mémoire, par. 36, note de bas de page 22.

> la Suisse, se trouve intégralement dans la convention. La charte octroie à la banque la personnalité juridique du droit suisse, sanctionne ses statuts nonobstant toute contradiction avec les dispositions impératives de ce droit, et énonce ses privilèges fiscaux et administratifs . . . .[52]

110. De même, l'engagement de la Suisse à ne pas appliquer le droit suisse en particulier aux opérations et activités de la Banque était assorti de l'engagement des Parties au traité instituant la Banque de ne pas modifier les Statuts d'une façon qui imposerait un régime différent à la Suisse, sans le consentement de ce dernier État:

> Dans la charte, la Suisse reconnaît, en outre, les statuts de la banque, ainsi que leurs modifications éventuelles, même si les statuts portent atteinte aux dispositions impératives du droit suisse actuel ou futur . . . . Il y a lieu de noter, en particulier, que les dispositions statutaires essentielles ne peuvent être modifiées que par une loi additionnelle à la charte de la banque . . . . Le caractère de la banque – c'est une des conditions de la conclusion de la convention par la Suisse – ne peut donc être modifié sans l'assentiment de notre pays.[53]

111. De fait, les Statuts, qui font partie intégrante de la Convention, précisent, à l'article 60 (actuellement article 58), les dispositions des Statuts qui, outre l'adoption en vertu de la procédure de modification de la Banque, requièrent également l'adoption d'une loi "additionnelle à la Charte de la Banque." La même condition est énoncée au paragraphe 4 de la Charte de la Banque, qui fait aussi partie intégrante de la Convention.

112. Bien que la structure interne de la Banque soit, en vertu de l'article 1 des Statuts, celle d'une "société anonyme par actions" et que le Conseil d'administration de la Banque soit composé en permanence des gouverneurs des banques centrales des sept États fondateurs et des personnes qu'ils ont désignées, le caractère fondamentalement international de la Banque découle du fait qu'elle tire son origine d'un traité.

---

[52] Feuille fédérale de la Confédération suisse, vol. 1, p. 87 (1930).
[53] *Id.*, p. 92 et 93.

113. Par ailleurs, les fonctions de la Banque avaient un caractère international public par excellence. M. Auboin, un des premiers directeurs généraux de la BRI, a écrit:

> Après la première guerre mondiale, pourtant, et en particulier pendant les phases de stabilisation monétaire de la période 1922-1930, les principales banques centrales unissaient fréquemment leurs forces pour accorder des "crédits de stabilisation" spéciaux soit dans le cadre des travaux de reconstruction entrepris par le Comité financier de la Société des Nations, soit indépendamment de ces opérations. Il était dès lors assez naturel que les autorités politiques et monétaires commencent bientôt à s'intéresser à l'idée de remplacer ces associations temporaires et ponctuelles par un système permanent de coopération.[54]

114. Dès sa création, la Banque a été chargée d'accomplir une tâche internationale particulièrement urgente. L'article 3 des Statuts originaux (qui n'a pas été modifié dans les Statuts actuels) définit l'objet de la Banque en termes généraux:

> La Banque a pour objet: de favoriser la coopération des banques centrales et de fournir des facilités additionnelles pour les opérations financières internationales; et d'agir comme mandataire (trustee) ou comme agent en ce qui concerne les règlements financiers internationaux qui lui sont confiés en vertu d'accords passés avec les parties intéressées.

L'article 4 des Statuts originaux, qui a été abrogé en 1969 (longtemps après avoir perdu toute pertinence pour le travail de la Banque), indique clairement que la principale raison de la création de la Banque était la gestion du plan connu sous le nom "Nouveau Plan" ou "Plan Young" pour le règlement des réparations allemandes, qui était à l'époque un problème international et intergouvernemental majeur.

---

[54] R. Auboin, The Bank for International Settlements, 1930-1955, Essays in International Finance, n° 22, carte 1955, p. 1-2 (Documents juridiques de la Banque n° 25).

115. La Banque a cité plusieurs instruments internationaux qui reconnaissent explicitement que la Banque est une organisation internationale:[55] l'Accord de siège avec la Suisse de 1987,[56] l'Accord de pays hôte entre la Banque et la République populaire de Chine de 1998[57] et l'Accord de pays hôte avec le Mexique de 2002.[58]

116. Dr. Reineccius et M. Mathieu reconnaissent que la Banque a l'identité d'une organisation internationale. First Eagle pose des questions sur l'identité de la Banque.[59] First Eagle affirme à tort que les accords de siège précités ne reconnaissent pas que la Banque est une organisation internationale. Cette reconnaissance découle manifestement des dispositions desdits accords. First Eagle élude la question, lorsqu'elle déclare qu'à la différence de la Banque mondiale et du Fonds monétaire international, la Banque des Règlements Internationaux a des actionnaires privés et ne peut donc pas être une organisation internationale. C'est précisément la question examinée.

117. De même, First Eagle déclare à tort que puisque la Banque exerce des activités commerciales courantes pour les banques du secteur privé, elle ne peut pas être une organisation internationale. Il se peut qu'une organisation internationale doive se lancer dans des activités propres au

[55] Contre-mémoire, par. 40.

[56] Accord entre le Conseil fédéral suisse et la Banque des Règlements Internationaux en vue de déterminer le statut juridique de la Banque en Suisse, 10 février 1987, RS 0.192.122.971.3 (Documents juridiques de la Banque n° 16).

[57] L'article 1 (personnalité et capacité juridiques) se lit comme suit: "Le gouvernement reconnaît la personnalité juridique internationale et la capacité juridique de la Banque sur le territoire de la République populaire de Chine, y compris la Région administrative spéciale de Hong-Kong." Accord de pays hôte entre la Banque des Règlements Internationaux et la République populaire de Chine relatif à la création et au statut d'un bureau de représentation de la Banque des Règlements Internationaux dans la Région administrative spéciale de Hong-Kong de la République populaire de Chine, 11 mai 1998 (Documents juridiques de la Banque n° 17).

[58] L'article 2, paragraphe 1, (personnalité et capacité juridiques) se lit comme suit: "L'État reconnaît la personnalité juridique internationale et la capacité juridique de la Banque sur le territoire de l'État." Accord de pays hôte entre la Banque des Règlements Internationaux et les États-Unis du Mexique relatif à la création et au statut d'un bureau de représentation de la Banque des Règlements Internationaux au Mexique, Diario Oficial de la Federación, 20 juin 2002, p. 3 (Documents juridiques de la Banque n° 18).

[59] Voir mémoire de First Eagle, par. 229-239.

secteur privé dans l'exercice de ses fonctions publiques, sans pour autant cesser automatiquement d'être un organe de droit international public. Le fait que des organisations internationales utilisent fréquemment les mêmes techniques comptables que les entités privées n'est pas concluant, car il s'agit de méthodes de contrôle et d'efficacité qui sont requises, sous l'une ou l'autre forme, dans toute collaboration à grande échelle. La Banque n'est pas non plus la seule organisation internationale à enregistrer des bénéfices. Cependant, même si la Banque était singulière à cet égard ou si ses bénéfices dépassaient largement ceux des autres organisations internationales, First Eagle elle-même admet qu'il existe une différence entre une entité à but lucratif et une entité qui recherche la maximisation du profit. Dans la déclaration du Conseil fédéral suisse (gouvernement fédéral suisse), citée plus haut,[60] il était précisé que

> La banque n'a pas pour but principal de faire des bénéfices. Sans doute, les statuts prévoient-ils la possibilité de gains considérables, mais ceux-ci reviendront, en première ligne, aux banques d'émission qui ont le droit de souscrire les actions. La banque des règlements internationaux tend à des buts d'intérêt général . . . .[61]

Ce n'est pas le fait que la Banque puisse faire des bénéfices qui importe, car cette possibilité est acquise, mais plutôt l'objet pour lequel la Banque a été créée et auquel les bénéfices sont destinés.

118. Par ces motifs, le Tribunal constate que la Banque des Règlements Internationaux est une création *sui generis* qui est une organisation internationale.

B. SECONDE QUESTION PRÉLIMINAIRE: DROIT APPLICABLE À LA QUESTION 1

119. Le Tribunal en vient à présent à la seconde question préliminaire concernant la question 1, à savoir: quel est le droit applicable à la

---

[60] Voir *supra* par. 109.

[61] Feuille fédérale de la Confédération suisse, *supra* note de bas de page 52, p. 95.

question de la licéité de la reprise des actions par la Banque à la date du 8 janvier 2001? La question du droit applicable en matière d'évaluation des actions reprises, si le Tribunal l'examine, doit être traitée séparément, comme il sera expliqué ci-dessous.

120. On se souviendra que ni Dr. Reineccius ni First Eagle n'ont contesté la licéité de la reprise ni n'ont fait valoir que ladite reprise outrepassait les compétences accordées par les Statuts. M. Mathieu, par contre, a avancé cet argument; il a en effet affirmé que les modifications des Statuts du 8 janvier 2001 étaient nulles de plein droit et a demandé la remise en état, impliquant le rétablissement des actionnaires privés.[62]

121. M. Mathieu a fondé son argument sur les Instruments constitutifs de la Banque; ainsi, il a déclaré que ce n'était qu'en cas de lacunes ou de manque de précision des Instruments constitutifs qu'il fallait se référer au droit international. Il a également fait valoir que les dispositions d'*ordre public international* néerlandaises et suisses devaient être prises en considération.

122. La Banque a convenu du rôle des Instruments constitutifs, mais elle s'est montrée particulièrement soucieuse de la non-application de la législation nationale et a allégué que

> Étant donné que la Banque est une organisation internationale, les questions intéressant ses principes organiques et sa gestion interne (comme les relations de la Banque avec ses actionnaires) sont nécessairement régies par le droit international public.[63]
>
> Les demandes formées contre les actes ou les omissions d'une organisation internationale dans l'exercice de ses pouvoirs souverains ne peuvent être régies que par le droit international public. En modifiant ses Statuts pour effectuer le retrait de ses actions détenues par des personnes privées, la BRI n'a pas agi en tant que partie privée. Plus exactement, elle a exercé son pouvoir législatif en vertu de l'article 57 des Statuts, qui autorise la BRI à modifier ses Statuts, notamment les droits statutaires

[62] Mémoire en Demande, p. 5-6; compte rendu, p. 89, lignes 18-27.
[63] Contre-mémoire, par. 48.

> des actionnaires privés. La résolution de l'Assemblée générale extraordinaire du 8 janvier 2001, qui a adopté les modifications permettant le rachat des actions détenues par des personnes privées constitue donc un acte *juri imperii* qui est régi par les Instruments constitutifs de la BRI et par le droit international public général applicable.[64]
>
> En somme, les droits des actionnaires de la BRI sont régis par les Instruments constitutifs de la BRI et par le droit international public général applicable, qui déterminent de même la validité et la légalité du rachat de leurs actions et de ses conséquences juridiques.[65]

123. La Banque affirme à juste titre que "les questions intéressant ses principes organiques ou sa gestion interne" sont régies par le droit international. Cependant, la Banque considère à tort que cette constatation signifie qu'elle a des "pouvoirs souverains" ou que des actes, comme la reprise d'actions, relèvent de la catégorie des *acta jure imperii*. Alors que les États jouissent de pouvoirs souverains, un acteur international, en sa qualité d'acteur international et en vertu de ce statut, n'est pas souverain. Quant à la distinction entre *acta jure imperii* et *acta jure gestionis*, elle est utilisée par les tribunaux nationaux, pour déterminer si un État étranger ou son agence qui n'a pas admis la juridiction locale jouira d'une immunité de juridiction et d'exécution. Cette distinction n'est pas pertinente devant un tribunal international public à l'égard d'un État ou de tout autre acteur international qui est soumis à sa juridiction.

124. M. Mathieu affirme à tort que les dispositions d'*ordre public international* néerlandaises et suisses sont applicables.[66] L'Accord entre les Pays-Bas et la Cour permanente d'Arbitrage du 30 mars 1999,[67] ainsi que l'Accord de siège entre la Banque des Règlements Internationaux et la

---

[64] *Id.*, par. 50.
[65] *Id.*, par. 51.
[66] Mémoire en Demande, p. 7-8.
[67] Accord concernant le siège de la Cour permanente d'Arbitrage entre le Royaume des Pays-Bas et la Cour permanente d'Arbitrage, 30 mars 1999, art. 3.

Suisse du 10 février 1987[68] avaient clairement pour intention d'exclure l'application respective de la compétence législative des Pays-Bas et de la Suisse. Par ailleurs, le but du paragraphe 5 de la Charte constitutive de la Banque, qui fait partie de l'Accord de La Haye de 1930, serait compromis si, par dérogation à ses dispositions, les principes d'*ordre public* suisses étaient applicables.

125. Tant M. Mathieu que la Banque tiennent pour acquis que les Instruments constitutifs de la Banque[69] règlent définitivement la question particulière de la licéité de la reprise des actions privées grâce à la modification des Statuts du 8 janvier 2001. Aucune de ces Parties n'a cité d'autres instruments juridiques qui pourraient régir cette question à l'exception de la Convention de Vienne sur le droit des traités de 1969, qui a été invoquée uniquement dans le but d'orienter de façon fiable l'interprétation. Néanmoins, M. Mathieu a fait valoir que le Tribunal devait dépasser les limites des Statuts; il a en effet affirmé que même si les modifications permettant la reprise étaient *intra vires* et valables en vertu des Statuts, elles étaient entachées de nullité en vertu du droit international général. Cette allégation sera examinée ci-dessous.

126. À la lumière de ce qui précède, le Tribunal en viendra à un examen de la licéité des actions entreprises par la Banque.

C. MODIFICATION DES STATUTS

127. Les Statuts de la Banque, dans leur version actuelle, comptent cinquante-huit articles. L'article 57 (dont le contenu n'a pas changé depuis 1930) dispose que:

> Des modifications à tous les articles des Statuts, à l'exception des articles énumérés à l'article 58, peuvent être proposées à l'Assemblée générale par le Conseil, statuant à la majorité des deux tiers. Si ces modifications sont adoptées par la majorité de

---

[68] *Supra* note de bas de page 56.

[69] La rédaction des Statuts a été achevée le 20 janvier 1930; le texte actuellement en vigueur est celui qui a été modifié le 8 novembre 1999.

> l'Assemblée générale, elles entrent en vigueur, pourvu qu'elles ne soient pas incompatibles avec les dispositions des articles énumérés à l'article 58.

L'article 58 dispose que:

> Les articles 2, 3, 8, 14, 19, 24, 27, 44, 51, 54, 57 et 58 ne peuvent être modifiés que dans les conditions suivantes: la modification doit être adoptée par une majorité des deux tiers du Conseil, approuvée par la majorité de l'Assemblée générale et sanctionnée par une loi additionnelle à la Charte de la Banque.

Le contenu des dispositions ci-dessus n'a pas non plus changé depuis 1930, bien que la numérotation des articles réservés cités à l'article 58 ait changé en raison d'autres ajouts et suppressions dont les Statuts ont fait l'objet au fil des années.

128. Bien que l'article 57 prévoie que des modifications peuvent être proposées à l'Assemblée générale, l'article 47 des Statuts dispose que:

> Les Assemblées générales extraordinaires sont convoquées pour statuer sur toute proposition du Conseil concernant:
>
> (a) les modifications aux Statuts;
>
> . . . .

Les Statuts n'imposent pas de préavis spécial pour les Assemblées générales extraordinaires; il semblerait que la règle du préavis de trois semaines fixé pour les Assemblées générales, comme prévu par l'article 44, s'applique également aux Assemblées générales extraordinaires. Il n'existe pas non plus de différence importante au niveau des conditions de vote lors des Assemblées générales et des Assemblées générales extraordinaires en ce qui concerne la modification des Statuts.

129. La modification de tous les articles des Statuts, à l'exception des douze articles réservés énumérés, requiert une proposition à l'Assemblée générale d'une majorité des deux tiers du Conseil et l'adoption par une majorité simple de l'Assemblée générale. La modification de l'un des douze articles réservés, cités à l'article 58 des Statuts, requiert l'*adoption*

par une majorité des deux tiers du Conseil et l'approbation par la majorité de l'Assemblée générale. Il semblerait qu'il n'y ait pas de différence importante entre la proposition d'une modification par une majorité des deux tiers du Conseil (article 57 des Statuts) et son adoption par une majorité des deux tiers du Conseil (article 58 desdits Statuts). La seule différence importante entre la modification des articles, exception faite des douze articles réservés, réside dans le fait que l'article 58 requiert une sanction par une loi suisse additionnelle à la Charte de la Banque, après approbation par la majorité de l'Assemblée générale, pour les raisons qui ont été expliquées plus haut. Par contre, la modification des articles non réservés des Statuts ne requiert pas l'adoption d'une telle loi.

130. Les articles réservés énumérés à l'article 58, pour lesquels la procédure de modification spéciale doit être appliquée, ont trait aux points suivants:

(i) Déplacement du siège social de la Banque établi à Bâle (article 2).

(ii) Modification de l'objet de la Banque (article 3).

(iii) Augmentation ou réduction du capital de la Banque et de la répartition imposée d'une augmentation du capital de la Banque (article 8).

(iv) Modification du régime qui accorderait un droit de vote ou de représentation aux actionnaires en cette qualité (article 14).

(v) Modification du principe selon lequel les opérations de la Banque doivent être conformes à la politique monétaire des banques centrales des pays intéressés (article 19).

(vi) Décision d'autoriser la Banque à exercer l'une des six activités expressément interdites (article 24).

(vii) Modification de la composition statutaire du Conseil d'administration (article 27).

(viii) Modification du droit de vote et du droit d'assister aux Assemblées générales (article 44).

(ix) Modification du régime d'affectation et de versement des bénéfices annuels (article 51).

(x) Changement des procédures de modification des articles non réservés dans les Statuts (article 57).

(xi) Changement des procédures de modification de l'un des articles réservés dans les Statuts (article 58).

Les articles réservés des Statuts concernent les intérêts particuliers des banques centrales et de la Suisse et ont manifestement été conçus pour les protéger. Ce sont uniquement les modifications aux Statuts qui entraînent une augmentation ou une réduction du capital de la Banque qui requièrent l'adoption par une majorité des deux tiers de l'Assemblée générale. Comme mentionné ci-dessus, à l'exception de l'article 8, les procédures de vote pour la modification des articles tant réservés que non réservés sont essentiellement les mêmes aussi bien au Conseil d'administration qu'à l'Assemblée générale. Cependant, la modification des articles réservés énumérés requiert en outre une adaptation de la Charte de la Banque en vertu d'une loi suisse, comme il a été expliqué ci-dessus.

D. Allégations de M. Mathieu concernant l'illicéité et réponse de la Banque

131. Lorsque la Banque a décidé de retirer toutes les actions détenues par des actionnaires privés lors de son Assemblée générale extraordinaire du 8 janvier 2001, la procédure suivie a été celle de la modification des articles non réservés des Statuts en conformité avec l'article 57 desdits Statuts. M. Mathieu a allégué que la modification des Statuts était illicite, car elle n'était pas conforme aux Instruments constitutifs de la Banque. Dans son mémoire, M. Mathieu déclare:

> La Résolution amendant les Statuts est illégale, ayant été adoptée en violation de la Charte et des Statuts. En effet, la Résolution a prévu l'ajout d'un nouvel article (1.1) ce que ne permettent pas les Instruments constitutifs de la Banque (1.2). Subsidairement, quand bien même il serait possible d'ajouter un

nouvel article, il aurait à tout le moins fallu le faire en application de la procédure renforcée (1.3).

Ainsi, M. Mathieu a soutenu que l'article 18A n'était pas la conséquence d'une modification d'un article existant mais l'ajout d'un nouvel article et, à ce titre, il s'agissait d'un type de modification des Statuts qui, selon lui, n'était pas autorisé par l'article 57 et était, par conséquent, nul et non avenu. À titre subsidiaire, il a fait valoir que même s'il était possible d'ajouter un nouvel article, il aurait fallu le faire en application de la procédure spéciale exposée à l'article 58, plutôt qu'en vertu de la procédure générale énoncée à l'article 57.

132. En ce qui concerne le premier argument de M. Mathieu, il a soutenu que l'article 18A ne résultait pas d'une modification au sens des Statuts, mais constituait un nouvel article que ni les Statuts ni la Charte n'autorisaient. Il a fait valoir que la Charte et les Statuts devaient être interprétés en conformité avec les règles du droit international, en particulier l'article 31 de la Convention de Vienne sur le droit des traités. En s'appuyant sur l'article 31, M. Mathieu a affirmé qu'une interprétation littérale visant à définir le "sens ordinaire" démontrait que les articles 57 et 58 des Statuts mentionnaient "des modifications à tous les articles des Statuts." Il est fait mention de *modifications* d'articles existants et non d'*additions* ou d'introduction de nouveaux articles. Le principal argument de M. Mathieu était donc que les termes du texte se référaient uniquement à des modifications d'articles spécifiques et non à l'addition de nouveaux articles.

133. M. Mathieu a fait valoir que son interprétation de ce qu'il pense être le sens naturel et ordinaire des Statuts est renforcée par une interprétation qui considère le contexte, au sens où ce terme est utilisé dans la Convention de Vienne sur le droit des traités. La Charte et les Statuts font la distinction entre les articles ordinaires, qui peuvent être amendés de façon ordinaire, et les articles réservés qui requièrent, en plus de la procédure ordinaire de modification, l'adoption d'une loi additionnelle. La spécification des articles indiquait, d'après M. Mathieu, que les Statuts envisageaient la modification de certains articles mais pas des Statuts dans leur ensemble.

134. Selon M. Mathieu, l'interprétation à la lumière de l'objet et du but de l'instrument qui est interprété renforcerait encore l'interprétation qu'il proposait. De son point de vue, la précision avec laquelle la disposition en matière de modification a été rédigée laissait transparaître l'intention des rédacteurs d'enserrer l'exercice des activités de la BRI dans des limites strictes et en particulier le pouvoir d'appréciation de la Banque. Selon M. Mathieu, ce fait démontrait que les États qui avaient créé une entité avec des pouvoirs strictement déterminés ne voulaient pas que ladite entité échappe à leur contrôle et prenne des libertés avec les pouvoirs qui lui avaient été accordés. En raison du caractère sensible des missions politiques de la Banque à l'époque de sa création, M. Mathieu a allégué que les États fondateurs étaient particulièrement soucieux de délimiter soigneusement le pouvoir discrétionnaire de la Banque. Il a par ailleurs soutenu qu'aucun nouvel article n'avait été ajouté aux Statuts depuis la constitution de la Banque et que le seul cas de suppression d'un article avait trait à l'expiration du plan Young. M. Mathieu a fait valoir que le fait que les activités de la Banque avaient évolué ne permettait pas à la Banque d'adapter les Statuts, car, comme le juge Bedjaoui l'a expliqué dans son opinion individuelle dans l'*affaire relative au projet Gabcíkovo-Nagymaros*, le droit qui doit présider à l'interprétation d'un traité est le droit contemporain de sa conclusion plutôt que le droit qui a ultérieurement évolué.[70] M. Mathieu a également cité l'Avis consultatif de la Cour internationale de Justice dans l'affaire relative à la *Namibie*.[71]

135. Par ailleurs, M. Mathieu a affirmé que même si le nouvel article n'était pas réputé illicite pour le motif qu'il s'agissait d'un ajout et non d'une modification, la Banque aurait dû appliquer la procédure de modification réservée prévue par l'article 58 des Statuts plutôt que la procédure moins rigoureuse de l'article 57. M. Mathieu a fait valoir qu'autoriser la Banque à introduire des articles nouveaux en application de la procédure ordinaire habiliterait la Banque non pas absolument à introduire des articles objectivement contraires aux articles réservés énumérés mais

---

[70] *Projet Gabcíkovo-Nagymaros (Hongrie/Slovaquie)*, opinion individuelle du juge Bedjaoui, Recueil CIJ 1997, par. 8.

[71] *Conséquences juridiques pour les États de la présence continue de l'Afrique du Sud en Namibie (Sud-Ouest africain) nonobstant la résolution 276 (1970) du Conseil de sécurité*, Avis consultatif du 21 juin 1971, Recueil CIJ 1971, p. 16, par. 53.

bien à créer de nouveaux éléments et à faire évoluer les Statuts dans une direction qui pourrait être conforme à la lettre des articles réservés énumérés, mais qui serait incompatible avec les buts originaires des États parties à l'Accord de La Haye de 1930. D'après M. Mathieu, pour éviter cela, il serait raisonnable d'exiger que les articles ajoutés fassent l'objet d'une loi additionnelle conformément à la procédure de l'article 58 des Statuts. Selon M. Mathieu, cette mesure préserverait l'intérêt de la Suisse en vertu du paragraphe 6, point (c),[72] de la Charte, ainsi que celui des États qui avaient conclu la convention de 1930.

136. Dans son contre-mémoire du 22 juillet 2002, la Banque a précisé que le sens ordinaire du mot anglais "amendment" (modification) était "[a] change made by addition, deletion or correction" (un changement apporté par ajout, suppression ou correction).[73] Par conséquent, la Banque a soutenu que le sens naturel et ordinaire des termes des Statuts concernait des modifications qui consisteraient à *ajouter* des articles et pas simplement des modifications qui consisteraient à *changer* les articles existants. De surcroît, la Banque a allégué que dans l'interprétation des instruments constitutifs des organisations internationales, il est tenu compte depuis longtemps de la pratique ultérieure de l'organisation, proposition étayée par l'article 31, paragraphe 3, point b, de la Convention de Vienne sur le droit des traités et confirmée dans un grand nombre d'avis rendus par la Cour internationale de Justice.[74]

137. À cet égard, la Banque a attiré l'attention du Tribunal sur des modifications importantes des Statuts qui ont donné lieu à l'ajout de

---

[72] Le paragraphe 6, point (c), dispose que: "La Banque est libre et exempte de tous impôts rentrant dans les catégories suivantes: tous impôts sur le capital de la Banque, ses réserves ou ses bénéfices distribués ou non, qu'ils frappent ces bénéfices avant distribution ou qu'ils soient perçus au moment de la distribution, sous forme d'une taxe à payer ou à retenir par la Banque sur les coupons. Cette stipulation ne porte pas atteinte au droit de la Suisse d'imposer les personnes résidant en Suisse autres que la Banque, comme elle le juge opportun."

[73] Contre-mémoire, par. 63, citation du dictionnaire "Black's Law Dictionary".

[74] *Certaines dépenses des Nations Unies*, avis consultatif du 20 juillet 1962, Recueil CIJ 1962, p. 165; *Réparation des dommages subis au service des Nations Unies*, *supra* note de bas de page 45, p. 174, 180; *Conséquences juridiques pour les États de la présence continue de l'Afrique du Sud en Namibie (Sud-Ouest africain) nonobstant la résolution 276 (1970) du Conseil de sécurité*, *supra* note de bas de page 71, p. 16, 22; *Jugements du Tribunal administratif de l'OIT sur requêtes contre l'Unesco*, Recueil CIJ 1956, p. 77, 91.

nouveaux articles en application de la procédure prévue à l'article 57. En 1969, une Assemblée générale extraordinaire a modifié l'article 5 (après renumérotation) et a ajouté le texte de l'article 6, ainsi qu'un nouvel article 9. À deux autres occasions, des Assemblées générales extraordinaires ont ajouté de nouvelles clauses à des articles existants.

138. La Banque a également fait valoir que plusieurs autres organisations internationales dont les instruments constitutifs autorisent la modification d'articles ont, dans la pratique, aussi bien ajouté que supprimé des articles de leurs instruments constitutifs.[75]

139. En ce qui concerne l'argument de M. Mathieu selon lequel les intentions des fondateurs de la Banque militent contre l'ajout de nouveaux articles en application de la procédure de modification, la Banque a relevé l'absence de toute preuve étayant cet argument et, au regard du droit, en se fondant sur l'avis rendu dans l'affaire *Certaines dépenses des Nations Unies*, a soutenu que des suppositions concernant les intentions des rédacteurs de ces instruments, "à l'exception de celles qui peuvent être déduites de ses termes mêmes,"[76] sont moins importantes dans l'interprétation des instruments constitutifs des organisations internationales.

140. En ce qui concerne l'argument de M. Mathieu selon lequel le retrait des actions devait être conforme à la procédure spéciale de l'article 58 applicable aux dispositions réservées énumérées des Statuts, la Banque a allégué que la procédure réservée s'appliquait uniquement aux dispositions précisées. Puisqu'il n'y avait pas d'incompatibilité entre les modifications visées ici et lesdites dispositions, il n'était pas nécessaire de se conformer aux procédures de l'article 58. La Banque a également déclaré que, dans la pratique, les modifications considérées ne changeaient ni la structure fondamentale, ni les objectifs, ni l'objet de la Banque et n'auraient donc pas requis la procédure spéciale prévue à l'article 58.

[75] Contre-mémoire, par. 67, note de bas de page 57, qui cite trois instruments constitutifs de cette nature.

[76] *Supra* note de bas de page 74, p. 184-185.

141. En ce qui concerne l'argument de M. Mathieu selon lequel la modification était illicite parce qu'elle était incompatible avec l'article 21, paragraphe g, des Statuts, qui limite la capacité de la Banque à "acheter et vendre des valeurs négociables autres que des actions, pour son propre compte ou pour celui des banques centrales", la Banque a fait remarquer que l'article 21, paragraphe g, ne faisait pas partie des dispositions réservées énumérées à l'article 58. Dès lors, même s'il y avait eu, *quod non*, conflit entre le nouvel article 18A et l'article 21, point g, préexistant, ledit conflit n'aurait pas requis la procédure spéciale de modification visée à l'article 58.

E. Examen par le Tribunal de l'illicéité alléguée

142. La licéité du rachat a été contestée principalement en vertu des Statuts de la Banque et accessoirement en vertu des principes de droit international en matière d'expropriation. Dans le premier cas, il convient de déterminer si la modification des Statuts, dans l'hypothèse où les principes du droit international ont été respectés, a été réalisée en conformité avec les articles 57 et 58 des Statuts (voir point 1 ci-dessous). Si la réponse à cette question est affirmative, il reste à examiner la validité de la modification en vertu des principes du droit international (voir point 2 ci-dessous). Il n'est pas nécessaire d'examiner cette question sous l'angle d'un droit interne quel qu'il soit.

1. Conformité de la reprise au regard des Statuts

143. En raison de l'importance du texte, il est utile de rappeler les termes des articles 57 et 58 des Statuts. L'article 57 dispose que:

> Des modifications à tous les articles des Statuts, à l'exception des articles énumérés à l'article 58, peuvent être proposées à l'Assemblée générale par le Conseil, statuant à la majorité des deux tiers. Si ces modifications sont adoptées par la majorité de l'Assemblée générale, elles entrent en vigueur, pourvu qu'elles ne soient pas incompatibles avec les dispositions des articles énumérés à l'article 58.

L'article 58 dispose que:

> Les articles 2, 3, 8, 14, 19, 24, 27, 44, 51, 54, 57 et 58 ne peuvent être modifiés que dans les conditions suivantes: la modification doit être adoptée par une majorité des deux tiers du Conseil, approuvée par la majorité de l'Assemblée générale et sanctionnée par une loi additionnelle à la Charte de la Banque.

À l'exception de l'obligation de sanction des modifications aux articles énumérés par une loi suisse additionnelle à la Charte de la Banque[77] visée à l'article 58, les procédures des articles 57 et 58 sont en fait les mêmes, hormis le fait que l'article 8 précise qu'une modification du capital requiert la majorité des deux tiers de l'Assemblée générale plutôt qu'une majorité simple.

144. Les termes de l'article 57 n'introduisent pas de limite importante à la compétence de modification de l'Assemblée générale si ce n'est l'obligation de compatibilité entre les modifications et les articles énumérés à l'article 58. Dès lors, en tant que simple question textuelle, une modification aux Statuts accomplie en conformité avec les procédures requises par l'article 57 serait *intra vires* et valable, tant qu'elle n'est pas incompatible avec l'une des dispositions réservées énumérées à l'article 58. L'article 57 ne précise pas si le mode de formulation d'une modification, qu'il s'agisse d'un ajout à un article existant ou d'un article entièrement nouveau désigné par un nouveau numéro, a une quelconque importance juridique. Par conséquent, une interprétation des Statuts de bonne foi et en conformité avec le sens ordinaire à donner aux termes du Traité doit amener à conclure que la modification considérée est valable et relève des compétences conférées par les Statuts.

145. L'article 31, paragraphe 3, point b, de la Convention de Vienne sur le droit des traités[78] requiert qu'il soit tenu compte "de toute pratique ultérieurement suivie dans l'application du traité par laquelle est établi

---

[77] Aux termes de l'article 1 de la Convention, la Suisse s'est engagée à ne pas sanctionner les modifications aux Statuts de la Banque visées au paragraphe 4 de la Charte si ce n'est d'accord avec les autres gouvernements signataires.

[78] *Supra* note de bas de page 23.

l'accord des parties à l'égard de l'interprétation du traité." Cette disposition revêt un sens particulier, lorsqu'elle est appliquée, en conformité avec l'article 5 de la Convention de Vienne, aux instruments constitutifs d'organisations internationales. Dans l'affaire *Réparation des dommages subis au service des Nations Unies*, la Cour internationale de Justice a dit que "les droits et devoirs d'une entité telle que l'Organisation [les Nations Unies] doivent dépendre des buts et des fonctions de celle-ci, énoncés ou impliqués par son acte constitutif et *développés dans la pratique*."[79] Le fait que la Banque ait, à de nombreuses occasions, modifié ses Statuts par l'introduction d'un nouvel article semble désigner l'interprétation des Statuts qui fait autorité à cet égard.

146. M. Mathieu a déclaré que les rédacteurs souhaitaient une interprétation stricte des pouvoirs de la Banque, de crainte que la Banque, une fois créée, n'échappe à leur contrôle et prenne des libertés avec les pouvoirs qui lui avaient été accordés.[80] Toutefois, la structure de décision de la Banque, comme elle a été définie aux chapitres IV et V des Statuts, requiert la majorité des deux tiers du Conseil pour proposer des modifications et la majorité simple de l'Assemblée générale pour les approuver. L'article 27 des Statuts, qui détermine la composition du Conseil, donne un siège permanent aux États fondateurs de la Banque. Il ne semblerait donc pas que l'inquiétude de M. Mathieu soit pertinente pour l'interprétation de cette partie des Statuts.

147. L'article 18A concernant le rachat forcé des actions détenues par des personnes privées ne peut pas raisonnablement être interpreté comme allant à l'encontre de l'un des articles réservés visés à l'article 58, ou de l'une des préoccupations ayant motivé cette disposition. Bien que la Banque eût été obligée d'obtenir le consentement de la Suisse (en accord avec les autres gouvernements signataires; voir l'article 1 de la Convention) s'il avait été prévu de modifier un des articles énumérés à l'article 58, ledit consentement aurait seulement été requis pour la modification d'un article réservé. En fait, comme il a été relaté à l'audience, la Banque a notifié à la Suisse la proposition de modification

[79] *Supra* note de bas de page 45, p. 174, 180 (les italiques ont été ajoutés).
[80] Mémoire en Demande, p. 12.

et la Suisse n'a pas formulé de réclamation ni d'objection.[81] De même, toutes les banques centrales qui étaient actionnaires de la Banque ont été informées, comme les Statuts de la Banque le requièrent, et il est dès lors raisonnable de supposer que la modification en cours avait également été portée à la connaissance de leurs gouvernements. Il ne semblerait pas non plus que les Statuts ou la Charte contiennent une disposition implicite qui aurait empêché la modification.

148. Par ces motifs, le Tribunal constate que la Banque avait la compétence d'ajouter l'article 18A aux Statuts, que le retrait forcé des actions, y compris les procédures par lesquelles il a été accompli, relevait de sa compétence en vertu des Statuts et que par conséquent, la Banque a valablement exercé ses pouvoirs. Néanmoins, le Tribunal insiste sur le fait que la constatation que le retrait des actions privées relevait de la compétence de la Banque en vertu de ses Instruments constitutifs n'a pas d'incidence sur la question de savoir si le retrait effectué par la Banque et l'évaluation par la Banque des actions détenues par des personnes privées étaient licites pour des raisons autres que la conformité avec les articles 57 et 58 des Statuts. Le Tribunal examine à présent cette question.

2. *Conformité de la reprise au regard des dispositions de fond du droit international*

149. M. Mathieu a fait valoir qu'outre le problème de l'insuffisance alléguée de l'indemnisation, l'action de la Banque était illicite, parce qu'elle violait deux des règles essentielles prévues par le droit international en cas d'expropriation licite: la cession doit présenter un caractère d'intérêt public et être non discriminatoire. Il convient de déterminer si la reprise par la Banque en 2001 des actions détenues par des personnes privées doit être examinée à la lumière du droit de la responsabilité des États, par assimilation des actionnaires privés à des étrangers et de la Banque à un État qui procède à une expropriation ou à la lumière de la législation des droits de l'homme, par assimilation des actionnaires privés à des ressortissants et de la Banque à leur État qui pose un acte de domaine éminent. Sans approfondir ici l'examen de ces analogies ou déterminer

[81] Prof. Giovanoli, compte rendu, p. 79.

si elles sont l'une et l'autre effectivement pertinentes, le Tribunal relève que les actions entreprises par la Banque le 8 janvier 2001 auraient satisfait aux critères de l'intérêt public et de la non-discrimination du droit international en matière d'expropriation que M. Mathieu a proposé d'appliquer.

a. CRITÈRE DE L'INTÉRÊT PUBLIC

150. Il est manifeste que la Banque n'est pas un État. S'il faut comprendre par intérêt public l'intérêt public d'un État, les actions de la Banque ne peuvent pas satisfaire au critère de l'intérêt public et seraient *eo ipso* illicites. La raison de cette conclusion ne tiendrait pas à la nature ni au but de l'action, mais au fait que la Banque n'est pas un État. Cet argument, qui serait une pétition de principe et serait stérile, ne correspond pas au sens du moyen avancé par M. Mathieu. Lorsqu'il concerne un acteur qui est une organisation internationale mais pas un État, l'intérêt public doit être compris, *mutatis mutandis*, comme une action rationnellement, proportionnellement et nécessairement liée à la réalisation de l'un des objectifs légitimes aux termes du droit international public de l'acteur qui le poursuit.

151. En ce qui concerne le critère de l'intérêt public, la Banque a produit des preuves étayant sa conclusion que la présence d'actionnaires privés au sein d'une organisation internationale augmentait certains coûts supportés par la Banque et gênait l'accomplissement de certaines de ses fonctions publiques internationales. Une note interne préparée par le Secrétariat de la Banque le 6 novembre 1998, présentant la proposition de reprise des actions de la Banque détenues par des personnes privées, faisait remarquer que:

> La nécessité de prendre en considération les intérêts des actionnaires privés limite sans aucun doute dans une certaine mesure la liberté d'action de la BRI dans sa politique de répartition des bénéfices. Il convient également de signaler qu'à diverses reprises, l'existence d'actionnaires privés a eu une incidence négative sur les négociations concernant les

> immunités juridictionnelles, fiscales et autres de la BRI dans plusieurs autres pays.[82]

Il est clair qu'il existe une incompatibilité latente entre les responsabilités liées aux fonctions publiques de la Banque et les responsabilités fiduciaires de la Banque à l'égard de ses actionnaires privés. À première vue, la Banque est capable de démontrer que, si les dispositions du droit international en matière d'expropriation étaient appliquées, elle pourrait satisfaire, *mutatis mutandis*, au critère de l'intérêt public.

b. PRINCIPE DE LA NON-DISCRIMINATION

152. Les actions de la Banque intéressant les actionnaires privés ne seraient pas non plus qualifiées de discriminatoires en vertu des dispositions du droit international en matière d'expropriation. D'un point de vue analytique, il convient de faire une distinction entre le référent factuel de "différenciations" et le référent juridique de "discriminations." Toutes les différenciations ne sont pas des discriminations. Une discrimination est une différenciation illicite. Les instruments juridiques indiquent qu'à partir de 1930, les actionnaires privés et les banques centrales, bien qu'ils jouissent de droits égaux en qualité d'actionnaires, avaient un statut différent. Les banques centrales uniquement ont le droit de vote. Bien que ce droit de vote ne soit pas directement attaché aux actions détenues par les banques centrales, il est indirectement lié aux actions souscrites par les banques centrales ou par leur intermédiaire. Cette constatation prouve que les banques centrales relèvent d'une catégorie différente de celle des actionnaires privés.

153. On rappellera qu'en 1969, la Banque a émis de nouvelles actions dont la vente a été réservée aux banques centrales. Aux termes de la troisième

---

[82] L-3 confidentielle, Capital-actions de la BRI, 6 novembre 1998, pièces jointes au mémoire de First Eagle, onglet 26, p. 2. Le même point de vue a été exprimé lors d'une réunion restreinte des membres du Conseil du 9 novembre 1998, p. 1, pièces jointes au mémoire de First Eagle, onglet 27. First Eagle a produit un document provenant des dossiers de M. Thomas McKittrick de la Harvard Library, qui est daté de juin 1938, mais n'est pas signé. Des commentaires sont également formulés sur l'incompatibilité d'actionnaires privés dans "une véritable banque des banques." Pièces jointes au mémoire de First Eagle, onglet 36, p. 10.

résolution de l'Assemblée générale extraordinaire du 9 juin 1969, le Conseil d'administration a donné l'autorisation

> (1) d'émettre, en une seule fois ou par intervalles, une troisième tranche de 200.000 actions de 2.500 francs or chacune, qui seront payées à la même valeur que les actions en circulation à la date d'émission et qui ne peuvent pas être souscrites ni achetées par le grand public.[83]

154. La nature même de la Banque en tant qu'organisation internationale créée notamment pour faciliter les relations entre les banques centrales et le fonctionnement du système monétaire international a instauré un traitement différent, à certaines fins, des banques centrales et des actionnaires privés, de la façon la plus radicale en matière de droits liés à la conduite des affaires, dont aucun ne pouvait être acquis par des actionnaires privés.

155. Par conséquent, même si, pour les besoins de l'argumentation, les dispositions du droit international en matière d'expropriation devaient être appliquées pour déterminer la validité de la reprise par la Banque des actions privées, cette opération aurait été licite au regard du critère de l'intérêt public et du principe de non-discrimination.

c. INDEMNISATION

156. Le droit international dispose également que pour être licite, une expropriation doit s'accompagner du versement d'une indemnité. En effet, la Banque a admis que la reprise avait eu pour conséquence que les actionnaires privés avaient perdu leurs droits. La Banque a d'emblée reconnu qu'une telle privation de propriété ne pouvait être licite que s'il y avait paiement d'une indemnité. Les questions ayant trait au montant de l'indemnité seront examinées séparément. Cependant, le Tribunal insiste sur le fait qu'une décision de la BRI qui a pour effet de priver les actionnaires privés de leurs droits patrimoniaux, à savoir leurs actions, ne peut pas être considérée comme licite s'il n'y a pas payement d'une

---

[83] Assemblée générale extraordinaire qui a eu lieu à Bâle le 9 juin 1969, Archives publiques, Pièces jointes au mémoire de First Eagle, onglet 22.

indemnité. Cette affirmation découle des dispositions du droit international général qui protège la propriété privée, ainsi que des principes généraux de droit applicables aux sociétés par actions, point que les Parties n'ont pas contesté.

157. Puisque la Banque a reconnu qu'elle était soumise à la juridiction du présent Tribunal et qu'elle s'est engagée à payer à tous les anciens actionnaires privés tout montant supplémentaire au montant qu'elle a déjà payé, si le Tribunal l'exige, ce troisième critère satisfait, *nunc pro tunc*, aux impératifs du droit international. Le Tribunal reviendra sur cette question ci-dessous.

158. Par conséquent, le Tribunal estime que la décision de retirer les actions détenues par des personnes privées, prise par l'Assemblée générale extraordinaire du 8 janvier 2001, relevait des compétences prévues dans les Statuts et correspondait à l'exercice licite des pouvoirs de la Banque. De même, l'exercice par la Banque de ses pouvoirs ne viole aucun principe de droit international qui pourrait s'appliquer.

159. Puisque le Tribunal estime que la modification des Statuts par l'ajout de l'article 18A relève des compétences prévues dans les Statuts et est licite, la question concernant les conséquences d'une constatation d'illicéité à l'égard de tous ceux qui étaient actionnaires privés à la date du 8 janvier 2001 est sans objet et ne doit dès lors pas être examinée.

CHAPITRE V – DEUXIÈME QUESTION DE L'ORDONNANCE DE PROCÉDURE N° 3

A. Introduction

160. Une question essentielle en l'espèce est le caractère approprié du montant que la Banque a versé pour les actions retirées. Que cette question relève du domaine des "réparations", ce qui implique que le retrait était illicite, ou du domaine de l'"indemnisation", ce qui implique que le retrait était une expropriation et que sa licéité dépend du payement par la Banque d'une indemnité conformément au droit international, ou encore du domaine du "prix équitable, ce qui implique, d'une manière plus neutre, qu'il convient simplement de déterminer la valeur correcte des actions retirées, tous les demandeurs, de même que la Banque ont admis que la question concernait l'évaluation. À cet égard, la Banque a invoqué et s'est largement fondée sur des principes du droit international.[84] Il est donc utile d'examiner en premier lieu le droit

---

[84] La Banque a également invoqué la pratique nationale apparentée. La Banque a mis en avant une pratique des États plutôt étendue concernant le phénomène particulier du retrait par des banques centrales des actions détenues par des actionnaires privés dans le cadre d'une opération à caractère forcé. La Banque a fait valoir que la pratique nationale semblait particulièrement pertinente en l'espèce, car les banques centrales, comme la Banque des Règlements Internationaux, ont conclu que la pratique antérieure autorisant des actionnaires privés au sein de banques qui étaient des institutions publiques était devenue anachronique et incompatible avec les fonctions publiques des banques centrales nationales. C'est pourquoi les banques centrales ont adopté des programmes de reprise, fort semblables à celui adopté par la BRI dans sa décision du 8 janvier 2001. Dans pratiquement tous ces programmes de reprise forcée, l'évaluation des actions était basée sur une moyenne du prix du marché des actions avant l'annonce de la reprise. Rien n'indique cependant que le cours de bourse était proche de l'actif net réévalué. Comme la Banque l'a décrit dans son contre-mémoire, la Banque du Canada a été nationalisée en 1938 en vertu de la loi portant modification de la loi sur la Banque du Canada (Documents juridiques de la Banque n° 119). La Banque du Canada a été organisée en société par actions avec un capital de 5.000.000 de dollars canadiens, chaque action ayant une valeur nominale de 50 dollars canadiens. Conformément à ladite loi, de nouvelles actions, détenues par le gouvernement canadien, ont été émises pour porter le capital à 5.100.000 dollars canadiens, ce qui a donné au gouvernement une majorité suffisante pour racheter les actions détenues par les actionnaires privés. Chaque ancien actionnaire privé a reçu 59,20 dollars canadiens par action, c'est-à-dire le prix du marché à cette époque (article 9 de la loi de 1938 portant modification de la loi sur la Banque du Canada (Documents juridiques de la Banque n° 119). De même, le gouvernement français a nationalisé la Banque de France en 1945 (Loi 45-14 (Documents juridiques de la Banque n° 115)). À l'époque, la Banque de France avait 46.809 actionnaires. Le prix d'une action était fixé à 28.029 francs, soit un montant égal au cours moyen des actions de la Banque de France pendant une période de référence antérieure de douze mois (arrêté de juillet 1946, J.O.,

international en la matière, même s'il se peut qu'il ne soit pas applicable lorsque les Parties ont établi une *lex specialis*.

B. JURISPRUDENCE INTERNATIONALE

161. Dans les cas d'expropriation d'actions détenues par des investisseurs étrangers, la pratique du droit international a, de façon assez constante, évalué les actions en se basant sur le prix du marché dans un contexte de marché efficient.

162. Dans l'affaire *American Int'l Group, Inc.*, le demandeur réclamait une indemnité pour sa participation minoritaire dans une société d'assurances iranienne qui avait été nationalisée par le gouvernement iranien.[85] Le demandeur réclamait la "valeur totale" de sa participation à la date de la nationalisation et le tribunal a conclu que l'indemnité due correspondait

21 juillet 1946, p. 6.538 (Documents juridiques de la Banque n° 115)). Contre-mémoire, par. 153-159. En 1949, le gouvernement norvégien a nationalisé la Norges Bank. La Norvège a repris les actions précédemment détenues par des actionnaires privés après payement d'une indemnité égale à 180% de la valeur nominale des actions (Norges Bank Bulletin, vol. 20, n° 4-5, 21 novembre 1949, p. 57, 59 (Documents juridiques de la Banque n° 121)). Ce chiffre de 180% était à peine supérieur au prix du marché correspondant à 178% de la valeur nominale de l'époque. En 1962, les actionnaires de Banco de España ont reçu une indemnité basée sur la juste valeur du marché de leurs actions après la nationalisation. L'indemnité versée aux anciens actionnaires correspondait à 5% de plus que la valeur la plus élevée soit du prix moyen en Bourse au cours des cinq années précédentes, soit du prix maximal de l'année précédente (Loi n° 2/162 du 14 avril 1962 (BOE du 16 avril 1962) (Documents juridiques de la Banque n° 123). La Nouvelle-Zélande a nationalisé la Reserve Bank of New Zealand en 1936; le prix de rachat a été fixé au prix de l'action à une certaine date de l'année précédente (New Zealand Parliamentary Debates, vol. 244, 25 mars-6 mai 1936, p. 144 (commentaires de M. Nash, ministre des finances) (Documents juridiques de la Banque n° 114)). Le Portugal a nationalisé sa banque centrale, la Banco de Portugal, et la Banco Nacional Ultramarino en 1974, en se fondant sur la moyenne du cours annuel de l'action pour fixer l'indemnité (article 5 du décret-Loi n° 452/74 du 13 septembre 1974 (Documents juridiques de la Banque n° 122); voir l'article 5 du décret-loi n° 451/74 du 13 septembre 1974, Relatório do Conselho de Administração (Documents juridiques de la Banque n° 122)). Le Venezuela a nationalisé sa banque centrale, la Banco Central de Venezuela, en 1974; les 6.170 actionnaires privés ont reçu un montant équivalant au prix moyen du marché au cours des six mois antérieurs (Banco Central de Venezuela, 1974 Memoria (rapport annuel), p. 14 (Documents juridiques de la Banque n° 118). Note de bas de page du contre-mémoire, par. 159).

[85] *American Int'l Group, Inc. v. Islamic Republic of Iran*, sentence n° 93-2-3, Recueil du Tribunal irano-américain de réclamations (Iran-U.S. C.T.R.), 19 décembre 1983, vol. 4.

à la part, revenant au demandeur, de la juste valeur du marché de la propriété nationalisée.[86] En calculant la juste valeur du marché, le tribunal a déterminé "les limites supérieures et inférieures de la fourchette dans laquelle la valeur de la société était raisonnablement censée se situer" et a ainsi obtenu le montant de l'indemnité grâce à une "approximation de cette valeur compte tenu de tous les éléments pertinents de l'espèce."[87]

163. Dans l'affaire *James Saghi*, les demandeurs étaient les actionnaires majoritaires de deux sociétés iraniennes placées sous l'administration du gouvernement iranien. Les demandeurs se sont plaints d'être privés de leurs droits patrimoniaux au sein desdites sociétés, bien qu'il n'y ait pas eu d'expropriation officielle. Le tribunal a fait observer que la juste valeur du marché serait la norme d'indemnisation applicable et a résumé comme suit le point de vue du droit international coutumier à l'égard de la juste valeur du marché:

> La juste valeur du marché peut être définie comme "le montant qu'un acheteur consentant aurait payé à un vendeur consentant pour l'achat des actions d'une société en activité, compte non tenu de toute dépréciation due à la nationalisation proprement dite ou à l'anticipation de celle-ci et sans considération de tout événement ultérieur qui aurait pu augmenter ou réduire la valeur des actions." Par ailleurs, bien que toute dépréciation causée par la privation de propriété proprement dite doive être prise en considération, "il convient de tenir compte de changements antérieurs du contexte politique, social et économique général qui auraient pu influencer les perspectives économiques de la société à la date où elle a été reprise."[88]

Pour obtenir la juste valeur du marché, le tribunal a appliqué la méthode d'"approximation raisonnable", tenant compte de l'impact de la révolution iranienne et de l'inflation monétaire.[89]

---

[86] *Id.*, par. 109.
[87] *Id.*
[88] *James M. Saghi v. Islamic Republic of Iran*, sentence n° 544-298-2, Recueil du Tribunal irano-américain de réclamations (Iran-U.S. C.T.R.), 22 janvier 1933, vol. 29, p. 20, 46.
[89] *Id.*, par. 103.

164. La jurisprudence internationale recommande de déterminer la juste valeur du marché par référence au cours de l'action, s'il est disponible. Dans l'affaire *Faith Lita Khosrowshahi*, le demandeur demandait réparation pour la perte de sa participation dans une société iranienne après son acquisition forcée par le gouvernement iranien.[90] Le demandeur a remis au tribunal d'autres évaluations possibles des actions perdues, notamment une évaluation basée sur "une moyenne pondérée de trois techniques d'évaluation différentes: une approche fondée sur l'accumulation d'actifs, une approche fondée sur la capitalisation des revenus et une approche fondée sur le marché" dérivée du prix de la dernière transaction des actions qui avaient été négociées publiquement à la Bourse de Téhéran.[91] L'évaluation de la défenderesse s'appuyait sur une analyse de la valeur comptable nette qui attribuait une valeur négative aux actions.[92] Après avoir appliqué la règle d'évaluation de la juste valeur du marché, le tribunal a constaté qu'"un prix du marché contemporain [était] manifestement la meilleure preuve disponible" de la valeur des actions expropriées.[93] Le tribunal a ainsi utilisé le dernier cours des actions mentionné dans le rapport annuel de la Bourse de Téhéran "au titre de base de l'analyse d'évaluation" et a appliqué une décote de 25% tenant compte de l'effet défavorable de la révolution iranienne sur le prix du marché des actions au cours de la période de huit mois comprise entre la dernière transaction et l'expropriation des actions.[94]

165. L'affaire *ACSYNGO* concernait des actions détenues par des investisseurs privés dans un conglomérat français dont la cession forcée à l'État français avait été réalisée en 1982.[95] Une indemnité a été versée aux actionnaires dépossédés sur la base du cours de bourse moyen des actions pendant une période de référence, après correction en raison des effets

---

[90] *Faith Lita Khosrowshahi v. Islamic Republic of Iran*, sentence n° 558-178-2, Recueil du Tribunal irano-américain de réclamations (Iran-U.S. C.T.R.), 30 juin 1994, vol. 30, p. 76.

[91] *Id.*, p. 90.

[92] *Id.*, p. 91.

[93] *Id.*, p. 92.

[94] *Id.*, p. 93-94.

[95] *"ACSYNGO" et autres c. Compagnie de Saint-Gobain (France) SA et autres*, International Law Reports, vol. 82, p. 127, p. 130 (1986).

de l'inflation et de la perte de dividendes.[96] S'agissant de l'indemnité payée par l'État français, le tribunal de commerce belge a déclaré que "[l]e fait que le cours de bourse moyen, les effets de l'inflation et les dividendes escomptés ont été pris en compte amène à conclure que, du point de vue du droit international public, le calcul de l'indemnité ne peut pas être désapprouvé."[97]

166. Dans l'affaire *Amoco Int'l Fin. Corp.*, bien que le Tribunal irano-américain de réclamations ait finalement constaté qu'en l'espèce il n'existait aucun "marché permettant de fixer un prix du marché objectif" pour la participation expropriée du demandeur dans une coentreprise iranienne, il a d'abord déclaré que le prix du marché était la "règle la plus recommandable" et qu'il y était "régulièrement fait référence en matière de nationalisation lorsque l'entreprise nationalisée [était] une société par actions dont le capital-actions [était] librement négocié en Bourse."[98] Le tribunal a précisé en outre que le prix du marché était "très facilement déterminé, lorsqu'il [existait] un marché pour des actifs identiques ou similaires, c'est-à-dire lorsque les actifs [faisaient] l'objet d'un flux continu de libres transactions."[99]

167. First Eagle a soutenu que la condition préalable à l'application du principe susvisé était l'existence d'un marché efficient et qu'il n'en existait pas pour les actions de la BRI. La Banque a fait valoir que les Bourses de Zurich et de Paris étaient tout à fait efficientes et que les problèmes de non-liquidité comparative des actions de la Banque découlaient de leur nature et non des marchés sur lesquels elles sont négociées. Il est sans nul doute exact que les actions de la Banque se distinguaient pas leur non-liquidité par rapport aux autres actions négociées sur le marché français ou suisse. Des facteurs, comme (i) le nombre limité d'actions de ce type qui étaient négociées; (ii) l'exigence de double agrément de la banque centrale par laquelle les actions avaient

---

[96] *Id.*, p. 135.
[97] *Id.*, p. 137.
[98] *Amoco Int'l Fin. Corp. v. The Government of the Islamic Republic of Iran and Others*, sentence partielle n° 310-56-3, Recueil du Tribunal irano-américain de réclamations (Iran-U.S. C.T.R.), 14 juillet 1987, vol. 15, p. 189, 255-256.
[99] *Id.*

été émises et de la Banque des Règlements Internationaux, avant que les actions puissent être vendues et (iii) la possibilité pour la Banque d'exiger le payement des 75% restants de la valeur des actions, ont contribué à la non-liquidité comparative de ces actions sur les marchés sur lesquels elles étaient achetées et vendues. Mais l'inefficience était due à la nature des actions et non aux marchés sur lesquels elles étaient négociées et le marché a introduit une décote du fait de ces inefficacités, comme le font les marchés. Abstraction faite des arguments concernant l'efficience ou la liquidité relative, il n'en reste pas moins que la Banque elle-même ne s'est jamais basée sur les cours de bourse pour évaluer les actions avant le présent arbitrage (voir par. 193 *et suiv.* ci-dessous).

168. Par ailleurs, le Tribunal n'est pas convaincu par le point de vue de la Banque, qui affirme que la norme d'indemnisation au regard du droit international est une norme d'indemnisation "appropriée". Bien qu'il soit exact que la jurisprudence de la Cour européenne des Droits de l'Homme a adopté une norme flexible, décrite comme une norme d'indemnisation "appropriée" en cas de reprise par un État de la propriété de ses ressortissants, l'assimilation de la Banque à un État qui prive de leur titre de propriété les actionnaires, considérés comme ses "ressortissants", n'est pas convaincante. Abstraction faite de la question de la pertinence générale de la législation régionale des droits de l'homme, les principes généraux du droit international général, s'ils sont appliqués à cette affaire, appellent l'indemnisation complète. Bien que cette norme ait été nuancée pendant la Guerre froide et ait sans doute été adaptée dans quelques cas où certains pays en voie de développement, en particulier s'agissant de pétrole, ont nationalisé leur unique ou principale ressource,[100] il est clair qu'elle a été rétablie dans la jurisprudence récente.

169. Ainsi, la norme d'indemnisation complète a été appliquée dans un arbitrage *ad hoc* en conformité avec le règlement d'arbitrage de la CNUDCI, aux termes duquel il a été constaté que le gouvernement du Ghana avait exproprié les investissements des demandeurs au Ghana.[101]

---

[100] *Aminoil v. Kuwait*, International Law Reports, vol. 66, p. 518 (1982).

[101] *Biloune and Marine Drive Complex Ltd v. Ghana Investments Centre and the Government of Ghana*, International Law Reports, vol. 95, p. 183 (1993).

Dans cette affaire, le tribunal a dit qu'"[e]n vertu des principes du droit coutumier international, un demandeur dont la propriété a été expropriée par un État étranger a droit à une indemnisation complète – c'est-à-dire rapide, adéquate et effective."[102]

170. De même, le Tribunal irano-américain de réclamations a généralement appliqué la norme d'indemnisation complète dans plusieurs affaires. Dans l'affaire *Sedco*, alors qu'il devait se prononcer sur la norme d'indemnisation à appliquer pour l'expropriation de la participation du demandeur dans la société de forage SEDIRAN, le tribunal a estimé que l'indemnisation complète était la norme applicable.[103] Le tribunal a déclaré que bien que certains commentateurs se soient déclarés favorables à une norme plus limitée dans des cas de nationalisations entreprises par des pays en voie de développement, l'indemnisation complète restait la norme généralement admise dans les cas d'expropriation individuelle.[104] Dans l'affaire *Sola Tiles*, le tribunal a accordé une indemnisation complète pour les actifs expropriés du demandeur.[105] Alors qu'il était amené à décider si le traité d'amitié entre les États-Unis et l'Iran constituait une *lex specialis* régissant la norme d'indemnisation, le tribunal a déclaré que la disposition du traité en vertu de laquelle l'indemnité "doit représenter l'équivalent complet de la propriété enlevée" correspondait à la norme imposée par le droit coutumier.[106] Bien que le tribunal ait admis que le terme "approprié" avait été largement appliqué à la norme d'indemnisation dans des cas d'expropriation, il a déclaré que le sens de ce terme pouvait englober l'"indemnisation complète".[107]

171. Enfin, il convient de préciser que sur le conseil de son consultant, J.P. Morgan, la Banque, appliquant le modèle des dividendes à perpétuité, a

---

[102] *Id.*, p. 211.

[103] *Sedco, Inc. v. National Iranian Oil Company, et al.*, sentence n° 59-129-3, Recueil du Tribunal irano-américain de réclamations (Iran-U.S. C.T.R.), 27 mars 1986, vol. 10, p. 180, 188.

[104] *Id.*, p. 188.

[105] *Sola Tiles, Inc. v. Islamic Republic of Iran*, sentence n° 298-317-1, Recueil du Tribunal irano-américain de réclamations (Iran-U.S. C.T.R.), 22 avril 1987, vol. 14, p. 223.

[106] *Id.*, p. 234.

[107] *Id.*, p. 236.

en fait payé aux actionnaires privés pratiquement le double de la valeur d'échange des actions retirées. En conformité avec la norme en matière d'expropriation au regard du droit international, si elle était appliquée, le montant de l'indemnité versée par la Banque aurait satisfait à la norme internationale. Mais, en fait, la Banque a payé le double du cours de bourse des actions retirées et a uniquement préconisé l'application du cours de bourse dans l'arbitrage. Les banques exercent leurs activités en vertu de règles strictes applicables aux capitaux qui leur sont confiés; elles ne peuvent pas donner de l'argent sans fondement juridique valable. De surcroît, le dossier révèle que les documents internes de la Banque indiquent que celle-ci n'utilisait pas le cours de bourse pour déterminer la prime d'émission pour les nouvelles tranches. Le comportement de la Banque suscite des doutes sur sa propre conviction contemporaine à l'égard de l'application du principe du prix du marché détaillé ci-dessus, en particulier dans une affaire qui ne concerne pas une expropriation mais plutôt un retrait forcé d'actions.

C. Instruments constitutifs de la Banque et droit international

172. Le Tribunal a déclaré que la Banque était une organisation internationale. Bien que la Banque soit dès lors soumise au droit international, toutes les Parties s'accordent à dire que les droits des actionnaires sont, au premier chef, déterminés par les Instruments constitutifs. Dr. Reineccius, qui a assuré lui-même sa représentation en justice, n'a pas explicitement examiné la question du droit applicable, mais a manifestement basé son argumentation sur son interprétation des Statuts et, selon son point de vue, sur leurs inévitables implications. Dans son mémoire, First Eagle a fondé sa demande, au premier chef, sur une interprétation des Statuts.[108] Dans son mémoire, M. Mathieu a fondé son argumentation, au premier chef également, sur les Instruments constitutifs de la Banque, faisant valoir qu'uniquement dans le cas où ils ne fournissaient pas de réponse, le Tribunal devait se référer au droit international général. Dans son mémoire en défense, la Banque a déclaré que "ses relations avec ses actionnaires [étaient] régies par ses Instruments constitutifs . . .

[108] Mémoire de First Eagle, par. 205.

complétés, au besoin, par le droit international public général."[109] Dans son contre-mémoire, la Banque a affirmé que "les droits attachés aux actions de BRI [devaient] être déterminés par référence aux dispositions des Statuts plutôt qu'en vertu de principes du droit interne des sociétés ou en vertu de définitions, données par les dictionnaires, de la propriété d'actions."[110]

173. Par conséquent, les Parties s'accordent à dire que la question qu'il faut trancher en l'espèce doit être réglée par référence aux Instruments constitutifs de la Banque et en vertu du droit international uniquement si les Instruments constitutifs n'apportent pas de réponse. Puisque les Parties conviennent que les questions soumises au Tribunal doivent être réglées au premier chef par référence aux Instruments constitutifs de la Banque, le lien entre les Statuts et le droit international doit être précisé. Les Instruments constitutifs de la Banque constituent une *lex specialis* entre les Parties. Dans la mesure où la *lex specialis* applicable à l'espèce – l'Accord de 1930, la Charte et les Statuts – apporte une réponse aux questions soulevées en l'espèce, le Tribunal ne serait pas autorisé à se référer au droit international – à moins que la *lex specialis* ne soit censée contenir un renvoi explicite au droit international général ou ne viole un principe fondamental du droit international.

174. En fait, ni la disposition applicable de la Convention de 1907 pour le règlement pacifique des conflits internationaux, ni l'Accord de La Haye de 1930 ne contiennent un renvoi au droit international à ce titre. L'article 15 de l'Accord de 1930 ne contient pas de clause explicite sur la loi applicable. L'annexe XII de l'Accord de 1930, qui a pour titre "Arbitrage – Règles de procédure", ne comporte pas non plus de clause explicite de choix de la loi applicable. Cependant, l'annexe XII englobe, par référence, le chapitre III de la Convention de La Haye de 1907 pour le règlement pacifique des conflits internationaux, dont les dispositions sont applicables, sauf et dans la mesure où elles sont modifiées par les dispositions de l'annexe XII ou de l'Accord de 1930. L'article 73 de la Convention de 1907 prévoit simplement l'application des "principes du droit." L'article 26 du "Règlement d'arbitrage entre la Banque des

---

[109] Mémoire en défense, par. 85.
[110] Contre-mémoire, par. 94.

Règlements Internationaux et des parties privées" dispose que "[l]e Tribunal doit appliquer les textes applicables à l'espèce ainsi que toute autre règle de droit pertinente." Somme toute, la *lex specialis* applicable à l'espèce – l'Accord de 1930, la Charte et les Statuts – a été élaborée pour se suffire à elle-même et n'intègre pas le droit international général, sauf si la *lex specialis* n'apporte pas de réponse à une question qui pourrait se poser ou qui viole un principe fondamental du droit international. Dans cette éventualité, un Tribunal saisi de l'affaire doit se tourner vers le droit international général.[111]

175. Le droit à indemnité relève tant du droit international général que du domaine spécifique des droits de l'homme et il est tout à fait possible qu'une action tendant à abroger ce droit puisse être déclarée nulle pour violation du droit international. Si les Statuts avaient eu pour intention de ne pas accorder d'indemnité aux actionnaires, un problème de droit international général aurait pu se former. Mais, en l'espèce, les Statuts exigent une indemnisation et le fait que la *lex specialis*, en raison des dispositions spécifiques des Statuts établissant l'égalité des droits des actions, pourrait recommander un montant plus élevé que ne le ferait le droit international général ne peut pas être considéré comme une violation du droit international. Dès lors, aucun motif ne justifie que le Tribunal déroge à la *lex specialis* applicable aux Parties et ait recours à la norme du droit international qui imposerait le prix du marché des actions.

D. Évaluation

176. Le Tribunal en vient à présent à la question de l'évaluation. La Banque a admis, dès les premières discussions sur l'opération de reprise, que la reprise devait être accompagnée d'une évaluation des actions et du payement d'une indemnité aux actionnaires. Par contraste avec M. Mathieu, qui a accusé la Banque d'avoir caché des informations et

---

[111] À cet égard, le régime juridique séquentiel créé par la *lex specialis* peut être comparé à l'article 42 de la Convention de 1965 pour le règlement des différends relatifs aux investissements entre États et ressortissants d'autres États ("Convention de Washington de 1965").

d'avoir fait confiance à des conseillers externes qui manquaient d'indépendance, Dr. Reineccius a exprimé sa conviction que la Banque avait présenté, de façon tout à fait correcte, des informations complètes sur ses données et méthodes d'évaluation. Le grief de Dr. Reineccius concernait la méthode que la Banque avait adoptée sur le conseil de ses consultants: le modèle des dividendes à perpétuité. Après avoir examiné le dossier, le Tribunal ne trouve aucune preuve de mauvaise foi de la part de la Banque.

1. Méthode de la valeur de rentabilité

177. Dr. Reineccius a soutenu que le modèle approprié à l'évaluation n'était pas le modèle des dividendes à perpétuité, mais plutôt la méthode de la valeur de rentabilité, qui, selon lui, est largement utilisée en Allemagne pour des situations comparables à certains égards à celle que le Tribunal examine, ou, à titre subsidiaire, une part proportionnelle de l'actif net réévalué. Il a fait valoir que le Tribunal devait choisir, entre ces deux méthodes, celle qui aboutissait au montant le plus élevé. First Eagle et M. Mathieu ont également allégué qu'une part proportionnelle de l'actif net réévalué était la méthodologie d'évaluation appropriée. En fait, la préférence de Dr. Reineccius pour la méthode de la valeur de rentabilité tient à l'hypothèse qu'il défend (partagée par M. Mathieu et, avec certaines réserves, par First Eagle) selon laquelle chaque action de la Banque des Règlements Internationaux donne droit à une part proportionnelle de ses bénéfices. La méthode de la valeur de rentabilité présume qu'un actionnaire peut prétendre aux bénéfices de la société. Dr. Reineccius estime que le modèle des dividendes à perpétuité "est approprié, lorsqu'une société distribue la majeure partie de ses bénéfices nets sous la forme de dividendes",[112] mais n'est pas approprié si la politique de la société consiste à économiser les bénéfices et à distribuer des dividendes très réduits.

178. À l'origine du point de vue de Dr. Reineccius, selon lequel le modèle des dividendes à perpétuité n'est pas une méthode d'évaluation appropriée, se trouve le postulat que les sociétés doivent veiller au bien-être de leurs actionnaires, dont l'intérêt est de percevoir les bénéfices sous la forme

[112] Compte rendu, p. 202, lignes 36-37.

de dividendes et qui, par conséquent, attendent de la société dont ils détiennent des actions qu'elle distribue autant de dividendes que l'autorise la préservation de la productivité future de la société. Ce postulat est valable pour la plupart des sociétés nationales et privées dans des systèmes capitalistes évolués. Mais comme il a été expliqué plus haut, la Banque des Règlements Internationaux est *sui generis*, dans le sens où c'est une organisation internationale mais organisée, selon les termes de l'article 1 des Statuts, comme une "société anonyme par actions." Elle est investie d'un mandat public international, dont l'accomplissement peut générer des bénéfices considérables. Les actionnaires privés souhaitaient que les bénéfices se traduisent par la distribution de dividendes plus élevés, alors qu'une réduction importante des dividendes et l'accumulation correspondante des bénéfices dans les diverses réserves statutaires de la Banque étaient préférables, de l'avis du Conseil, pour le mandat international public de la Banque.

179. Par conséquent, l'assimilation implicite de la pratique de la Banque en matière de bénéfices et de dividendes avec celle des politiques en cette matière de sociétés privées nationales, défendue par Dr. Reineccius, n'est pas pertinente. Par ailleurs, elle n'a pas de fondement au regard de la *lex specialis*. Les Statuts n'accordent pas aux actionnaires de la BRI un droit aux bénéfices *simpliciter*, mais aux bénéfices tels qu'ils sont déterminés en vertu d'un processus décisionnel décrit à l'article 51 des Statuts, qui concerne les bénéfices nets annuels. L'article 13 des Statuts dispose:

> Les actions jouissent de droits égaux dans la répartition des bénéfices de la Banque et dans toute distribution d'actifs faites conformément aux articles 51, 52 et 53 des Statuts.

Dr. Reineccius voudrait interpréter l'article 13 comme s'il disait uniquement: "[l]es actions jouissent de droits égaux dans la répartition des bénéfices de la Banque[.]" sans tenir compte des réserves qui suivent. Si l'article 13 était effectivement tronqué de la façon dont Dr. Reineccius interprète la disposition, c'est-à-dire avec un point après les termes "la Banque", les bénéfices nets seraient nécessairement équivalents aux dividendes, qui devraient alors être distribués de façon égale. Toutefois, l'article 51 assortit de réserves les "droits égaux dans la répartition des bénéfices" visés à l'article 13, puisqu'il confère à l'Assemblée générale, sur la recommandation du Conseil, une grande liberté d'appréciation dans la fixation des dividendes (article 51, paragraphes 2 et 4). Par conséquent, dans l'hypothèse où les procédures prévues sont respectées, un décalage entre des bénéfices élevés et de faibles dividendes, s'il est décidé en vertu de la procédure correcte, serait valable pour la Banque conformément aux Statuts.

180. À la réunion des Gouverneurs du 9 avril 1936, il avait été décidé à l'unanimité de tenter de racheter les actions détenues par des personnes privées correspondant aux émissions française et belge et, fait particulièrement important dans ce contexte, de modifier la politique des dividendes visée à l'article 53 des Statuts:

> Au cours des années 1936-1937, des mesures ont été prises pour modifier l'article 53, paragraphes b et c, des Statuts dans le but d'abolir le caractère cumulatif des dividendes . . . et de créer une disposition en vertu de laquelle tout solde de bénéfices nets . . . est inscrit au crédit d'un fonds de réserve de dividendes qui sera distribué aux actionnaires, si et lorsque l'Assemblée générale le décide; cela signifie que ce fonds sera uniquement distribué au moment où l'Assemblée générale décide (sur la proposition du Conseil) que ledit fonds n'est plus nécessaire à titre de réserve.
>
> La modification de l'article 53 établira clairement que cette mesure sera également applicable à la réserve de dividendes existante, qui ne sera donc pas distribuée tant que l'Assemblée générale n'en aura pas décidé; dès lors, ladite assemblée ne sera pas tenue de distribuer ledit fonds, même si moins de 6% des bénéfices nets sont versés sous la forme de dividendes.[113]

En 1975, à l'Assemblée générale extraordinaire, les articles 51 et 52 des Statuts ont été modifiés, selon les termes du président du Conseil d'administration,

> pour mettre fin au concept d'un dividende lié au montant du capital libéré. Par conséquent, le Conseil et l'Assemblée générale auraient une liberté d'appréciation plus grande qu'ils n'en ont eu jusqu'ici, pour décider de l'affectation des bénéfices nets

[113] Projet de procès-verbal, Bâle, 9 avril 1936, pièces jointes au mémoire de First Eagle, onglet 20.

> soit sous la forme de dividendes, soit par un versement aux réserves.[114]

L'administrateur a ajouté

> [c]ompte tenu de l'importance de la réforme proposée, il a cependant été jugé approprié de donner à ces actionnaires, s'ils le souhaitent, la possibilité de vendre leurs actions en toute équité, c'est-à-dire au prix de 3.100 francs suisses par action.[115]

Ce prix était basé sur le prix moyen des actions de l'émission américaine à Bâle, arrondi à la centaine de francs directement supérieure, au cours des six semaines antérieures. Quelques actionnaires seulement ont accepté l'offre.

181. Les responsabilités différentes et potentiellement incompatibles que la Banque assume dans le cadre de la politique en matière de bénéfices et de dividendes en faveur des actionnaires privés, d'une part, et dans le cadre de ses fonctions publiques, d'autre part, constituent précisément un des motifs d'intérêt public qui peuvent justifier le retrait des actions privées en conformité avec le droit international, comme il a été expliqué au paragraphe 151 ci-dessus.

182. Par ces motifs, le Tribunal conclut que la méthode de la valeur de rentabilité, en dépit de son importance pour les sociétés nationales du secteur privé, n'est pas une méthode appropriée pour l'évaluation des actions de la Banque des Règlements Internationaux.

2. *Méthode de l'actif net réévalué*

183. Les trois demandeurs ont tous fait valoir que la méthode appropriée d'évaluation était soit exclusivement, soit, pour Dr. Reineccius, à titre subsidiaire, une part proportionnelle par action de l'actif net réévalué

---

[114] Extrait du discours prononcé par le Président du Conseil d'administration lors de l'Assemblée générale extraordinaire de la Banque des Règlements Internationaux du 8 juillet 1975, annexe III à la note aux actionnaires (autres que les banques centrales) de l'émission américaine du capital de la Banque, pièces jointes au mémoire de First Eagle, onglet 8, p. 7.

[115] *Id.*, p. 8.

sans décote de la Banque. Comme il a été déclaré plus haut, toutes les Parties s'accordent à dire qu'une interprétation des Instruments constitutifs est essentielle pour trancher cette question et que c'est uniquement si elle ne fournit pas de réponse que le Tribunal doit se référer au droit international général.

184. First Eagle a basé son argumentation, tout d'abord, sur les articles 1 et 13 des Statuts et sur leurs inévitables implications, à savoir que "les actions de la Banque dans leur ensemble, comme celles de toute autre société anonyme par actions, constituent la participation totale de la société."[116] Contrairement à Dr. Reineccius, cependant, First Eagle a invoqué l'article 13 pour démontrer que toutes les actions, selon les termes de la Banque, "jouiss[ai]ent de droits patrimoniaux identiques."[117] First Eagle, de même que Dr. Reineccius, interpréterait l'article 13 des Statuts de la Banque, comme si aucune réserve n'était formulée. Cependant, à la différence de Dr. Reineccius dans son argument principal, First Eagle allègue également que

> le seul moyen qu'ont les actionnaires de continuer à participer de façon égale aux bénéfices de la Banque qui ne sont pas distribués sous la forme de dividendes au cours de l'année pendant laquelle ils sont réalisés est de jouir d'un droit égal aux actifs accumulés de la Banque et à ses réserves accumulées.[118]

Cet argument n'a pas d'incidence sur le pouvoir statutaire, conféré au Conseil et à l'Assemblée générale en vertu de l'article 51 des Statuts, de déterminer, le cas échéant, le montant des bénéfices qui doivent être distribués sous la forme de dividendes.

185. Bien que les Statuts aient été soigneusement rédigés pour régler la gamme habituelle des activités d'une entreprise, ils ne parlent pas, que ce soit directement ou implicitement, du droit de procéder à un retrait

---

[116] Mémoire de First Eagle, par. 213.

[117] Banque des Règlements Internationaux, Note aux actionnaires privés: Reprise de la totalité des actions de la Banque des Règlements Internationaux détenues par ses actionnaires privés, 15 septembre 2000, p. 2. Citation du mémoire de First Eagle, par. 218.

[118] *Id.*, par. 221.

forcé d'actions quelles qu'elles soient et de ses conséquences. Mais, pour First Eagle, si un rachat forcé des actions est autorisé,

> l'égalité des droits patrimoniaux dans la répartition des bénéfices réalisés et la distribution des actifs en cas de liquidation, que les Statuts reconnaissent explicitement, serait applicable avec autant de force dans le contexte de l'exclusion nouvellement autorisée.[119]

First Eagle a allégué que le retrait d'actions équivalait à une liquidation partielle, parce que le payement de ces actions était financé par la conversion d'actifs de la Banque, le montant correspondant étant déduit desdits actifs. De même, la participation des actionnaires, qui a été convertie en espèces, a également été liquidée.[120] Ainsi, l'éventualité prévue pour l'application des articles 13 et 52, troisième paragraphe, était réalisée.

186. M. Mathieu a fait valoir, comme First Eagle, qu'une interprétation adéquate des articles 13, 51, 52 et 53 démontrait que l'égalité des actions impliquait l'égalité en ce qui concerne les bénéfices et les répartitions.

187. La Banque a admis que la question devait au premier chef être tranchée en conformité avec les Instruments constitutifs. Le principal argument de la Banque est que l'article 13:

> ne confér[ait] pas aux actionnaires des droits absolus de participer aux bénéfices et aux actifs de la BRI, car il subordonn[ait] clairement lesdits droits et les détermin[ait] par un renvoi spécifique aux articles 51, 52, et 53.[121]

La Banque a ajouté que puisque (i) la vente des actions était subordonnée à l'approbation tant de la Banque que de la banque centrale à l'origine de l'émission nationale à laquelle les actions correspondaient et puisque (ii) les actions ne donnaient pas de droits dans la conduite des affaires de la Banque, lesdites actions ne présentaient pas les caractéristiques

---

[119] *Id.*, par. 224.
[120] *Id.*, par. 225.
[121] Contre-mémoire, par. 95.

fondamentales de la participation.[122] La Banque a fait valoir que ces diverses contraintes étaient prises en compte par les marchés qui imposaient une décote de 75% à l'actif net réévalué proportionnel des actions.[123]

188. Cette interprétation des Statuts formulée par la Banque n'est que partiellement correcte. En raison de la nature des actions, des contraintes particulières auxquelles elles sont soumises et de l'absence de droits dans la conduite des affaires de la Banque, cette dernière a raison de déclarer que ses actions sont différentes des actions de sociétés privées traditionnelles. La Banque affirme à juste titre également que, comme il a été expliqué ci-dessus, les Statuts ne confèrent pas aux actions des droits égaux aux bénéfices *simpliciter*, mais aux bénéfices tels qu'ils sont déterminés par le Conseil et l'Assemblée générale en conformité avec l'article 51 des Statuts.[124]

189. Toutefois, le terme "participer" cité dans l'argument de la Banque selon lequel l'article 13:

> ne confère pas aux actionnaires des droits absolus de participer aux bénéfices et aux actifs de la BRI, car il subordonne clairement lesdits droits et les détermine par un renvoi spécifique aux articles 51, 52, et 53[125]

se rapporte sans distinction aux droits dans la conduite des affaires de la Banque et aux droits de participer à la répartition des bénéfices. L'article 13 dispose que "[l]es actions jouissent de droits égaux . . . dans toute distribution d'actifs." L'absence de participation aux décisions, que les Statuts imposent aux actionnaires, en qualité d'actionnaires, en ce qui concerne la conduite des affaires doit être distinguée des droits substantiels des actionnaires à la distribution des actifs de la Banque.

---

[122] *Id.*, par. 97 et 98.
[123] *Id.*, par. 102.
[124] *Id.*, par. 95.
[125] *Id.*

190. De même, la Banque laisse entendre à tort que les droits clairement restreints visés aux articles 13, 51 et 52 concernant les bénéfices vont de pair avec les droits également restreints concernant les actifs en cas de liquidation. Alors que les actionnaires, en qualité d'actionnaires, n'ont pas le droit de participer à une décision de liquidation, les termes impératifs de l'article 52, troisième paragraphe, indiquent clairement qu'en cas de liquidation, les actionnaires jouissent de droits égaux:

> En cas de liquidation après règlement des obligations de la Banque et des frais de liquidation, ces fonds de réserve seront répartis entre les actionnaires.

Les restrictions, énoncées à l'article 13, au droit aux bénéfices qui est subordonné aux procédures de l'article 51 et qui transforme effectivement un droit de participer aux bénéfices en un droit aux dividendes que les organes directeurs de la Banque pourraient décider de distribuer, ne sont pas applicables à une liquidation. Dès lors, on déduit des Statuts que les actionnaires jouissent effectivement de droits égaux à l'ensemble des actifs de la Banque.

191. S'agissant de la demande de First Eagle que les dispositions des Statuts relatives à la liquidation soient appliquées à l'espèce, la Banque a fait valoir que les dispositions en matière de liquidation étaient uniquement applicables en cas de dissolution totale de la Banque et que cette opération requérait une décision à la majorité des trois quarts de l'Assemblée générale, qui n'a pas été prise le 8 janvier 2001.[126] La Banque a comparé le retrait des actions à une opération de rachat volontaire d'actions, qui est licite dans plusieurs systèmes nationaux.[127] Mais, bien entendu, l'origine du différend porté devant le Tribunal tient au fait que le retrait était involontaire. En raison de son caractère forcé, la procédure interne la plus proche, s'il fallait y avoir recours, serait la "cession forcée." Comme il a été dit, la Banque a rejeté le principe que tout droit interne des sociétés est applicable à l'espèce.[128]

---

[126] *Id.*, par. 107 et 109. En fait, la décision du 8 janvier 2001 a été adoptée à l'unanimité.
[127] *Id.*, par. 113 et voir également la note de bas de page 83.
[128] *Id.*, par. 153, note de bas de page 61.

192. Ni la Banque ni First Eagle n'ont été en mesure de trouver dans les Statuts une preuve convaincante pour étayer leur argumentation respective. Comme il a déjà été signalé, les Statuts n'envisageaient pas directement une reprise forcée des actions détenues par des parties privées. En effet, en 1936, alors qu'il envisageait de "se débarrasser des actionnaires privés", le président de la Banque a apparemment été averti qu'une telle opération outrepasserait les compétences conférées par les Statuts.[129] De même, s'agissant de l'argumentation de First Eagle, il est exact que l'un des sens juridiques du terme "liquidation" est la transformation d'un actif ou d'une créance en une somme d'argent. Mais il semble évident que l'article 52, troisième paragraphe, a été rédigé dans l'éventualité d'une dissolution de la Banque.

193. Pour l'interprétation à donner aux instruments juridiques pertinents, il est manifestement important d'examiner comment la BRI a elle-même compris les dispositions relatives à la reprise des actions détenues par des personnes privées. Une note datée de juin 1938 provenant des archives de l'ancien président de la Banque, M. McKittrick, qui avait envisagé le rachat des actions des actionnaires privés, proposait, à titre de méthode d'évaluation des actions, de déterminer "la valeur réelle ou la valeur de liquidation des actions de la BRI."[130] Une note interne préparée par le Secrétariat pour la 318e réunion du Conseil d'administration de la Banque du 8 septembre 1969, tenait pour acquis que les actionnaires privés jouissaient d'une "part potentielle des provisions et des réserves de la Banque."[131] Il est également instructif que la méthode d'évaluation recommandée par le Secrétariat pour fixer le prix d'une nouvelle émission d'actions était basée sur un actif net réévalué avec application d'une décote.[132] La recommandation a été adoptée par le Conseil lors de la 319e réunion du Conseil du 17 novembre 1969.[133] Une note interne du 6 novembre 1998, préparée par le service juridique de la Banque, a fait remarquer la nécessité "de respecter le principe de l'égalité des droits de

[129] Note de Weiser de 1936, p. 3-4, pièces jointes au mémoire de First Eagle, onglet 35.

[130] Document sans titre, pièces jointes au mémoire de First Eagle, onglet 36, p. 11.

[131] Ordre du jour de la 318e réunion, Ajustement du capital de la Banque et modification de ses Statuts, pièces jointes au mémoire de First Eagle, onglet 23, p. 2.

[132] *Id.*, p. 4.

[133] Ordre du jour de la 319e réunion, onglet 24, p. 7.

tous les actionnaires dans la répartition des bénéfices ou dans la distribution des actifs, principe énoncé à l'article 13 des Statuts."[134] Il convient de faire observer que la note concernant l'exclusion fait état de la nécessité de payer la valeur patrimoniale complète de chaque action de la Banque. En l'espèce, la valeur "patrimoniale" ne peut que concerner la valeur réelle des actifs de la Banque. Dans aucune des délibérations internes de la Banque concernant le rachat forcé, il n'a été considéré que le prix du marché des actions était la règle appropriée pour calculer la valeur des actions. Le rapport de J.P. Morgan du 7 septembre 2000, qui sera examiné plus en détail ci-dessous, a également relevé que "lors de sa récente émission d'actions destinées aux 4 nouveaux membres de la BRI, le prix de l'action a été calculé par la BRI sur la base de l'actif net réévalué."[135] L'actif net réévalué pour cette émission s'élevait à 20.080 dollars américains par action et après décote de 30%, le montant était de 14.056 dollars américains ou 5.020 francs or par action. Le rapport signalait également que "pour une émission d'actions précédente d'un total de [sic] 44.000 actions destinées à 13 banques centrales membres en novembre 1996, le calcul de l'actif net réévalué donnait une valeur de 18.772 dollars américains par action, soit l'équivalent de [. . .] 3.643 [francs or]."[136]

194. En somme, à partir de 1936, il semble à la lumière des éléments dont le Tribunal dispose que la Banque, dans ses délibérations internes, ait admis que toutes les actions ouvraient le droit à une part égale proportionnelle des actifs de la Banque, qu'elle ait fixé le prix des nouvelles actions sur cette base (avec application d'une décote qui sera examinée plus loin) et qu'elle ait tenu pour acquis que si elle devait procéder au rachat forcé de ses actions détenues par des personnes privées, les Statuts lui imposeraient de fixer le prix des actions en appliquant une méthode d'évaluation des actions tenant compte des actifs nets de la Banque. Dans aucune des délibérations internes de la Banque concernant le rachat

---

[134] L-3 confidentielle, Capital-actions de la BRI, 6 novembre 1998, *supra* note de bas de page 82, p. 3.

[135] J.P. Morgan, Projet Primus – Présentation au Conseil d'administration de la Banque des Règlements Internationaux (BRI) – Rapport d'évaluation et fourchette de prix suggérée pour l'opération, 7 septembre 2000. Pièces jointes au mémoire de First Eagle, onglet 43, p. 24; mémoire en défense, pièce 23.

[136] *Id.*, note de bas de page non numérotée.

forcé, le cours de bourse n'a été présenté comme la règle à appliquer pour calculer le prix des actions.

3. Pertinence et montant d'une décote éventuelle

195. Après avoir constaté qu'une part proportionnelle de l'actif net réévalué est la méthode imposée par les Instruments constitutifs, comme le confirme la pratique antérieure de la Banque, le Tribunal en vient à la question de savoir si et dans quelle mesure il faut appliquer une décote à l'actif net réévalué proportionnel par action. À cet égard, le Tribunal considère particulièrement instructif le document interne déjà mentionné, qui a pour titre ORDRE DU JOUR DE LA TROIS CENT DIX-HUITIÈME RÉUNION DU CONSEIL D'ADMINISTRATION DE LA BANQUE DES RÈGLEMENTS INTERNATIONAUX,[137] qui a été préparé par le Conseiller juridique, a ensuite été approuvé par le Comité consultatif du Conseil d'administration et a finalement été approuvé par le Conseil d'administration du 17 novembre 1969.[138] Le point 8 dudit document, qui a pour titre "Ajustement du capital de la Banque et modification de ses Statuts (318/E (1) & (2))", a été préparé dans le but de fournir des éléments d'appréciation et de présenter une recommandation au Conseil d'administration concernant le prix d'une nouvelle tranche de 200.000 actions de 2.500 francs or chacune, qui ne pouvaient être souscrites que par des banques centrales. Le document fait observer que la question d'une prime pour les actions n'avait jamais été soulevée auparavant[139] et passe en revue les différentes considérations qui pourraient influencer la décision à prendre.

196. Le rapport poursuit: "[l]e Conseil . . . doit trouver une base objective à partir de laquelle il calculera la prime . . . ."[140] Le rapport procède à l'examen des "trois méthodes les plus généralement admises"[141] qui étaient

---

[137] *Supra* note de bas de page 131, onglet 23.
[138] *Supra* note de bas de page 133.
[139] *Supra* note de bas de page 131, p. 1.
[140] *Id.*, p. 2-3.
[141] *Id.*

(i) la rentabilité future de la société;

(ii) le prix du marché des actions;

(iii) la méthode mathématique.

La méthode de la rentabilité future (qui est apparentée au modèle des dividendes à perpétuité utilisé par J.P. Morgan et adopté par le Conseil dans sa décision prise à l'Assemblée générale extraordinaire du 8 janvier 2001) présentait plusieurs problèmes. Les bénéfices avaient connu de grandes fluctuations, l'évolution future des prix n'était pas prévisible et la politique de la Banque en matière de dividendes était dictée par des préoccupations liées à l'objet de la Banque plutôt qu'au profit des actionnaires. Par conséquent, le rapport a rejeté cette méthode. S'agissant de la méthode basée sur le prix du marché, le rapport a fait remarquer que, compte tenu de la nature des actions de la Banque, des divers marchés boursiers sur lesquels elles étaient achetées et vendues et du statut particulier de la Banque elle-même, cette méthode constituait "une base peu fiable pour calculer la prime."[142]

197. S'agissant de la méthode mathématique, apparentée à l'actif net réévalué, le rapport a estimé, dans le cas de la BRI, qu'elle constituait:

> . . . le seul moyen fiable . . . , car elle évite autant qu'il est possible la nature capricieuse des autres méthodes considérées plus haut et elle n'est pas influencée par des circonstances extérieures. Elle comporte aussi un avantage supplémentaire par le fait que le bilan de la BRI donne une image plus exacte de la valeur de la société que le bilan d'une société commerciale ordinaire; la BRI n'a pas de réserve occulte et hormis la valeur qui peut être attribuée à ses bâtiments et terrains totalement amortis, qui serait bien entendu toujours sujette à discussion, le bilan donne une image assez précise de la valeur réelle de la société.[143]

---

[142] *Id.*
[143] *Id.*, p. 4.

Le rapport procède au calcul de l'actif net réévalué, si la Banque devait être liquidée sur-le-champ. Mais comme l'actif net réévalué ordinaire ne tient pas compte d'une liquidation hypothétique, le rapport a essayé de prendre en considération les incidences qu'une liquidation aurait entraînées, telles que:[144]

(i) lourdes pertes, donnant lieu à une forte réduction des réserves;

(ii) dépréciation des terrains et des bâtiments en cas de liquidation;

(iii) épuisement du Fonds spécial de réserve de dividendes.

Le rapport conclut

> . . . il semble que la prime doive être calculée en vertu de la méthode mathématique, mais qu'il serait équitable d'appliquer une décote au total des fonds propres de la Banque, afin de tenir compte de l'ensemble des considérations examinées ci-dessus. Cette constatation tend à indiquer qu'une décote de 30% serait appropriée.[145]

198. Le rapport de J.P. Morgan du 7 septembre 2000 considère également la question d'une décote de la valeur des actions dans le cadre de la méthode de l'actif net réévalué. Bien que plusieurs des résultats de ses calculs rejoignent approximativement ceux présentés dans le rapport du Conseil d'administration de 1969, la méthode utilisée alors était assez différente. D'une part, le rapport de J.P. Morgan ne mentionne pas les articles 1 et 13 des Statuts, qui consacrent l'égalité des actions. Il est utile de rappeler que l'article 1 dispose que:

> Il est constitué sous le nom de Banque des Règlements Internationaux . . . une société anonyme par actions.

---

[144] *Id.*, p. 5.
[145] *Id.*, p. 5-6.

et que l'article 13 dispose:

> Les actions jouissent de droits égaux dans la répartition des bénéfices de la banque et dans toute distribution d'actifs faites aux articles 51, 52 et 53 des Statuts.

D'autre part, dans le rapport du Conseil d'administration, la décote est obtenue en grande partie par l'introduction de variables correspondant à une liquidation hypothétique, dont on pouvait prévoir qu'elle réduirait la valeur; le rapport de J.P. Morgan ne fait pas état d'un prix de liquidation corrigé, mais applique une décote du fait (i) de l'absence de droit de vote; (ii) de la négociabilité réduite et (iii) des contraintes dues au double veto sur les ventes d'actions.[146]

199. Bien que l'analyse réalisée par J.P. Morgan soit rigoureuse et élaborée, le Tribunal fait remarquer qu'elle confond deux méthodes d'évaluation: le prix de l'action tel qu'il est déterminé par le marché et l'évaluation de l'actif net réévalué. Les trois facteurs que le rapport de J.P. Morgan identifie peuvent contribuer à expliquer la disparité entre le prix du marché et le prix de l'actif net réévalué proportionnel, mais ils ne sont pas pertinents pour une analyse de l'actif net réévalué dans le cas d'une entité dont les instruments constitutifs consacrent l'égalité fondamentale de toutes les actions au regard de leurs droits aux actifs de la Banque. Dès lors, une grande partie des données à partir desquelles J.P. Morgan a obtenu sa décote de 30% en raison de l'absence de droit de vote est dérivée des tendances du marché.[147] De même, la proposition de J.P. Morgan d'appliquer une décote supplémentaire de 15% liée à la négociabilité peut être appropriée pour déterminer le prix du marché correct d'une action négociée, mais n'est pas adéquate dans une analyse de l'actif net réévalué dans le cas d'une entité dont les instruments constitutifs consacrent l'égalité du droit de toutes les actions aux actifs de la société.

---

[146] *Id.*, p. 28 *et suiv.* Le rapport de J.P. Morgan crée aussi une catégorie supplémentaire, "autres considérations", mais conclut finalement qu'elle n'est pas applicable.

[147] *Id.*, p. 29.

200. Le rapport d'Arthur Andersen, qui a également reconnu le caractère inapproprié d'une méthode basée sur le cours de bourse en raison des caractéristiques de la Banque, a passé en revue le rapport de J.P. Morgan et a conclu que le prix de 16.000 francs suisses par action était "équitable."[148] Cependant, quelques-unes de ses brèves observations ne sont pas tout à fait compatibles avec l'approche du rapport de J.P. Morgan. Le rapport d'Arthur Andersen, par exemple, fait remarquer que "la valeur d'une action cotée ne peut pas être supérieure au prix payé par les banques centrales à la date d'une augmentation de capital";[149] en fait, le rapport de J.P. Morgan a fixé le prix des actions retirées à un montant considérablement inférieur "au prix payé par les banques centrales à la date d'une augmentation de capital." Bien qu'il soulève plusieurs autres questions à propos des estimations présentées dans le rapport de J.P. Morgan, il ignore également la *lex specialis* des Statuts et partage en général les principales hypothèses sur lesquelles J.P. Morgan s'est basée.

201. Par ces motifs, le Tribunal n'estime pas que les analyses de la décote présentées dans les rapports de J.P. Morgan et d'Arthur Andersen soient juridiquement pertinentes en l'espèce. Par contre, le Tribunal déclare que l'analyse de la décote exposée par le Conseil d'administration en 1969, qui a été appliquée pour fixer le prix des différentes tranches des nouvelles émissions d'actions destinées à être vendues aux nouvelles banques centrales par la suite, est appropriée pour déterminer une décote de l'actif net réévalué. L'usage d'une valeur de liquidation hypothétique, qui était l'approche adoptée par le Conseil d'administration en 1969 et par la suite, est également pertinent, eu égard au fait que First Eagle a allégué que la situation analogue la plus appropriée envisagée dans les Statuts était une liquidation ou une "liquidation partielle"; l'approche du Conseil d'administration était basée sur une valeur de liquidation projetée. Par ailleurs, il semble que le prix résultant par action qui se dégage de cette analyse corresponde à un prix qu'au moins un des demandeurs, First Eagle, a estimé être un prix approprié, lorsqu'il s'est adressé à la Banque le 23 juin 2000 pour proposer un rachat public d'action "dans des conditions similaires à celles d'émissions récentes

---

[148] Pièces jointes au mémoire de First Eagle, onglet 45, p. 16; mémoire en défense, pièce 21, p. 7-8.
[149] *Id.*

d'actions."[150] Mais la preuve la plus révélatrice en faveur d'une décote de 30% est son usage constant pour la fixation par la Banque du prix des actions émises destinées aux nouvelles banques centrales. Par conséquent, le Tribunal estime que la décote appropriée de l'actif net réévalué s'élève à 30%.

202. Par ces motifs, le Tribunal déclare que l'indemnisation appropriée pour les actions reprises, comme les Statuts l'exigent, était une part proportionnelle de l'actif net réévalué de la Banque avec application d'une décote de 30%, sous réserve d'une évaluation supplémentaire de l'actif net réévalué en ce qui concerne les biens immobiliers. Puisque la Banque a payé un montant inférieur, elle est tenue de verser la différence à chaque actionnaire privé.

4. Actif net réévalué de la Banque à la date du 8 janvier 2001

203. Le rapport de J.P. Morgan a évalué l'actif net réévalué de la Banque, en calculant la moyenne d'évaluations faites à trois dates différentes. Le rapport de J.P. Morgan mentionne un chiffre de 10.072.000.000 de dollars américains ou 19.034 dollars américains (33.820 francs suisses) par action pour les 529.165 actions de la Banque. Dr. Reineccius a indiqué qu'il accepterait ce chiffre comme actif net réévalué. M. Mathieu souhaitait avoir la possibilité de présenter ses arguments concernant la valeur des biens immobiliers de la Banque, puisqu'elle n'est pas incluse dans le rapport de J.P. Morgan.[151] First Eagle a laissé entendre qu'elle accepterait l'actif net réévalué mentionné dans le rapport de J.P. Morgan, si une évaluation des biens immobiliers était réalisée par un expert.[152] Le Tribunal réservera la question de l'actif net réévalué de la Banque avec application d'une décote pour la phase suivante, qui sera la dernière phase de l'arbitrage.

---

[150] Mémoire en défense, pièce 22.
[151] Voir par. 84 *supra*; compte rendu, p. 318.
[152] Voir par. 76 *supra*; compte rendu, p. 329.

CHAPITRE VI – AUTRES QUESTIONS

A. INTÉRÊTS

204. À la lumière de ce qui précède, une somme précise à déterminer lors de la phase suivante, ainsi que les intérêts sont dus. S'agissant des intérêts, l'état actuel du dossier ne permet pas au Tribunal de déterminer le montant des intérêts dus, ainsi que le taux à appliquer, la date à partir de laquelle ils doivent être versés, le montant sur lequel ils doivent être calculés et si des intérêts simples ou composés sont dus.

B. ÉVALUATION DES BIENS IMMOBILIERS

205. Puisque l'actif net réévalué retenu ne comprend pas les biens immobiliers de la Banque, cette évaluation doit également être réalisée lors de la phase suivante de l'arbitrage. L'évaluation des biens immobiliers sera confiée à un expert. Le choix de l'expert, son mandat et le calendrier de l'évaluation seront arrêtés par le Tribunal après consultation des Parties.

C. DEMANDE RECONVENTIONNELLE DE LA BANQUE

206. Il convient de rappeler que la Banque a présenté une demande reconventionnelle contre First Eagle, réclamant des dommages-intérêts pour violation par First Eagle de l'article 54 des Statuts du fait qu'elle a ignoré à tort cet engagement relatif à la juridiction et a intenté une action contre la Banque aux États-Unis, afin d'éviter la juridiction du Tribunal, et pour les frais de l'arbitrage.

207. Dans l'état actuel de la procédure, le Tribunal ne dispose pas d'informations suffisantes sur les arguments de la Banque et de First Eagle en ce qui concerne ladite demande reconventionnelle, notamment sa quantification. Par conséquent, le Tribunal décide que la question de la demande reconventionnelle sera réglée lors de la phase suivante de l'arbitrage selon un calendrier qui sera fixé en concertation avec les Parties.

D. Frais

208. Le Tribunal ne dispose pas d'informations suffisantes en ce qui concerne les frais de l'arbitrage. Le Tribunal décide que la question des frais sera réglée lors de la phase suivante de l'arbitrage selon un calendrier à fixer en concertation avec les Parties, en tenant compte, pour autant qu'elles le jugent pertinent, de l'*Ordonnance dans l'affaire entre M. Reginald H. Howe et la Banque des Règlements Internationaux*, rendue par le Tribunal.

CHAPITRE VII – DÉCISIONS

209. PAR CES MOTIFS, le Tribunal arbitral prend à l'unanimité les décisions suivantes:

1. DIT que la modification des Statuts de la Banque des Règlements Internationaux du 8 janvier 2001 tendant à exclure les actionnaires privés en tant qu'actionnaires de la Banque était licite;

2. DIT que les demandeurs n° 1, 2 et 3 ont droit à une indemnité pour chacune des actions reprises qu'ils détenaient dans la Banque des Règlements internationaux, ladite indemnité étant égale à une part proportionnelle de l'actif net réévalué de la Banque avec application d'une décote de 30%;

3. CONSTATE qu'aux fins de l'indemnisation visée dans la décision n° 2, les demandeurs n° 1, 2 et 3 acceptent que l'actif net réévalué de la Banque des Règlements Internationaux s'élève à 10.072.000.000 de dollars américains, soit 19.034 dollars américains (équivalant à 33.820 francs suisses) par action, compte non tenu de la valeur des biens immobiliers de la Banque;

4. FAIT DROIT À la demande présentée par les demandeurs n° 1, 2 et 3 dans la mesure où elle est compatible avec les décisions cidessus et REJETTE toute autre mesure demandée par les demandeurs n° 1, 2 et 3 non compatible avec lesdites décisions, ainsi que la mesure demandée par la Banque des Règlements Internationaux afférente auxdites décisions;

5. RESTE compétent en ce qui concerne l'évaluation des biens immobiliers de la Banque des Règlements Internationaux, la fixation du montant exact, y compris les intérêts, que la Banque doit verser aux demandeurs n° 1, 2 et 3, la demande reconventionnelle de la Banque des Règlements Internationaux contre le demandeur n° 2 (First Eagle) et les frais de l'arbitrage, ainsi que toute mesure demandée par l'une des Parties quelle qu'elle soit en ce qui concerne ces questions;

6. DIT qu'il rendra une ou plusieurs ordonnances de procédure concernant le déroulement de la phase suivante de l'arbitrage

ayant trait aux questions visées dans la décision n° 5 après concertation avec les Parties.

Fait au Palais de la Paix, La Haye, le 22 novembre 2002,

Prof. W. Michael Reisman

Prof. Dr. Jochen A. Frowein

Prof. Dr. Mathias Krafft

Prof. Dr. Paul Lagarde

Prof. Dr. Albert Jan van den Berg

Phyllis P. Hamilton, Secrétaire

ANNEXE A

Accord concernant le règlement complet et définitif de la question des réparations (signé à La Haye le 20 janvier 1930)

ANNEXE XII

Arbitrage. Règles de procédure

1. A l'occasion de tout arbitrage la procédure sera réglée par les dispositions du chapitre III de la convention de La Haye de 1907 pour le règlement pacifique des conflits internationaux, dans la mesure où elles ne sont pas modifiées ci-après ou par les dispositions de l'accord de La Haye de janvier 1930.

   Notamment l'article 85 de la convention de La Haye recevra application et chaque partie supportera ses propres frais et une fraction égale des frais du tribunal.

2. Le tribunal siégera à La Haye ou en tout autre lieu qu'il pourra lui-même désigner.

   La date des sessions sera fixée par le président et préavis de 14 jours au moins sera donné aux Parties.

3. Chacune des Parties nommera un représentant.

   Toutes communications, soit entre les Parties et le tribunal, soit entre les Parties, seront faites par l'intermédiaire de ces représentants.

   Le tribunal désignera un secrétaire à qui les communications devront être adressées.

4. La procédure comprendra deux phases:

   (1) L'instruction écrite; et

(2) Les débats oraux.

Les débats oraux seront publics.

5. La partie demanderesse présentera son mémoire dans un délai de six semaines à compter de la date du compromis ou d'une date à fixer par le président ou par le tribunal et l'autre partie présentera son contre-mémoire dans un délai de six semaines à partir du jour où elle aura reçu le mémoire de la demanderesse.

Si une contestation s'élève sur le point de savoir, dans une espèce donnée, quelle partie est demanderesse, le question sera résolue en procédure sommaire par le président du tribunal ou tout autre de ses membres désigné à cet effet par le président.

6. Les mémoires comprennent:

(1) un exposé des faits sur lesquels la demande est fondée;

(2) un exposé de droit;

(3) les conclusions;

(4) le bordereau des pièces à l'appui; ces pièces devront être annexées au mémoire.

Les contre-mémoires comprennent:

(1) la reconnaissance ou la contestation des faits mentionnés dans le mémoire;

(2) le cas échéant, un exposé additionnel des faits;

(3) un exposé de droit;

(4) des conclusions fondées sur les faits énoncés; ces conclusions peuvent comprendre des demandes reconventionnelles, pour autant que ces dernières rentrent dans la compétence du tribunal;

(5) le bordereau des pièces à l'appui; ces pièces devront être annexées au contre-mémoire.

7. Les Parties auront également le droit de présenter respectivement une réplique et une duplique dans un délai de trois semaines à partir de la réception de l'élément antérieur de procédure.

Tous les mémoires seront imprimés. Six exemplaires au moins seront remis à la partie adverse et douze exemplaires au moins au tribunal. Chacune des Parties accusera réception de tout document à la partie qui l'a remis et informera le tribunal de la date de réception; tous documents invoqués à l'appui seront annexés en copies certifiées conformes.

8. Les délais ci-dessus indiqués peuvent être prolongés, soit par accord entre les Parties, soit par décision du président ou du tribunal.

9. La procédure écrite pourra être rédigée en français, anglais ou, au cas où l'Allemagne est partie, en allemand. Tout membre du tribunal aura toutefois la faculté de demander que toute pièce de procédure ou autre document (y compris toute traduction) remis dans l'une de ces trois langues soit traduit en une autre de ces langues et que la traduction soit, le cas échéant, dûment certifiée.

10. Aucune des Parties ne pourra avoir, pour chaque question distincte soumise à l'arbitrage, plus de deux avocats.

11. Les avocats pourront plaider en leur propre langue, sous réserve du droit de tout membre du tribunal ou de la partie adverse de réclamer une traduction en français et en anglais.

12. Il sera établi des comptes rendus sténographiques de tous le débats oraux et des transcriptions en clair en seront fournies, avec toute la célérité possible, aux membres du tribunal et aux Parties. L'exécution de la présente clause et la rédaction des procès-verbaux nécessaires incombent au secrétaire du tribunal.

13. Pour tout ce qui concerne l'arbitrage et jusqu'au début des débats oraux, le président ou deux membres du tribunal, désignés par le président,

auront qualité pour prendre, au nom du tribunal, toutes décisions que celui-ci est autorisé à prendre.

14. Aucune des Parties ne pourra, sans le consentement de l'autre partie, utiliser, au cours des débats, un document qui n'aura pas été préalablement communiqué à cette dernière.

15. Tout membre du tribunal pourra poser aux Parties, au cours des débats, toutes questions qu'il jugera utiles.Le tribunal pourra, à tout moment, jusqu'au prononcé de sa décision, faire usage de tous moyens d'information qu'il jugera nécessaire et il pourra demander toutes notes, mémoires, documents ou explications supplémentaires qu'il jugera désirables.Toutefois, au cas où le tribunal voudrait faire usage d'autres moyens d'information que ceux qui lui ont été fournis par les Parties, il leur donnera la faculté de présenter leurs observations à ce sujet.

16. Aucune explication orale ne sera reçue de l'une des Parties si l'autre partie n'est présente ou n'a été dûment citée.

17. Toute requête ou communication adressée au tribunal par l'une des Parties sera en même temps communiquée à l'autre partie.

18. Le secrétaire du tribunal notifiera à toutes les Parties à l'accord de La Haye de janvier 1930 toutes procédures instituées devant le tribunal.

19. Lorsqu'une puissance signataire ou la banque des règlements internationaux estime que, dans un différend, un intérêt d'ordre juridique est pour elle en cause, elle peut adresser au Tribunal une requête aux fins d'intervention.

    Faute d'accord entre les Parties, le président, ou tout membre du tribunal désigné par lui à cet effet, fixera le délai dans lequel la partie intervenante devra présenter son mémoire.

    Sous réserve de toutes dispositions contraires prises par le tribunal, les règles qui précèdent et les stipulations de l'accord de La Haye de janvier 1930 relatives à l'arbitrage, notamment celles ayant trait à la désignation en certains cas d'un membre additionnel, s'appliqueront à la partie intervenante comme à toute partie primitivement en cause.

ANNEXE B

Accord concernant le règlement complet et définitif de la question des réparations (signé à La Haye le 20 janvier 1930)

Article XV

1. Tout différend, soit entre les gouvernements signataires du présent accord, soit entre un ou plusieurs d'entre eux, et la banque des règlements internationaux au sujet de l'interprétation et de l'application du nouveau plan, sera soumis, sous réserve des dispositions spéciales prévues aux annexes I, V*bis*, VI*bis* et IX, pour décision définitive, à un tribunal arbitral de cinq membres nommés pour 5 ans, dont un, qui remplira les fonctions de président, devra être citoyen des Etats-Unis d'Amérique, dont deux devront être ressortissants d'Etats ayant été neutres pendant la dernière guerre, et dont les deux derniers seront respectivement ressortissants de l'Allemagne et de l'une des puissances créancières de l'Allemagne.

   Pour la première période de cinq ans, à dater de la mise à exécution du nouveau plan, ce tribunal sera composé des cinq membres qui constituent actuellement le tribunal arbitral institué par l'accord de Londres du 30 août 1924.

2. Il sera pourvu, soit au renouvellement des membres du tribunal à l'expiration de chaque période, soit à toute vacance qui pourrait se produire en cours de période: en ce qui concerne le membre ayant la nationalité de l'une des puissances créancières de l'Allemagne, par le gouvernement français qui s'entendra préalablement à cet effet avec les gouvernements belge, britannique, italien, japonais; en ce qui concerne le membre ayant la nationalité allemande, par le gouvernement allemand, et, en ce qui concerne les trois autres membres, par les six gouvernements précédemment mentionnés agissant d'un commun accord, ou, faute de cet accord, par le président en exercice de la cour permanente de justice internationale.

3. Dans tous les cas où, soit l'Allemagne, soit la banque sera partie demanderesse ou défenderesse, si le président du tribunal estimait, à la requête d'un ou plusieurs d'entre les gouvernements créanciers parties au litige, que ce ou ces gouvernements sont principalement intéressés, il invitera ce ou ces gouvernements à désigner, d'un commun accord, si plusieurs gouvernements sont en cause, un membre qui remplacera dans le tribunal le membre nommé par le gouvernement français.

   Au cas où, lors d'un différend entre deux ou plusieurs gouvernements créanciers, le tribunal ne compterait pas sur le siège un ressortissant d'un ou de plusieurs d'entre ces gouvernements, ce ou ces gouvernements auraient le droit de désigner chacun un membre qui siégera à cette occasion. Le président, s'il estime que certains de ces gouvernements ont un intérêt commun au litige, les invitera à désigner un seul membre; toutes les fois que, par l'effet de cette disposition, le tribunal sera composé d'un nombre pair de membres, le président aura voix prépondérante.

4. Avant toute décision finale et sans préjudice du fond, le président du tribunal ou, en cas d'empêchement de sa part, dans un cas quelconque, tout autre membre désigné par lui, pourra, sur requête de la partie la plus diligente, ordonner des mesures conservatoires destinées à garantir les droits des parties.

5. En recourant au tribunal, les Parties peuvent toujours se mettre d'accord pour soumettre leur différend au président ou à un des membres choisi comme arbitre unique.

6. Sauf dispositions spéciales prévues au compromis qui ne sauraient en aucun cas porter atteinte au droit d'intervention d'une tierce partie, la procédure du tribunal ou celle de l'arbitre unique sera réglée conformément à l'annexe XII.

   Ces règles de procédure s'appliquent également, sous la même réserve, à toute instance devant le tribunal prévue aux annexes du présent accord.

7. Faute d'entente sur les termes du compromis, toute partie pourra saisir directement et par simple requête le tribunal qui statuera, fût-ce par défaut, sur toute question dont il sera de la sorte saisi.

8. Le tribunal et l'arbitre unique sont juges de leur compétence. Toutefois, au cas où, dans un conflit s'élevant entre gouvernements, la question de la compétence serait soulevée, elle sera, à la demande de l'une des parties, déférée à la cour permanente de justice internationale.

9. Les présentes dispositions seront dûment acceptées par la banque en vue du règlement de tout différend pouvant surgir entre elle et un ou plusieurs des gouvernements signataires en ce qui concerne l'interprétation ou l'application de ses statuts ou du nouveau plan.

COUR PERMANENTE D'ARBITRAGE

TRIBUNAL ARBITRAL ÉTABLI CONFORMÉMENT
À L'ARTICLE XV DE L'ACCORD SIGNÉ À
LA HAYE LE 20 JANVIER 1930

Prof. W. Michael Reisman
Prof. Dr. Jochen A. Frowein
Prof. Dr. Mathias Krafft
Prof. Dr. Paul Lagarde
Prof. Dr. Albert Jan van den Berg

Phyllis Hamilton, Secrétaire
Cour Permanente d'Arbitrage, Greffe

DR. HORST REINECCIUS, DEMANDEUR (DEMANDE N° 1)
FIRST EAGLE SOGEN FUNDS, INC., DEMANDERESSE (DEMANDE N° 2)
M. PIERRE MATHIEU ET LA SOCIÉTÉ DE CONCOURS HIPPIQUE
DE LA CHÂTRE, DEMANDEURS (DEMANDE N° 3)

-CONTRE-

BANQUE DES RÈGLEMENTS INTERNATIONAUX, DÉFENDERESSE

SENTENCE DÉFINITIVE
CONCERNANT LES DEMANDES D'INDEMNISATION POUR LES ACTIONS ANCIENNEMENT DÉTENUES PAR LES DEMANDEURS, LES INTÉRÊTS DUS EN CONSÉQUENCE ET LES FRAIS D'ARBITRAGE ET CONCERNANT LA DEMANDE RECONVENTIONNELLE FORMÉE PAR LA BANQUE CONTRE FIRST EAGLE SOGEN FUNDS, INC.

La Haye, le 19 septembre 2003

Table des Matières

CHAPITRE I – INTRODUCTION

1. Le 22 novembre 2002, le Tribunal concernant la Banque des Règlements Internationaux (ci-après le "Tribunal") a rendu à l'unanimité une sentence partielle (ci-après la "sentence partielle") dans les affaires concernant Dr. Horst Reineccius (ci-après "Dr. Reineccius" ou "le demandeur n° 1"), First Eagle SoGen Funds, Inc. (ci-après "First Eagle" ou "le demandeur n° 2") et M. Pierre Mathieu et la Société de Concours Hippique de La Châtre (ci-après dénommés collectivement "M. Mathieu" ou "le demandeur n° 3") contre la Banque des Règlements Internationaux (ci-après la "Banque" ou la "BRI"). Dans ladite sentence partielle, le Tribunal a rendu les décisions suivantes:

> 1. DIT que la modification des Statuts de la Banque des Règlements Internationaux du 8 janvier 2001 tendant à exclure les actionnaires privés en tant qu'actionnaires de la Banque était licite;
>
> 2. DIT que les demandeurs n° 1, 2 et 3 ont droit à une indemnité pour chacune des actions reprises qu'ils détenaient dans la Banque des Règlements Internationaux, ladite indemnité étant égale à une part proportionnelle de l'actif net réévalué de la Banque avec application d'une décote de 30%;
>
> 3. CONSTATE qu'aux fins de l'indemnisation visée dans la décision n° 2, les demandeurs n° 1, 2 et 3 acceptent que l'actif net réévalué de la Banque des Règlements Internationaux s'élève à 10.072.000.000 de dollars américains, soit 19.034 dollars américains (équivalant à 33.820 francs suisses) par action, compte non tenu de la valeur des biens immobiliers de la Banque;
>
> 4. FAIT DROIT À la demande présentée par les demandeurs n° 1, 2 et 3 dans la mesure où elle est compatible avec les décisions ci-dessus et REJETTE toute autre mesure demandée par les demandeurs n° 1, 2 et 3 non compatible avec lesdites décisions, ainsi que la mesure demandée par la Banque des Règlements Internationaux afférente aux dites décisions;
>
> 5. RESTE compétent en ce qui concerne l'évaluation des biens immobiliers de la Banque des Règlements Internationaux, la fixation du montant exact, y compris

les intérêts, que la Banque doit verser aux demandeurs n° 1, 2 et 3, la demande reconventionnelle de la Banque des Règlements Internationaux contre le demandeur n° 2 (First Eagle) et les frais de l'arbitrage, ainsi que toute mesure demandée par l'une des Parties quelle qu'elle soit en ce qui concerne ces questions;

6. DIT qu'il rendra une ou plusieurs ordonnances de procédure concernant le déroulement de la phase suivante de l'arbitrage ayant trait aux questions visées dans la décision n° 5 après concertation avec les Parties.[1]

[1] Sentence partielle, par. 209.

CHAPITRE II – HISTORIQUE DE LA PROCÉDURE

2. Après réception de la sentence partielle, les Parties se sont entendues sur la communication de pièces et sur le calendrier des conclusions écrites concernant les questions encore pendantes devant le Tribunal: la demande reconventionnelle de la Banque contre First Eagle, la valeur des immeubles de la Banque et de leurs biens mobiliers (ci-après les "biens immobiliers"), le montant restant dû à chaque actionnaire privé, la question des intérêts, des frais de l'arbitrage et des frais judiciaires[2], ainsi que toutes les questions connexes.[3] Au cours de la seconde phase de l'arbitrage, Dr. Reineccius, First Eagle et la Banque sont convenus que si le Tribunal appliquait le taux de change du 7 septembre 2000, la valeur correcte de l'actif net réévalué par action s'éléverait à 33.936 francs suisses.[4]

3. Les Parties ont notifié au Tribunal leur accord concernant le calendrier de procédure de la seconde phase de l'arbitrage, que le Tribunal a confirmé le 31 janvier 2003 dans l'ordonnance de procédure n° 9 homologuant un accord entre les Parties relatif au calendrier de procédure, aux demandes de production de pièces et à la désignation d'un Expert dans la seconde phase (ci-après "ordonnance de procédure n° 9").

---

[2] Voir également l'ordonnance concernant les frais du 5 octobre 2001. Le texte intégral de toutes les ordonnances de procédure citées peut être consulté sur le site Internet www.pca-cpa.org.

[3] Sentence partielle, par. 209, point 5.

[4] Le Tribunal a relevé au paragraphe 203 de la sentence partielle que le rapport de J.P. Morgan concluait à un actif net réévalué de la Banque égal à 10.072.000.000 de dollars américains, soit 19.034 dollars américains (33.820 francs suisses) par action. Ainsi que la Banque et First Eagle en conviennent tous deux (voir mémoire de First Eagle suivant la sentence partielle (ci-après le "mémoire de FE suivant la sentence partielle"), par. 59), il s'agissait vraisemblablement d'une erreur d'écriture, étant donné que ce chiffre correspond en fait au montant d'un seul des trois mois dont J.P. Morgan a calculé la moyenne de l'actif net réévalué. Le rapport conclut que J.P. Morgan obtient un actif net réévalué de la BRI égal à 19.099 dollars américains (33.936 francs suisses) par action. Voir rapport d'évaluation (21) de J.P. Morgan du 7 septembre 2000 (Rapport de J.P. Morgan (pièce jointe n° 54). Contre-mémoire suivant la sentence partielle (ci-après "contre-mémoire de la BRI suivant la sentence partielle"), par. 2, note de bas de page 2. Le demandeur n° 1 retient également cette valeur dans sa demande de décision. Compte rendu, p. 386, ligne 29; voir également *infra* par. 19. Le demandeur n° 3 cite le montant de 33.936 francs suisses dans son mémoire en duplique. Mémoire en duplique de M. Mathieu sur la seconde phase de l'arbitrage ("Mémoire en duplique de M. Mathieu seconde phase"), p.5.

4. Conformément aux dispositions de la sentence partielle, le Tribunal a reçu: (1) une demande datée du 17 janvier 2003 émanant de First Eagle tendant à ce que la Banque communique des pièces, (2) une demande datée du 17 janvier 2003 émanant de la Banque tendant à ce que First Eagle communique des pièces, (3) une demande corrigée datée du 21 janvier 2003 émanant de First Eagle tendant à ce que la Banque communique des pièces, (4) les objections de First Eagle à la demande de la Banque datées du 28 janvier 2003, (5) la réponse et les objections de la Banque à la demande de First Eagle datées du 28 janvier 2003, (6) une réplique de la Banque aux objections de First Eagle datée du 30 janvier 2003 et (7) une réplique de First Eagle aux objections de la Banque datée du 4 février 2003. La Banque et First Eagle n'ont pu s'entendre sur:

(i) la demande par First Eagle de pièces relatives à la constitution du Tribunal,

(ii) la demande par First Eagle de pièces qui permettraient de calculer l'actif net réévalué de la Banque à la date du 8 janvier 2001 et

(iii) la demande par la Banque de pièces relatives, d'une part, à la décision de First Eagle de poursuivre la Banque et, d'autre part, aux communications entre First Eagle et ses actionnaires ou des personnes de droit public concernant l'opération visant à exclure les actionnaires privés.[5]

5. Le Tribunal a examiné les communications des Parties et a rendu l'ordonnance de procédure n° 10 décidant que:

> la demande de First Eagle dont il est fait état au point (i) ci-dessus ne tient pas compte du calendrier de procédure accepté d'un commun accord par les Parties et dans le cadre duquel les objections relatives à la juridiction ou au défaut d'indépendance devaient être déposées. La demande de pièces relatives à la constitution du Tribunal dans cette phase de l'arbitrage, après

---

[5] Ordonnance de procédure n° 10 du 9 mars 2003 ("ordonnance de procédure n° 10").

acceptation explicite[6] des Parties quant à la juridiction et à l'indépendance du Tribunal, est déplacée.

Le Tribunal a déclaré que la décision concernant la demande de First Eagle dont il est fait état au point (ii) ci-dessus serait examinée à une date ultérieure "si le Tribunal décid[ait] que la date du 8 janvier 2001 [était] celle qui d[evait] être retenue pour fixer le taux de change entre le dollar américain et le franc suisse aux fins de déterminer le montant à payer aux demandeurs."[7]

6. Le Tribunal a fait droit à la demande de la Banque dont il est fait état au point (iii) ci-dessus, relative à la déclaration de la Banque selon laquelle First Eagle aurait violé l'article 54, paragraphe 1, des Statuts de la Banque des Règlements Internationaux du 20 janvier 1930, tel qu'il a été modifié le 8 janvier 2001 (ci-après les "Statuts de la Banque"). First Eagle a été enjointe de communiquer à la Banque:

    a. Tous les documents non confidentiels relatifs à la décision de First Eagle de poursuivre la Banque sur le territoire des Etats-Unis et relatifs au déroulement de cette procédure ("Action de First Eagle aux Etats-Unis"), autres que les dossiers, affidavits et autres documents déposés par First Eagle auprès des tribunaux américains;

    b. Tous les documents créés le 11 septembre 2000 ou après cette date (date de l'annonce publique faite par la Banque de son intention de modifier les Statuts pour exclure les actionnaires privés) et avant le 31 août 2001 (date de la notification d'arbitrage de First Eagle) se rapportant aux communications entre First Eagle et les actionnaires (ou prétendus actionnaires) de la Banque (y compris les conseils de tels actionnaires) et concernant (i) l'opération par laquelle la Banque a procédé au retrait de ses actions détenues par des personnes autres que les banques centrales ("l'opération visant à exclure les actionnaires privés") et (ii) l'Action de First Eagle aux Etats-Unis;

---

[6] L'ordonnance de procédure n° 3 (Acte de mission) du 5 mars 2002 rapporte au paragraphe 1 que lors de la réunion du 26 février 2002 entre les Parties et le Tribunal visant à établir l'acte de mission, les Parties ont déclaré "ne pas soulever d'exceptions d'incompétence."

[7] Ordonnance de procédure n° 10, par. B.

c. Toutes les communications entre First Eagle et ses propres actionnaires concernant (i) l'opération visant à exclure les actionnaires privés et (ii) l'Action de First Eagle aux Etats-Unis; et

d. Tous les documents se rapportant aux communications de First Eagle aux Etats-Unis avec toutes personnes de droit public (autres que les tribunaux) cherchant à faire obstacle à l'opération visant à exclure les actionnaires privés.[8]

7. Par ailleurs, le Tribunal a entériné la désignation du bureau de Zurich de C.B. Richard Ellis, société proposée par les Parties, aux fins d'évaluer les immeubles de la Banque situés à Bâle et leurs biens mobiliers, dès lors que les Parties se sont entendues pour choisir la société Ellis et pour exiger de l'Expert qu'il fournisse une déclaration d'indépendance pour cette affaire.[9] La Secrétaire a demandé une proposition et une estimation des honoraires de la société Ellis pour ladite expertise, lesquelles ont été fournies et communiquées aux Parties le 5 avril 2003. Les Parties ont confirmé qu'elles acceptaient la proposition de la société Ellis.

8. Les Parties ont communiqué des pièces conformément à l'ordonnance de procédure n° 9 homologuant un accord entre les Parties et aux dispositions de l'ordonnance de procédure n° 10. Le Tribunal a reçu de Dr. Reineccius une lettre datée du 24 janvier 2003 exposant ses arguments et la décision demandée et renvoyant à ses lettres des 27 novembre 2002 et 3 janvier 2003. Le Tribunal a reçu des demandeurs n° 2 et 3: (1) un mémoire de First Eagle daté du 28 février 2003, (2) un mémoire de la Banque relatif à sa demande reconventionnelle, daté du 28 février 2003, (3) un mémoire de M. Mathieu daté du 3 mars 2003, (4) un contre-mémoire de First Eagle daté du 21 avril 2003, (5) un contre-mémoire de la Banque daté du 21 avril 2003, (6) une réplique de First Eagle datée du 16 mai 2003, (7) une réplique de M. Mathieu datée du 16 mai 2003 et (8) une réplique de la Banque datée du 16 mai 2003.

9. Le 16 mai 2003, le Tribunal a rendu l'ordonnance de procédure n° 11 homologuant un accord entre les Parties (ci-après ("ordonnance de procédure n° 11"), qui constate que:

---

[8] *Id.*, par. C.
[9] *Id.*, par. D.

> [L]e Tribunal a reçu de l'Expert sa déclaration d'indépendance dans cette affaire, comme les Parties l'avaient demandé le 7 avril 2003. Accompagné de la Secrétaire du Tribunal, l'Expert a inspecté tous les biens le 16 avril 2003 et a remis, le 28 avril 2003, un certificat d'évaluation, ainsi que les rapports d'évaluation correspondants qui ont été transmis aux Parties et acceptés par celles-ci . . . .
>
> . . . .
>
> B. Le Tribunal retient la valeur de 168.094.000 francs suisses (cent soixante-huit millions quatre-vingt-quatorze mille francs suisses), déterminée par l'Expert, aux fins de l'évaluation des immeubles de la Banque et de leurs biens mobiliers à la date du 7 septembre 2000, comme la sentence partielle rendue le 22 novembre 2002 le requiert.[10]

En outre, le Tribunal a entériné l'ordre du jour du débat oral.

10. Le 25 mai 2003, le Tribunal a rendu une ordonnance de procédure n° 12 homologuant un accord entre les Parties (proposition d'une nouvelle pièce jointe n° 104), faisant droit à la demande de First Eagle de déposer la nouvelle pièce jointe n° 104.

11. Le 27 mai 2003, le Tribunal a rendu l'ordonnance de procédure n° 13 homologuant un accord entre les Parties, faisant droit à la demande de Dr. Reineccius de déposer un relevé bancaire d'une seule page en tant que pièce jointe n° 1.

12. Conformément à l'article XV de l'Accord concernant le règlement complet et définitif de la question des réparations, signé à La Haye le 20 janvier 1930 (ci-après l' "Accord de La Haye de 1930") et à l'article 20 du règlement d'arbitrage, les audiences publiques relatives à la dernière

---

[10] Lors de l'audience du 28 mai 2003, les demandeurs n° 1 et 2 ont contesté la valeur que l'Expert avait fixée. Voir également *supra*, par. 7 et 9, et *infra* note de bas de page 17 et par. 18, 19 (ii) et 32. La Banque a demandé que le Tribunal se conforme à la décision contenue dans la sentence partielle, selon laquelle un seul expert fixe la valeur des biens immobiliers, et qu'il s'en tienne au choix explicite de la société Ellis par les Parties aux fins d'en fixer la valeur. Compte rendu, p. 604 et 605.

phase de l'arbitrage ont eu lieu les 28 et 29 mai 2003 dans la Grande Salle de Justice du Palais de la Paix à La Haye. A la demande des Parties, les demandes séparées ont été entendues en parallèle mais avec une certaine intégration pour l'efficacité et la commodité des Parties. Pendant les audiences, First Eagle était représentée par M. Donald Francis Donovan et M. Dietmar W. Prager du cabinet Debevoise & Plimpton. M. Mathieu était représenté par M. Elie Kleiman et M. Guillaume Tattevin du cabinet Freshfields Bruckhaus Deringer. La Banque était représentée par M. Jonathan I. Blackman, M. Laurent Cohen-Tanugi et Mlle Claudia Annacker du cabinet Cleary, Gottlieb, Steen & Hamilton. Le professeur Mario Giovanoli et M. James Freis étaient également présents pour le compte du Secrétariat de la BRI. Dr. Reineccius a comparu sans avocat le 28 mai.

13. En conformité avec la Convention concernant la Banque des Règlements Internationaux conclue le 20 janvier 1930 (ci-après la "Convention de La Haye de 1930"), des traductions simultanées en anglais, français et allemand ont été fournies pendant les audiences.

CHAPITRE III – LES PARTIES ET LEURS DEMANDES

A. Dr. Reineccius, demandeur n° 1

1. *Arguments*

a. Calcul de l'indemnité

14. Par lettre du 27 novembre 2002, Dr. Reineccius a demandé qu'il plaise au Tribunal de décider qu'un montant de 33.820 francs suisses[11] majoré du montant proportionnel des biens immobiliers de la Banque lui soit versé en francs suisses. Dr. Reineccius a indiqué à l'audience d'août 2002[12] qu'il convenait expressément que les calculs de l'actif net réévalué présentés par J.P. Morgan étaient corrects aux fins du calcul du montant supplémentaire à payer aux actionnaires privés. Dans sa lettre du 24 janvier 2003, Dr. Reineccius a demandé à nouveau qu'il plaise au Tribunal de lui accorder, conformément au paragraphe 209, point 5, de la sentence partielle, un montant de 33.820 francs suisses, majoré du montant fixé par l'Expert pour la valeur des immeubles.

b. Intérêts

15. Il a demandé des intérêts portant sur ce montant au taux minimal de 3¼% par an, qu'il assimile au *Geldmarktzins* en francs suisses avant le 17 septembre 2001. Il a relevé que le taux était inférieur après septembre 2001, mais a fait valoir que l'évaluation avant cette date était adéquate.[13]

c. Frais de l'arbitrage

16. Par lettre du 3 janvier 2003, Dr. Reineccius a demandé qu'il plaise au Tribunal d'ordonner à la Banque de rembourser la somme qu'il a déposée pour les frais de l'arbitrage.

d. Conclusions

17. Par lettre du 24 janvier 2003, Dr. Reineccius a notifié au Tribunal son intention de participer aux audiences des 28 et 29 mai 2003. Il a

[11] Voir *supra* note de bas de page 4, mais voir *infra* par. 19(i).
[12] Compte rendu, p. 331.
[13] *Id.*, p. 388.

approuvé le calendrier pour le dépôt des conclusions figurant dans l'ordonnance de procédure n° 9 homologuant un accord entre les Parties et a demandé que lui soient envoyées des copies: (1) des documents échangés par les Parties en application de l'ordonnance de procédure n° 9, paragraphes 5 à 8; et (2) des conclusions écrites visées dans l'ordonnance.

e. DÉCLARATIONS EXPRESSES

18. Dr. Reineccius s'est déclaré disposé à accepter le calcul de l'actif net réévalué de la Banque présenté par J.P. Morgan, tel qu'il est décrit au paragraphe 2 *supra*. S'agissant de l'évaluation des biens immobiliers conformément au paragraphe 205 de la sentence partielle, Dr. Reineccius a écrit le 27 novembre 2002:

> Ich überlasse es First Eagle in ihrem und in meinen Namen einen Vorschlag für die Benennung eines Immobilien-Experten und seinen Zeitplan für die Bewertung zu machen.[14]

First Eagle a explicitement consenti à la désignation d'un expert.[15]

2. Décision demandée

19. Dr. Reineccius a demandé qu'il plaise au Tribunal de dire que:

(i) ainsi que le Tribunal l'a déclaré au paragraphe 209, point 3, de la sentence partielle, il doit recevoir, pour ses actions ayant fait l'objet d'une reprise forcée, une indemnité proportionnelle de l'actif net réévalué de la Banque, présenté dans le rapport de J.P. Morgan et s'élevant, selon ses calculs, à 33.936 francs suisses par action;[16]

(ii) la valeur proportionnelle des immeubles de la Banque et de leurs

[14] Je charge First Eagle de faire, en son nom et en mon nom, une proposition concernant la désignation d'un expert immobilier et le calendrier de l'évaluation. [Traduction fournie par le Tribunal.]

[15] Voir *infra*, par. 32.

[16] Compte rendu, p. 386.

biens mobiliers qui lui est due doit être de 767 francs suisses par action;[17]

(iii) la Banque doit lui verser des intérêts portant sur l'indemnité susvisée au taux minimal de 3¼% l'an à compter du 8 janvier 2001 jusqu'à la date du paiement;[18]

(iv) les frais de l'arbitrage qui lui incombent (le dépôt fait sur le compte du Tribunal auprès de la BRI), à savoir 1.852,64 euros, doivent lui être remboursés et une indemnité doit lui être versée pour ses frais judiciaires et les efforts (*Bemühungen*) qu'il a consentis pour défendre sa cause devant le Tribunal;[19]

(v) une date précise doit être fixée pour le paiement de ladite indemnité, y compris les intérêts;[20]

(vi) le Tribunal doit "expressément interdire à la Banque de subordonner les paiements ultérieurs à la signature d'une renonciation".[21]

B. FIRST EAGLE, DEMANDEUR N° 2

1. Arguments

a. CALCUL DE L'INDEMNITÉ

20. First Eagle fait valoir que conformément à la sentence partielle, elle a droit à une indemnité de 7.755,20 francs suisses (non compris la valeur des biens immobiliers) pour chacune des 9.110 actions qu'elle détenait,[22]

---

[17] *Id.*, p. 387. A l'audience du 28 mai 2003, Dr. Reineccius a demandé qu'il plaise au Tribunal de substituer la valeur pour laquelle les biens immobiliers de la Banque étaient assurés à la valeur fixée par l'Expert. Voir également *supra*, par. 7 et 9 et note de bas de page 10, et *infra*, par. 32.

[18] Compte rendu, p. 388.

[19] Lettre du 27 novembre 2002 adressée à la Secrétaire du Tribunal par Dr. Reineccius.

[20] Compte rendu, p. 387.

[21] *Id.*, p. 388.

[22] Mémoire en réplique de First Eagle suivant la sentence partielle (ci-après "Mémoire en réplique de FE suivant la sentence partielle"), par. 186, point a.

majorée d' "intérêts composés mensuels[23] au taux d'au moins 7%[24] . . . à compter du 8 janvier 2001 jusqu'à la date du paiement",[25] plus les frais, honoraires et frais judiciaires qu'elle a supportés du fait de la présente procédure.[26]

21. Dans ses conclusions des 28 février 2003 et 16 mai 2003, First Eagle a soutenu que l'actif net réévalué de la Banque aux fins de déterminer l'indemnité due à First Eagle devait être fixé à 33.936 francs suisses par action, soit la valeur calculée par J.P. Morgan dans son rapport du 7 septembre 2000.[27]

> [C]e résultat s'impose du fait que les Parties ont déclaré expressément, à l'audience d'août 2002, accepter le calcul de l'actif net réévalué de la Banque présenté par J.P. Morgan. Par cette déclaration, les Parties sont convenues de considérer comme irréfutable une évaluation à la date de septembre 2000. . . dans l'hypothèse où le taux de change en vigueur en janvier 2001 serait retenu, l'actif net réévalué devrait être recalculé à compter de cette date également.[28]

A défaut de ce calcul, First Eagle serait contrainte de "supporter l'effet négatif de l'évolution des coefficients de conversion des monnaies . . . sans prise en considération de la hausse compensatrice de l'actif net réévalué de la Banque à la date ultérieure."[29]

22. Selon First Eagle, l'argument invoqué par la Banque selon lequel la date du taux de change entre le franc suisse et le dollar américain doit être le 8 janvier 2001 et non le 7 septembre 2000 constitue "une tentative de priver First Eagle de l'indemnité à laquelle elle a droit en vertu de la sentence partielle."[30] First Eagle affirme que lors de l'opération

---

[23] *Id.*, par. 162.
[24] *Id.*, par. 154.
[25] *Id.*, par. 151 et 186, point e.
[26] *Id.*, par. 186, points d et e.
[27] Mémoire de FE suivant la sentence partielle, par. 10; mémoire en réplique de FE suivant la sentence partielle, par. 4.
[28] Mémoire en réplique de FE suivant la sentence partielle, par. 5.
[29] Mémoire de FE suivant la sentence partielle, par. 70.
[30] Mémoire en réplique de FE suivant la sentence partielle, par 3.

d'exclusion, la Banque s'est effectivement basée sur le rapport de J.P. Morgan, dont elle a tenu compte des calculs en francs suisses.

> Lors de l'opération d'exclusion à l'origine de la réclamation de First Eagle, la Banque a d'abord fixé, le 10 septembre 2000, un prix de rachat en francs suisses. A cet effet, elle s'est basée sur le rapport de J.P. Morgan, qui a appliqué les taux de change en vigueur en septembre 2000 . . . . Ainsi, le 8 janvier 2001, la Banque s'est engagée à payer (et a par la suite payé) ce même prix de rachat en francs suisses.[31]

23. First Eagle fait valoir que la pratique antérieure de la Banque en matière d'émission d'actions n'est pas pertinente, mais qu'elle a pourtant justifié la référence à la date de septembre 2000 pour l'évaluation en francs suisses de l'actif net, présentée par J.P. Morgan:[32]

> [L]es pratiques antérieures en matière d'actions n'ont pas eu ou ont eu peu d'importance en comparaison avec la pratique utilisée par la Banque lors de l'opération d'exclusion, qui a consisté à fixer un prix de rachat en francs suisses à la date de septembre 2000 sur la base des taux de change en vigueur à cette date et à considérer que ce prix restait constant pendant toute la période de rachat des actions.[33]

24. First Eagle considère que l'argument de la Banque[34] selon lequel trois documents prouvent qu'elle suivait les fluctuations des taux de change après septembre 2000 est dénué de pertinence, car la Banque n'a pris aucune mesure en conséquence.[35] Par ailleurs, First Eagle fait remarquer que si J.P. Morgan a actualisé l'ensemble de son évaluation, les documents "révèlent que la Banque elle-même n'a pas appliqué à l'actif net réévalué de septembre 2000 les taux de change postérieurs à septembre 2000 . . . . La Banque a recalculé l'actif net réévalué en même

---

[31] Mémoire de FE suivant la sentence partielle, par. 76.

[32] Mémoire en réplique de FE suivant la sentence partielle, par. 83.

[33] *Id.*

[34] La Banque "a activement suivi l'évolution des taux de change du franc suisse et du dollar américain sur le marché jusqu'à la décision de l'Assemblée générale extraordinaire." Contre-mémoire de la BRI suivant la sentence partielle, par. 77.

[35] Mémoire en réplique de FE suivant la sentence partielle, par. 79.

temps qu'elle recalculait le taux de change, mais n'a pas appliqué de nouveaux taux de change à l'actif net réévalué de septembre . . . ."[36]

b. FRAIS DE L'ARBITRAGE ET FRAIS JUDICIAIRES

25. First Eagle affirme ce qui suit.

> First Eagle a également droit au remboursement par la Banque des frais de l'arbitrage et des honoraires d'avocat et frais judiciaires qu'elle a supportés. Premièrement, en sa qualité de partie gagnante, First Eagle a droit à se voir rembourser ses frais et honoraires, de manière à être pleinement dédommagée du refus de la Banque de payer l'indemnité légale au moment où elle était due. Deuxièmement, étant donné que la présente procédure était nécessaire pour rectifier l'indemnité au demeurant illicite versée par la Banque et dès lors pour assurer la conformité de l'opération aux impératifs du droit international, les frais, honoraires et frais judiciaires supportés par First Eagle relèvent des frais opérationnels nécessaires pour réaliser l'opération d'exclusion. Troisièmement, étant donné que tous les actionnaires exclus de la Banque ont largement bénéficié des efforts de First Eagle, lesdits actionnaires doivent au minimum partager proportionnellement les frais judiciaires de First Eagle.[37]

c. INTÉRÊTS

26 First Eagle soutient qu'elle a droit à des intérêts avec capitalisation sur une base mensuelle à un taux d'au moins 7% à compter du 8 janvier 2001 portant "sur le paiement de l'indemnité due, ainsi que sur les frais, honoraires et frais judiciaires qu'elle a supportés."[38] First Eagle fait valoir qu'un taux d'intérêt de 7%

> correspond au rendement minimal que First Eagle aurait attendu d'autres investissements possibles présentant le même risque, si elle avait reçu l'indemnité complète au moment où elle était due. Si First Eagle devait recevoir des intérêts calculés à un taux

---

[36] *Id.*, par. 80.
[37] *Id.*, par. 9.
[38] *Id.*, par. 12.

> inférieur à 7%, la Banque percevrait un revenu imprévu . . . et s'enrichirait donc de façon injuste.[39]

First Eagle affirme que les intérêts doivent être calculés avec capitalisation sur une base mensuelle "en conformité avec le droit international et la pratique financière actuellement en vigueur, y compris celle de la Banque elle-même".[40]

d. JUGEMENTS DÉCLARATIFS

27. First Eagle s'oppose à la demande de la Banque requérant une sentence définitive déclarant que "le Tribunal a la compétence exclusive pour toute action intentée contre la Banque, découlant ou liée à la validité, aux procédures et au montant de l'indemnité prévue pour le [rachat forcé] du 8 janvier 2001".[41] First Eagle soutient que le Tribunal ne peut pas rendre "un avis consultatif sur des questions ne relevant pas de sa compétence."[42]

28. Par ailleurs, First Eagle fait valoir qu'elle a droit à une sentence ordonnant à la Banque de verser une indemnité et des intérêts dus sur l'ensemble des 9.110 actions revendiquées par First Eagle, tant celles enregistrées au nom de First Eagle que celles détenues par un dépositaire. Le 8 janvier 2001, First Eagle était le titulaire enregistré de 5.250 actions de la Banque.[43] Or, First Eagle réclame une indemnité pour 9.110 actions de la Banque. First Eagle fait savoir que les 3.860 actions pour lesquelles elle réclame une indemnité mais dont elle n'est pas le titulaire enregistré,

> étaient détenues par deux dépositaires au nom desquels les actions étaient enregistrées . . . . En qualité de sous-dépositaire suisse de Bank of New York, Crédit Suisse First Boston . . . détenait 3.655 actions et en qualité de sous-dépositaire suisse de J.P. Morgan Chase, UBS détenait 205 actions . . . . Aux fins de la présente procédure, tant Bank of New York que J.P. Morgan ont confirmé que si elles-mêmes, et non First Eagle, recevaient une indemnité

[39] *Id.*, par. 13.

[40] *Id.*

[41] Mémoire (ci-après "mémoire de la BRI"), par. 70.

[42] Mémoire en réplique de FE suivant la sentence partielle, par. 14.

[43] Mémoire de FE suivant la sentence partielle, par. 28 et 29.

> pour les actions dont elles sont dépositaires, elles reverseraient ladite indemnité à First Eagle.[44]

En outre, First Eagle explique qu'elle a

> introduit précédemment, dans le cadre de la présente procédure, une demande pour 9.085 actions, soit 25 actions de moins que le total visé dans sa demande actuelle . . . en janvier 2001, une opération prévue était en cours . . . [qui] a été annulée après que l'opération d'exclusion l'a empêchée de la mener à bien . . . . Elle réclame à présent l'indemnité supplémentaire due pour ces actions également.[45]

e. DÉFENSE DE FIRST EAGLE EN RÉPONSE À LA DEMANDE RECONVENTIONNELLE DE LA BANQUE

29. First Eagle soutient qu'elle avait le droit d'intenter une action devant le tribunal de district aux Etats-Unis en ce qui concerne tant sa demande au titre des lois sur les valeurs mobilières que le litige relatif à la compétence arbitrale; elle requiert qu'il plaise au Tribunal de rejeter la demande de dommages-intérêts présentée par la Banque pour violation de l'article 54, paragraphe 1, des Statuts de la Banque, étant donné que ladite demande ne relève pas de la convention d'arbitrage.

30. First Eagle affirme que l'essentiel du litige porté devant les tribunaux américains concerne des demandes ayant trait aux lois sur les valeurs mobilières[46] et "découle de la demande de mesures conservatoires présentée par First Eagle."[47] Pour sa défense, First Eagle allègue que son recours devant le tribunal de district ne constitue pas une violation de l'article 54, paragraphe 1, parce que les juridictions nationales ne donnent pas en général à l'arbitre le droit de statuer d'emblée sur la compétence.[48] C'est pourquoi First Eagle soutient qu'elle avait le droit de porter en justice "tant ses demandes au titre des lois sur les valeurs

---

[44] *Id.*, par. 30 et 31.

[45] *Id.*, par. 32 et 33.

[46] Compte rendu, p. 533 et 534.

[47] Contre-mémoire de First Eagle formant opposition à la demande reconventionnelle (ci-après "Contre-mémoire de FE demande reconventionnelle"), p. 77.

[48] *Id.*, par. 89.

mobilières que le litige relatif à la compétence arbitrale et étant donné que les honoraires supportés par la Banque . . . sont uniquement dus à l'introduction d'une action concernant ces deux questions, la demande présentée par la Banque pour violation de l'article 54, paragraphe 1, doit être rejetée."[49]

31. First Eagle fait également valoir que l'article 54 n'est pas applicable. Lorsque First Eagle a introduit l'action en justice aux Etats-Unis, le Tribunal n'existait pas encore et "la nomination, après que le litige est survenu, de chacun des membres par les gouvernements intéressés au litige ne correspond pas aux principes fondamentaux de l'ordre public."[50]

f. DÉCLARATIONS EXPRESSES

32. First Eagle a déclaré au cours des audiences qu'elle était disposée à ne pas contester, si la Banque en faisait de même, que l'actif net réévalué correspondait à la valeur déterminée par J.P. Morgan, telle qu'elle est mentionnée dans la pièce jointe n° 43 annexée au mémoire de First Eagle (ci-après "pièce jointe de FE"). S'agissant d'une déclaration concernant la valeur des biens immobiliers de la Banque, First Eagle a déclaré ce qui suit.

> Dans leur déclaration du 7 janvier 2003, les Parties sont convenues qu'elles "tenteraient de se mettre d'accord sur la valeur de l'actif immobilier de la Banque et à défaut d'accord sur cette valeur, elles s'efforceraient de proposer une procédure et un calendrier convenus grâce auxquels la question pourrait être réglée." Les Parties ont ensuite accepté la désignation par le Tribunal d'un expert pour évaluer les biens immeubles.[51]

First Eagle, de même que les autres Parties, a proposé que le bureau de Zurich de la société C.B. Richard Ellis soit désigné par le Tribunal pour

[49] *Id.*, par. 97.
[50] *Id.*, par. 118.
[51] Mémoire de FE suivant la sentence partielle, par. 58.

fixer la valeur des immeubles de la Banque et de leurs biens mobiliers dont l'évaluation serait définitive et serait ajoutée à l'actif net réévalué.[52]

2. Droit applicable

33. Dans son mémoire, First Eagle déclare que les principes généraux du droit international sont applicables au présent différend et que, comme la Banque, elle est d'avis que "les règles du droit international public général président à l'interprétation des Statuts et donc à l'appréciation de la participation des actionnaires exclus dans la Banque."[53]

34. First Eagle conteste que la compétence du Tribunal se fonde sur une *lex specialis*. Elle affirme que dès lors qu'elle s'est manifestement soumise à la compétence du Tribunal, la compétence se fonde sur ce consentement et non sur la *lex specialis*. Elle se prévaut de l'affaire *Siemens AG c. Dutco Constr. Co.*[54] pour faire valoir qu'elle a le droit de demander à un tribunal national de se prononcer sur la validité de la convention d'arbitrage. Pour étayer davantage l'argument afférent à l'inapplicabilité de l'article 54, First Eagle invoque[55] la Convention de New York, car "la composition de l'instance arbitrale . . . n'est pas conforme à la convention des parties."[56]

3. Décision demandée

35. Dans son mémoire en réplique, First Eagle a demandé qu'il plaise au Tribunal de rendre une sentence définitive enjoignant à la Banque de:

   a) verser à First Eagle une indemnité supplémentaire de 7.755,20 francs suisses par action (soit 70% de l'actif net

---

[52] Voir également l'ordonnance de procédure n° 9 homologuant un accord entre les Parties; la sentence partielle, par. 205; Mémoire en demande sur la seconde phase de l'arbitrage (ci-après "Mémoire en demande de Mathieu seconde phase"), p. 4; compte, rendu, p.329 à 331.

[53] Mémoire de First Eagle (ci-après "Mémoire FE"), par. 205.

[54] Cour de cassation française, 7 janvier 1992, réimprimé dans XVIII Y.B. Comm. Arb., p. 141 et 142 (1993).

[55] Compte rendu, p. 520.

[56] Convention des Nations Unies pour la reconnaissance et l'exécution des sentences arbitrales étrangères, New York, le 10 juin 1958, art. V, paragraphe 1, point d, UST, vol. 21, p. 2517, Nations Unies, Recueil des traités, vol. 330, p. 38 (ci-après la "Convention de New York").

réévalué s'élevant à 33.936 francs suisses par action, diminués de l'indemnité déjà payée, à savoir 16.000 francs suisses par action) pour chacune des 9.110 actions détenues par First Eagle, soit au total 70.649,872 francs suisses;

b) payer à First Eagle la part de la valeur des biens immobiliers de la Banque qui lui revient;

c) payer les frais de l'arbitrage qui incombent à First Eagle, qui s'élèvent actuellement à 546.913,40 dollars, ou au moins la fraction de ces frais supérieure à la part proportionnelle des actions détenues par First Eagle par rapport au total des actions faisant l'objet de l'opération d'exclusion;

d) payer les honoraires d'avocats et les frais judiciaires qui incombent à First Eagle, le montant étant fixé après l'audience de mai 2000 (*sic*) dans la présente affaire de la façon que le Tribunal déterminera, ou au moins la fraction des honoraires d'avocat et des frais judiciaires supérieure à la part proportionnelle des actions détenues par First Eagle par rapport au total des actions faisant l'objet de l'opération d'exclusion;

e) payer à First Eagle un intérêt avec capitalisation sur une base mensuelle à un taux d'au moins 7% à compter, s'agissant de l'indemnité supplémentaire, du 8 janvier 2001 jusqu'à la date du paiement de ladite indemnité et, s'agissant des frais et honoraires d'avocat de First Eagle, à compter de la date de paiement par First Eagle jusqu'à la date de remboursement par la Banque;

f) rejeter toutes les demandes présentées par la Banque, contre-mémoire n° 2 de la BRI, p. 91;

g) accorder à First Eagle toute autre indemnité que le Tribunal estime équitable et appropriée.[57]

---

[57] Mémoire en réplique de FE suivant la sentence partielle, par. 186; le 22 mai 2003, First Eagle a effectué un autre dépôt d'un montant de 259.173,00 dollars américains pour les frais de l'arbitrage, ce qui porte sa contribution totale aux frais de l'arbitrage à 806.086,40 dollars américains.

C. M. MATHIEU, DEMANDEUR N° 3

1. Arguments

a. CALCUL DE L'INDEMNITÉ

36. M. Mathieu demande qu'il plaise au Tribunal de calculer l'indemnité supplémentaire due aux anciens actionnaires privés en conformité avec la sentence partielle du 22 novembre 2002, en appliquant le taux de change en vigueur à la date du 6 septembre 2000.

> Dire que la date devant être retenue pour déterminer le taux de change applicable en vue de la conversion en francs suisses de l'actif net réévalué de la BRI libellé en dollars américains a d'ores et déjà été fixée par le Tribunal au 6 septembre 2000.[58]

37. M. Mathieu fait valoir que la proposition faite par la Banque de choisir la date du 8 janvier 2001 est en contradiction avec la déclaration expresse des Parties concernant l'actif net réévalué présenté dans le rapport de J.P. Morgan.[59] Par ailleurs, M. Mathieu soutient que l'allégation de la Banque selon laquelle sa pratique antérieure justifie l'application du taux de change en vigueur à la date du 8 janvier 2001 n'est pas adaptée au rachat forcé.

> [L]a BRI a en effet soutenu dans son Contre-mémoire que le calcul de l'indemnité doit se faire sur la base de son procédé habituel de calcul des montants en matière d'émission d'actions nouvelles. Cependant, cet usage n'a aucun titre à être appliqué à l'instance. La BRI fait en réalité une interprétation contestable du raisonnement du Tribunal dans la Sentence partielle. Qui plus est, la méthode proposée n'est pas adaptée à la situation du retrait forcé.[60]

38. Si le Tribunal devait retenir la date du 8 janvier 2001 proposée par la Banque, l'actif net réévalué de la Banque devrait être recalculé par un expert désigné par le Tribunal, aux frais de la Banque:

---

[58] Mémoire en duplique de M. Mathieu seconde phase, p. 15.
[59] *Id.*, p. 5.
[60] *Id.*, p. 3.

> A titre subsidiaire, si le Tribunal devait décider qu'il convient de retenir le taux de change applicable au 8 janvier 2001, dire que l'actif net de la BRI devra être réévalué à cette même date et désigner à cette fin, aux frais de la BRI, tel expert indépendant qu'il plaira au Tribunal de nommer . . . .[61]

b. DATE DU TAUX DE CHANGE À APPLIQUER

39. M. Mathieu fait valoir que, conformément à la sentence partielle et à l'évaluation de J.P. Morgan, il convient de retenir la date du 6 septembre 2000 pour fixer le taux de change à appliquer pour l'indemnité supplémentaire à verser aux anciens actionnaires:

> La différence est en effet significative: en appliquant le taux de change ayant cours au 6 septembre 2000, à savoir 0,5628 dollar américain pour un franc suisse, une action de la banque évaluée à 19.034 dollars américains se convertit à la somme de 33.820 francs suisses. Si, comme le soutient la Banque, le taux de change devant être retenu était celui applicable au 8 janvier 2001, à savoir 0,6256 dollar américain pour un franc suisse, la contre-valeur en francs suisses de cette même action ne serait plus que de 30.425,80. La controverse porte donc sur un enjeu d'un montant de 3.394,20 francs suisses par action. Ce montant correspond, pour la Banque, à l'économie qu'elle espère réaliser sur l'indemnisation que le droit international lui impose de verser en contrepartie des actions, dont elle conserve pour l'avenir la propriété et les espérances de plus values qui leur sont attachées – ne serait-ce qu'en considération de la décote de 30% sur la valeur d'actif net retenue aux termes de la Sentence.[62]

c. INTÉRÊTS

40. M. Mathieu demande le paiement d'intérêts portant sur le montant supplémentaire à verser aux actionnaires privés à dater du 8 janvier 2001.[63]

---

[61] *Id.*, p. 15.
[62] Mémoire en demande de M. Mathieu Seconde phase, p. 5 (citations internes omises).
[63] Mémoire en duplique de M. Mathieu Seconde phase, p. 11 et 12.

41. Par ailleurs, M. Mathieu demande que lui soient payés les intérêts portant sur le montant de 16.000 francs suisses que la Banque a offert à titre de dédommagement mais que M. Mathieu a refusé jusqu'au prononcé par le Tribunal de la sentence partielle du 22 novembre 2002.

> Le Demandeur, dans son Mémoire en demande du 13 mai 2002, développe ainsi trois moyens: (i) l'illégalité de la résolution amendant les statuts, (ii) l'illicéité de l'opération de rachat forcé des actions et (iii) l'insuffisance de l'indemnité accordée aux actionnaires privés.
>
> Le Demandeur aura par conséquent, du premier jour du litige jusqu'à la Sentence du 22 novembre 2002, toujours soutenu que l'opération de rachat forcée était illégale et qu'en raison de cette illégalité, il possédait toujours sa qualité d'actionnaire de la Banque. Il n'est dès lors pas surprenant que ce dernier se soit toujours opposé à percevoir l'indemnité qui lui était proposée, afin de rester cohérent dans sa démarche à l'encontre de la Banque. L'on ne saurait, en effet, demander une chose et son contraire.[64]

42. M. Mathieu demande qu'il plaise au Tribunal d'accorder des intérêts composés de 7% sur la base du rapport de J.P. Morgan selon lequel le coût en capital de la Banque est de l'ordre de 6,7 à 7%.[65] Des intérêts composés sont dus en conformité avec le droit international et la pratique commerciale moderne:

> Le principe de réparation intégrale exige enfin que les intérêts soient capitalisés. En effet les intérêts à percevoir contribuent à former un capital et doivent donc eux-mêmes être porteurs d'intérêts, ainsi que l'exige une jurisprudence établie en droit international. Conformément aux usages du commerce international, ces intérêts seront capitalisés sur une base mensuelle.[66]

---

[64] Mémoire en demande de M. Mathieu seconde phase, p. 14.
[65] *Id.*, p. 15.
[66] *Id.*, p. 16.

d. FRAIS DE L'ARBITRAGE ET FRAIS JUDICIAIRES

43. M. Mathieu soutient que la Banque doit, en tant que partie perdante, supporter les frais de l'arbitrage, y compris les frais judiciaires. Toutefois, si le Tribunal ne condamne pas la Banque aux frais de l'arbitrage, les frais judiciaires, ainsi que les honoraires d'avocat des demandeurs doivent être répartis entre l'ensemble des actionnaires privés. Ladite répartition est équitable, car les frais judiciaires ont été encourus au titre d'actions qui ont conféré un avantage à l'ensemble des anciens actionnaires privés. M. Mathieu déclare que la Banque doit supporter les frais et les frais judiciaires qu'il a encourus, ainsi que verser des intérêts portant sur ces sommes au même taux que celui fixé pour le payement supplémentaire. Par ailleurs, M. Mathieu demande le remboursement des frais et débours que lui-même et ses avocats ont encourus au cours de l'arbitrage, à savoir 4.321,67 euros.[67]

e. JUGEMENT DÉCLARATIF

44. Par ailleurs, M. Mathieu soutient que le Tribunal ne doit pas faire droit à la demande de la Banque requérant que la sentence arbitrale soit définitive, ait force obligatoire pour toutes les Parties etait valeur de règlement pour toutes les actions que pourraient être intentées.[68]

f. DÉCLARATION EXPRESSE

45. M. Mathieu a indiqué qu'il se joignait aux autres demandeurs quant aux déclarations expresses visées au paragraphe 32 ci-dessus concernant l'utilisation de l'actif net réévalué, tel qu'il est déterminé dans le rapport de J.P. Morgan (pièce jointe n° 43 de FE), majoré de la valeur des biens immobiliers de la Banque.[69]

---

[67] *Id.*, p. 18; voir *infra,* par. 48.

[68] Mémoire en Duplique de M. Mathieu Seconde phase, p. 13.

[69] Compte rendu, p. 330; voir *supra,* par. 18 et *infra,* par. 67; mémoire en demande de M. Mathieu seconde phase, p. 4.

2. *Droit applicable*

46. M. Mathieu fait valoir que les instruments constitutifs de la Banque et le droit international général doivent présider à la définition des droits des actionnaires. Par ailleurs, M. Mathieu soutient que l'ordre public international tant de la Suisse que des Pays-Bas doit être pris en compte en raison du lieu de l'arbitrage et du lieu de l'exécution éventuelle.[70]

3. *Décision demandée*

47. Dans ses conclusions du 16 mai 2003, M. Mathieu demande ce qui suit:

> Le Demandeur requiert qu'il plaise au Tribunal Arbitral de:
>
> Dire que la date devant être retenue pour déterminer le taux de change applicable en vue de la conversion en francs suisses de l'actif net réévalué de la BRI libellé en dollars américains a d'ores et déjà été fixée par le Tribunal au 6 septembre 2000;
>
> A titre subsidiaire, si le Tribunal devait décider qu'il convient de retenir le taux de change applicable au 8 janvier 2001, dire que l'actif net de la BRI devra être réévalué à cette même date et désigner à cette fin, aux frais de la BRI, tel expert indépendant qu'il plaira au Tribunal de nommer;
>
> Dire que les intérêts dus par la BRI au Demandeur ont couru, à compter du 8 janvier 2001, et à titre subsidiaire à compter du 14 février 2001, tant sur le complément d'indemnité en cours de détermination et ce jusqu'à parfait paiement, que sur la somme de 16.000 francs suisses entre le 8 janvier 2001 et le 9 janvier 2003 par la BRI, au taux minimum de 7%; ordonner la capitalisation des intérêts sur une base mensuelle;
>
> Dire que la BRI supportera seule l'intégralité des frais liés au présent arbitrage; à titre subsidiaire, dans l'hypothèse où le Tribunal déciderait du contraire, donner acte au Demandeur de l'engagement de la BRI de supporter en toute hypothèse la moitié des frais d'arbitrage, et dire que toute partie de ces frais qui ne sera pas mise à la charge de la BRI sera répartie entre la totalité

[70] Mémoire en demande (ci-après "Mémoire de M. Mathieu"), p. 7 et 8.

des actionnaires privés de celle-ci proportionnellement au nombre d'actions dont chacun de ces actionnaires était propriétaire au 8 janvier 2001 rapporté au nombre total de 74.952 (sic) actions ; réserver la justification des frais (pour mémoire);

Dire que des intérêts portant sur les frais d'arbitrage sont dus par la BRI à compter de la date du déboursement effectif de ces sommes jusqu'à parfait paiement par la BRI, au taux minimum de 7% avec capitalisation sur une base mensuelle;

Condamner, en toute hypothèse, la BRI à régler au Demandeur la totalité des honoraires d'avocat encourus dans le cadre du présent arbitrage (pour mémoire);

Enfin, rectifier dans la sentence finale le nom de la Société de Concours hippique de La Châtre.[71]

48. Par ailleurs, M. Mathieu demande le remboursement des frais judiciaires qu'il a encourus, soit 4.436,75 euros, et le remboursement des sommes déposées pour les frais de l'arbitrage, soit 760,25 euros.[72]

D. Banque des Règlements Internationaux, défenderesse

1. Arguments

a. Demande reconventionnelle

49. La Banque soutient que l'action intentée aux Etats-Unis par First Eagle[73] contestant (1) le droit de la Banque de procéder au rachat et (2) le montant de l'indemnité prévue par l'article 18A des Statuts de la Banque et exigeant des dommages-intérêts "équivalant à la valeur totale de la participation des demandeurs dans la Banque par rapport à l'ensemble

---

[71] Mémoire en duplique de M. Mathieu seconde phase, p. 15 et 16.

[72] Mémoire en demande de M. Mathieu seconde phase, p. 18; lettre du 27 août 2003 adressée par M. Mathieu au Tribunal et à la Banque.

[73] *First Eagle SoGen Funds, Inc.* c. *Bank for Int'l Settlement*, n° 01 Civ. 0087(RO), 2001 WL 1150323, (S.D.N.Y. 28 septembre 2001).

des participations"[74] constitue une violation de l'article 54. "En conséquence de cette violation, la Banque a subi un préjudice économique direct de plus de 587.000 dollars américains pour se défendre dans l'action en justice intentée par First Eagle et a gaspillé des ressources juridiques et administratives internes."[75]

50. La Banque conteste la déclaration de First Eagle selon laquelle elle entendait obtenir des informations[76] et "déterminer la validité" de sa "convention" d'arbitrage en vertu de l'article 54.[77] La Banque fait valoir que même si le "recours concernant les valeurs mobilières avait été indépendant des demandes relatives à la conversion, à la violation du contrat et à la violation des responsabilités fiduciaires . . . , First Eagle n'en serait pas pour autant dispensée de son obligation de soumettre ces dernières demandes à l'arbitrage en conformité avec l'article 54. "[78]

51. La Banque cite le texte de l'article 54, paragraphe 1:

> Si un différend vient à s'élever quant à l'interprétation ou à l'application des Statuts de la Banque, soit entre la Banque, d'une part, et telle banque centrale, établissement financier ou autre banque visé aux Statuts, d'autre part, soit entre la Banque et ses actionnaires, ce différend sera soumis, pour décision définitive, au Tribunal prévu par l'Accord de La Haye de janvier 1930.[79]

La Banque fait valoir ce qui suit:[80]

> First Eagle a tenté de se soustraire à son obligation de soumettre ces questions à l'arbitrage en conformité avec l'article 54, en prétendant que le retrait des actions consistait en une offre d'achat volontaire plutôt qu'en un rachat forcé. Cependant, le tribunal de district n'a pas été dupe, puisqu'il a déclaré que "la seule véritable

---

[74] Mémoire en réplique suivant la sentence partielle (ci-après "Mémoire en réplique de la BRI suivant la sentence partielle"), par. 4 (citations internes omises).
[75] *Id.*, par. 2.
[76] Contre-mémoire de FE demande reconventionnelle, par. 38.
[77] *Id.*, par. 5.
[78] Mémoire en réplique de la BRI suivant la sentence partielle, par. 5.
[79] *Id.*, par. 10.
[80] *Id.*, par. 14.

> question soulevée par le demandeur concern[ait] le prix et la méthode d'évaluation."[81] ... La cour d'appel n'a pas non plus été dupe, car elle a reconnu que "de fait, le principal recours présenté par First Eagle sembl[ait] tenir au fait que les méthodes d'évaluation appliquées par J.P. Morgan et Arthur Andersen [avaient] sous-évalué les actions détenues par des personnes privées."[82]
>
> L'article 54, paragraphe 2, dispose expressément que le Tribunal "statuera ... sur toute question [concernant l'acte de mission en conformité avec l'article 54, paragraphe 1], y compris celles relatives à l'étendue de sa compétence" et l'article 16, paragraphe 1, du règlement du Tribunal dispose que "le Tribunal a le pouvoir de décider de sa propre compétence."[83] Toutes les questions de compétence dans des litiges qui opposent la Banque à ses actionnaires concernant l'interprétation ou l'application des Statuts doivent dès lors être portées exclusivement devant le Tribunal.[84]

52. La Banque souligne que les documents juridiques cités par First Eagle laissent supposer l'existence d'une "convention d'arbitrage signée à l'initiative des Parties ou un régime spécifique d'arbitrage qui prévoit explicitement ou implicitement un recours devant les juridictions nationales."[85]

53. La Banque fait valoir que les règles qu'elle est tenue de respecter, y compris celles afférentes à l'instance chargée du règlement des litiges qui la concernent, ne font pas l'objet d'une convention privée.

> L'obligation de la Banque et de ses actionnaires de porter les questions d'arbitralité exclusivement devant le Tribunal est ... une obligation créée par le système conventionnel à l'origine de la constitution de la Banque, qui met en place un mécanisme

---

[81] Pièces jointes au mémoire ("pièces BRI") n° 25 (*First Eagle So Gen Funds, Inc.* c. *Bank for Int'l Settlements*, n° 01 Civ. 0087 (RO), 2001 WL 66321, p. *3 n. 6 (S.D.N.Y. 26 janvier 2001)).

[82] Pièce jointe de la BRI n° 50 (*First Eagle So Gen Funds, Inc.* c. *Bank for Int'l Settlements*, 252 F. 3d, p. 607 (2e cir. 2001).

[83] Documents juridiques de la BRI, p. 39.

[84] Mémoire en réplique de la BRI suivant la sentence partielle, par. 21.

[85] *Id.*, par. 22.

> exclusif propre pour le règlement des litiges internes relatifs à "l'interprétation ou l'application des Statuts de la Banque." Ces litiges auxquels le droit interne d'une organisation internationale est applicable ne relèvent pas de la compétence législative, administrative et juridictionelle d'un Etat.[86]

54. La Banque dénie "l'assertion avancée par First Eagle qu'il existe un principe universel en vertu duquel les parties à un arbitrage peuvent requérir d'un tribunal des mesures conservatoires".[87] La Banque cite le Groupe de travail (arbitrage et conciliation) de la Commission des Nations Unies pour le droit commercial international (CNUDCI), qui déclare ce qui suit au paragraphe 22 de sa note de janvier 2002 sur la préparation de dispositions uniformes en matière de mesures conservatoires de protection:

> D'autres droits disposent que le pouvoir de prendre des mesures conservatoires appartient exclusivement au tribunal arbitral et que les tribunaux n'ont pas la compétence de prendre des mesures conservatoires pour soutenir l'arbitrage. Le défaut de compétence du tribunal peut être le résultat de dispositions qui excluent la compétence du tribunal, lorsqu'une convention d'arbitrage existe.[88]

55. Par ailleurs, la Banque relève les documents juridiques cités par First Eagle, laissant présumer que dans le contexte d'une convention d'arbitrage commercial, l'une des parties a le droit de requérir d'un tribunal des mesures conservatoires, si les règles applicables à l'arbitrage ou la convention signée par les parties prévoient cette possibilité. La Banque fait valoir que le mécanisme conventionnel créé par la Convention pour le règlement des différends relatifs aux investissements entre Etats et ressortissants d'autres Etats ("CIRDI")[89] présente une plus grande analogie.

---

[86] *Id.*, par. 23 (citations internes omises).
[87] *Id.*, par. 34.
[88] *Id.*, par. 35.
[89] Washington, 18 mars 1965, TIAS, p. 6090, Nations Unies, Recueil des traités, vol. 575, p. 159.

> [L]es règles de procédure en matière d'arbitrage, c'est-à-dire le règlement d'arbitrage établi conformément à la Convention de 1965 pour le règlement des différends relatifs aux investissements, disposent qu'une partie peut requérir que des mesures conservatoires soient recommandées par un tribunal extérieur au CIRDI, seulement si la convention d'arbitrage autorise telle requête.[90]

56. La Banque fait valoir que les arguments de First Eagle concernant la validité de l'article 54 ont échoué aux Etats-Unis et ont été abandonnés par First Eagle dans la procédure devant le Tribunal.[91]

57. La Banque signale que:

> [L]es membres de cours et tribunaux internationaux, y compris les cours et tribunaux qui connaissent des différends entre les Etats concernés et des parties privées, sont habituellement désignés par les gouvernements. Le rôle joué par les gouvernements nationaux dans la désignation des membres des cours et tribunaux internationaux n'a jamais été considéré comme incompatible avec l'indépendance des membres desdits cours et tribunaux internationaux. S'agissant des différends internes aux organisations internationales, ces différends sont généralement portés devant les tribunaux internes ou soumis à l'arbitrage. Du point de vue organisationnel, les cours ou tribunaux institués par une organisation internationale ou au sein de celle-ci sont des organes de l'organisation concernée. Par conséquent, l'organisation ou les gouvernements de ses Etats membres, et non les parties au différend, exercent les droits concernant la composition, la compétence et la procédure du tribunal saisi, qui ne sont pas réservés audit tribunal. Dans l'affaire *Waite et Kennedy* c. *Allemagne,* la Cour européenne des Droits de l'Homme a confirmé que la procédure de règlement des différends prévue dans la Convention portant création d'une Agence spatiale européenne (ESA), qui renvoie les différends entre l'Agence et les membres ou anciens membres de son personnel devant la commission de recours de l'Agence, satisfait aux critères de la Convention européenne des Droits de l'Homme.[92]

---

[90] Mémoire en réplique de la BRI suivant la sentence partielle, par. 35.

[91] *Id.*, par. 54.

[92] *Id.*, par. 58 (citations internes omises).

58. La Banque relève que First Eagle ne fait pas valoir que la procédure de désignation donne lieu d'une quelconque façon à une distorsion ou à un préjudice pour l'une des parties.[93]

59. La Banque déclare qu'elle doit être dédommagée des frais encourus dans l'affaire portée devant le tribunal américain, et qui aurait dû être soumise à l'arbitrage, et qu'elle doit recevoir la totalité des frais et honoraires d'avocat qu'elle réclame.[94]

b. POSITION DE LA BANQUE À L'ÉGARD DU CALCUL DE L'INDEMNITÉ

60. La Banque apporte la réponse suivante aux arguments des demandeurs concernant le calcul du montant dû aux anciens actionnaires privés.

> La Banque est convaincue que [sa déclaration lors de l'audience d'août concernant le calcul de l'actif net réévalué par J.P. Morgan] revient à reconnaître l'exactitude de l'actif net réévalué calculé par J.P. Morgan, à savoir 19.099 dollars américains, et rien de plus . . . . Conformément au raisonnement suivi par le Tribunal lorsqu'il a adopté la formule de l'actif net réévalué diminué de 30% et au principe sous-jacent de l'égalité de traitement de tous les actionnaires (tant les banques centrales que les anciens actionnaires privés), cette formule doit être appliquée à l'actif net réévalué calculé par J.P. Morgan de la même manière que la Banque l'a régulièrement appliquée pour la fixation du prix des actions pour les souscriptions des banques centrales. Si la formule de l'actif net réévalué diminué de 30% était appliquée de façon cohérente aux actions retirées, comme il est présenté dans la partie III, point A.2. *infra*, le montant total de l'indemnité supplémentaire s'élèverait à 4.494 francs suisses par action.
>
> En revanche, si au lieu de suivre la pratique antérieure, le Tribunal retenait simplement l'actif net réévalué calculé par J.P. Morgan et l'appliquait à l'obligation statutaire, imposée au retrait des actions du 8 janvier 2001 en vertu de l'article 18A, de verser une indemnité en francs suisses correspondant à la participation des actionnaires privés dans l'actif net réévalué, la méthode la plus simple de convertir l'actif net réévalué avec décote libellé en

[93] *Id.*, par. 59.
[94] *Id.*, par. 47.

dollars américains pour obtenir le montant de l'indemnité en francs suisses serait d'appliquer le taux de change du 8 janvier 2001. Le calcul donnerait une indemnité supplémentaire de 5.458 francs suisses par action.[95]

c. DATE DU TAUX DE CHANGE À APPLIQUER

61. La Banque soutient que l'actif net réévalué calculé par J.P. Morgan doit être ajusté compte tenu du taux de change entre le franc suisse et le dollar américain à la date de janvier 2001. La Banque fait valoir

> que son bilan est effectivement établi en dollars américains (son unité de compte officielle pendant la période en question était le franc or, qui avait une parité fixe de 1,94149 dollar américain) et que par suite sa pratique antérieure dans l'application de la formule de l'actif net réévalué avec décote a été pour le Conseil d'Administration de décider d'une émission d'actions, à un prix en franc or fixe, avec des paiements en monnaie forte auxquels a été appliqué le taux de change à la date du paiement; qu'ainsi, l'actif net réévalué avec décote, établi en dollars américains tel qu'il figure dans le rapport de J.P. Morgan, devrait être converti en francs suisses à la date du 8 janvier 2001, date de la reprise des actions détenues par des actionnaires privés, plutôt que soumis au taux de change du 6 septembre 2000 comme prévu dans le rapport de J.P. Morgan . . . .[96]

d. DEMANDE D'UN JUGEMENT DÉCLARATIF PRÉSENTÉE PAR LA BANQUE

62. La Banque présente une demande, à laquelle s'oppose First Eagle, requérant qu'il plaise au Tribunal de dire qu'il a “compétence exclusive pour toute action intentée contre la Banque et découlant ou liée à la validité, aux procédures et au montant de l'indemnité prévue pour le rachat des actions de la Banque détenues par des personnes privées à la date du 8 janvier 2001”.[97]

---

[95] Contre-mémoire de la BRI suivant la sentence partielle, par. 2 et 3 (citations internes omises).

[96] Ordonnance de procédure n° 9 homologuant un accord entre les Parties.

[97] Contre-mémoire de FE demande reconventionnelle, par. 140; mémoire en réplique de la BRI suivant la sentence partielle, par. 70, point a.

e. INTÉRÊTS

63. La Banque soutient que:

1. ni le droit international ni les règles particulières applicable à la BRI ne requièrent que le Tribunal accorde des intérêts aux demandeurs dans ces procédures;

2. si le Tribunal décidait néanmoins d'accorder des intérêts portant sur le montant supplémentaire de l'indemnité, le taux d'intérêt ne devrait pas être supérieur au taux du marché du franc suisse pour la période comprise entre le 8 janvier 2001 et la date de la sentence définitive;

3. il n'est pas justifié d'accorder un intérêt composé;

4. dans le cas de First Eagle et de M. Mathieu, aucun intérêt ne doit être accordé.[98]

64. La Banque propose de payer des intérêts, si le Tribunal estime "qu'un intérêt est dû sur l'indemnité supplémentaire à verser aux anciens actionnaires privés . . . à compter de la date de prise d'effet du droit à l'indemnité initiale, c'est-à-dire le 8 janvier 2001, jusqu'à la date du prononcé de la sentence définitive par le Tribunal."[99] La Banque justifie le choix de la date de la sentence définitive par analogie avec les paiements décidés le 8 janvier 2001. Ainsi, aucun intérêt n'a été payé pour la période comprise entre le 8 janvier et le paiement effectif aux actionnaires.

65. Par ailleurs, la Banque fait valoir[100] que la demande présentée par First Eagle concernant l'octroi d'intérêts portant sur les frais et les honoraires d'avocat qu'elle a supportés à compter de la date du paiement desdits frais et honoraires[101] n'est pas accompagnée de document juridique. La Banque soutient que toute obligation de payer les frais ou frais

[98] Contre-mémoire de la BRI suivant la sentence partielle, par. 114.
[99] *Id.*, par. 138.
[100] *Id.*, par. 147.
[101] Mémoire de FE suivant la sentence partielle, par. 163.

judiciaires encourus par First Eagle, le cas échéant, ne peut produire d'intérêts avant la date de la décision du Tribunal.

f. FRAIS DE L'ARBITRAGE ET FRAIS JUDICIAIRES

66. La Banque affirme que la *lex specialis* de la Banque exclut le dédommagement des frais et honoraires.

> Ces demandes ne trouvent pas de fondement dans la *lex specialis* de la Banque, dont le Tribunal a décidé qu'elle était la loi applicable à la présente procédure. En vertu de la *lex specialis*, constituée des Statuts de la Banque et des traités en application desquels ils ont été adoptés, il convient de répartir également les frais judiciaires entre les demandeurs et la Banque; le Tribunal a la compétence de répartir entre les différents demandeurs la part de ces frais judiciaires incombant auxdits demandeurs, mais n'a pas la compétence d'imposer cette dernière part à la Banque. De même, la *lex specialis* requiert expressément que chaque partie supporte ses propres frais, dont les frais judiciaires.[102]

g. DÉCLARATIONS EXPRESSES

67. La Banque a fait savoir qu'elle acceptait l'utilisation des calculs présentés dans le rapport de J.P. Morgan pour toute constatation relative à l'actif net réévalué.[103] La Banque s'est associée aux autres Parties pour proposer que le Tribunal désigne le bureau de Zurich de la société C.B. Richard Ellis afin d'évaluer les biens immobiliers de la Banque.

h. IDENTITÉ DES BÉNÉFICIAIRES DU PAIEMENT

68. La Banque s'oppose à la demande de First Eagle concernant le paiement à First Eagle de dommages-intérêts pour 9.110 actions.

> La BRI n'enregistre pas les actions au nom d'un "personne dénommée" agissant en tant que porteur inscrit pour le compte d'un propriétaire effectif non identifié . . . . L'article 18 [des Statuts de la Banque] dispose de façon incontestable que First

[102] Contre-mémoire de la BRI suivant la sentence partielle, par. 6.

[103] Compte rendu, p. 331.

> Eagle ne détient une participation valable et juridiquement protégée que pour les actions enregistrées à son nom dans les livres de la Banque. Le registre des actionnaires de la Banque révèle que le 8 janvier 2001, First Eagle détenait 5.250 actions et non les 9.110 actions que First Eagle a prétendu détenir . . . . Toute participation effective que First Eagle prétend détenir en conséquence de relations contractuelles avec des tiers n'est pas valable, ni pertinente ni opposable à la Banque.[104]

2. *Droit applicable*

69. Dans son contre-mémoire, la Banque affirme que "les droits des actionnaires de la BRI sont régis par les Instruments constitutifs de la BRI et par le droit international public général applicable".[105] De la sorte, la Banque fait échec à l'affirmation de First Eagle selon laquelle la Banque est une organisation privée et fait valoir qu'il est important qu'une organisation internationale soit régie par le droit international public. S'appuyant sur son statut d'organisation internationale, la Banque dénonce également l'argument de First Eagle selon lequel un droit national doit être appliqué, en déclarant qu' "il n'y a pas lieu d'appliquer un droit national des sociétés à ces questions et les tentatives visant à imposer un droit national . . . au régime juridique significativement différent institué par les Statuts de la Banque doivent être écartées."[106]

3. *Décision demandée*

70. La Banque requiert qu'il plaise au Tribunal de rendre une sentence:

(a) déclarant que le Tribunal a la compétence exclusive pour toute action intentée contre la Banque, découlant ou liée à la validité, aux procédures et au montant de l'indemnité prévue pour le rachat des actions de la Banque détenues par des personnes privées à la date du 8 janvier 2001;

(b) constatant que First Eagle a violé l'article 54, paragraphe 1, des Statuts en intentant une action contre la Banque

---

[104] Contre-mémoire de la BRI suivant la sentence partielle, par. 159 à 161.
[105] Contre-mémoire (ci-après "Contre-mémoire de la BRI"), par. 51.
[106] *Id.*

devant les tribunaux aux Etats-Unis pour des affaires relevant de la compétence exclusive du Tribunal;

(c) condamnant First Eagle à payer à la Banque des dommages-intérêts s'élevant à 587.413,49 dollars américains au titre du remboursement des frais judiciaires directs et accordant à la Banque toute mesure de réparation supplémentaire que le Tribunal juge appropriée du fait de la violation par First Eagle de l'article 54, paragraphe 1, des Statuts;[107]

[d] déclarant que la sentence du Tribunal n'est pas susceptible d'appel et a force obligatoire pour les Parties et que le paiement de l'indemnité supplémentaire de 4.494 francs suisses par action aux demandeurs pour chaque action enregistrée en leurs noms dans les registres de la Banque à la date du 8 janvier 2001 libère la Banque de toute obligation envers les demandeurs en rapport avec le retrait forcé de ses actions détenues précédemment par des personnes privées;

[e] rejetant les demandes des demandeurs concernant les honoraires d'avocat et les frais;

[f] rejetant les demandes des demandeurs concernant les intérêts, ou à titre subsidiaire, accordant un intérêt au taux du marché du franc suisse à compter du 8 janvier 2001 jusqu'à la date de la sentence définitive;

[g] accordant à la Banque d'autres mesures de réparation, si le Tribunal l'estime juste et approprié.[108]

---

[107] Mémoire de la BRI suivant la sentence partielle, par. 70.

[108] Contre-mémoire de la BRI suivant la sentence partielle, Décision demandée.

CHAPITRE IV – LA SENTENCE

A. FIXATION DU MONTANT EXACT DÛ PAR LA BANQUE DES RÈGLEMENTS INTERNATIONAUX PAR ACTION

71. Le rapport de J.P. Morgan du 7 septembre 2000 expose son point de vue quant au montant à verser aux actionnaires dans le cadre du rachat forcé des actions de la Banque détenues par des personnes privées.[109] Le rapport indique le montant en dollars américains, suivi, entre parenthèses, du montant équivalent en francs suisses au cours en vigueur à la date du rapport. Les demandeurs insistent pour recevoir la valeur du paiement supplémentaire - dont la sentence partielle a jugé qu'il était dû par la Banque - en francs suisses au taux de change dollar américain/franc suisse à la date du 7 septembre 2000. La Banque insiste pour que le montant du paiement supplémentaire soit calculé au taux de change dollar américain/franc suisse à la date du 8 janvier 2001, c'est-à-dire la date de mise en oeuvre du rachat forcé des actions ou, à titre subsidiaire, au taux de change dollar américain/franc suisse à la date de paiement retenue dans la sentence définitive. Etant donné que la valeur du franc suisse s'est appréciée d'environ 10% par rapport au dollar américain entre le 7 septembre 2000 et le 8 janvier 2001, la décision du Tribunal en l'espèce aura un effet considérable sur le montant dû par la Banque.

72. L'ordonnance de procédure n° 9 homologuant un accord entre les Parties dispose dans sa partie pertinente:

> Attendu que les Parties sont convenues que dans la sentence définitive, l'actif net réévalué en dollars américains de la Banque doit être identique à celui figurant dans le rapport de J.P. Morgan (et auquel sera ajoutée la valeur de l'actif immobilier), mais que
>
> (a) la Banque soutient que son bilan est effectivement établi en dollars américains (son unité de compte officielle pendant la période en question était le franc or, qui avait une parité fixe de 1,94149 dollars américains) et que par suite sa pratique antérieure dans l'application de la formule de l'actif net réévalué avec décote a été pour le Conseil d'administration de décider d'une émission d'actions, à un prix en franc or fixe, avec des paiements en

[109] Voir *supra* note de bas de page 4.

monnaie forte auxquels a été appliqué le taux de change à la date du paiement; qu'ainsi, l'actif net réévalué avec décote, établi en dollars américains tel qu'il figure dans le rapport de J.P. Morgan, devrait être converti en francs suisses à la date du 8 janvier 2001, date de la reprise des actions détenues par des actionnaires privés, plutôt que soumis au taux de change du 6 septembre 2000 comme prévu dans le rapport de J.P. Morgan, et que

(b) [First Eagle soutient que] le Tribunal devrait retenir la valeur de l'actif net réévalué en francs suisses telle qu'elle figure dans le rapport de J.P. Morgan (comme indiqué au paragraphe 209, point 3, de la sentence partielle), mais que, si la valeur du dollar américain était convertie à la date du 8 janvier 2001 (ce qui ne devrait pas être) et non à la date prévue dans le rapport de J.P. Morgan, l'actif net réévalué de la Banque devrait alors être réévalué à cette date pour tenir compte de l'impact du changement de taux de change sur les actifs de la Banque non libellés en dollars, et par suite sur son actif net réévalué, ainsi que sur tous les bénéfices non distribués depuis la date de l'évaluation par J.P. Morgan.

73. Bien que les Parties aient débattu longuement du sens de la déclaration formulée dans l'ordonnance de procédure n° 9 (ordonnance homologuant un accord entre les Parties), le Tribunal ne la juge pas déterminante, étant donné que l'ordonnance déclare simplement dans sa partie pertinente que "les Parties sont convenues que dans la sentence définitive, l'actif net réévalué en dollars américains de la Banque doit être identique à celui figurant dans le rapport de J.P. Morgan . . . ." Cet accord ne règle pas la question portée devant le Tribunal et de fait, la suite de la citation extraite de l'ordonnance de procédure n° 9 expose précisément la question examinée ici. De même, le Tribunal estime non concluante la conclusion de la Banque selon laquelle:

> Conformément au raisonnement suivi par le Tribunal lorsqu'il a adopté la formule de l'actif net réévalué diminué de 30% et au principe sous-jacent de l'égalité de traitement de tous les actionnaires (tant les banques centrales que les anciens actionnaires privés), cette formule doit être appliquée à l'actif net réévalué calculé par J.P. Morgan de la même manière que la Banque l'a régulièrement appliquée pour la fixation du prix des

> actions pour les souscriptions des banques centrales. Si la formule de l'actif net réévalué diminué de 30% était appliquée de façon cohérente aux actions retirées, comme il est présenté dans la partie III, point A.2. *infra*, le montant total de l'indemnité supplémentaire s'élèverait à 4.494 francs suisses par action.
>
> En revanche, si au lieu de suivre la pratique antérieure, le Tribunal retenait simplement l'actif net réévalué calculé par J.P. Morgan et l'appliquait à l'obligation statutaire, imposée au retrait des actions du 8 janvier 2001 en vertu de l'article 18A, de verser une indemnité en francs suisses correspondant à la participation des actionnaires privés dans l'actif net réévalué, la méthode la plus simple de convertir l'actif net réévalué avec décote en dollars américains pour obtenir le montant de l'indemnité en francs suisses serait d'appliquer le taux de change du 8 janvier 2001. Le calcul donnerait une indemnité supplémentaire de 5.458 francs suisses par action.[110]

Il n'est pas non plus utile d'examiner la pratique de la Banque en matière de paiement des dividendes, car l'opération en cause ne relève pas du paiement de dividendes, mais bien du rachat forcé d'actions.

74. Dans la sentence partielle, le Tribunal a constaté que la pratique suivie par la Banque lors de la fixation des prix des différentes tranches des nouvelles émissions d'actions donnait des indications sur l'évaluation, par la Banque et les nouveaux actionnaires, de chacune des actions de la Banque, c'est-à-dire la valeur que la Banque et les banques centrales donnaient aux actions.[111] En revanche, le Tribunal ne découvre pas d'indications comparables dans les procédures par lesquelles les banques centrales pouvaient acheter les nouvelles actions émises, car il s'agissait d'une opération entièrement consensuelle pour laquelle, en outre, les délais de paiement pour l'achat pouvaient, dans certaines limites, être décidés par l'acheteur. Cette opération consensuelle est tout à fait différente de la procédure de rachat forcé visée à l'article 18A des Statuts.

---

[110] Contre-mémoire de la BRI suivant la sentence partielle, par. 2 et 3.

[111] Sentence partielle, par. 201.

75. Cela étant, le Tribunal conclut que la pratique de la Banque en ce qui concerne le mécanisme de fixation des prix et du taux de change que la Banque a elle-même utilisé pour le programme de rachat forcé est déterminante en l'espèce. On se souviendra que la Banque a adopté une méthode d'évaluation au 7 septembre 2000 qu'elle a appliquée dans sa décision du 8 janvier 2001; le montant fixé en francs suisses le 7 septembre 2000 a été payé en francs suisses le 8 janvier 2001 indépendamment du taux de change par rapport à d'autres monnaies convertibles. Dans sa sentence partielle, le Tribunal a estimé que le retrait lui-même relevait de l'exercice valable des pouvoirs de la Banque et que la procédure suivie pour retirer les actions détenues par des personnes privées était licite.[112] Seule la méthode d'évaluation appliquée par la Banque pour le rachat forcé des actions n'était pas correcte. Mais c'est un fait que le 8 janvier 2001, la Banque a payé le montant qu'elle avait fixé en francs suisses au taux de conversion dollar américain/franc suisse arrêté au 7 septembre 2000. Comme il a été dit plus haut, pendant la période comprise entre le 7 septembre 2000 et le 8 janvier 2001, la valeur du franc suisse s'est appréciée par rapport au dollar américain, de telle manière que si la Banque avait appliqué la théorie de paiement qu'elle propose à présent au Tribunal, elle aurait recalculé le taux de conversion entre le dollar américain et le franc suisse à la date du 8 janvier 2001 et aurait versé aux actionnaires privés une somme inférieure d'environ 10% à celle qu'ils auraient reçue le 7 septembre 2000. En fait, la Banque n'a pas agi de la sorte. Plutôt que de tirer avantage de la dépréciation du dollar américain et faire un bénéfice grâce au change, la Banque a versé aux actionnaires le montant en francs suisses par action, qui avait été fixé dans le rapport du 7 septembre 2000. La Banque n'est pas une institution à but lucratif,[113] mais elle recherche par nature à maximiser les bénéfices et a, en outre, des responsabilités fiduciaires à l'égard de ses actionnaires. Si la Banque avait pensé qu'elle était légalement habilitée à tirer avantage de l'opération de change, elle aurait été obligée en droit de le faire et l'aurait fait.

76. Comme il a été dit, la sentence partielle a jugé que le programme de rachat forcé des actions de la Banque était licite, mais qu'une méthode

---

[112] *Id.*, par. 142 à 158.

[113] Cela ne signifie pas qu'elle ne peut pas réaliser des bénéfices, comme le Conseil fédéral suisse l'a relevé en 1930. Voir sentence partielle, par. 117.

d'évaluation incorrecte avait été appliquée: la Banque aurait dû payer pour chaque action un montant proportionnel de l'actif net réévalué de la Banque, diminué de 30%. Dès lors, le Tribunal a enjoint à la Banque de le faire. Cela étant, le Tribunal a estimé que pour le reste, la structure et la procédure de paiement conçues et adoptées par la Banque ne présentaient pas de défaut. En conséquence, l'évaluation par action du 7 septembre 2000 doit désormais être remplacée par une évaluation par action de l'actif net réévalué (telle qu'il est fixé dans le rapport de J.P. Morgan et accepté par les Parties) diminué de 30% et la différence entre le montant versé au 8 janvier 2001 et le montant légalement dû doit désormais être versée. Dans ces circonstances, la procédure adoptée par la Banque le 8 janvier 2001 doit être reproduite *mutatis mutandis*.

77. A cet égard, le Tribunal relève que la Banque elle-même a tenu pour acquis que ce taux de change serait conforme aux dispositions de la sentence partielle. Le 25 novembre 2002, c'est-à-dire 3 jours après la publication de la sentence partielle, la Banque a publié un communiqué de presse dans lequel elle résume l'essentiel de la décision du Tribunal et déclare qu' "[e]n conséquence, la BRI sera appelée à effectuer un paiement supplémentaire correspondant à la moitié environ de la somme déjà versée . . . ."[114] La Banque a manifestement fondé ses prévisions du 25 novembre concernant le montant dû sur l'hypothèse que la date de conversion du dollar américain et du franc suisse était le 7 septembre 2000.

78. Dès lors, le montant en francs suisses dû aux actionnaires privés pour l'achat forcé de leurs actions correspond à la valeur par action de l'actif net réévalué de la Banque tel qu'il a été calculé par J.P. Morgan dans son rapport, diminué de 30% et majoré de la valeur par action des biens immobiliers de la Banque avec application d'une décote de 30%. Comme il a été dit, Dr. Reineccius, First Eagle et la Banque sont convenus que si le Tribunal retenait le taux de change du 7 septembre 2000, la valeur par action serait de 33.936 francs suisses.[115] Après application de la décote de 30% ordonnée par la sentence partielle, ce montant s'élève à

[114] Communiqué de presse de la BRI du 25 novembre 2002, *Décision du Tribunal arbitral de La Haye concernant la reprise des actions de la Banque des Règlements Internationaux détenues par ses actionnaires privés*.

[115] Voir *supra*, note de bas de page 4.

23.755 francs suisses. Etant donné que la Banque a versé à chacun des actionnaires privés un montant de 16.000 francs suisses, la Banque doit à chacun des demandeurs (compte tenu de certaines réserves exposées ci-dessous) un montant supplémentaire de 7.755,20 francs suisses par action. Il y a lieu d'ajouter à ce montant 70% de la valeur par action des biens immobiliers; le Tribunal reviendra sur cette question plus loin.

B. IDENTITÉ DES BÉNÉFICIAIRES

79. First Eagle requiert[116] qu'il plaise au Tribunal d'enjoindre à la Banque de verser à First Eagle l'indemnité supplémentaire due en vertu de la sentence partielle, en tenant compte des informations communiquées par First Eagle selon lesquelles elle détient 9.110 actions, soit directement soit par l'intermédiaire d'un dépositaire.[117] La Banque préfère se baser sur son registre des actionnaires, dans lequel figurent les propriétaires des actions, pour effectuer le paiement, comme elle l'a fait pour le paiement de l'indemnité approuvé par l'Assemblée générale extraordinaire du 8 janvier 2001.[118] Etant donné que l'article 18 des Statuts de la Banque dispose que "[l]a propriété de l'action s'établit par l'inscription du nom de l'actionnaire sur les registres de la Banque" (ce que, par ailleurs, First Eagle a reconnu),[119] le Tribunal estime que la Banque a le droit d'adresser le paiement uniquement aux actionnaires inscrits, dont le nom apparaît dans le registre des actionnaires de la Banque.

C. INTÉRÊTS: APPLICABILITÉ ET TAUX

80. Dr. Reineccius réclame des intérêts portant sur l'indemnité supplémentaire due aux termes de la sentence partielle, en soutenant qu'à la date du 8 janvier 2001, il est devenu ". . . un créancier de la Banque. Dès lors, l'indemnité qui m'est due porte intérêt . . . l'intérêt du marché monétaire en francs suisses à cette date précise . . .",[120] qu'il chiffre à pas

[116] Mémoire de First Eagle suivant la sentence arbitrale, par. 28 à 33; compte rendu, p. 371.
[117] Voir *supra* par. 19.
[118] Contre-mémoire de la BRI suivant la sentence partielle, par. 159 à 161.
[119] Compte rendu, p. 371.
[120] Compte rendu p. 387.

moins de 3 ¼% l'an.[121] First Eagle fait valoir qu'elle a droit à percevoir, sur l'indemnité impayée, ainsi que sur les frais, honoraires et frais judiciaires, un intérêt d'au moins 7% avec capitalisation sur une base mensuelle à compter du 8 janvier 2001. M. Mathieu requiert également un intérêt minimal de 7% avec ". . . capitalisation des intérêts sur une base mensuelle".[122] First Eagle et M. Mathieu fondent leur demande d'intérêts sur le principe de réparation intégrale. Comme M. Mathieu l'affirme:

> En tout état de cause, les intérêts ayant pour fonction d'*"(. . .) indemniser un créancier de l'absence, pendant un certain temps, des fonds qui lui sont dus (. . .)"*, le Demandeur a droit aux intérêts portant sur la somme qui *aurait dû* être versée le 8 janvier 2001.[123]

81. First Eagle et M. Mathieu font valoir que le le taux d'intérêt doit correspondre au rendement que la Banque aurait obtenu des fonds non versés. First Eagle soutient également que le taux d'intérêt de 7% correspond au rendement minimal qu'elle aurait pensé obtenir d'autres investissements possibles présentant le même risque, si elle avait reçu l'indemnité complète au moment où elle était due. First Eagle allègue également que si la Banque versait des intérêts dont le taux serait inférieur à 7%, elle retirerait un revenu imprévu de l'indemnité retenue et s'enrichirait donc de façon injuste. First Eagle affirme ce qui suit:

> Un taux d'intérêt raisonnable doit avant tout tenir compte du fait que la Banque a conservé une partie de l'indemnité due aux actionnaires privés et qu'elle a pu disposer de ces fonds en tant que capitaux propres.[124]

82. De même, M. Mathieu faire valoir ce qui suit:

> Le Tribunal tiendra également compte du fait que la Banque a réalisé une économie substantielle en retenant le complément d'indemnité dû aux actionnaires évincés et qu'elle a pu faire libre

---

[121] *Id.*

[122] Mémoire en demande de M. Mathieu seconde phase, p. 19.

[123] *Id.*, p. 10 (citations internes omises).

[124] Mémoire de FE suivant la sentence partielle, par. 166.

> usage de ce capital obtenu sans rien débourser entre la date de rachat forcé et la date où elle devra effectivement verser le complément d'indemnité.[125]

83. First Eagle et M. Mathieu requièrent à titre subsidiaire que le taux d'intérêt doit correspondre au taux appliqué par J.P. Morgan pour réduire les paiements futurs de dividendes dans le modèle des dividendes à perpétuité[126], car le paiement d'intérêts est analogue en l'espèce à un paiement de dividendes.[127]

84. M. Mathieu réclame en outre des intérêts sur le versement initial de l'indemnité à compter du 8 janvier 2001.[128]

85. A l'audience de mai 2003,[129] la Banque a répondu que l'octroi d'intérêts n'était pas prévu par les Statuts de la Banque, ni par la *lex specialis* de l'arbitrage et, selon les allégations de la Banque, n'était pas imposé par le droit international. Néanmoins, si le Tribunal devait accorder des intérêts portant sur l'indemnité supplémentaire due en vertu de la sentence, la Banque estime qu'elle devrait payer un intérêt simple au taux LIBOR (London Interbank Offered Rate) à trois mois pour le franc suisse, portant sur l'indemnité supplémentaire que la Banque a accepté de payer à tous les anciens actionnaires privés.

86. La Banque allègue ce qui suit:

> [L]a *lex specialis* de la Banque n'aborde pas directement la question des intérêts. Néanmoins, l'article 18A des Statuts dispose clairement que l'indemnité liée au retrait des actions du 8 janvier 2001 sera versée aux anciens actionnaires privés uniquement après présentation à la Banque de leurs certificats d'action et ne comprend pas l'accumulation ni le paiement d'intérêts pendant la période indéfinie de présentation des certificats d'action, de vérification par la Banque et de paiement du prix de rachat. Par ailleurs, l'octroi d'intérêts n'est pas requis

---

[125] Mémoire en demande de M. Mathieu seconde phase, p. 15.
[126] Sentence partielle, par. 171.
[127] Mémoire de FE suivant la sentence partielle, par. 170; mémoire de M. Mathieu, p. 14 et 15.
[128] Mémoire en demande de M. Mathieu seconde phase, p. 10.
[129] Compte rendu, p. 427.

par les principes généraux du droit international. Toutefois, si le Tribunal devait accorder des intérêts portant sur le complément d'indemnité, le taux appliqué devrait être le taux d'intérêt du marché suisse (non composé), étant donné que l'indemnité est due en francs suisses et que la Suisse est le lieu où le paiement est exigible.[130]

87. En outre, la Banque répond à l'argument des demandeurs selon lequel les intérêts doivent être fixés par référence au taux de rendement de ses investissements, mentionné dans le rapport de J.P. Morgan:

> [T]out autre argument soutenant que les anciens actionnaires privés doivent recevoir des intérêts liés d'une quelconque manière aux bénéfices ou revenus de la Banque est fondamentalement incompatible avec la décision du Tribunal confirmant la licéité du retrait des actions. En tant qu'actionnaires, ils jouissaient d'un droit sur les bénéfices de la Banque (sous la forme attenuée de dividendes, comme le Conseil d'administration l'a déclaré en conformité avec l'article 51); néanmoins, le 8 janvier 2001, ce droit de propriété a été transformé en un droit quelque peu différent, à savoir un droit statutaire à réparation, qui n'est aucunement lié aux revenus ou bénéfices de la Banque.[131]

88. S'agissant de la demande de M. Mathieu concernant le paiement d'intérêts portant sur l'indemnité initialement offerte par la Banque, cette dernière fait valoir qu'aucun intérêt n'est dû. La Banque fait remarquer qu'il dépendait de M. Mathieu de recevoir l'indemnité initiale. Son refus de remettre ses actions ne doit pas entraîner pour la Banque l'obligation de payer des intérêts.

89. Comme il a été dit plus haut, les demandeurs ont proposé des taux d'intérêt variant entre 3¼% et 7%, sur la base de différentes théories de droit international public (y compris des théories d'enrichissement injuste), du droit commercial international et de la pratique suisse. Le Tribunal a également entendu des arguments détaillés fondés sur de récentes décisions rendues par des instances d'arbitrage international

[130] Contre-mémoire de la BRI suivant la sentence partielle, par. 7.

[131] *Id.*, par. 133.

accordant des intérêts composés et sur l'éventualité que lesdites décisions fassent désormais partie du droit international coutumier.

90. Ni l'Accord de La Haye de 1930, ni la Convention de La Haye de 1907,[132] ni les Statuts de la Banque n'imposent *expressis verbis* un taux d'intérêt dans quelque but que ce soit et d'autant moins dans le cas d'un rachat forcé d'actions détenues par des personnes privées. Cependant, comme il l'a déclaré dans la sentence partielle, le Tribunal estime que des intérêts sont dus,[133] car il est habituel que des intérêts soient versés, lorsque des paiements doivent être effectués à une date précise et qu'ils ne le sont pas. Le Tribunal constate que ladite règle s'applique également à la Banque s'agissant des relations qu'elle entretient avec ses actionnaires. Il convient à présent de déterminer le taux d'intérêt à appliquer.

91. Le droit international n'impose pas un taux d'intérêt spécifique, mais plusieurs autres ordres juridiques qui en imposent un pourraient être pertinents. Dans des circonstances où le droit de plusieurs ordres juridiques différents pourrait être appliqué à une opération ou à un événement particulier, il est de pratique courante de choisir le droit de l'ordre juridique avec lequel la question à trancher est, dans le cas d'espèce, le plus étroitement liée. A cet égard, le Tribunal relève que l'article 2 des Statuts de la Banque désigne Bâle (en Suisse) comme lieu où le siège social de la Banque doit être situé et que la Suisse a constamment été le siège et le centre opérationnel des activités de la Banque. En outre, la Banque a effectué des versements de dividendes en francs suisses et la monnaie dans laquelle les intérêts doivent être payés est le franc suisse. Par ailleurs, les actionnaires privés traitaient avec la Banque en Suisse et leurs dividendes étaient payés en francs suisses. Ces relations réciproques entre la Banque et ses actionnaires constituent des éléments de la pratique. Tous ces faits, qui ont perduré tout au long des soixante-dix ans et plus d'activité continue de la Banque, révèlent que l'ordre juridique suisse est le système auquel la question examinée est plus étroitement liée.

---

[132] Convention (II) pour le règlement pacifique des conflits internationaux, conclue à La Haye, le 18 octobre 1907 (ci-après la "Convention de La Haye de 1907").

[133] Sentence partielle, par. 204.

92. Du point de vue du Tribunal, ces faits conduisent à penser qu'il est pertinent de se reporter au droit suisse[134] pour en dégager des orientations en matière de taux d'intérêt. L'article 73 du Code des obligations dispose ce qui suit:

> 1. Celui qui doit des intérêts dont le taux n'est fixé ni par la convention, ni par la loi ou l'usage, les acquitte au taux annuel de 5 pour cent.
>
> 2. La répression des abus en matière d'intérêt conventionnel est réservée au droit public.

L'article 104 *(intérêt moratoire)* du Code dispose ce qui suit:

> 1. Le débiteur qui est en demeure pour le paiement d'une somme d'argent doit l'intérêt moratoire à 5 pour cent l'an, même si un taux inférieur avait été fixé pour l'intérêt conventionnel.
>
> 2. Si le contrat stipule, directement ou sous la forme d'une provision de banque périodique, un intérêt supérieur à 5 pour cent, cet intérêt plus élevé peut également être exigé du débiteur en demeure.
>
> 3. Entre commerçants, tant que l'escompte dans le lieu de paiement est d'un taux supérieur à 5 pour cent, l'intérêt moratoire peut être calculé au taux de l'escompte.

Par conséquent, le droit suisse applique un intérêt moratoire au taux simple de 5%.

93. Il apparaît que la décision d'appliquer l'intérêt moratoire suisse est le résultat de l'application de plusieurs facteurs liés à la pratique de la Banque et à la prépondérance des liens avec le droit suisse. Ladite décision ne se fonde pas sur l'hypothèse que la Banque est soumise au droit suisse. Il ne faut pas non plus voir dans la décision du Tribunal une prise de position en faveur ou contre les tendances récentes en matière

---

[134] Code des obligations (Loi fédérale complétant le Code civil suisse, Livre cinquième: Droit des obligations, 30 mars 1911).

d'application d'intérêts composés en droit international contemporain; cette question ne se pose pas en l'espèce compte tenu de l'effet déterminant de la pratique de la Banque et de la prépondérance des liens avec l'ordre juridique suisse en ce qui concerne les intérêts dans la présente affaire.

94. En conséquence, le Tribunal décide que la Banque doit verser des intérêts simples de 5%.

D. DATE À COMPTER DE LAQUELLE LES INTÉRÊTS SONT DUS

95. First Eagle soutient que l'intérêt doit être calculé pour la période comprise entre la date à laquelle le paiement était échu, soit le 8 janvier 2001, et la date du paiement effectif.[135] Dr. Reineccius[136] et M. Mathieu[137] réclament également des intérêts à compter du 8 janvier 2001 jusqu'à la date du paiement effectif. En outre, M. Mathieu réclame des intérêts sur le paiement de 16.000 francs suisses pour la période comprise entre le 8 janvier 2001 et le 9 janvier 2003, date à laquelle il a présenté ses actions et demandé le paiement.[138]

96. La Banque propose, pour le cas où le Tribunal déciderait que des intérêts sont dus sur l'indemnité supplémentaire, de payer des intérêts à partir du 8 janvier 2001 jusqu'à la date de la sentence définitive. Par ailleurs, la Banque propose de ne pas payer d'intérêts postérieurs à la sentence, à moins qu'elle ne reste en défaut de payer l'indemnité supplémentaire dans un délai raisonnable qui pourrait être fixé par le Tribunal.[139]

97. L'intérêt moratoire en droit suisse est dû à compter du jour où la dette est exigible jusqu'à la date du paiement par le débiteur. S'agissant du rachat forcé des actions de la Banque détenues par des personnes privées, le terme "dette" comporte plusieurs éléments. Pour tous les demandeurs, la Banque est redevable d'un montant supplémentaire, correspondant à la

---

[135] Compte rendu, p. 373 à 375.
[136] *Id.*, p. 388.
[137] Mémoire en demande de M. Mathieu seconde phase, p. 19.
[138] Compte rendu, p. 395 et 396.
[139] *Id.*, p. 432 et 433.

différence entre la somme versée par la Banque le 8 janvier 2001 et l'application de la formule de l'actif net réévalué diminué de 30% que le Tribunal, dans la sentence partielle, a déclaré être la norme légale d'évaluation des actions distinctes. Dès lors, est calculé pour tous les demandeurs un intérêt simple de 5% portant sur ledit complément à compter du 8 janvier 2001 jusqu'à la date de la présente sentence.

98. A la différence de Dr. Reineccius, demandeur n° 1, qui a remis ses actions à la Banque conformément à la décision de l'Assemblée générale extraordinaire (en réservant son droit au paiement supplémentaire auquel il pouvait prétendre) et a reçu le paiement correspondant, les demandeurs n° 2 et 3 n'ont remis leurs actions qu'à des dates ultérieures, la Banque leur versant le montant fixé le 8 janvier 2001. Le demandeur n° 3 a réclamé des intérêts sur ce montant à compter du 8 janvier 2001 jusqu'à la date à laquelle il a remis ses actions contre paiement.

99. La condition préalable à l'octroi de l'intérêt moratoire est le défaut de paiement de la part du débiteur; l'intérêt moratoire n'est pas dû dans des situations où, le débiteur manifestant sa volonté et sa capacité de payer, le retard de paiement est dû uniquement au refus ou au défaut du créancier de prendre les mesures nécessaires pour recevoir le paiement. S'agissant du demandeur n° 3, le débiteur, en l'espèce la Banque, était disposé à effectuer le paiement dès le 8 janvier 2001 et, de surcroît, à respecter toute réserve de droits concernant l'évaluation des actions. Dès lors, l'intérêt moratoire n'est pas dû au demandeur n° 3 pour la période comprise entre le 8 janvier 2001 et la date à laquelle les actions ont été remises contre paiement et payées dans les délais.

E. ÉVALUATION DES BIENS IMMOBILIERS

100. Le calcul de l'actif net réévalué, présenté dans le rapport de J.P. Morgan et auquel toutes les Parties, comme il a été précisé aux paragraphes 18, 32, 45 et 67 *supra,* ont donné leur accord, ne comprend pas d'évaluation actualisée des biens immobiliers de la Banque. Au paragraphe 205 de la sentence partielle, le Tribunal déclare que l'évaluation des biens immobiliers serait confiée à un expert, dont l'identité, le mandat et le calendrier de l'évaluation seraient arrêtés par le Tribunal après consultation des Parties. Etant donné que les Parties n'ont pas pu se

mettre d'accord sur la valeur de l'actif immobilier de la Banque, conformément au paragraphe 209, point 5, de la sentence partielle, les Parties ont notifié au Tribunal qu'elles désignaient le bureau de Zurich de la société C.B. Richard Ellis pour déterminer la valeur des biens immobiliers. Dans l'ordonnance de procédure n° 10, le Tribunal a confirmé aux Parties la désignation de la société Ellis. Le Tribunal a reçu de l'Expert la déclaration d'indépendance demandée par les Parties et l'Expert, accompagné de la Secrétaire du Tribunal, a inspecté tous les biens et a remis un rapport d'évaluation à la date du 28 avril 2003, date à laquelle la Secrétaire du Tribunal a transmis des copies du rapport aux Parties, en les invitant à faire part de leurs observations. Aucune observation n'a été communiquée. Le 16 mai 2003, dans l'ordonnance de procédure n° 11 homologuant un accord entre les Parties, le Tribunal a déclaré ce qui suit.

> Le Tribunal retiendra la valeur de 168.094.000 francs suisses (...) fixée par l'Expert aux fins d'évaluer à la date du 7 septembre 2000 les immeubles de la Banque, ainsi que leurs biens mobiliers, comme requis par la sentence partielle rendue le 22 novembre 2002.

101. A l'audience de mai 2003, Dr. Reineccius et First Eagle ont soulevé, pour la première fois, certaines objections à l'égard du rapport d'Ellis.[140] Etant donné que les Parties ont approuvé le rapport et que, néanmoins, elles ont eu une autre possibilité suffisante de faire part de leurs observations sur le rapport avant que l'ordonnance de procédure n° 11 homologuant un accord entre les Parties ne soit rendue à la date du 16 mai 2003, le Tribunal estime que les objections soulevées à l'audience ont été présentées hors délai et ne sont pas recevables et confirme que le rapport Ellis est définitif.

102. La valeur totale des actions, soit 168.094.000 francs suisses, correspond à une valeur par action de 317,66 francs suisses, qui, après décote de 30%[141], donne un montant supplémentaire de 222,36 francs suisses par action à verser aux demandeurs. Ce montant sera ajouté à la somme

---

[140] Voir *supra,* par. 31.
[141] Sentence partielle, par. 209, points 2 et 3.

mentionnée au paragraphe 78 *supra*, soit 7.755,20 francs suisses par action.

F. CONCLUSIONS CONCERNANT LES CALCULS

103. Le Tribunal conclut que la Banque doit verser à chacun des demandeurs un montant supplémentaire de 7.977,56 francs suisses. Ce montant représente 70% de l'actif net réévalué total de la Banque par action, soit 33.936 francs suisses par action (c'est-à-dire l'actif net réévalué par action calculé dans le rapport de J.P. Morgan[142]) et 317,66 francs suisses par action (la valeur des biens immobiliers de la Banque[143]), diminué de 30%, moins le montant de 16.000 francs suisses par action déjà payé par la Banque à chaque actionnaire privé. Des intérêts moratoires sont dus sur ledit montant à compter du 8 janvier 2001 jusqu'à la date de la présente sentence au taux simple de 5%.

G. DEMANDE RECONVENTIONNELLE

104. La Banque fait valoir que l'action en justice intentée aux Etats-Unis[144] par First Eagle, qui (1) mettait en cause le droit de la Banque de procéder au rachat et le montant de l'indemnité prévue par l'article 18A des Statuts de la Banque et (2) réclamait des dommages-intérêts "équivalant à la valeur totale de la participation des demandeurs dans la Banque par rapport à l'ensemble des participations", constitue une violation de l'article 54 des Statuts de la Banque.[145]

> En conséquence de cette violation, la Banque a subi un préjudice économique direct de plus de 587.000 dollars américains pour se défendre dans l'action en justice intentée par First Eagle et y a consacré des ressources juridiques et administratives internes.[146]

---

[142] Voir *supra* note de bas de page 4.

[143] Voir *supra* par. 99 à 101.

[144] *First Eagle SoGen Funds, Inc. v. Bank for Int'l Settlements,* n° 01 Civ. 0087(RO), 2001 WL 1150323 (S.D.N.Y. 28 septembre 2001).

[145] Mémoire en réplique de la BRI suivant la sentence partielle, par. 1.

[146] *Id.*, par. 2.

105. La Banque met en cause la déclaration de First Eagle selon laquelle sa "tentative d'interdire le retrait des actions"[147] visait à obtenir des informations[148] et que son refus de soumettre l'affaire à l'arbitrage avait pour but de "déterminer la validité" de sa "convention" d'arbitrage en vertu de l'article 54.[149] Au contraire, de l'avis de la Banque, First Eagle a "ignoré l'article 54 et a intenté une action contre la Banque aux Etats-Unis pour obtenir un jugement [et] des dommages-intérêts équivalant à la valeur totale de la participation du demandeur dans la Banque par rapport à l'ensemble des participations, ainsi que les intérêts y afférents".[150] La Banque soutient que même si le "recours concernant les valeurs mobilières avait été indépendant des demandes de First Eagle relatives à la conversion, à la violation du contrat et à la violation des responsabilités fiduciaires . . . , First Eagle ne serait pas pour autant dispensée de son obligation de soumettre ces dernières demandes à l'arbitrage en conformité avec l'article 54."[151]

106. La Banque allègue que le deuxième moyen de défense de First Eagle, à savoir qu'elle a invoqué la compétence des tribunaux des Etats-Unis "pour déterminer la validité et le caractère applicable de [sa] convention d'arbitrage",[152] est "doublement erroné":

> [D]'un point de vue juridique, parce que l'article 54 n'est pas une "convention [privée] d'arbitrage" commercial, mais fait partie intégrante d'un régime juridique indépendant qui exclut la compétence des juridictions nationales en ce qui concerne l'"interprétation ou l'application des Statuts de la Banque", notamment les questions de compétence du Tribunal; d'un point de vue factuel, parce que First Eagle n'a, en tout état de cause, pas demandé une déclaration concernant la validité de l'article 54, mais a intenté une action contre la Banque pour obtenir des dommages-intérêts en violation dudit article.[153]

---

[147] *Id.*, par. 3.
[148] Contre mémoire de FE demande reconventionnelle, par. 38.
[149] *Id.*, par. 5.
[150] Mémoire en réplique de la BRI suivant la sentence partielle, par. 4 (citations internes omises).
[151] *Id.*, par. 5.
[152] Contre-mémoire de FE demande reconventionnelle, par. 59.
[153] Mémoire en réplique de la BRI suivant la sentence partielle, par. 17.

La Banque fait remarquer qu'elle est une organisation internationale:[154]

> régie . . . par un régime juridique statutaire indépendant, créé par l'Accord de La Haye de 1930, la Convention et la Charte constitutive de la Banque. En vertu de ce régime, les droits et devoirs des actionnaires envers la Banque, y compris leurs droits et devoirs en vertu de l'article 54, doivent être réglés à la lumière des Instruments constitutifs de la Banque. *Voir* sentence partielle, par. 173 et 174 . . . . Les tribunaux nationaux n'ont pas la compétence de trancher les différends internes d'une organisation internationale, à moins que cette compétence ne soit spécifiquement et expressément prévue par les instruments régissant l'organisation . . . . L'article 55, paragraphe 1, des Statuts confirme l'*immunité* de la Banque à l'égard de la juridiction des tribunaux nationaux, sous réserve uniquement des exceptions restrictives (et inapplicables) prévues par lesdits Statuts.[155]
>
> L'article 54, paragraphe 2, dispose expressément que le Tribunal "statuera . . . sur toute question [concernant l'acte de mission en conformité avec l'article 54, paragraphe 1], (y compris celles relatives à l'étendue de sa compétence") . . . [tandis que] l'article 16, paragraphe 1, du règlement du Tribunal dispose que "le Tribunal a le pouvoir de décider de sa propre compétence." Toutes les questions de compétence dans des litiges qui opposent la Banque et ses actionnaires concernant l'interprétation ou l'application des Statuts doivent dès lors être portées exclusivement devant le Tribunal.[156]

107. La Banque fait valoir que "la nature de la Banque qui est celle d'une organisation internationale" requiert un règlement des questions sur une base uniforme et cohérente. La probabilité d'incohérences inhérentes aux décisions rendues par des tribunaux nationaux ponctuels requiert "que les différends relevant du droit interne d'une organisation internationale soient portés devant des cours ou tribunaux internes ou soumis à l'arbitrage."[157]

---

[154] *Id.*, par. 19.
[155] *Id.*, par. 19 et 20 (certaines citations internes ont été omises).
[156] *Id.*, par. 21 (citations internes omises)
[157] *Id.*, par. 24.

108. S'agissant de l'allégation de First Eagle selon laquelle il lui est loisible de demander à un tribunal national de prendre des mesures conservatoires, la Banque soutient que la *lex specialis* des Statuts de la Banque prévoit des mesures conservatoires de protection:

> Avant de prendre toute décision finale, et sans préjuger du fond, le président du tribunal, ou, en cas d'empêchement de sa part dans un cas quelconque, tout autre membre désigné par lui d'urgence, pourra, sur requête de la partie la plus diligente, ordonner des mesures conservatoires provisoires pour sauvegarder les droits respectifs des parties.[158]

109. En outre, la Banque affirme qu'il n'y a pas "concurrence entre [ce pouvoir de prendre des mesures provisoires et] la compétence des tribunaux nationaux. Au contraire, l'article 55 confirme l'immunité de la Banque à l'égard de la juridiction nationale, sous réserve d'exceptions très restrictives et expresses."[159] La Banque soutient que l'article 54 ne prévoit pas d'exception à cette immunité, bien que, comme l'article 55 le donne à entendre, les Etats parties à l'Accord de La Haye de 1930 auraient pu prévoir cette exception.

110. First Eagle affirme qu'elle avait le droit de saisir le tribunal de district aux Etats-Unis en ce qui concerne tant sa demande au titre des lois sur les valeurs mobilières que le litige relatif à la compétence arbitrale; elle requiert qu'il plaise au Tribunal de rejeter la demande de dommages-intérêts de la Banque pour violation de l'article 54, paragraphe 1, des Statuts de la Banque. First Eagle s'efforce de démontrer la nature différente de sa demande au titre de la loi américaine sur les valeurs mobilières, en faisant valoir que tant la Banque que le tribunal de district aux Etats-Unis ont reconnu que ces demandes ne relevaient pas de la convention d'arbitrage. First Eagle soutient que lorsque la Banque a demandé au tribunal de district de se prononcer sur le fond en ce qui concerne les demandes au titre des lois sur les valeurs mobilières, elle a "confirmé que les demandes de First Eagle au titre des lois sur les valeurs

---

[158] *Id.*, par. 31 (qui cite l'article 54, paragraphe 3, des Statuts de la Banque).
[159] *Id.*, par. 32.

mobilières ne relevaient pas du champ d'application de l'article 54, paragraphe 1."[160]

111. First Eagle affirme que l'essentiel du litige porté devant les tribunaux américains concerne des demandes ayant trait aux lois sur les valeurs mobilières et "découle de la demande de mesures conservatoires présentée par First Eagle."[161] En outre, First Eagle cite plusieurs documents[162] étayant son allégation selon laquelle "en vertu de toutes les lois en matière d'arbitrage, les parties à une convention d'arbitrage peuvent requérir les tribunaux de prendre des mesures conservatoires sans entrer en conflit avec la convention d'arbitrage."[163] Par ailleurs, First Eagle a produit des citations de documents examinant le rapport entre la Convention de New York et les actions intentées devant les tribunaux nationaux.[164]

112. A titre de moyen de défense justifiant son recours devant le tribunal de district, First Eagle fait valoir que cette action ne constitue pas une violation de l'article 54, paragraphe 1, parce que les "tribunaux sont habilités à examiner l'existence et la validité de la convention d'arbitrage sur laquelle la compétence des arbitres est fondée . . . ."[165] Dès lors, First Eagle soutient qu'elle avait le droit d'intenter une action concernant "tant les demandes au titre des lois sur les valeurs mobilières que le différend relatif à la compétence arbitrale et étant donné que les frais encourus par la Banque . . . découlent uniquement de l'action portant sur ces deux questions, la demande de la Banque au titre de la violation de l'article 54, paragraphe 1, doit être rejetée."[166]

113. Le Tribunal relève d'emblée que la *lex specialis* de la Banque des Règlements Internationaux comprend la Convention de La Haye de 1930, la Charte constitutive de la Banque des Règlements Internationaux

---

[160] Contre-mémoire de FE demande reconventionnelle, par. 64.

[161] *Id.*, par. 77.

[162] *Id.*, par. 85 à 88.

[163] Klaus Peter Berger, INTERNATIONAL ECONOMIC ARBITRATION 331 (1993).

[164] Contre-mémoire de FE demande reconventionnelle, par. 91 à 93.

[165] FOUCHARD, GAILLARD & GOLDMAN ON INTERNATIONAL COMMERCIAL ARBITRATION, p. 667 (E. Gaillard & J. Savage, ed. 1999).

[166] Contre-mémoire de FE demande reconventionnelle, par. 97.

du 20 janvier 1930 (ci-après la "Charte constitutive") et les Statuts de la Banque. Il s'agit d'instruments internationaux, fait particulièrement important pour l'examen du rapport entre ces derniers et la législation nationale. L'article 54, paragraphe 1, des Statuts dispose ce qui suit:

> Si un différend vient à s'élever quant à l'interprétation ou à l'application des Statuts de la Banque, soit entre la Banque, d'une part, et telle banque centrale, établissement financier ou autre banque visé aux Statuts, d'autre part, soit entre la Banque et ses actionnaires, ce différend sera soumis, pour décision définitive, au Tribunal prévu par l'Accord de La Haye de janvier 1930.

L'article 55 des Statuts dispose ce qui suit:

> La Banque bénéficie de l'immunité de juridiction, sauf:
>
> a) dans la mesure où cette immunité a été formellement levée pour des cas déterminés par le Président, le Directeur Général ou par leurs représentants dûment autorisés;
>
> b) dans le cas d'actions civiles ou commerciales découlant de transactions bancaires ou financières, intentées par des cocontractants de la Banque, sous réserve des cas pour lesquels des dispositions d'arbitrage ont ou auront été prises.

114. Le régime qui en découle est tout à fait unique. Outre le fait qu'il fasse partie de la structure juridique internationale de la Banque, l'article 55 des Statuts constitue un engagement bilatéral applicable parallèlement aux articles 54 et 17. En acceptant les Statuts conformément à l'article 17, les actionnaires acceptent aussi l'article 54 et par conséquent, la compétence d'un tribunal établi en vertu de l'Accord de 1930 et conviennent de ne pas porter devant les tribunaux nationaux toute affaire relevant de la compétence de tel tribunal. Il ressort clairement du régime institué par ces dispositions que les litiges entre notamment la Banque et ses actionnaires quant à l'interprétation ou à l'application des Statuts doivent être portés devant un tribunal établi en conformité avec l'Accord de La Haye de 1930. Un tel tribunal a le pouvoir de "statuer sur toute question, y compris celles relatives à l'étendue de sa compétence" et, en plus, d'"ordonner des mesures conservatoires provisoires pour

sauvegarder les droit respectifs des parties."[167] L'article 55 met en lumière le caractère exclusif de la compétence du tribunal, puisqu'il établit l'immunité de la Banque à l'égard d'autres juridictions nationales, sous réserve de deux exceptions expresses, dont aucune n'est pertinente dans le cas d'espèce.

115. Un actionnaire privé de la Banque ne pouvait pas être officiellement partie à l'Accord de La Haye de 1930. Cependant, un actionnaire privé achetant des actions était tenu à un type particulier et également contraignant d'obligation à l'égard du régime de règlement des conflits décrit ci-dessus. L'article 17 des Statuts de la Banque dispose que "la propriété d'actions de la Banque emporte adhésion aux Statuts de la Banque." Tous les certificats d'action portaient la même mention. Les brochures présentant les actions signalaient le régime de la compétence exclusive. Une déclaration d'acceptation des actions impliquait l'accord de se soumettre au régime de règlement des litiges. En somme, les acteurs privés qui achetaient des actions acceptaient, au moyen de divers instruments dont la multiplicité et la réitération excluaient toute possibilité de malentendu, le régime de règlement des litiges, y compris l'immunité de la Banque à l'égard des tribunaux nationaux et la compétence d'un tribunal créé en vertu de l'Accord de 1930 et des Statuts afin de décider de sa propre compétence et de prendre des mesures conservatoires. Le Tribunal insiste sur le facteur déterminant de l'*acceptation* du régime. S'agissant de la question de la juridiction compétente, les actionnaires privés ont accepté sans réserve le statut juridique international de la Banque.

116. Une grande attention a été accordée à la pratique nationale relative à l'application de l'article II de la Convention de New York. Le Tribunal ne doit pas examiner si, en dépit des termes explicites de l'article II dudit instrument, il existe un droit général en vertu de ce traité de vérifier, devant les tribunaux nationaux des Etats contractants, la validité d'une convention d'arbitrage au-delà de la constatation que ladite convention est "caduque, inopérante ou non susceptible d'être appliquée."[168] De même, le Tribunal ne doit pas examiner si une sentence arbitrale en vertu

---

[167] Statuts de la Banque, article 54, paragraphes 2 et 3.
[168] *Supra* note de bas de page 56, article II.

de l'Accord de La Haye de 1930 relève effectivement du champ d'application de la Convention de New York. La question portée devant le Tribunal est beaucoup plus restreinte. Il se peut que les parties éventuelles à une convention d'arbitrage puissent introduire une procédure aux Etats-Unis pour vérifier la validité de ladite convention. Néanmoins, même s'il en est ainsi, aucun impératif juridique n'impose le recours à ladite procédure. Il s'agit d'un droit ou d'une option, mais pas d'une obligation. Une option ou un droit prévu par le droit des Etats-Unis ne peut pas servir à justifier la violation d'une obligation qui relève du droit international. En essayant d'exercer une option qui peut lui être ouverte par le droit des Etats-Unis, First Eagle a violé ses obligations en vertu des Statuts de la Banque et en particulier en vertu de l'article 54.

117. Le Tribunal n'est pas non plus convaincu par l'affirmation selon laquelle le Tribunal n'existait pas à l'époque où First Eagle a essayé de détourner son différend vers une juridiction des Etats-Unis. Beaucoup de tribunaux arbitraux ne sont pas permanents, mais doivent être constitués après la naissance d'un différend. Puisque un mécanisme praticable était prévu pour la constitution du tribunal, l'action intentée par First Eagle violait ses obligations en vertu des Statuts de la Banque. L'affaire *Siemens AG c. Dutco Constr. Co.*,[169] sur laquelle les demandeurs n° 2 et 3 se fondent, ne livre pas d'autres enseignements. L'affaire *Dutco* concernait des parties qui contestaient une convention d'arbitrage contractuelle privée. La compétence du Tribunal découle de l'Accord de La Haye de 1930, de la Charte constitutive et des Statuts de la Banque, un cadre international que les actionnaires privés ont accepté, lorsqu'ils ont acheté les actions.

118. First Eagle a fait valoir que certaines des demandes qu'elle a présentées devant le tribunal aux Etats-Unis ne relevaient pas de la compétence du présent Tribunal et ne pouvaient être introduites qu'auprès d'un tribunal compétent situé aux Etats-Unis. La Banque soutient que ces demandes n'étaient que des prétextes, conclusion à laquelle les tribunaux concernés aux Etats-Unis semblent avoir abouti. Quoi qu'il en soit, les deux parties ont reconnu que les questions étaient étroitement liées. Il est indubitable que les questions essentielles relevaient de la compétence exclusive du Tribunal.

[169] *Supra* note de bas de page 55.

119. Pour les raisons exposées ci-dessus, le Tribunal estime qu'en présentant ses demandes contre la Banque devant un tribunal aux Etats-Unis, First Eagle a violé ses obligations en vertu des Statuts de la Banque et a illicitement obligé la Banque à consacrer une somme considérable à la défense de ses droits aux termes des Statuts, donnant à la Banque un droit à réparation. En conséquence, First Eagle doit rembourser à la Banque les frais que celle-ci a encourus aux fins de l'action intentée aux Etats-Unis. Le montant de 587.413,49 dollars américains réclamé par la Banque, que le Tribunal estime raisonnable, peut être déduit par la Banque, au taux de change entre le dollar américain et le franc suisse à la date de la présente sentence, des sommes dues à First Eagle en conséquence de la présente sentence.

H. DEMANDE DE DÉCISION DÉCLARATIVE

120. Au titre de sa demande reconventionnelle, la Banque a demandé la décision déclarative suivante.

> Pour toutes les raisons exposées ci-dessus, la Banque requiert que le Tribunal rende une sentence:
>
> a. déclarant que le Tribunal a la compétence exclusive pour toute action intentée contre la Banque, découlant ou liée à la validité, aux procédures et au montant de l'indemnité prévue pour le rachat des actions de la Banque détenues par des personnes privées à la date du 8 janvier 2001 . . .[170]

121. Dans sa demande de décision, Dr. Reineccius a requis qu'il plaise au Tribunal d' "interdire expressément à la Banque de subordonner les paiements ultérieurs à la signature d'une renonciation" du droit de saisir des tribunaux ordinaires pour obtenir un jugement plus favorable.[171]

122. First Eagle s'est opposée à la demande de la Banque requérant la sentence déclarative exposée ci-dessus.[172] First Eagle a soutenu que le

---

[170] Mémoire de la BRI, par. 70.
[171] Compte rendu, p. 388.
[172] Mémoire en réplique de FE suivant la sentence partielle, par. 170 à 175.

Tribunal ne pouvait pas donner un avis consultatif "sur des questions ne relevant pas de sa compétence." Par ailleurs, selon First Eagle, le Tribunal ne doit pas imposer de conditions à la réception par les actionnaires exclus du paiement des sommes auxquelles ils ont droit.[173]

123. Le Tribunal est confronté à une demande de jugement déclaratif et doit établir si la Banque a démontré un intérêt particulier que le Tribunal doit examiner. Etant donné que le demandeur n° 2 a manifestement envisagé de s'adresser à une autre juridiction[174] et que le demandeur n° 1 n'a apparemment pas exclu cette possibilité,[175] cette condition est remplie.

124. Par nature, une sentence, qui a l'autorité de la chose jugée entre les parties, désigne le droit qui s'applique aux parties en ce qui concerne la question soumise à l'arbitrage. Ladite décision est définitive et a force obligatoire pour les Parties au présent arbitrage; aucune autre voie de droit n'est ouverte aux Parties *inter se* s'agissant des questions faisant l'objet du présent arbitrage. En outre, un tribunal doit interpréter les instruments invoqués par les Parties dans l'exercice de ses compétences. En vertu de la compétence exclusive du présent Tribunal en matière d'interprétation et d'application des Statuts de la Banque, les décisions qu'il rend à propos du sens des Statuts en ce qui concerne les questions qui lui sont soumises constitue l'interprétation des Statuts qui fait autorité en l'espèce. Dès lors, les décisions du Tribunal interprétant les Statuts afin de déterminer la compétence en l'espèce, la validité des procédures suivies par la Banque lors de la reprise forcée des actions détenues par des parties privées en vertu de sa décision du 8 janvier 2001 et la règle à appliquer pour évaluer les actions reprises constituent l'interprétation des Statuts de la Banque qui fait autorité à l'égard de tous ceux auxquels lesdits Statuts sont applicables.

---

[173] *Id.*, par. 173.
[174] Compte rendu, p. 590 à 600.
[175] *Id.*, par. 388.

I. FRAIS JUDICIAIRES DES PARTIES

125. Le Tribunal en vient à présent aux frais judiciaires des Parties. Le Tribunal fait remarquer que les demandeurs n° 1, 2 et 3 ont demandé à être remboursés des frais judiciaires qu'ils ont encourus et le demandeur n° 2 a réclamé le remboursement des honoraires d'avocat qu'il a supportés. Le Tribunal rappelle que l'annexe XII de l'Accord de La Haye de 1930, relative à l'arbitrage, dispose que chaque partie doit payer "ses propres frais". Le Tribunal estime que cette disposition doit être interprétée et appliquée à la lumière du principe de l'accès effectif à la justice, comme il a été exposé plus haut dans le contexte spécifique d'une action en justice opposant des actionnaires privés et la Banque.

126. Dans l'affaire *Waite*[176], la Cour européenne des Droits de l'Homme a jugé que l'immunité des organisations internationales avait pour corollaire l'obligation de garantir un accès équitable à la justice. De l'avis du Tribunal, cette décision est en accord avec un principe général du droit. La Banque a expliqué qu'elle était consciente que les frais liés à l'accès à la justice devaient être réglementés de façon à ce que les actionnaires isolés, qui ne disposent pas des mêmes ressources que les personnes morales de grande dimension, aient, dans la pratique, la possibilité d'avoir accès à la justice. Les demandeurs n° 1 et 3 sont des demandeurs individuels dont les ressources financières sont limitées. Le demandeur n° 1 n'était pas représenté par un avocat. Le demandeur n° 3 était représenté *pro bono* par le bureau parisien du cabinet juridique Freshfields Bruckhaus Deringer.[177] C'est pourquoi la Banque ne doit payer que les frais judiciaires encourus par le demandeur n° 3, à savoir 4.436,75 euros [178]. Le Tribunal relève avec satisfaction que la Banque, reconnaissant pleinement le principe de l'accès effectif à la justice, a dès le début manifesté son consentement à accepter la compétence du Tribunal en matière de répartition des coûts afférents à l'accès à la justice de demandeurs individuels, de manière à ne pas entraver leurs possibilités de recourir aux procédures formelles. Dès lors, les frais

---

[176] *Waite & Kennedy c. Allemagne,* requête n° 26083/94, CEDH, vol. 30, p. 261 (1999).

[177] Compte rendu, p. 477.

[178] Mémoire en demande de Mathieu seconde phase, p. 18; lettre du 27 août 2003 adressée par M. Mathieu à la Secrétaire du Tribunal, copie à la Banque.

judiciaires (à savoir 4.436,75 euros) du demandeur n° 3 seront supportés par la Banque et remboursés par elle directement audit demandeur.

127. Le demandeur n° 2 est une personne morale qui dispose de ressources financières importantes. Par ailleurs, le paiement par la Banque d'indemnités supplémentaires substantiels lui est assuré en raison du succès qu'il a obtenu au terme de la présente procédure. Le Tribunal souligne également que la Banque, pour sa part, a obtenu gain de cause au titre de la demande reconventionnelle. S'agissant de déterminer si les frais et honoraires d'avocats doivent être remboursés par la Banque au demandeur n° 2, le Tribunal souligne d'emblée que l'accès effectif à la justice n'a pas fait problème, relativement, à la possibilité pour First Eagle de faire valoir ses demandes. En effet, First Eagle a d'abord intenté une action coûteuse aux Etats-Unis avant de s'adresser au présent Tribunal.

128. Le Tribunal estime qu'il est aussi en son pouvoir d'accorder au demandeur n° 2 le remboursement des frais judiciaires et honoraires d'avocat, si cela est requis en vertu du principe de l'accès effectif à la justice ou de tout autre principe lié à l'équité de la procédure d'arbitrage. Cependant, le Tribunal ne considère pas qu'un tel principe s'applique en l'espèce. Le Tribunal relève l'argument avancé par le demandeur n° 2 selon lequel la présente procédure a bénéficié à de nombreux autres actionnaires. Le demandeur n° 2, qui était anciennement titulaire d'une des plus grandes participations privées, défendait ses propres droits et intérêts. En conséquence, First Eagle est tenue de supporter ses propres frais.

129. S'agissant des frais judiciaires de la Banque, le Tribunal estime qu'il n'y a pas lieu de déroger à la règle en vertu de laquelle chaque partie supporte ses propres frais. C'est pourquoi la Banque doit supporter les frais judiciaires et honoraires d'avocat qu'elle a encourus.

130. Sous réserve des circonstances particulières exposées au paragraphe 126 *supra*, chaque Partie supportera donc les honoraires d'avocat qu'elle a encourus.

J. FRAIS DE L'ARBITRAGE

131. Le Tribunal en vient à présent aux frais de l'arbitrage.[179] Le Tribunal relève que l'annexe XII, "Arbitrage. Règles de procédure", de l'Accord de la Haye de janvier 1930[180] dispose que "[n]otamment l'article 85 de la Convention de La Haye recevra application et chaque partie supportera ses propres frais et une fraction égale des frais du tribunal." L'article 85 de la Convention de La Haye de 1907 dispose que "[c]haque Partie supporte ses propres frais et une part égale des frais du Tribunal."

132. Il est clair que les dispositions citées ci-dessus s'imposent au Tribunal dans le cas de procédures interétatiques ou de procédures entre un Etat et la Banque, telles qu'envisagées par l'article XV de l'Accord de La Haye de 1930. Néanmoins, il y a lieu de se demander si les règles prévues pour les organismes gouvernementaux inscrites dans les articles cités sont entièrement applicables aux différends qui opposent la Banque et d'autres actionnaires privés. Tous les actionnaires sont visés par la disposition en matière d'arbitrage de l'article 54 des Statuts de la Banque. Cependant, les procédures impliquant des actionnaires autres que des Etats ne sont pas relevées dans l'annexe relative à l'arbitrage ni dans la Convention de 1907.

133. En imposant les obligations énoncées à l'article 54, paragraphe 1, tant aux actionnaires privés qu'aux banques centrales, les auteurs du texte entendaient manifestement instaurer un régime qui permettrait aux actionnaires privés d'exercer ce droit plutôt que de les en empêcher. C'est pourquoi le Tribunal estime que l'article 54 des Statuts de la

---

[179] L'article 33 des règles de procédure dispose que:

> "[l]e Tribunal fixe le montant des frais d'arbitrage dans sa sentence. Les "frais" comprennent: (a) les honoraires des membres du Tribunal fixés par le Tribunal lui- même; (b) les frais de déplacement et autres dépenses des arbitres; (c) les frais encourus pour toute expertise ou pour toute autre aide demandée par le Tribunal; (d) les honoraires et les frais du secrétaire du Tribunal et du Bureau international."

[180] Accord de La Haye de 1930, annexe XII, paragraphe 1.

Banque[181] réglant l'arbitrage entre les actionnaires et la Banque doit être interprété de manière à permettre à chaque actionnaire d'avoir accès à la justice non seulement en théorie mais aussi en pratique. Ce principe a été reconnu par la Banque dès le début de la présente procédure.[182] Le renvoi à l'article 85 de la Convention de La Haye de 1907 doit être compris à la lumière dudit principe d'accès effectif à la justice, qui est aujourd'hui pleinement reconnu par la législation des droits de l'homme. Même si cette règle n'était pas complètement développée en 1930, le droit international a évolué et le Tribunal doit appliquer le droit dans son acception contemporaine.

134. Dans l'ordonnance de procédure sur la demande de mesures exceptionnelles de M. Howe rendue le 31 août 2001, le Tribunal a déclaré:

> H. Quant à la répartition des sommes consignées et des frais : le Tribunal a-t-il compétence ou pouvoir discrétionnaire d'équité pour procéder à la répartition des sommes consignées et des frais en prenant en considération les circonstances particulières à chacun des demandeurs?
>
> H.1. Le Traité de 1930 et la Convention de 1907 envisageaient une répartition en parts égales entre les parties, des frais de l'arbitrage. Le contexte dans lequel ces instruments ont été établis étant celui d'arbitrages interétatiques et non d'arbitrages entre un État ou une organisation internationale, d'une part, et des demandeurs individuels, d'autre part, ce système de répartition en parts égales était conforme à la notion d'égalité souveraine des États et peut avoir donné lieu à une formule susceptible d'aboutir à un résultat équitable dans des affaires déterminées.

---

[181] En vertu de l'article 54, paragraphe 1:

> Si un différend vient à s'élever quant à l'interprétation ou à l'application des Statuts de la Banque, soit entre la Banque, d'une part, et telle banque centrale, établissement financier ou autre banque visé aux Statuts, d'autre part, soit entre la Banque et ses actionnaires, ce différend sera soumis, pour décision définitive, au Tribunal prévu par l'Accord de La Haye de janvier 1930.

[182] Voir *infra*, par. 134, H. 5.

H.2. L'article 54 des Statuts de la Banque a étendu la compétence du Tribunal aux litiges entre la Banque et ses actionnaires individuels. Dans ce type de rapport, la répartition en parts égales des frais, qui, non sans raison, était prescrite en cas d'arbitrage interétatique, pourrait créer des injustices et même restreindre voire décourager l'accès à l'arbitrage par des particuliers. À cet égard, le Tribunal prend note de la déclaration de la Banque dans sa lettre du 23 août 2001, selon laquelle "[l]a Banque ne souhaite pas que la question des frais empêche d'anciens actionnaires privés individuels de déférer à l'arbitrage leur demande." L'expression du souhait de la Banque mise à part, une interprétation d'une disposition figurant dans l'un des instruments régissant l'organisation du Tribunal qui aurait pour effet d'empêcher le recours à l'arbitrage de particuliers ayant qualité pour introduire pareil recours, ne pourrait être légitime. L'article 9 (1) du Règlement du Tribunal stipule en effet que:

> Sous réserve des dispositions du présent Règlement, de l'Accord de La Haye de 1930, de la Convention de 1907 et de l'acte de mission, le Tribunal peut procéder à l'arbitrage comme il le juge approprié, pourvu que les parties soient traitées sur un pied d'égalité et qu'à tout stade de la procédure, chaque partie ait toute possibilité de faire valoir ses droits et proposer ses moyens.

Une répartition des sommes consignées et des frais qui aboutirait à priver une partie de "la possibilité de faire valoir ses droits et proposer ses moyens" ne satisferait pas aux dispositions de l'article 9 (1).

H.3. Le "Règlement d'arbitrage entre la Banque des Règlements Internationaux et des Parties Privées", qui a été adapté ainsi que l'Accord de La Haye en donne la possibilité, pour pouvoir s'appliquer à des arbitrages entre la Banque et des actionnaires privés, autorise le Tribunal en son article 33, à 'fixer' le montant des frais, un terme qui, dans le contexte de ce type d'arbitrages, comprend la compétence de répartir les frais d'une façon qui serve les objectifs communs poursuivis par les parties à la procédure arbitrale, dans le but de garantir un procès équitable et un résultat juste, conformément au droit.

H.4. Le Tribunal a donc compétence s'agissant d'arbitrages tombant sous le coup de l'article 54 des Statuts de la Banque, pour répartir les frais d'une façon qui conduise à un usage optimal de l'arbitrage ainsi qu'envisagé par l'article 54, et garantisse justice et équité dans le déroulement de chaque procédure arbitrale.

H.5. Le Tribunal prend note de la déclaration de la Banque dans sa lettre du 23 août 2001, laquelle:

> "l'article 33 du Règlement du Tribunal signifie, selon la Banque, que le Tribunal répartit les frais en équité de la façon qu'il estime appropriée, les adjugeant par exemple à un demandeur victorieux. Nous sommes également d'avis que toute consignation à titre d'avance à valoir sur les frais conformément à l'article 34 pourrait faire l'objet de pareille répartition équitable, laquelle prendrait en considération de façon appropriée les circonstances particulières à tout demandeur. Il appartient néanmoins au Tribunal de déterminer, en fonction du nombre total de demandes finalement introduites et de tous les autres faits et circonstances les caractérisant, la façon dont la somme à consigner à titre d'avance sur les frais devrait être répartie."

H.6. Compte du caractère factuel et contextuel s'attachant à toute répartition équitable, le Tribunal ne peut à l'avance statuer sur la répartition des frais, d'autant plus que pareille répartition doit " prendre en considération de façon appropriée les circonstances particulières à tout demandeur." Néanmoins, même sans avoir connaissance de ces circonstances s'agissant d'affaires en cours ou devant encore être introduites, le Tribunal prend bonne note de la déclaration faite par la Banque selon laquelle "[l]a Banque n'est certes pas d'avis qu'en cas de pluralité de demandeurs, ceux ci doivent collectivement prendre en charge plus de la moitié des frais encourus par le Tribunal . . . ."

> H.7. Les observations précédentes s'appliquent mutatis mutandis aux sommes consignées en vue de la procédure arbitrale tel que stipulé dans les articles 33 et 34 du Tribunal.
>
> H.8. Il s'en suit que le Tribunal a compétence légale et pouvoir discrétionnaire, pour répartir les frais d'une façon qui favorise l'accès à la procédure arbitrale prévue à l'article 54 des Statuts, qui assure le déroulement en équité de la procédure et qui garantisse le prononcé d'une sentence significative.

Il convient de rappeler que la Banque, pour sa part, a déclaré au point H.5. *supra* que: "l'article 33 du Règlement du Tribunal signifie, selon la Banque, que le Tribunal répartit les frais en équité de la façon qu'il estime appropriée, les adjugeant par exemple à un demandeur victorieux."

135. S'agissant d'un litige entre deux Etats ou entre un Etat et la Banque, les articles cités prévoient une répartition égale entre les parties. Pour la Banque, qui est une organisation internationale disposant d'avoirs financiers importants, cette répartition ne constituerait pas un obstacle à la justice. En revanche, si cette disposition était appliquée à des demandeurs individuels, contraints dès lors de payer la moitié des frais encourus par le Tribunal, leur accès à la justice serait illusoire. Compte tenu de tous ces éléments, notamment le fait que la Banque a été déboutée sur des questions importantes du litige tout en ayant obtenu gain de cause sur d'autres et compte tenu par ailleurs de l'accord conclu par les Parties reconnaissant la compétence du Tribunal en matière de répartition des frais en équité de la façon qu'il juge appropriée, le Tribunal estime que la Banque doit supporter la totalité des frais de l'arbitrage.

136. Les frais de l'arbitrage, visés à l'article 33 du Règlement d'Arbitrage, doivent être entièrement supportés par la Banque comme suit: la Banque doit rembourser directement au demandeur n° 1 la somme de 1.852,64 euros; la Banque doit rembourser directement au demandeur n° 2 la somme de 806.086,40 dollars américains; la Banque doit rembourser directement au demandeur n° 3 la somme de 760,25 euros.

137. En vertu de son pouvoir d'appréciation, le Tribunal rejette les demandes[183] présentées par les demandeurs en vue d'obtenir des intérêts sur les montants versés pour les frais de l'arbitrage.

[183] Voir *supra* par. 26, 35 (e), 43 et 47.

CHAPITRE V - DECISIONS

138. PAR CES MOTIFS, le Tribunal arbitral prend à l'unanimité les décisions suivantes:

1. DIT que le montant dû à chacun des demandeurs s'élève à 7.977,56 francs suisses par action;

2. DIT que s'agissant des actions revendiquées par le demandeur n° 2 (First Eagle) qui ne sont pas enregistrées à son nom, la Banque est en droit de ne verser le montant susvisé qu'aux titulaires des actions enregistrées, tels qu'ils sont inscrits dans le registre des actionnaires de la Banque;

3. DIT que le demandeur n° 2 (First Eagle) doit rembourser à la Banque la somme de 587.413,49 dollars américains, soit les frais encourus par la Banque pour défendre sa cause dans l'action intentée aux Etats-Unis par le demandeur n° 2 (First Eagle), que la Banque peut déduire des sommes dues au demandeur n° 2 (First Eagle) en conséquence de la présente sentence;

4. DIT qu'un intérêt simple de 5% est dû à tous les demandeurs sur la somme mentionnée au paragraphe 138, point 1, *supra* à compter du 8 janvier 2001 jusqu'à la date de la présente sentence;

5. REJETTE la demande du demandeur n° 3 (M. Mathieu), requérant un intérêt sur le montant fixé par l'Assemblée générale extraordinaire du 8 janvier 2001 en vertu de l'article 18A des Statuts de la Banque;

6. DIT que la Banque doit rembourser directement au demandeur n° 3 (M. Mathieu) la somme de 4.436,75 euros pour ses frais judiciaires. Le Tribunal dit également que le demandeur n° 2 (First Eagle) doit supporter les honoraires d'avocat et autres frais qu'il a encourus;

7. DIT que les frais de l'arbitrage doivent être entièrement payés par la Banque comme suit: la Banque doit rembourser directement au demandeur n° 1 (Dr. Reineccius) la somme de 1.852,64 euros; la Banque doit rembourser directement au demandeur n° 2 (First Eagle) la somme de 806.086,40 dollars américains; la Banque doit

rembourser directement au demandeur n° 3 (M. Mathieu) la somme de 760,25 euros;

8. REJETTE les demandes présentées par les demandeurs en vue d'obtenir des intérêts sur les montants versés pour les frais de l'arbitrage;

9. DIT que tous les montants mentionnés ci-dessus doivent être payés dans un délai de 90 jours;

10. DIT qu'aucune autre voie de droit n'est ouverte aux Parties *inter se* en ce qui concerne les questions résolues dans le présent arbitrage;

11. REJETTE toute autre mesure demandée non compatible avec les décisions exposées ci-dessus.

Fait au Palais de la Paix, La Haye, le 19 septembre 2003,

Professeur W. Michael Reisman

Professeur Dr. Jochen A. Frowein

Professeur Dr. Mathias Krafft

Professeur Dr. Paul Lagarde

Professeur Dr. Albert Jan van den Berg

Phyllis P. Hamilton, Secrétaire

MIX
Papier aus verantwortungsvollen Quellen
Paper from responsible sources
FSC® C105338

If you have any concerns about our products,
you can contact us on
ProductSafety@springernature.com

In case Publisher is established outside the EU,
the EU authorized representative is:
Springer Nature Customer Service Center GmbH
Europaplatz 3, 69115 Heidelberg, Germany

Printed by Libri Plureos GmbH
in Hamburg, Germany